American Evangelical Christianity

To
Rich Mouw
and
Luder Whitlock

American Evangelical Christianity

An Introduction

Mark A. Noll

Copyright © Mark A. Noll 2001

The right of Mark A. Noll to be identified as author of this work has been
asserted in accordance with the Copyright, Designs and Patents Act 1988.

First published 2001

2 4 6 8 10 9 7 5 3 1

Blackwell Publishers Ltd
108 Cowley Road
Oxford OX4 1JF
UK

Blackwell Publishers Inc.
350 Main Street
Malden, Massachusetts 02148
USA

British Library Cataloguing in Publication Data

A CIP catalogue record for this book is available from the British Library.

Library of Congress Cataloging-in-Publication Data

Noll, Mark A., 1946–
    American evangelical Christianity : an introduction / Mark A. Noll.
        p. cm.
Includes bibliographical references and index.
    ISBN 0–631–21999–4 (alk. paper) — ISBN 0–631–22000–3 (pbk. : alk.
paper)
    1. Evangelicalism—United States. I. Title.
    BV3773 .N65 2000
    277.3′082—dc21

                                                                00-010082

Typeset in 11 on 13 pt Ehrhardt
by Best-set Typesetter Ltd., Hong Kong
Printed in Great Britain by
T. J. International, Padstow, Cornwall

This book is printed on acid-free paper.

Contents

99994

Tables

Introduction

This book describes, interprets, and evaluates a stream of Christianity that was the predominant form of religion in the early history of the United States, that existed as a large but disintegrating force in the first half of the twentieth century, and that has been an increasingly visible but frequently misunderstood political presence over the past fifty years. Although *American Evangelical Christianity* exploits research by sociologists, political scientists, and theologians, its shape is dictated by my own interests as a historian. A great deal of the book is directed toward explaining evangelicals as they exist at the start of a new century, but its explanations of current situations rely extensively on historical narration and analysis.

As a historian of religion in America I am concerned to make all such description and analysis as accurate and interesting as possible. But since I am myself by upbringing and personal conviction an evangelical Christian, the book is more than an objective report. Straightforward description predominates through the first group of chapters in efforts to show where modern evangelicals came from (chapter 1), how they can be defined and counted (chapter 2), why Billy Graham has been such an important representative of modern evangelical Christianity (chapter 3), what evangelicals believe (chapter 4), and where evangelicals may be located by region, class, race, and gender (chapters 5 and 6).

The second part of the book continues the descriptive task, but with a difference. Evangelical relations with Roman Catholics (chapter 7), evangelical engagements with science (chapter 8), and the contemporary mobilization of evangelicals in politics (chapter 9) are important subjects in themselves. But they are also subjects in which I have considerable personal interest – and opinions. The interest has produced longer chapters with more documentation. The opinions translate into a more polemical, less objective form of writing.

In the last part of the book, historical analysis continues, but its three chapters also express opinions even more clearly than earlier in the volume. My proposal for how exploiting the resources of evangelical theology might improve the quality of evangelical politics (chapter 10), for how a glance north of the border into Canada might likewise provide helpful instruction (chapter 11), and for how popular hymns display evangelical Christianity at its best (chapter 12) give way, at least in part, to the persistent evangelical tendency to preach. The book's Epilogue on the future and its Guide to Further Reading return to a more analytical style, but of course readers should be on their guard for the way prejudices can shape even those innocuous looking addenda.

The central concern of the book is to portray American evangelical Christianity as a form of "culturally adaptive biblical experientialism" and to show why that portrayal makes sense of both evangelical religion and the place of evangelicals in American history. Evangelicals stress the reality of religious experience before God. They also stress the Bible as the source of the authoritative stories and precepts by which they define their own existence. But the evangelical movements in America have also always been adaptive to broad trends in national culture. As examples, evangelicals learned how to "sell" the gospel in popular forms once marketplace realities came to dominate American public life. Evangelicals mastered successive new technologies of the United States' mass communications systems (public speaking, print, radio). Evangelicals also have adapted themselves to important American ideologies like republicanism, the Victorian home, and (more recently) therapeutic individualism.

This book has been written to provide insight for evangelicals, but even more for those who are not evangelicals, into the meaning of evangelical activities, aspirations, and ideologies throughout American history. A key to fulfilling that goal is to understand, when considering different subjects, which evangelical element has been exerting the most force – when, that is, the experiential religion of born-again Christianity predominates, when the evangelical trust in Scripture is ascendant, or when the evangelical propensity for adapting to American culture takes over.[1] More, of course, is involved in understanding American evangelical Christianity than following this one interpretive strategy, but certainly never less.

The original stimulus for the book came from a general course on evangelical Protestantism that I was asked to teach in the spring semester 1998 as the Alonzo L. McDonald Family Visiting Professor of Evangelical Theological Studies at the Harvard Divinity School. That assignment afforded the opportunity to revise scattered writings on various subjects that had been published over the years and also to prepare new lectures. As the semester went on, realization dawned that this collection of reworked and new material might have the makings of a book. A friendly invitation from Alex Wright at Blackwell to submit a manuscript proposal brought the volume into being.

I hope the chapters of this book fit together, and that the progression from objective analysis, through engaged description, to historically informed argument is compelling in its own right. But should any be curious as to where the parts of the book came from, they may be tracked down as follows.

Chapters 2, 4, 5, 6, and the Guide to Further Reading appear in print for the first time here.

Chapter 1 is an extensively rewritten and expanded version of an essay published with Lyman Kellstedt as "The changing face of evangelicalism," in *Pro Ecclesia*, 4 (Spring), 1995, pp. 146–64. Used by permission.

Chapter 3 is an extensively rewritten conflation of material that first appeared in *The Reformed Journal*, January 1989, pp. 3–4; and *First Things*, January 1998, pp. 34–40. The material from *The Reformed Journal* is used by permission of the publisher, Wm. B. Eerdmans Publishing Co.; all rights reserved. Likewise the material from *First Things*, a monthly journal published in New York City by the Institute on Religion and American Life.

Chapter 7 is expanded and revised from "The history of an encounter: Roman Catholics and Protestant evangelicals," in *Evangelicals and Catholics Together: Toward a Common Mission*, eds Charles Colson and Richard John Neuhaus (Word, 1995), pp. 81–114. This material is used by permission of Word Publishing, Nashville, Tennessee. All rights reserved.

Chapter 8 is a revision and expansion of material from two articles, "Evangelicalism, fundamentalism, and science" from *The History of Science and Religion in the Western Tradition: an Encyclopedia*, eds Gary B. Ferngren, Edward J. Larson, and Darrel W. Amundsen (Garland, 2000); and "Science, theology, and society: from Cotton Mather to

William Jennings Bryan," from *Evangelicals and Science in Historical Perspective*, eds David Livingstone, D. G. Hart, and Mark A. Noll (Oxford University Press, 1999), pp. 99–119. The adaptation from the latter source is used by permission of Oxford University Press, Inc.

Chapter 9 is an abridgment of "Evangelicals in the American founding and evangelical political mobilization today," from *Religion and the New Republic: Faith in the Founding of America*, ed. James H. Hutson (Rowman and Littlefield, 2000), pp. 137–58. This material is used by permission of Rowman and Littlefield. All rights reserved.

Chapter 10 is a revision of "Adding cross to crown," which was published in a volume of the same title with contributions also by Luis Lugo, James Bratt, Max Stackhouse, and James Skillen (Baker, 1996). It was first presented as the Kuyper Lecture at Calvin College in November 1995. This material is used by permission of Baker Book House. All rights reserved.

Chapter 11 is a revision of "Canadian evangelicalism: a view from the United States," in *Aspects of the Canadian Religious Experience*, ed. G. A. Rawlyk (McGill-Queen's University Press, 1997), pp. 3–20, 434–7. It was presented publicly at a conference on the evangelical tradition in Canada at Queen's University, Kingston, Ontario, in May 1995. This revision is used by permission of McGill-Queen's University Press. All rights reserved.

Chapter 12 is a revision of "Evangelicalism at its best," from *Where Shall My Wond'ring Soul Begin?*, eds Mark A. Noll and Ronald F. Thiemann (Eerdmans, 2000), pp. 1–26. A colloquium in February 1998 sponsored by the Alonzo L. McDonald Chair in Evangelical Theological Studies at the Harvard Divinity School was the occasion for its preparation. Used by permission of William B. Eerdmans Publishing Co.; all rights reserved.

For unusually efficient help in preparing this book for the press, I am very grateful to Rachel Maxson and especially Joel Moore. I am also grateful to Angus Reid and Andrew Grenville of the Angus Reid Group for allowing me to use material from their 1996 cross-border survey and their later World Surveys. Bud Kellstedt at Wheaton College has been a long-suffering colleague and good friend in taking me by the hand through forests of survey research data. For general orientation to the study of evangelical traditions, I am grateful to the extraordinarily cooperative network of scholars – many themselves evangelicals, but also many who are not – who have taken part over the past two decades in the activities of Wheaton College's Institute for the Study of American Evangelicals. To the members and pastors of Immanuel Presbyterian Church, Warrenville, Illinois, I am thankful for supporting my faltering efforts at trying to live as a Christian. For making life in the round worthwhile, I am always pleased to thank my wife Maggie and my children Mary, David, and Robert. The book is dedicated to two long-treasured exemplars and friends who also represent evangelicalism at its best.

Note

1   My conviction that it means a great deal to note which evangelical emphasis is predominant for any one group at any one time comes from the work of the late George Rawlyk; for example, the "Introduction" to *Amazing Grace: Evangelicalism in Australia, Britain, Canada, and the United States*, eds Rawlyk and Mark A. Noll (Montreal and Kingston: McGill-Queen's University Press, 1993), pp. 17–18. This is a good place for noting that to Rawlyk, as also to George Marsden, a long-time and continuing mentor, I am conscious of owing unusually profound debts of intellectual and personal influence.

Part I
Who Are Evangelicals?

1

Historical Overview

In the century that followed the close of religious warfare in early modern Europe – that is, from the Peace of Westphalia on the Continent in 1648 and the Restoration of the English monarchy in 1660 – Protestant Christianity was transformed. That transformation involved many factors. Some of the factors were obviously religious, but others (like accommodation to the beginnings of commercial society or resistance to theories of divine-right monarchy) were more subtle in their relationship to faith. The most overt religious factor in the transformation of Protestantism was spiritual renewal expressed as a multifaceted protest against ecclesiastical formalism and an urgent appeal for living religion of the heart. The form of Christianity that contemporary Americans recognize as evangelicalism originated in this pietistic revival.[1]

This chapter provides a historical overview of that movement with special attention to developments during the twentieth century. This historical positioning then leads on to chapters considering the complex question of identifying the size of contemporary evangelical constituencies in North America and around the world, and assessing the significance of Billy Graham as the most visible American evangelical of the post-war era. This groundwork will then make it possible to examine in greater detail what evangelicals believe, how they are located by region, race, class, gender, and why their attitudes toward Roman Catholics, their imbroglios with modern science, and their political activities have been centers of controversies in American history. Only after these largely descriptive and analytical chapters will I try to employ standards from within evangelical religion itself to evaluate the character of American evangelical Christianity.

Historical Origins of Modern Evangelicalism

On the European continent the emergence of pietistic emphases is usually dated from the publication in 1675 of Philip Jakob Spener's *Pia Desideria*, an appeal for reform in the Lutheran state-churches of Germany. But a surging longing for "true religion" was also heralded by the nearly simultaneous appearance in England of John Bunyan's *Pilgrim's Progress* (1678, 1684) and by similarly spiritual activity in late seventeenth-century colonial America, like the intricate poems of Edward Taylor, the Congregationalist minister of Westfield, Massachusetts, written as his preparation for the celebration of communion.

During the first half of the eighteenth century pietist protests against religious formalism gathered increasing strength even as the widening search for a "true religion of the heart" broadened and deepened.[2] For the English-speaking world the result was evangelicalism. From the 1720s and 1730s – in London and English market towns, the Scottish Highlands and Lowlands, Wales, Ireland, and the North American colonies – English-speaking Protestantism was significantly renewed through a series of often intense religious "awakenings." The most visible human agents of these revivals were larger-than-life figures – the spell-binding preacher George Whitefield, the indefatigable evangelist John Wesley, and the brilliant theologian Jonathan Edwards. But if these and other leaders, who were almost as well known in their day (like Howel Harris in Wales, John McLaurin in Scotland, or Gilbert Tennent in America), defined the revivals on a large canvass, experiences of countless ordinary men and women sustained the life of the evangelical awakening.[3]

From the start, news about evangelical experiences in particular places was passed on with great excitement to other interested parties in the North Atlantic region. In Scotland, Wales, Ireland, and England concerned Protestants read about the experiences of Abigail Hutchinson of Northampton, Massachusetts, who on a Monday morning in 1735 was turned from despair and alienation to God. As her minister explained the event, when "these words came to her mind, 'The blood of Christ cleanses from all sin' [they were] accompanied with a lively sense of the excellency of Christ, and his sufficiency to satisfy for the sins of the whole world. . . . By these things," Jonathan Edwards concluded, Abigail "was led into such contemplations and views of Christ, as filled her exceeding full of joy."[4] Not long thereafter Protestants throughout the English-speaking world could read in the published journal of John Wesley what had befallen him at a small-group meeting on Aldersgate Street in London. It was on Wednesday, May 24, 1738, "where one was reading Luther's preface to the *Epistle to the Romans*. About a quarter before nine, while he was describing the change which God works in the heart through faith in Christ, I felt my heart strangely warmed. I felt I did trust in Christ, Christ alone for salvation; and an assurance was given me that He had taken away *my* sins, even *mine*, and saved *me* from the law of sin and death."[5] Many English-speaking Protestants followed just as closely the extraordinary revival at Cambuslang, near Glasgow in Scotland, which began in February 1742 and continued for several months.

Soon congregations and conventicles through the North Atlantic region were singing hymns describing such experiences. Most of evangelicalism's early hymn-writers wrote of what they had personally experienced, as did John Newton, the slave-trader become Anglican priest, who taught the world to sing:

> Amazing grace! how sweet the sound
> that saved a wretch like me!
> I once was lost, but now am found,
> was blind, but now I see. . . .
> 'Twas grace that taught my heart to fear,
> and grace my fears relieved;
> how precious did that grace appear
> the hour I first believed.[6]

Along with the public preaching of repentance and free grace, new institutions arising to perpetuate that message, and hymns memorializing its effects, experiences like those of Abigail Hutchinson and John Wesley constituted the evangelical movement. Such experiences were not unique to English-speaking Protestants, for a general turn to inwardness characterized European religion of the eighteenth century among Roman Catholics as well as Protestants, Jews as well as Christians. Nor did these experiences constitute a new religion, for the individuals who were awakened in the evangelical revivals sustained many of the convictions, ecclesiastical practices, and moral expectations of earlier British Protestantism, especially as that tradition had passed through seventeenth-century Puritanism. If neither unique nor unprecedented, the eighteenth-century English-speaking evangelical awakening still created a distinct set of new emphases in the Christian world. These distinctives are the subjects of the later chapters of this book.

Since the mid-eighteenth century, evangelicals have played a significant role in the history of Christianity, especially on the North American continent and wherever the British or American empires spread. For much of the nineteenth century white evangelical Protestants constituted the largest and most influential body of religious adherents in the United States (as also in Britain and Canada). Methodists, Baptists, Presbyterians, Congregationalists, and some Episcopalians shared broadly evangelical convictions – though they could battle each other aggressively on the details of those convictions. Evangelical elements were prominent among Lutherans, German and Dutch Reformed, and the Restorationist churches (Churches of Christ, Disciples of Christ) as well. During this era, evangelicals provided the backbone of the English-speaking missionary activity and of many movements of social reform at home and abroad. Today, groups descended from those eighteenth- and nineteenth-century movements are more visible than they have been for several decades. In the Church of England, a majority of those in full-time preparation for the ministry have, for some years, been trained in evangelical colleges. In Canada, a majority of the Protestants in church on any given Sunday attend evangelical congregations. For the United States, the number of evangelicals, as we note in chapter 2, depends on how they are defined. But however defined, they are a substantial and growing number. Throughout the world, pentecostal and charismatic movements, which trace their lineage to developments within Anglo-American evangelicalism early in the twentieth century, are far and away the fastest growing segments of worldwide Christianity.[7]

Preliminary Definitions

The evangelicalism that began in the English-speaking world during the eighteenth century and has blossomed in so many varieties over the centuries since is a more complicated phenomenon than either its adherents or its foes usually admit. The complexity is immediately obvious when definitions are proposed. We probe the issue of definition much further in chapter 2, but here it is important to provide some preliminary orientation.

The word "evangelical" has several legitimate senses, all related to the etymological meaning of "good news." For Christians of many types throughout history the word has been used to describe God's redemption of sinners by the work of Christ. In the Reformation of the sixteenth century it became a rough synonym for "Protestant." That history explains why many Lutherans still employ the term (for example, the Evangelical Lutheran Church in America). The most common use of the word today, however, stems from the renewal movements of the eighteenth century and from practitioners of revival in the nineteenth and twentieth centuries, especially as personified by such noteworthy preachers as Charles Grandison Finney, D. L. Moody, and Billy Graham.

Whatever its other legitimate uses, "evangelical" is also the best word available to describe the fairly discrete network of Protestant Christian movements arising during the eighteenth century in Great Britain and its colonies. Two complementary perspectives undergird this usage. "Evangelical" refers to the heirs of these Anglo-American religious revivals, but it also designates a consistent pattern of convictions and attitudes. In one of the most useful summaries of that pattern, the British historian David Bebbington has identified the key ingredients of evangelicalism as conversionism (an emphasis on the "new birth" as a life-changing experience of God), biblicism (a reliance on the Bible as ultimate religious authority), activism (a concern for sharing the faith), and crucicentrism (a focus on Christ's redeeming work on the cross, usually pictured as the only way of salvation).[8] These evangelical traits have never by themselves yielded cohesive, institutionally compact, or clearly demarcated groups of Christians. But they do serve to identify a large family of churches and religious enterprises.

The prominence of the Bible and focus on Christ as the means of salvation link evangelical traditions with earlier Protestant movements like English and American Puritanism. But where the Puritans worked for purified state–church establishments, most modern evangelicals have been independent-minded people delighted with the separation of church and state. In addition, where Puritanism retained an exalted role for the clergy and great respect for formal learning, evangelicals since

the eighteenth century have been powered by lay initiative and in the
twentieth century have been wary of formal scholarship.

The relationship of African-American churches to evangelical traditions is complex.[9] Blacks in America only began to accept Christianity
in the mid-eighteenth century, when the Christian message was presented to them by evangelists like Whitefield or the Virginia Presbyterian Samuel Davies. To this day, most African-American denominations
and independent congregations share many evangelical characteristics,
including belief in the "new birth," trust in the Scriptures, and commitment to traditional morality. Some white evangelicals in the early
years of the new United States, like the New England Congregational
theologian Samuel Hopkins and the founder of American Methodism
Francis Asbury, were also early leaders in the fight against slavery. Yet
other evangelicals, North as well as South, either tolerated or defended
the institution.[10] Throughout the nineteenth century almost all white
evangelicals also frowned on elements of African ritual retained in the
worship of black Christians. The fact that in the twentieth century white
evangelicals have mostly supported the social and political status quo
that marginalized African-Americans means that ties between black
Protestants and white evangelicals are not as close as their shared religious beliefs might lead one to expect.

Several observations are pertinent concerning evangelical history
since the mid-eighteenth century.

1   Evangelicalism has been an extraordinarily complex phenomenon.
Since its origins, the movement has always been *diverse, flexible, adaptable*, and *multiform*. In particular, contextual settings have regularly
colored the shape of evangelicalism (making, for example, some expressions very conservative politically and at least a few quite radical). Evangelical movements have been shapers of culture (as, for example, in the
Scottish Highlands, in the early nineteenth century throughout all of
Scotland, as well as in wide areas of Canada, Britain, and the United
States into the twentieth century). Yet the degree to which evangelicals
have adapted to local situations has also sometimes left evangelicals per-
vasively shaped by their particular cultures.

2   Evangelicalism has always been profoundly affected by its popular
character. This reality is illustrated mostly clearly by the path-breaking
arguments in Nathan Hatch's *The Democratization of American Christianity*, a book describing how eager many evangelicals were to exploit

the new political and social freedoms of the United States.[11] At the same time, evangelical populism is often ambiguous in its appeals to authority. Sometimes evangelicals grant unusual influence to charismatic leaders or organizational geniuses who (with populist rhetoric) replace traditional autocracy with their own iron discipline. Yet evangelicals have also added traditional aspects of Christianity (especially the doctrines of the Reformation) to innovative religious beliefs and behaviors. If evangelicalism can be characterized in terms of its religious form, it is best seen as a persistent mixing of innovation and tradition.

3 Innovative but informal networks of communication have sustained the transnational character of evangelicalism and given it much of its distinctive shape. The critical agents of transmission have been voluntary associations (e.g. Bible societies), personal ties (e.g. George Whitefield or Billy Graham), books (e.g. William Wilberforce's *Practical View of the Prevailing Religious System of Professed Christians* or Hal Lindsey's *Late Great Planet Earth*), periodicals (e.g. *The Christian History* of the 1740s or *Christianity Today* since the 1950s), and hymns (e.g. by Charles Wesley or Fanny Crosby). These agents and strategies of communication defined the specific character of evangelical expressions in the different regions of the North Atlantic and, later, around the world.

The Recent Past

The twentieth-century history of American evangelicals may be divided into four general periods: (a) into the 1920s, (b) from the Great Depression through the Second World War, (c) from after the war until about 1970, and (d) from about 1970 to the present.[12]

Through the 1920s

Divisions among Protestants – especially the fundamentalist–modernist battles of the first quarter of the twentieth century – greatly weakened the public presence of evangelicalism in the years surrounding the First World War.[13] Evangelical cultural influence had, in fact, been declining for several decades owing to the large-scale immigration of non-Protestants, the growth of cities as multicultural sites, and the secularization of university learning. The passing of evangelical cultural dominance, however, was also accompanied by significant innovations. The most important of these was the emergence of pentecostalism, which began early in the twentieth century from emphases on Christian "holiness" that had long existed in several Protestant bodies. With its emphasis on the direct work of the Holy Spirit, pentecostalism has become a major worldwide force in the twentieth century. Its influence is seen in denominations like the mostly white Assemblies of God and mostly African-American Church of God in Christ, but also in a wide variety of other denominations and traditions, especially through the charismatic movement after the Second World War.[14] Politically, during this period, evangelicals united behind the drive for Prohibition, but otherwise did not take distinctive political positions.

From the Great Depression through the Second World War

In the period of the Great Depression and the Second World War, evangelicalism was less visible than it has ever been – before or since – in North American life.[15] Self-identified fundamentalists largely dropped out of sight after losing control of the Northern mainline denominations and also suffering the ignominy of the Scopes Trial in 1925.[16] Yet appearances were deceptive. Shut out of the Northern denominations and ignored by university elites, fundamentalists were still anything but idle. Fundamentalists advanced their version of evangelical faith in many arenas, and set in motion activities that shape evangelicalism to this day. These arenas included higher education, where a number of Bible schools, led by the Moody Bible Institute, expanded dramatically throughout the 1920s and 1930s. The period was also characterized by considerable vitality in local congregations. The Southern Baptist Convention, the Assemblies of God, the Christian and Missionary Alliance, and the Church of the Nazarene were only some of the evangelical denominations that grew more rapidly than the population during the 1930s. Innovations in publishing, especially from networks created by widely read magazines like *The Sunday School Times*, established alternatives to the traditional denominations.

Fundamentalists also pioneered in exploiting the airwaves for religious purposes. Leaders of ecumenical Protestantism negotiated with the new national radio networks for time to present a generic form of religious uplift. For their pains they were granted occasional half-hours on Sunday mornings and other out-of-the-way corners of the week. By

contrast, fundamentalists and evangelicals continued the entrepreneurial habits of the nineteenth century and bought their own radio time in
prime listening hours. With this strategy, several evangelical or fundamentalist broadcasters like Aimee Semple McPherson, Charles Fuller,
and (in Alberta) William Aberhart established regional or national
reputations that rivaled the most popular radio hosts of the day. By the
mid-1930s, McPherson, Fuller, and Aberhart were joined by scores, if
not hundreds, of imitators who blanketed North America with evangelical and fundamentalist broadcasts.[17]

During the 1920s and 1930s a number of groups that earlier had little
contact with English-speaking evangelicals continued processes of
assimilation and education that would one day bring them into the evangelical coalition. Around the Great Lakes, for example, radio broadcasts
from Moody Bible Institute in Chicago found receptive listeners among
the Dutch Reformed of western Michigan, some Lutherans, and a
number of migrants from Southern churches who had come North to
find work during the Great Depression and the Second World War. A
similar phenomenon took place in the Upper Midwest with the radio
broadcasts emanating from William Bell Riley's conservative Baptist
empire in Minneapolis, Minnesota. In similar fashion, Scandinavian
bodies like the Swedish Covenant Church and the Evangelical Free
Church began to define themselves less by the old-world circumstances
that had brought them into existence and more by the new-world evangelicals with whom – especially after they had set aside European languages for the use of English – they found congenial fellowship and
helpful Christian instruction. From the other side, when such groups
became Americanized, they made a distinctly pietist contribution to
twentieth-century evangelicalism.

By the 1940s, a few evangelical liberal arts colleges like Gordon in
Massachusetts, Wheaton near Chicago, and Westmont in California
had also grown to significant size. They were educating an increasingly
diverse mix of fundamentalists, members of holiness denominations,
pentecostals, conservative mainline Protestants, immigrant confessionalists, and others who found common cause in a denominationally
diverse evangelical environment.

While evangelicals went about building an independent institutional
base, politics revolved around economic issues, in particular the appropriate role for government in the economy. Evangelicals reacted to these
issues more in terms of their dominant regional subculture and their

lower socioeconomic status than in terms of their religious values. With a few exceptions for radical fringe groups, religion seemed largely irrelevant to political life, and participation rates were low.

The era of Billy Graham: from the Second World War through about 1970

The quarter-century or so after the Second World War marked a distinct era in American evangelical history. Convenient boundaries for this period are 1949 (and the first national publicity for Billy Graham) and 1974 (when the Graham-sponsored Lausanne Congress on World Evangelization took place).

By the late 1940s, the fluid, shifting life in the shadows that had prevailed for evangelicals since the First World War was giving way to an apparently more monolithic movement. New public attention was well deserved, for conservative evangelicals had faded away only in the eyes of culturally influential beholders, not in actual fact. The impression that a well unified, coherent evangelicalism had returned – resembling in influence the Protestant revivalism of the nineteenth century – was, however, a mirage. It was a mirage, nonetheless, with great staying power, largely because of the impact of Billy Graham. For nearly thirty years, from the end of the war into the 1970s, the great visibility of Billy Graham and the heightened influence of institutions that he favored gave the impression that a unified, culture-shaping evangelicalism had returned to America. If the impression was false, it still testified powerfully to the charismatic impact of Graham. We look in chapter 3 at Graham's career specifically. What remains largely unexplored, however, is the dense network of evangelical institutions that radiated from his ministry.

Post-war "neo-evangelicalism," to use a phrase popular in the 1950s and 1960s, was, however, considerably more than just Billy Graham. If Graham broke through walls created by fundamentalist–modernist battles, and if he virtually ignored some of the cultural shibboleths that had come to define fundamentalism (for example, absolute prohibitions on wine and beer, or strict avoidance of the cinema), others were eager to join him in shaping a new, more positive evangelicalism.

In New England, the Philadelphia area, the Upper Midwest, and California a small, but vocal generation of articulate post-fundamentalists came of age as willing colleagues of Billy Graham.[18] These leaders were mostly content with the doctrinal "fundamentals" of conservative evangelicalism, but they sought a positive spirituality and an intellectual incisiveness that had become rare among militant fundamentalists. After the Second World War, the personal aspirations of such figures led to a spurt of institutional reinvigoration – some as new creations (often with Billy Graham as mediator), others as renovations of already existing bodies.

During the war itself, these leaders founded the National Association of Evangelicals in 1943 as a promoter of general evangelical concerns. But soon the combined efforts of pastor-educator Harold John Ockenga, theologian-administrator E. J. Carnell, editor-theologian Carl Henry, philanthropists J. Howard Pew and Herbert J. Taylor, and a host of missionary-minded young people led to the creation or expansion of many institutions, including Fuller, Gordon-Conwell, and Trinity seminaries, *Christianity Today* and several other periodicals, a number of active youth ministries, and a raft of new mission agencies.

The spread of this "neo-evangelicalism" was also aided greatly by the further assimilation of European ethnic communities; for example, members of the (largely Dutch-American) Christian Reformed Church. Evangelicals offered the Dutch Reformed an important reference point as their immigrant community moved closer to American ways. For their part, the Dutch confessionalists gave their American counterparts a heritage of serious academic work and experienced philosophical reasoning. The Christian Reformed also provided evangelicals with a flourishing network of serious publishers to replace the New York firms that had largely excluded evangelical authors since the 1920s. By the late 1940s, Baker, Eerdmans, and Zondervan (all located in Grand Rapids, Michigan) had become the publishers of choice for many of the "new evangelicals" like Carl Henry and E. J. Carnell.

The Wm B. Eerdmans Publishing Company also played a major role in bringing a British influence to bear on the emerging neo-evangelical coalition. Beginning in the 1930s, a number of British evangelicals inside and out of the Church of England had united in efforts to expand the evangelical presence in the universities. The cradle for this effort was the British InterVarsity Fellowship, while the nursemaids were graduate students and young professors convinced of the intellectual integrity of evangelical faith. Led by preachers like Martin Lloyd-Jones, scholars like F. F. Bruce and David Wenham, and organizers like Douglas Johnson, these British evangelicals made significant progress in a relatively short time. The British InterVarsity Press published many products of this renewed evangelicalism, often with Eerdmans as a co-sponsor or the American distributor. In addition, by the 1950s, American evangelicals were regularly traveling across the Atlantic to pursue graduate work with British scholars who were either evangelicals or open to evangelical emphases. More generally, throngs of American evangelicals read with great appreciation the works of British evangelicals, especially the Brethren Bible scholar F. F. Bruce and the evangelical Anglicans John R. W. Stott and James I. Packer.[19]

What may have been the most important encouragement for American evangelicals from Britain did not come from an evangelical, but from the "mere Christian" C. S. Lewis, whose books have enjoyed a phenomenal success on this side of the Atlantic. Billy Graham promoted Lewis, Eerdmans joined several secular publishers in bringing out his books in America, and countless evangelicals seeking a conception of Christian faith with beauty and intellectual substance found what they were looking for in Lewis and his friends. Wheaton College even created a specially funded center to promote the work of Lewis and other British Christian writers (including Dorothy Sayers and G. K. Chesterton), even though none of these authors – for doctrinal or behavioral reasons – could ever have been hired to teach at the college.

The neo-evangelicalism that after the Second World War defined itself in the shadow of Billy Graham's activities and influence was vigorous, articulate, intellectually ambitious, and culturally visible. But even in the 1940s and 1950s, it was far from the whole story. Many other evangelical groups existed that were related only marginally, if at all, to Graham and his connections. Graham, Henry, Ockenga, and their circle may have communicated a sense of cohesion, but, on the ground, evangelicalism remained profoundly pluralistic.

Even in its heyday, the Billy Graham network possessed few connections with many other vibrant denominations, groups, and movements whose convictions, practices, and heritages placed them securely within the evangelical tradition. Pentecostals continued to expand in denominations like the Assemblies of God and the Church of God in Christ that were only marginally noticed by many members of the Billy Graham entourage. The large healing revivals associated with figures of great regional popularity like William Marion Branham and Oral Roberts also went unnoticed.[20] These revivals were, however, especially important for what came later, since they prepared the way for the rapid spread among evangelicals in the 1960s and following decades of charismatic styles of music, emphases on healing, and approaches to spirituality.

In this era evangelical pluralism was regional as well as denominational. Since the late nineteenth century, the South has been the one region with a majority of born-again, Bible-believing Protestants. Yet the relative isolation of the South from the rest of the country's religious organizations – as well as the South's distinctive history – has meant that the Billy Graham orbit did not actively engage much of the country's largest reservoir of evangelicals, despite Graham's own Southern roots.[21]

Other evangelical groups not related as directly to the Billy Graham orbit included African-Americans. As mentioned above, black Protestants in North America have always shared many of the personal convictions and religious practices of white evangelicals. But their experiences – at first under slavery and then in a racially segregated society – have been so radically different from white evangelicals that their story is difficult to incorporate in the larger picture. That difficulty is ironic, for black Christians are the ones who have experienced the cross most dramatically in American history. More than white evangelical bodies, they are the ones who have most deeply lived out the pietist themes of comfort in Jesus and security in his cross. It was a black hymn-writer, Thomas Dorsey, who wrote in 1938,

> Precious Lord, take my hand, lead me on, let me stand,
> I am tired, I am weak, I am worn.
> Thru the storm, thru the night, lead me on to the light,
> Take My Hand, Precious Lord, lead me home.[22]

Whites also eventually sang these words, but positions of social superiority may have kept them from sensing the meaning of such lyrics as profoundly as did African-American Christians.

Besides Pentecostals and blacks (and many black Pentecostals), other evangelical groups flourished beyond the Billy Graham orbit, including Southern Baptists, Mennonites, several of the Holiness churches, and many Lutherans.[23] Missionaries and speakers from the Nazarenes, the Christian and Missionary Alliance, the Baptist Bible Fellowship, or other large, growing denominations would occasionally show up in circles identified with Graham, but these appearances represented tokens rather than substantial interaction. Yet all these and more were evangelical in conviction, practice, and disposition, even if only a few felt at home with the mostly Northern, mostly white evangelicals who in the 1940s and 1950s seemed to define a movement.

In marked contrast to the distinctive political actions of evangelical Protestants in the nineteenth century, evangelicals from the election of Herbert Hoover in 1928 to the early 1970s remained largely quiescent. Southern evangelicals were Democrats like most of the rest of the South. Northern evangelicals were divided between the two parties and not very active politically, but, when they did enter the political arena, they were less thoroughly Republican than mainline Protestants.

From about 1970 to the present

The diversity that always existed within North American evangelicalism has become much more obvious over the past decades. Changes within American society as well as changes in the character of religious practice have contributed to a new awareness of this diversity. Some of the broad cultural changes with the greatest direct impact on evangelicals have included: the growing importance of university-based intellectuals as arbiters for the general culture; an expanding awareness of the world as a whole due to heightened media coverage of famine, war, and economic conflict; an unprecedented attention to the status of women in modern society; and the rise of higher education as a norm for more and more people. In the religious domain, the phenomenal growth of the charismatic movement and of non-denominational Protestant churches has left a major mark. Partly because such changes pushed evangelicals in several different directions, the Billy Graham orbit has shrunk relative to other expanding evangelical influences. New leaders and new concerns have created a more pluralistic evangelicalism than has ever existed in American history. The sources of that diversity are many.

For one, the rulings by the United States Supreme Court in the 1960s that eliminated prayer in the public schools and in 1973 that legalized abortion contributed to the politicization of American religion.[24] Evangelicals differed among themselves on how best to respond to these decisions. Most objected but for different reasons and with different alternative solutions. More generally, *Roe* v. *Wade* and the school prayer decisions were widely perceived as indicating a decline in national moral values. They also represented heightened efforts by the national government to regulate the daily lives of citizens. That expanding involve-

Table 1.1 Partisan change of evangelicals defined by beliefs and denominational affiliation, 1960s to 1980s (regular church attenders only, percentages)

	1960s		1980s		Republican gain 1960s to 1980s
	Dem.	Rep.	Dem.	Rep.	
Northern	35	57	22	72	15 points
Southern	69	21	51	39	18 points

ment has almost inevitably politicized local communities and heightened the political self-consciousness of religious groups. In response, evangelicals of the Billy Graham sort have remained either apolitical or, if politically engaged, relatively unobtrusive. By contrast, other leaders, like the Baptists Jerry Falwell and Timothy LaHaye or the lay psychologist James Dobson, entered politics with a vengeance during the 1970s and 1980s. These figures were all marked by unusual enterprise in putting to use media of mass communications. They, rather than the "neo-evangelicals," were the ones who created the New Religious Right and have made conservative evangelical support so important for the Republican Party since the campaigns of Ronald Reagan.

Their efforts transformed evangelicals from a political constituency that was more Democratic than Republican and relatively passive politically to one that has become more Republican than, and almost as active as, the American population at large. It took a second phase of Christian Right activism to mobilize the pentecostal and charismatic wings of American evangelicalism, led by the Rev. Pat Robertson during his 1988 presidential campaign. Robertson's candidacy did not fare all that well, but it did succeed in politicizing a large segment of the evangelical community that had not been involved before. This second phase led on to a third, the founding of a grassroots organization, the Christian Coalition, with a goal of mobilizing evangelicals for political action at local, state, and national levels. These mobilizing efforts have had considerable success. Already by the 1980s, evangelicals who were active in their churches had swung substantially in a Republican direction, as table 1.1 suggests.[25] Below in chapters 9 and 10 we will observe how that partisanship became even stronger in the 1990s.

Recent decades have also witnessed a repositioning of old religious and ideological antagonisms. With secularizing changes at work across

North America, even the very deep, historic antagonism between Catholics and Protestants is breaking down. As examined more fully in chapter 7, although American evangelicals still mostly keep their distance from institutional Roman Catholicism, a wide array of social, political, theological, academic, and reforming efforts now link some evangelicals with some Catholics. Evangelicals have also helped once sectarian groups like the Seventh-day Adventists and the Worldwide Church of God in their move toward more traditional Christian affirmations. At the end of the twentieth century, there were even a few signs of improved relations between some evangelicals and some Mormons, whom most evangelicals had long considered far beyond the pale.[26] In addition, the fall of communism in Eastern Europe left American evangelicals without a well identified external enemy. With the decreasing influence of the older, mainline Protestant churches, evangelicals now worry less about theological liberalism and more about multiculturalism, postmodernism, and the general secularization of public life. Evangelicals also now expend considerable energy in debating modes of public worship, with much support in many churches for innovative contemporary styles (as on display, for example, at the 17,000-member Willow Creek Community Church in suburban Chicago), while others promote older patterns, and many vacillate in between.

North American evangelicals are participating fully in the increasing turn to images that is replacing the historic Protestant reliance on the written word. A culture dominated by television, advertising, and therapy has presented both problems and opportunities for evangelical outreach. What it has not provided is unity. As people who have served on the worship committee of a local evangelical church realize, evangelicalism embraces a full spectrum of musical tastes and a thoroughly diverse set of responses to contemporary culture – from those who race to baptize the most visible products of modern life to those who reject soft rock, client-centered preaching, and the cult of celebrity as dangerous threats to the faith.

At the beginning of the twenty-first century, there are very few generalizations that apply to all American evangelicals. To be sure, David Bebbington's four defining characteristics are still generally valid. A reliance on Scripture remains, though how that reliance is expressed differs widely. Some evangelicals rejoice in themes they find in the Bible for the liberation of women. Others, by contrast, think that the Bible teaches traditional patriarchy. Some think that the notion of "inerrancy" is the best way to express the Bible's authority, while others look for doctrinal formulas less tied to the controversies from the late nineteenth century. The belief that the earth was created less than 10,000 years ago has spread very widely in evangelical circles, and sometimes this conviction is used to test the faithfulness of others to Scripture. But in these same circles are found vigorous defenders of evolution who contend that *they* are the ones reading the Bible correctly. Later chapters in this book treat some of these questions much more extensively.

Concern for conversion also remains, though conversion is understood differently in, for example, charismatic, confessional, or Baptist circles. Sometimes conversion is even described with the language popularized by Alcoholics Anonymous's "Twelve Step" program to combat addiction. Yet the conviction that life-changing encounters with God can, do, and should take place remains a fixture in evangelical churches.

Evangelicals are as active as ever, but that activity spreads over every point on the compass. Most North American evangelicals oppose the liberalization of abortion laws that has occurred over the past thirty years in Canada and the United States. But how that opposition is expressed – passively, apolitically, or through civil disobedience – ranges widely, as do religious conclusions about the basic issues at stake. The Religious Right has galvanized the political energies of many Christians, but a surprising spectrum of economic, political, and social viewpoints can be found in evangelical communities. Even among evangelicals with the highest religious commitment and most active involvement in Christian activities, over one-fifth are not militantly pro-life and do favor increased civil rights for homosexuals, about one-half favor aggressive governmental policies on the environment and in the fight against poverty, and one-half support the idea of national health insurance.[27]

Finally, the death of Christ on the cross is still at the heart of evangelical religion, although the formal doctrines that once defined the message of atonement receive much less attention today than thirty or sixty or a hundred years ago. The continuing spread of pentecostalism and the growth of the charismatic movement has meant more concentration on doctrines of sanctification (becoming holy oneself) than on doctrines of justification (how God accepts a sinner). In addition, an appeal to the consolations of redemption is now much more common than detailed theological exposition of its nature. In biblical terms, the

Psalms have taken precedence over Isaiah, the gospels are edging out the epistles of Paul.

Much, in other words, separates contemporary evangelical Christians from the first modern evangelicals two and one-half centuries ago. But much also remains to provide continuity with those predecessors. The earliest evangelicals might be amazed at the number and extent of evangelical adherents at the start of the twenty-first century, though exactly how many and how widely spread these evangelicals now are pose complicated questions that deserve full treatment in their own right. To that subject we now turn.

Notes

1 The two best general accounts of this period and the origins of modern evangelicals are by W. R. Ward, *The Protestant Evangelical Awakening* (New York: Cambridge University Press, 1992), and *Christianity under the Ancien Régime* (New York: Cambridge University Press, 1999).

2 See, for example, Ted Campbell, *The Religion of the Heart: European Religious Life in the Seventeenth and Eighteenth Centuries* (Columbia: University of South Carolina Press, 1991).

3 For expanded treatment of these themes, see the early chapters and the Introduction (which is the source for the next few paragraphs) of *Evangelicalism: Comparative Studies of Popular Protestantism in North America, the British Isles, and Beyond, 1700–1990*, eds Mark A. Noll, David W. Bebbington, and George A. Rawlyk (New York: Oxford University Press, 1994).

4 *The Works of Jonathan Edwards, volume 4: The Great Awakening*, ed. C. C. Goen (New Haven, CT: Yale University Press, 1972), p. 193.

5 Nehemiah Curnock, ed. *The Journal of John Wesley*, 8 vols (London: Epworth, 1938), volume 1, pp. 475–6.

6 See especially D. Bruce Hindmarsh, *John Newton and the English Evangelical Tradition* (New York: Oxford University Press, 1996).

7 On that recent and dramatic spread of such movements, see Karla Poewe, ed., *Charismatic Christianity as a Global Culture* (Columbia: University of South Carolina Press, 1994); Murray Dempster, Bryon D. Klaus, and Douglas Peterson, eds, *The Globalization of Pentecostalism* (Oxford: Regnum, 1999); and Richard Shaull and Waldo Cesar, *Pentecostalism and the Future of the Christian Churches* (Grand Rapids, MI: Eerdmans, 2000).

8 David Bebbington, *Evangelicalism in Britain: a History from the 1730s to the 1980s* (London: Unwin Hyman, 1989), pp. 2–17.

9 See the section on race in chapter 5.

10 Compare James Essig, *The Bonds of Wickedness: American Evangelicals Against Slavery, 1770–1808* (Philadelphia: Temple University Press, 1982), with the accounts of Scripture being used to support slavery in Mark A. Noll, "The Bible and slavery," in *Religion and the American Civil War*, eds Randall M. Miller, Harry S. Stout, and Charles Reagan Wilson (New York: Oxford University Press, 1998), pp. 43–73.

11 Nathan O. Hatch, *The Democratization of American Christianity* (New Haven, CT: Yale University Press, 1989).

12 For general treatments that cover much twentieth-century material, see George M. Marsden, *Understanding Fundamentalism and Evangelicalism* (Grand Rapids, MI: Eerdmans, 1991); and Randall Balmer, *Mine Eyes Have Seen the Glory: a Journey into the Evangelical Subculture in America* (New York: Oxford University Press, 1989).

13 The best study is George M. Marsden, *Fundamentalism and American Culture: the Shaping of Twentieth-century Evangelicalism, 1870–1925* (New York: Oxford University Press, 1980); but also valuable, from quite different perspectives, are Ernest R. Sandeen, *The Roots of Fundamentalism: British and American Millenarianism, 1800–1930* (Chicago: University of Chicago Press, 1970); and George W. Dollar, *A History of Fundamentalism in America* (Greenville, SC: Bob Jones University Press, 1973).

14 Especially helpful studies are Robert Mapes Anderson, *Vision of the Disinherited: the Making of American Pentecostalism* (New York: Oxford University Press, 1979); Edith L. Blumhofer, *Restoring the Faith: the Assemblies of God, Pentecostalism, and American Culture* (Champaign: University of Illinois Press, 1993); and Grant Wacker, *Heaven Below: Early Pentecostals and American Culture* (Cambridge, MA: Harvard University Press, 2001).

15 The key book is Joel A. Carpenter, *Revive Us Again: the Reawakening of American Fundamentalism* (New York: Oxford University Press, 1997).

16 See especially Edward J. Larson, *Summer for the Gods: the Scopes Trial and America's Continuing Debate over Science and Religion* (New York: Basic, 1997).

17 See Quentin Schultze, ed., *Evangelicals and the Mass Media* (Grand Rapids, MI: Zondervan, 1990).

18 Especially useful is George M. Marsden, *Reforming Fundamentalism: Fuller Seminary and the New Evangelicalism* (Grand Rapids, MI: Eerdmans, 1987).

19 See Derek J. Tidball, *Who Are the Evangelicals? Tracing the Roots of Today's Movements* (London: Marshall Pickering, 1994); and the latter portions of Kenneth Hylson-Smith, *Evangelicals in the Church of England, 1734–1984* (Edinburgh: T. & T. Clark, 1988).

20   See especially David Edwin Harrell, Jr, *All Things Are Possible: the Healing and Charismatic Revivals in Modern America* (Bloomington: Indiana University Press, 1975).

21   A good account of recent contacts is found in David S. Dockery, ed., *Southern Baptists and American Evangelicals: the Conversation Continues* (Nashville: Broadman & Holman, 1993).

22   See especially Michael W. Harris, *The Rise of Gospel Blues: the Music of Thomas Andrew Dorsey in the Urban Church* (New York: Oxford University Press, 1992).

23   For an example of how accelerating osmosis between evangelicals and a formerly separated denomination has worked, see Perry Bush, *Two Kingdoms, Two Loyalties: Mennonite Pacifism in Modern America* (Baltimore: Johns Hopkins University Press, 1998).

24   See chapter 9.

25   Material in this table is taken from polls conducted by the University of Michigan's Center for Political Studies and is reproduced from Mark A. Noll and Lyman Kellstedt, "Religion, voting for President, and party identification, 1948–1984," in *Religion and American Politics*, ed. Mark A. Noll (New York: Oxford University Press, 1990), p. 372.

26   See the breakthrough represented by mutually respectful dialogue in Craig L. Blomberg and Stephen E. Robinson, *How Wide the Divide? A Mormon and an Evangelical in Conversation* (Downers Grove, IL: InterVarsity Press, 1997).

27   This information is from Lyman Kellstedt and draws on several national surveys conducted by Kellstedt, along with John Green, James Guth, and Corwin Smidt.

2

Constituencies in North America and the World

Charting the size of the American evangelical constituency at the start of the twenty-first century depends upon which criteria are used for definition. The same dependency of results upon criteria exists for the task of counting evangelicals around the world. Trying out alternative definitions and noting complexities in the defining process itself may look like typical academic obfuscation. It is not. Rather, care over definitions and comparison of results from differing definitions is the only way forward in better understanding who evangelicals are and where they are located. This chapter carries out such an exercise for Canada and the United States; it then goes on to examine a significant survey that makes possible an estimate of the number of evangelicals in over thirty other countries around the world.

There are at least three well supported strategies for carrying out these tasks. Each method has a persuasive logic of its own, but, not surprisingly, each method yields different results. One is to ascertain how many people tell survey researchers that they embrace traditional evangelical convictions concerning the Bible, the new birth, and related matters. This method is the technique regularly used by the Gallup Organization in asking people if they have been born again. In somewhat more detail, it has also been used for several recent surveys conducted by the Angus Reid Group of Toronto.[1] A second method is to count the people adhering to the churches and denominations most strongly linked to the historical evangelical and revival movements. This method has been put to especially good use by political scientists, one group of which has published a series of perceptive works on the political behavior of American religious groups.[2] A third method is to figure out how many people use the term "evangelical" to describe their own religious beliefs and practices. A research team headed by the sociologist Christian Smith of the University of North Carolina has recently brought out important books and articles on those who use the term "evangelical" for themselves, their churches, and their wider connections.³

To indicate how and why these various ways of locating evangelicals overlap, but also contrast, it would be ideal to possess a single research project that uses all three. Fortunately, one recent survey included enough questions to test out all these definitions. An added benefit of the same survey was that it asked virtually the same questions of a large sample of Canadians as well as Americans. For the sake of clarity in defining just who evangelicals are and how many exist in North America, that survey deserves careful attention.

Evangelical Constituencies in the United States and Canada

In October 1996, the Angus Reid Group of Toronto conducted an unusually extensive cross-border poll in which nearly identical questions were asked to 3,000 Americans and 3,000 Canadians.⁴ One-fifth of the Canadian interviews were conducted in French, while interviewers used Spanish for 7 percent of the calls in the United States. The survey included a number of questions about religion, which were originally drafted by the late Canadian historian, George Rawlyk, in an effort to frame questions that came as close to David Bebbington's fourfold definition of "evangelical" as such survey research allows.⁵ Yet the poll also gathered information that allowed for counting evangelicals by the other two methods as well. The following paragraphs describe how the three methods were put to work.

Self-definition. One question asked directly about self-identity. ("Do you consider yourself to be any of the following?" The answers provided were, "A Charismatic Christian," "A Pentecostal Christian," "An Evangelical Christian," "A Fundamentalist Christian," and "A Liberal or Progressive Christian.") The following results tabulate as self-defined evangelicals those who responded with any combination of "evangelical," "fundamentalist," "charismatic," or "pentecostal."

Beliefs. Several questions inquired about beliefs or practices that have been associated in theological and historical writing with evangelical identity. These were the questions that Rawlyk hoped would come close to operationalizing the Bebbington definition. Four of these questions were tabulated for the following tables. It was, thus, considered a sign of "evangelical" conviction, if:

- a respondent strongly agreed that "through the life, death and resurrection of Jesus, God provided a way for the forgiveness of my sins" (crucicentrism);
- a respondent strongly agreed that "the Bible is the inspired word of God"; or agreed to whatever degree that "the Bible is God's word, and is to be taken literally, word for word" (biblicism);
- a respondent strongly agreed that "I have committed my life to Christ and consider myself to be a converted Christian" (conversionism);
- a respondent agreed or agreed strongly that "it is important to encourage non-Christians to become Christians" (activism).

By tallying the number of those who responded positively to all four measures (sometimes three or four), it is possible to obtain a rough picture of the prevalence of traditional evangelical convictions.

Denominations. The survey also made it possible to group respondents by ecclesiastical traditions. The categories below follow the important work that Green, Guth, Kellstedt, and Smidt have done on religion and politics in the United States, although the categories are also similar to ones developed by Reginald Bibby and Donald Posterski for Canada.⁶

- Evangelical Protestants: people who are affiliated with the following churches: Adventist, Alliance, Baptist, Brethren, Church of Christ, Church of God, Mennonite; who identified their denomination or church as charismatic, evangelical, fundamentalist, holiness, pentecostal; or who offered an indeterminate answer to the question of religious affiliation but who could be placed with these churches through other means.
- Mainline Protestants: people who responded Anglican, Episcopal, Congregational, Methodist, United Church (Canada); United Church of Christ (USA); most Lutherans, most Presbyterians, most Reformed; or who likewise gave an indeterminate answer but who could be placed with these churches through other means.
- Black Protestants (USA only): as we discuss in greater detail in chapter 5 below, African-American Protestants share many doctrinal

and behavioral characteristics with those in evangelical Protestant denominations, but they are treated as a separate category because their responses to almost all social, political, or cultural questions set them apart dramatically from the white evangelicals.

- Roman Catholics.
- Secular/nominal: these people responded that they were agnostic, atheist, or nothing in particular; also added to this category were those who, though they responded with a religious affiliation, showed no or virtually no religious commitment – for example, people who said they were Baptist, Catholic, or the like, but who rarely prayed, almost never went to church, did not consider religion important, and thought that the idea of God is a superstition.
- Other: this is a grab bag category that includes Mormons, Jehovah's Witnesses, Eastern Orthodox, Unitarian-Universalists, Jews, and others not readily classifiable with the other larger groups. (The numbers for all such groups, as well as for members of other religions, even in a survey of 6,000 respondents, is quite low.)

With these general categories we are able to make important comparisons between denominational traditions that are usually considered evangelical and those that are not.

Testing the Definitions

When constituencies defined by these three methods are compared, it is not surprising that a high correlation exists between those who call themselves "evangelical," those who affirm the beliefs historically associated with evangelical movements, and those who are members or adherents of traditionally evangelical denominations. Yet it is also important to stress that this correlation is not absolute. Quite a few people who call themselves evangelical or who belong to traditionally evangelical denominations do not affirm all of the traditionally evangelical beliefs and practices. And many mainline Protestants and Roman Catholics, especially in Canada, affirm all or most of the evangelical beliefs. Brief discussion of tables 2.1 to 2.9 will show how important care in definition actually is.

Using the first method, about 19 percent of Americans use some combination of the labels "evangelical," "pentecostal," "charismatic," or

Table 2.1 Percentage of population affirming the evangelical beliefs

	USA	Canada
No beliefs	13	33
One belief	14	22
Two beliefs	17	17
Three beliefs	20	14
Four beliefs	36	13

Table 2.2 Percentage of population in various denominational traditions

	USA	Canada
Evangelical Protestant	26	10
Mainline Protestant	15	17
Black Protestant	9	–
Roman Catholic	20	26
Other	10	7
Secular	20	40

"fundamentalist" for themselves. In Canada the comparable number is 12 percent. Tables 2.1 and 2.2 present overall totals for the numbers of evangelicals in the United States and Canada as defined by the two other methods.

Table 2.1 reveals that many more in both countries affirm at least three or four of the traditional beliefs than call themselves "evangelical." Thus, over half of the Americans queried affirmed three or four of these convictions, and slightly over one-fourth of the Canadians. When we compare the two countries, about 60 percent more Americans than Canadians call themselves "evangelicals," nearly three times as many Americans as Canadians affirm all four traditional evangelical convictions, and about twice as many Americans as Canadians affirm at least three of those convictions.

Table 2.2 shows that, as with evangelical self-identification and profession of evangelical convictions, there are more Americans than Canadians in the historic evangelical denominations, by a ratio of 2.6 to 1.

Table 2.3 Percentage of self-defined evangelicals who affirm various numbers of evangelical beliefs

	USA	Canada
No beliefs	1	3
One belief	3	6
Two beliefs	8	13
Three beliefs	15	27
Four beliefs	74	51

Table 2.4 Percentage of self-defined evangelicals who are found in the various denominational traditions

	USA	Canada
Evangelical Protestant	61	50
Mainline Protestant	16	17
Black Protestant	8	–
Roman Catholic	13	25
Other	1	1
Secular	1	7

The more interesting results surface when the definitions are crossed. Tables 2.3 and 2.4 examine those who call themselves evangelicals (or a similar term). In table 2.3 it is seen that, not surprisingly, most of the self-identified evangelicals affirm most of the traditional evangelical beliefs. But not all. More than 10 percent of American self-defined evangelicals and more than 20 percent of Canadian self-defined evangelicals do not affirm even three of the traditional evangelical convictions. The numbers in table 2.4 are even more revealing. While half (Canadian) or more than half (US) of self-defined evangelicals are found in the evangelical denominations, solid minorities are also present among mainline Protestants and Roman Catholics. In Canada a full one-fourth of those calling themselves evangelical are Roman Catholic.

An even greater blurring of labels occurs when we look at those who affirm three or four of the traditional evangelical convictions. Thirty-three percent of Canadians and 31 percent of Americans who affirm three or four of the traditional evangelical beliefs also use the label evan-

Table 2.5 Percentage of those affirming three of four evangelical beliefs as found in the various denominational traditions

	USA	Canada
Evangelical Protestant	41	30
Mainline Protestant	15	22
Black Protestant	13	–
Roman Catholic	18	32
Other	6	5
Secular	7	10

Table 2.6 Percentage of those affirming all four evangelical beliefs as found in the various denominational traditions

	USA	Canada
Evangelical Protestant	51	45
Mainline Protestant	14	19
Black Protestant	13	–
Roman Catholic	13	25
Other	5	7
Secular	4	4

gelical for themselves. Tables 2.5 and 2.6 show that those who hold to the traditional evangelicals beliefs of course show up substantially in the evangelical denominations. But these denominations by no means monopolize the ones who affirm the evangelical convictions. Table 2.6 is especially striking since it specifies where those who hold the evangelicals beliefs are found ecclesiastically. In the United States 13 percent of those who affirm all of the survey's four evangelical convictions are African-American Protestants (who only sometimes call themselves "evangelicals"), 14 percent are found in mainline Protestant churches, and another 13 percent are Roman Catholics. The distribution is even more counter-intuitive in Canada, where fewer than half of those who affirm all four evangelical beliefs are found in evangelical denominations, while one-fourth are Roman Catholics and nearly one-fifth are mainline Protestants.

Table 2.7 Percentage of those in the various denominational traditions who called themselves evangelicals

	USA	Canada
Evangelical Protestant	44	57
Mainline Protestant	21	12
Black Protestant	17	–
Roman Catholic	12	11
Other	1	2
Secular	1	2

Table 2.8 Percentage of those in the various denominational traditions who affirmed three or four of the evangelical beliefs

	USA	Canada
Evangelical Protestant	88	80
Mainline Protestant	57	37
Black Protestant	79	–
Roman Catholic	50	34
Other	37	21
Secular	20	7

Tables 2.7 and 2.8 put the denominational traditions in the spotlight. As table 2.7 indicates, a slight majority of Canadians in the evangelical denominations call themselves evangelical, but fewer than half in the American evangelical denominations do so. Significant minorities among mainline Protestants, Roman Catholics, and African-American Protestants also used that self-designation. Table 2.8 shows the most correspondence between evangelical beliefs and evangelical denominations, but even here the fit is not tight. On the one hand, small minorities in the evangelical denominations do not affirm even three of the evangelical beliefs. On the other hand, large numbers of black Protestants, mainline Protestants, Roman Catholics, and even the miscellaneous category affirm the beliefs.

Implications of the Angus Reid Survey

Precision in terminology is important. It is natural to use the term "evangelical" to mean those who hold certain Christian beliefs and exercise certain Christian practices. It is also legitimate to use the term historically for designating certain churches and religious traditions deriving ultimately from the Reformation and also identifying strongly with more recent revival traditions. But it is also precarious when those two usages are merged without discrimination. As the survey shows, considerable differences result from defining "evangelicals" as those who hold evangelical convictions when compared to defining as "evangelicals" those who identify with the historic Protestant denominations where those beliefs have been most prominent.

The distribution of beliefs and practices traditionally known as "evangelical" is surprisingly wide. As we would expect, a high proportion of those affiliated with explicitly evangelical denominations hold evangelical convictions and a high proportion of all who hold such beliefs are affiliated with evangelical denominations. Yet it is also striking how much mainline and black Protestants contribute to the total of those who hold evangelical beliefs. African-American Protestants, in fact, contribute a higher proportion, relative to their overall population, of those who affirm the evangelical beliefs than do adherents of the mostly white evangelical denominations. It is even more striking how much Roman Catholics contribute to the total of evangelical believers, especially in Canada.

On all issues of belief and practice Canada is now more secular than the USA. Even with regional variations taken into account, by measures used in the Angus Reid survey, Canada is less religiously active than the United States, and evangelical believers (however measured) are proportionally a much larger part of the population in the United States.

Historical explanations remain important. The considerable differences between Canada and the United States in levels of religious belief and practice pose a major interpretive problem. Although sophisticated surveys like the 1996 Angus Reid poll did not exist a generation ago, earlier, less sophisticated measures nonetheless suggested that until the 1970s Canada actually enjoyed higher rates of religious practice than the

USA.[7] Historical accounts suggest that as far back as the early nineteenth century, Christian belief and practice were considerably more widespread (and more deeply rooted) in Canada than in the United States.[8] If those impressions about earlier situations are valid, it means that Canada has undergone a massive decline in religious practice over just the past thirty years. Some study has gone into that situation for Quebec, almost none for the rest of Canada. For both Christian and academic reasons, study of that secularization is an absolute imperative.

For the United States, the search for evangelical Protestants must proceed cautiously. Each of the methods outlined above provides a valid way for talking about evangelicals, but each must be used carefully to avoid category mistakes and simple uninformed ignorance.

Contemporary Evangelical Constituencies in the World

Over the past several years, the Angus Reid Group of Toronto has included numerous questions bearing on religion in its worldwide comparative surveys as well as in its work in North America. Those surveys make it possible to approach an even more difficult question than the number of evangelicals in North America.[9] That question concerns the number of evangelicals in various individual countries around the world.

Modern survey research yields inexact results. People lie. People say what they think their neighbors would want them to tell the pollsters. Surveys about the Clinton sex scandal illustrate the problem – only a small percentage of Americans said they were interested, but a very large number thought other people were fascinated by l'affaire Lewinsky.

The best survey research firms, like the Angus Reid Group, are aware of these problems. When the good ones present their data, they are at pains to specify degrees of reliability and to highlight doubts about the representativeness of sample populations. The "World Poll" that Angus Reid conducted in 1997 is no exception. In its own publications reporting on results from 33 different nations, it took pains to spell out limitations. For example, in a few of the countries, surveys were restricted to residents in urban areas or to the part of the population that possessed telephones. In addition, the sample size of 500 per country, while entirely adequate for large-scale generalizations, does not allow for results to be fine-tuned. Such limitations obviously skew results and qualify the impact of nation-to-nation comparisons.[10]

Yet once necessary precautions have been taken, the Angus Reid World Survey still produced very interesting findings, especially from its queries about religion. The Angus Reid Group's concern for connections between faith and public life, along with strategic exploitation of questions related to political and economic matters, meant that a solid group of religious questions were included in the World Survey. Thus, along with queries about attitudes toward the United States, on politics in the respondents' countries, and on a range of economic and consumer matters, the World Survey included the following questions on religion:

- To what extent is your religious faith important to you in your day-to-day life?
- Are you a Roman Catholic Christian, Christian but not a Roman Catholic, Jewish, or Muslim/Islam?
- Please tell me whether you agree or disagree, moderately or strongly, with the following statement: "I have committed my life to Christ and consider myself to be a converted Christian."
- How often do you pray outside of formal religious services?
- Other than on special occasions such as weddings, funerals, or baptisms, how often did you attend religious services or meetings in the past 12 months?

Of most obvious interest for a book on evangelicals is the question on conversion. A legitimate doubt remains whether the translation of this question into the various languages of the survey measured exactly the same thing that the original might measure in North America. Choice of wording is critical. The translation of the key assertion, for example, used more wooden words for "committed" and "converted" in German-speaking Switzerland ("Ich habe mein Leben Christus gegenüber *verpflichtet* und fühle mich als *konvertierten* Christen") than in Germany itself, where a better idiomatic translation was made ("Ich habe mein Leben Jesus Christus *gewidmet* und betrachte mich als *überzeugten* Christen").

Again to set aside details, however, the general results of the poll were significant. The Angus Reid Group tabulated in all 33 countries those respondents who scored "high" on the religious questions – that is, people who affirmed that religion was very important *and* who prayed at least once a day *and* who attended church at least weekly *and* who have committed their lives to Christ and consider themselves converted Christians. This total, in turn, was divided between non-Roman Catholics and the Catholics (in Greece, Ukraine, and Russia, Orthodoxy was substituted for Catholicism). In light of the importance within evangelical traditions of personal commitment to Christ and of the conversion experience, it is tempting to call those who scored "high" on these questions "evangelicals." Yet because that term can be used in so many different ways, it is probably more accurate to call those falling into this Angus Reid category something like Protestant "True Believers" Who Come Close to Traditional Evangelical Definitions.

As indicated in table 2.9, the highest proportion of such Protestant "True Believers" is found in the United States and urban South Africa, with substantial segments as well in Brazil, the Philippines, and South Korea. Several other European and North American countries, as well as Australia, have somewhat fewer. On the Catholic side, the highest proportion of "True Believers" is found in the Philippines, Italy, Poland, Spain, South Korea, Brazil, Mexico, and Argentina. Orthodox "True Believers" total 19 percent in Greece, 7 percent in Ukraine, and 1 percent in Russia. When Catholics and non-Catholics are combined, the highest proportion of "True Believers" among the surveyed countries is found in the Philippines. Other countries with more than one-fourth of the population in that same category include the United States (35 percent), South Africa (33 percent), Italy (27 percent), South Korea (26 percent), and Brazil (25 percent).

The Angus Reid survey researchers admitted that their work touched only parts of the world, but even with its limitations the poll contains much useful information. Among other conclusions, it indicates that the high proportion of evangelical Christians (however defined) in the United States makes that country very unusual in the world. The Canadian situation, with a proportion of "True Believers" at around 10 percent of the population, is more typical. The survey also suggests that one of the major opportunities, as well as major challenges, in years to come will be whether Protestant "True Believers" are able to negotiate successfully with Catholic "True Believers," since when considering the world as a whole, there seem to be quite a few more of them than of the Protestant variety.

Table 2.9 Percentage of "True Believers" in 1997 Angus Reid World Survey (ranked by Protestant totals)

	Protestant	Roman Catholic	Orthodox	Total
USA	28	7	–	35
South Africa	28	5	–	33
Brazil	10	15	–	25
Philippines	10	28	–	38
South Korea	10	16	–	26
Canada	8	7	–	15
Australia	7	5	–	12
Norway	6	–	–	6
UK	5	2	–	7
Netherlands	5	2	–	7
Switzerland	4	5	–	9
Finland	3	–	–	3
Mexico	3	14	–	17
Germany	3	4	–	7
Hong Kong	3	1	–	4
Taiwan	3	–	–	3
Indonesia	2	1	–	3
Sweden	2	1	–	3
Argentina	2	10	–	12
Ukraine	1	–	7	8
Czech Republic	1	3	–	4
China	1	–	–	1
Malaysia	1	2	–	3
Greece	1	–	19	20
Italy	1	26	–	27
Poland	–	22	–	22
Spain	–	17	–	17
Belgium	–	4	–	4
India	–	2	–	2
Russia	–	–	1	1
France	–	1	–	1

This chapter has tried to give some specificity to the question of who are evangelicals, in North America and elsewhere. Surveys of the populace in general go a long way in answering such questions. But so do efforts at understanding something about the leaders who are most widely recognized as standard-bearers for the evangelical movement and finding out about what formally evangelical organizations say they believe. Those are the subjects of the next two chapters.

Notes

1   For useful discussion of evangelicals, defined as those who say they have been born again, see George Gallup, Jr and Jim Castelli, *The People's Religion: American Faith in the 90s* (New York: Macmillan, 1989), pp. 92–8. Popular reports on religion in Canada using the Angus Reid surveys are found in "God is alive – special report: the religion poll," *Maclean's*, April 12, 1993, pp. 32–50; "How very different: a poll shows how Canadian and US attitudes vary on family, politics and religion," *Maclean's*, November 4, 1996, pp. 36–40; and Mark A. Noll, "Religion in Canada and the United States," *Crux* [Regent College], December 1998, pp. 13–25, with commentary by John G. Stackhouse on "Who are the evangelicals?" pp. 26–8. For a sophisticated essay using Angus Reid data, see Andrew S. Grenville, "The awakened and the spirit-moved: the religious experiences of Canadian evangelicals in the 1990s," in *Aspects of the Canadian Evangelical Experience*, ed. G. A. Rawlyk (Montreal and Kingston: McGill-Queen's University Press, 1997), pp. 417–31.

2   For a wide-ranging survey of their results and conclusions, see John Green, James Guth, Lyman Kellstedt, and Corwin Smidt, *Religion and the Culture Wars: Dispatches from the Front* (Lanham, MD: Rowman & Littlefield, 1996). Further examples include Kellstedt and Green, "The mismeasure of evangelicals," *Books & Culture*, January/February 1996, pp. 12–13; Kellstedt and Smidt, "How to count the Spirit-filled," *Books & Culture*, July/August 1996, pp. 24–5; Green, Guth, Kellstedt, and Smidt, "Who elected Clinton: a collision of values," *First Things*, August/September 1997, pp. 35–40; Green, Guth, Kellstedt, Smidt, and Margaret Poloma, *The Bully Pulpit: The Politics of Protestant Ministers* (Lawrence: University Press of Kansas, 1997); Green, Guth, Kellstedt, and Smidt, "Bringing in the sheaves: the Christian right and white Protestants, 1976–1996," in *Sojourners in the Wilderness: the Christian Right in Comparative Perspective*, eds James Penning and Corwin Smidt (Lanham, MD: Rowman & Littlefield, 1997), pp. 75–91; Green, Guth, Kellstedt, and Smidt, "Evangelicalism," in *The Encyclopedia of Religion and Society*, ed. William H. Swatos, Jr. (Walnut Creek, CA: AltaMira Press, 1998), pp. 175–8; Green and Guth, "United Methodism and American political culture: a statistical portrait," in *The People Called Methodists*, eds William Lawrence, Dennis Campbell, and Russell E. Richey (Nashville, TN:

Abingdon, 1998), pp. 27–52; and Green, Guth, Kellstedt, and Smidt, "The 'spirit filled' movements in contemporary America: a survey perspective," in *Pentecostal Currents in American Protestantism*, eds Edith L. Blumhofer, Russell P. Spittler, and Grant Wacker (Champaign: University of Illinois Press, 1999), pp. 111–30.

3   Christian Smith, *American Evangelicalism: Embattled and Thriving* (Chicago: University of Chicago Press, 1998); Michael Emerson and Christian Smith, *Divided by Faith: Evangelical Religion and the Problem of Race in America* (New York: Oxford University Press, 2000); and Christian Smith, *Christian America? What Evangelicals Really Want* (Berkeley: University of California Press, 2000).

4   I am grateful to Angus Reid and Andrew Grenville for the use of this data and to Lyman Kellstedt for assistance with interpretation.

5   See above, p. 13.

6   See Reginald W. Bibby, *Fragmented Gods: the Poverty and Potential of Religion in Canada* (Toronto: Irwin, 1987); *Mosaic Madness: the Poverty and Potential of Life in Canada* (Toronto: Stoddart, 1990); and *Unknown Gods: the Ongoing Story of Religion in Canada* (Toronto: Stoddart, 1993). Donald Posterski has put Angus Reid survey data to good use in regular columns for the Winnipeg-based periodical *Christian Week*.

7   As late as the early 1970s, church attendance in Canada, as reported in Gallup polls, was higher than in the United States; in the 1950s and early 1960s it was much higher.

8   See, for example, John Webster Grant, *A Profusion of Spires: Religion in Nineteenth-century Ontario* (Toronto: University of Toronto Press, 1988), pp. 224–5.

9   For exploring Angus Reid's own concerns about morality, modern economic life, and social capital, especially in Canada, see Angus Reid, *Shakedown: How the New Economy Is Changing Our Lives* (Toronto: Doubleday Canada, 1996).

10 General discussion of this world poll is found in *Angus Reid World Monitor*, 1, January 1998.

3

The Significance of Billy Graham

Evangelicalism has always been a populist religion in which the ability of persuasive leaders to gain a following is central. Over the past century there have been a great number of charismatic revivalists, industrious editors, and energetic builders of institutions whose labors defined the movement's public face. In Britain, John Stott, a preacher and author of careful biblical exposition, has been a focal point of evangelism, cultural analysis, and social criticism for a large constituency.[1] Evangelical leaders in the United States are usually more flamboyant than Stott, although the editor-theologian Carl Henry has displayed some of the same combination of evangelistic zeal, thoughtful writing, and movement mobilization.[2] Earlier in the twentieth century, William Bell Riley used his platform as a popular Baptist pastor in Minneapolis to become an early leader of the fundamentalist movement.[3] His near contemporary, Aimee Semple McPherson, also gained national attention, but as a largely nonconfrontational promoter of pentecostal themes.[4] Thomas F. Zimmerman, long-time general superintendent of the Assemblies of God, exercised low-key but effective leadership in guiding the very rapid growth of the Assemblies of God.[5] By exemplifying and institutionalizing the practice of divine healing, Oral Roberts became a larger-than-life figure for millions.[6] More recently, Jerry Falwell, Pat Robertson, James Dobson, and Charles Colson have – in quite different ways – parlayed religious zeal, media savvy, and political polemic into wide recognition as evangelical leaders.[7] Of all notable evangelicals in the United States' recent past, however, none has come close to the visibility, influence, and sheer presence of William Franklin Graham.

The recent publication of Billy Graham's memoirs offers a propitious opportunity for taking stock of his career.[8] Along with several other recent developments – the frailties of his age, the encroachments of

Parkinson's disease, the death or retirement of many of the Billy Graham Evangelistic Association's original team players, the extension of the evangelist's mantle to his son Franklin, and a growing number of solid assessments from outside Graham's immediate circle – the appearance of this autobiography provides an apt moment for assessment.[9]

Billy Graham became popular because he had a gift for public speaking, and because he simply exuded charisma. Who could turn aside from such a winsome Southerner even when he was describing the broad way leading to destruction. Russell Mixter, a retired professor of biology who once caught heat at Graham's alma mater, Wheaton College, for daring to explore the relationship between Christianity and evolution, was a member of the United Gospel Tabernacle in Wheaton where Graham received his first regular preaching assignment in the early 1940s. "I heard him every Sunday for two years," Professor Mixter recently recalled. "He was a straightforward, plain-spoken, honest, direct and very competent man who was obviously devout."[10]

An impressive preacher from an early age, Graham became in 1944 the first full-time employee of the Youth for Christ Movement, whose purpose was to evangelize the young people of the nation. He traveled extensively on behalf of Youth for Christ, was briefly president of a Bible college in the Twin Cities, and conducted periodic tent crusades. In the summer of 1949, Graham and associates planned such a gathering in Los Angeles, thinking it would last three weeks. Spectacular conversions of athletes, mobsters, and entertainers led to an extension. Publisher William Randolph Hearst got wind of the event and instructed his newspapers to "puff Graham." The results were spectacular. The rallies extended for another nine weeks; crowds jammed the 6,000-seat "Canvas Cathedral"; and a new star had arisen on the nation's religious horizon.

Graham has remained popular over the succeeding half-century because he has aged well – the fiery young evangelist became the distinguished senior evangelist. In addition, he remains popular because he does not have extra-marital affairs, nor does he exploit the sums of money contributed by his followers for lavish personal consumption. In an America where the sexual and fiscal indiscretions of popular revivalists make up a considerable chronicle, these are not small virtues. Graham's appeal has even reached heights usually reserved for rock stars and lifetime .330 hitters. Parents are known to take very small children to Graham's public meetings so that the youngsters can later say they heard him preach in person. I even have a friend who proudly boasts of once having changed his clothes in a room where Graham formerly resided.

Graham's autobiography, *Just as I Am*, does many of the things that memoirs from such a stage of life often do. Graham's choice of title, for instance, evokes much that has been memorable about his public activity. The phrase is from a hymn written by Charlotte Elliott (1789–1871), sister of an evangelical Anglican clergyman:

> Just as I am, without one plea,
> But that Thy Blood was shed for me,
> And that Thou bidst me come to Thee,
> O Lamb of God, I come.

The hymn's use of the language of the Authorized Version, its reminder of the freighted spiritual significance of saintly women (usually slightly in the background), as also its quintessentially evangelical mixture of Christo-centric self-resignation and spiritual self-assertion – all of these are pure Billy Graham. The title also evokes the scene played out at the end of thousands of Graham's sermons where, with this hymn being sung slowly in the background by a massed choir under the direction of Cliff Barrows, Graham appeals to his listeners to get up out of their seats and proceed to the front of the auditorium (or stadium or hall or amphitheater) in order to make a decision for Christ.

Just as I Am is also characteristic for taking a few pages in trying to set the record straight. The book is not at its best in these sections, which include a concession about perhaps overstressing the spiritual danger of international communism in his early preaching, a defense of incautious statements about the relative freedom of Christian worshipers made after Graham's first visits behind the Iron Curtain in the late 1970s and 1980s, several obviously painful efforts to describe the difficulties in raising a family of five children while being perpetually away from home, and an account (once again) of loyalty to Richard Nixon. What sets this memoir apart is not the effectiveness of such rebuttals, for (whatever their merits) self-justifications of this sort are almost impossible to pull off. Rather, it is the mood or tone of voice with which such infrequent efforts at score-settling are attempted, for even in such situations Billy Graham comes across as an almost unbelievably nice person.

Graham seems to like everyone. He has a good word to say about even the enemies who railed at him from the theological far right as a tool of Satan (for consorting with modernists) and from the theological far left as an ignoramus, bigot, or front man for American Big Business. Graham has had personal contact with all of the Presidents since Truman, he has been invited to provide words of spiritual counsel to many other high-ranking American officials, and he has met the heads of state from dozens of countries around the world. No one, it seems, could get his goat, at least for long. In 1954, a hard-bitten columnist pounded Graham in print shortly before he arrived in London. Graham responded by seeking out the reporter in a pub (lemonade for Billy), whereupon the reporter softened up enough to write a commendatory column. The great Swiss theologian Karl Barth once stood in the rain to hear Graham preach in Basel. When he told Graham that the sermon from John 3:3 was good but should not have stressed the *must* in "you must be born again," Graham begged to differ (and was soon gratified to hear another great theologian, Emil Brunner, affirm his position). But then Graham closes this account concerning Barth with these words: "In spite of our theological differences, we remained good friends." That line, with variations for politics, region, ethnicity, and other appropriate variables, could be the epitome for his life.

Graham's apparently bottomless kindness, combined with the lightning pace of this narrative – so many visits, so many high and mighty, so many good friends, so many celebrities – means that *Just as I Am* is not a particularly challenging book. It is, nonetheless, worth reading carefully, both because Graham is the genuine article and because many of the book's details and much of its tone are in fact quite useful for attempting a more complex assessment.

Such a complex assessment could begin by trying to summarize important aspects of his career and by offering theses interpreting its major direction. In what follows I offer three of each.

Observations

As a first observation on his career, Graham has shown a capacity, rare among those possessing great gifts at an early age, for maturing as he grew older. For Graham, that maturity has been primarily political and social. Early in his career Graham's conventional evangelical faith was matched by a conventional faith in America. In 1950, the first broadcast of his long-running radio program, "The Hour of Decision," offered what was then a typical mixture of religious and anti-communist fervor. "The Battle Hymn of the Republic" preceded an appeal for spiritual repentance, and the evangelist's message was filled with alarm about "the tragic end of America" and the "hour of tragic crisis all across the world." As time wore on, such rhetoric would gradually tone down.

Graham also matured in his judgment on political figures. He has enjoyed particularly close relationships with conservative political leaders, especially Richard Nixon. Only last-minute intervention by Bobby Kennedy kept Graham from publishing an endorsement of then Vice President Nixon on the eve of the 1960 presidential election between Nixon and John F. Kennedy. The resignation of President Nixon in 1974 and, even more, the earlier revelations of sordid doings in the Nixon White House sobered Graham politically. Since then, he has been more circumspect and more determinedly non-partisan in his political associations. He has also advanced well beyond the conventional views of his evangelical constituency to advocate greater controls on nuclear arms and increased efforts to establish world peace. In the 1980s he made several well received visits to China and the Soviet Union, during which he went out of his way to cooperate with local officials and to encourage the Christian churches in these countries. Almost as remarkable as the consistent appeal of Graham's preaching, therefore, is the evolution of his politics, from aggressive cold warrior to widely respected advocate for world peace and international toleration.

Second, for a popular preacher Graham has played a surprisingly positive part in the reawakening of evangelical intellectual life that has taken place since the Second World War. By his own admission, Graham is not a scholar. Yet he has supported many of the main ventures that have advanced evangelical learning. Graham was the major force behind the founding of *Christianity Today*, which he envisaged as a magazine "that would give theological respectability to evangelicals," one which would, among other things, "also show that there was concern for scholarship among evangelicals." He has served as a board member for many evangelical institutions of higher education. And he has gone out of his way to present an evangelistic message at many major universities in the United States and abroad. By his friendship with Howard John Ockenga, Carl Henry, and like-minded leaders he provided the evangelical equivalent of an *imprimatur* for serious engagement with the academic world. Perhaps more than any other figure, Graham has protected evangelical scholars from the anti-intellectual tendencies of the broader evangelical community. If, in my limited experience, I know of several instances where Graham has effectively turned aside evangelical Mau-Maus on the warpath against even small outbursts of intellectual creativity, there must be many more such moments.

Third – and what must be most important for evangelicalism as such – Graham has remained a man with a message. Day in, day out he has proclaimed what, in a trademark phrase, "the Bible says" about human sin and the need for divine redemption. His gospel message is a simple one of the need for faith in Christ, but not simplistic, for it does not deny the struggles of faith. Graham has been remarkably eager to cooperate with a wide range of Christians. A major campaign in New York City in 1957 marked a turning point in his career. When Graham insisted on including representatives of mainline Protestant churches in the planning for the crusade, and on directing some who made decisions for Christ at these meetings to those same churches, he won the undying wrath of separatistic fundamentalists. In subsequent years, Graham has even gained the guarded support of Catholic officials for his work. Earlier he had been a pioneer in integrating blacks and whites in his crusades, even in the South. All this is to say that for Graham, the gospel – not in-group, nationalistic, racial, privileged, partisan, or sectarian appropriations of the gospel – has remained the guiding light.

But more needs to be said by way of assessment. Graham's status as a celebrity, the kinds of sermons he has preached, and his basic theological stance all require further consideration.

Assessment

First, Graham's nose for the powerful has taken some of the edge off his message but also allowed him to become an extraordinary symbol for the universality of Christian faith. Whether consciously or not, Graham practiced a strategy of access from his earliest days as a student preacher. Always charismatic as a speaker, always friendly face to face, always morally upright, always careful about funds, he has worn his own fame very well. Over time, especially after Watergate, he became more consistent in keeping his own political and international views out of sight, even as he continued to exploit political and diplomatic friendships. The result was access to the absolutely top levels of political decision-making as well as his position as one of the twentieth century's most widely recognized human beings. (Think, for example, of Graham in the three-year period 1958–60, preaching before large crowds at multiple sites in the Caribbean, Africa, Europe, Australia, New Zealand, and the United States, and then again in the three-year period 1988–90, doing the same thing at multiple sites in the People's Republic of China, the USSR, Canada, England, Hungary, West Germany, Hong Kong, and again the United States – and carrying on the same way for most of the intervening thirty years. It is a pace that no mere politician, basketball star, or rock band could hope to match.) To maintain this level of well regarded fame has taken work at reducing friction – moral, political, public relational, and personal. But he has done it. Graham, in short, has traded angularity for access. If the two following theses are valid, it was a good trade.

Second, Graham has minimized offense at his preaching by restricting his enumeration of sins mostly to those that received close attention in his evangelical culture: malicious neglect of spouse and children, overindulgence in drink, sexual immorality, and capitulation to anomie. While he gives many indications of realizing that sin also manifests itself as heedless egotism, self-aggrandizement, greed, callousness to the poor, excessive self-protection, and lust for the main chance, these sins (more the pride of life than the lusts of the flesh or eyes) have not featured large in his witness. Since in his sermons the sense of sin is the beginning point for the balm of the gospel, the charge of self-protecting spiritual myopia might be reasonable. Why witness about how Christ forgives sins to X (fill in the name of the public person you best love to hate, since Graham is almost certain to have maintained some level of friendship with that individual) if you won't speak plainly to that person about the sin he or she seems most obviously to be committing? It is a good question, but perhaps a misdirected question, since Graham's preference for generic (and hence not too threatening) sins has enabled him to keep speaking to all sorts of people in all sorts of places and, moreover, has enabled the innumerable schemes, ventures, publications, movies, programs, educational institutions, and miscellaneous ventures to which he has lent his name to benefit from the almost universal fondness for Graham himself.

In other words, Graham has brokered his particularly inoffensive way of reminding people that they are sinners in need of grace into one of the most powerful forces for Christian ecumenicity ever seen – that is, himself.

Graham emerged from a divisive brand of Protestant fundamentalism that in the 1930s and 1940s – for example, at Bob Jones University in South Carolina and Wheaton College in Illinois – was fighting for its life, in all senses of the phrase. Graham took to heart the cross- and Christ-centered focus of that tradition but very early on began to outgrow its combatively compulsive boundary-setting. In 1957, fundamentalists broke with Graham (not Graham with fundamentalists) when he invited non-fundamentalist churches to his New York City crusade. Graham likewise reached out across racial lines earlier than all but a few of his Southern (or even Midwestern) evangelical peers, and that at a time when Graham's publishing brainchild, *Christianity Today*, was being funded by wealthy evangelicals who equated civil rights agitation with the communist threat. He was also one of the first Protestants, evangelical or mainline, to exploit the common ground of the Apostles' Creed ("my own basic creed," he calls it in *Just As I Am*) with Roman Catholics and then the Orthodox. By so doing, Graham has done more than any person in the twentieth century, with the possible exception of C. S. Lewis, to promote from the Protestant side the enriching concerns of a meaningfully specific "mere Christianity." In his memoirs, Graham takes particular delight in highlighting mutual supporting relationships with Cardinal Cushing, Rose Kennedy, John Paul II, Bishop Fulton Sheen, and other well known Catholics.

As early as the mid-1950s, Graham had determined to maintain a broad basis for cooperation: "If a man accepts the deity of Christ and is living for Christ to the best of his knowledge, I intend to have fellowship with him in Christ." The fact that he has maintained that basis allows for a balanced judgment. The Graham who portrays sin in a relatively unthreatening way is also the Graham who reaches out very widely to redeemed sinners of every description. The result is a Christian witness that has knitted together an incredibly far-flung network of Christian believers from all over the globe and from every stratum on the social hierarchy.

The third thesis concerns the most important matter. Whatever the assessment of Graham's view of sin, what about his view of God? Here

the question is whether Graham's strategies of access and orthodox ecumenicity undermine his message. The charge that perhaps they do arises
from two ways in which Graham has seemed to reduce the Christian
gospel to a utilitarian device existing for other, more ultimate purposes.
In the first instance, it is possible to glimpse pressure on his message
from the moral calculus, singularly American in its outworking, of
republican citizenship. This calculus suggests that in a republic the good
health of the polity depends upon the morality of the citizenry; that the
best thing for personal morality is religion; and that, since Christianity
is the best religion, it is positioned to do the most for America.
Especially in the first part of his career, Graham was prone to statements
that seemed to make the destiny of the United States loom larger than
the fate of the Christian gospel; for example, "I seriously doubt if
the old America is going to exist another generation unless we have a
turning to Christ." Some who share Graham's beliefs would agree with
him, but also wonder if he was making the penultimate over into the
ultimate.

In a second instance, Graham throughout his career has spoken of
Christianity, again in his words, as "alone" pointing "the way to individual peace, social harmony, life adjustment, and spiritual satisfaction."
From a Christian angle, true enough again. But are priorities arranged
as they should be arranged when sermons conclude as one did, for
example, in New York in 1957: "All your life you've been searching
for peace and joy, happiness, forgiveness. I want to tell you, before you
leave Madison Square Garden this night of May 15, you can find everything that you have been searching for, in Christ. He can bring that
inward, deepest peace to your soul. He can forgive every sin you've ever
committed."

The charge that can be laid against the utilitarian drift of Graham's
Christian message is the charge that so troubled Martin Luther for a
decade or more in the early sixteenth century as he struggled to find a
merciful God. The heart of Luther's spiritual dilemma was the fear that
his supposed search for God was really a search for his own ease of soul,
the fear that he was seeking God primarily for what God could do for
him. Luther may have been overly scrupulous, but he could tell idolatry when he saw it, and tell it most clearly when he saw it up close.

Billy Graham claims for himself neither Luther's theological acumen
nor his penetrating powers of self-analysis. Yet what rescued Luther
from himself is also what has preserved the authenticity of Billy

Graham's message. The reason why Graham's message, though admittedly soft at the edges, remains solid as a rock at the center is its focus on the cross of Christ. In the early 1950s Graham solidified early practice by dedicating himself to the saving work of Christ as the heart of his message: "I made a commitment never to preach again without being sure that the Gospel was as complete and clear as possible, centering on Christ's sacrificial death for our sins on the Cross and His resurrection from the dead for our salvation."

At the close of his memoirs, as at the close of so many sermons, Graham restates an appeal for conversion that is the trademark of his career. As he makes that appeal in the book there is his customary attention to what the gospel does for us. But undergirding the appeal, from first to last, is an equally full sense of what the gospel does *to* us:

> We are not here by chance. God has put us here for a purpose, and our lives are never fulfilled and complete until His purpose becomes the foundation and center of our lives. . . .
>
> When you [open your heart to Jesus Christ], you become a child of God, adopted into His family forever. He also comes to live within you and will begin to change you from within. No one who truly gives his or her life to Christ will ever be the same, for the promise of His Word is true: "Therefore, if anyone is in Christ, he is a new creation; the old has gone, the new has come! All this is from God, who reconciled us to himself through Christ and gave us the ministry of reconciliation" (2 Corinthians 5:17–18).
>
> We have seen this happen countless times all over the world, and it can happen in your life as well. Open your life to Christ today.

If in the hands of Billy Graham, as an American of his age, the gospel bends, nonetheless it does not break. To conclude that Graham has remained faithful to the message that God saves sinners for his own purposes, as well as for theirs, is the highest accolade a fellow-believer can bestow on this remarkable man.

But Graham, of course, has become more than just a rallying point for Christian believers. He is also the most attractive public face that evangelical Protestantism has offered to the wider world in the half-century since the Second World War. And so one other thing needs to be said when we consider the other dynamic personalities who might have fulfilled that leadership role had Graham not remained faithful to his message: the only people with more cause to be thankful for the life of Billy Graham than those who share his beliefs are those who do not.

Notes

1   Reliable information is found in two works by Timothy Dudley-Smith, *John Stott: The Making of a Leader* (Leicester: InterVarsity Press, 1999); and *John Stott: a Comprehensive Bibliography* (Downers Grove, IL: Inter-Varsity Press, 1995). For an even clearer measure of Stott's contributions, see his own books – including many volumes of biblical commentary: *Basic Christianity* (Grand Rapids, MI: Eerdmans, 1958, and many subsequent editions); *Between Two Worlds: the Art of Preaching in the Twentieth Century* (Grand Rapids, MI: Eerdmans, 1982); *The Cross of Christ* (Downers Grove, IL: InterVarsity Press, 1986); and *Evangelical Truth* (Downers Grove, IL: InterVarsity Press, 1999) – and the helpful exchanges recorded in a jointly authored book, David L. Edwards and John Stott, *Essentials: a Liberal–Evangelical Dialogue* (Downers Grove, IL: InterVarsity Press, 1988).

2   See Carl F. H. Henry, *Confessions of a Theologian: an Autobiography* (Dallas: Word, 1986).

3   See William Vance Trollinger, *God's Empire: William Bell Riley and Midwestern Fundamentalism* (Madison: University of Wisconsin Press, 1990).

4   See Edith L. Blumhofer, *Aimee Semple McPherson: Everybody's Sister* (Grand Rapids, MI: Eerdmans, 1993).

5   Edith L. Blumhofer, *Restoring the Faith: the Assemblies of God, Pentecostalism, and American Culture* (Urbana: University of Illinois Press, 1993), pp. 231–49 passim.

6   See David Edwin Harrell, Jr, *Oral Roberts: an American Life* (Bloomington: Indiana University Press, 1985).

7   See Jerry Falwell, *Falwell: an Autobiography* (Lynchburg, VA: Liberty House, 1997); David Edwin Harrell, Jr, *Pat Robertson* (San Francisco: Harper & Row, 1987); Wendy Murray Zoba, "Daring to discipline America" [on James Dobson], *Christianity Today*, March 1, 1999, pp. 31–8; and Charles W. Colson, *Born Again* (Old Tappan, NJ: Chosen Books, 1995).

8   *Just as I Am: the Autobiography of Billy Graham* (San Francisco: Harper-SanFrancisco/Zondervan, 1997). Unless otherwise indicated, all quotations from Graham are from this volume.

9   The best general biography is William Martin, *A Prophet with Honor: the Billy Graham Story* (New York: Morrow, 1991), but also noteworthy are John Pollock, *Billy Graham, Evangelist to the World* (San Francisco: Harper

& Row, 1979); Marshall Frady, *Billy Graham: a Parable of American Right-eousness* (Boston: Little, Brown, 1979); and the treatment of Graham in the last sections of Joel A. Carpenter, *Revive Us Again: the Reawakening of American Fundamentalism* (New York: Oxford University Press, 1997).

10 Personal conversation with the author, December 1988.

4
Beliefs

It is one thing for historians, sociologists, survey researchers, and other curious investigators to debate who may be considered an evangelical and to describe what such classifications mean in practice. It is another for denominations and special-purpose organizations to define prescriptively for themselves their own convictions. An important, if often neglected, path to understanding evangelical Christianity is to find out what groups widely recognized as evangelical actually put in writing concerning their beliefs. The British sociologist Steve Bruce once came to a startling realization early in his research on Americans who identified with the New Christian Right: "What we need to know to explain the genesis of a popular social movement . . . is why people become involved. The obvious thing to do is to ask them."[1] Pursuing a similar strategy for evangelical organizations – though by no means a way of answering all possible questions – will nonetheless provide a clearer picture of the formal religious shape of evangelical Christian conviction.

At the mid-point of his long public ministry in eighteenth-century England, John Wesley paused to attempt a succinct definition of what it meant theologically to be committed to the principles of the evangelical revival. This master of the terse summation could put it into 18 words: "I. Original Sin. II. Justification by Faith. III. Holiness of Heart and Life provided their life be answerable to their doctrine."[2]

In 1999, a well regarded leader of contemporary American evangelicalism attempted a similarly concise response to the question "What is an evangelical?" Timothy George is the president of the Beeson Divinity School at Samford University in Birmingham, Alabama. Beeson is an unusual seminary because, although it is Southern Baptist, it also supports studies in Anglicanism, Methodism, and Presbyterianism, and carries out under George's direction a number of pan-evangelical enterprises that regularly cross boundaries between Baptists and non-Baptists, whites and blacks, as well as Southerners and Northerners. George began his attempt at answering the question with a one-paragraph expansion of Wesley's effort from 235 years earlier:

> Evangelicals are a worldwide family of Bible-believing Christians committed to sharing with everyone everywhere the transforming good news of new life in Jesus Christ, an utterly free gift that comes through faith alone in the crucified and risen Savior. To put it more simply, evangelicals are gospel people and Bible people. We do not claim to be the only true Christians, but we recognize in one another a living, personal trust in Jesus the Lord, and this is the basis of our fellowship across so many ethnic, cultural, national, and denominational divides.[3]

For good and for ill, denominations and self-defined evangelical institutions cannot be as brief as Wesley or George. Almost all such organizations publish a doctrinal statement or confession of faith that sets out their religious beliefs. For some groups these statements remain in the background. For others they are a source of constant tinkering. For still others they become flashpoints of controversy when disputes force boundary-setting definitions to be applied in specific cases. Whatever the different ways they are employed, however, the formal belief statements constitute a valuable resource for understanding contemporary evangelical Christianity. To anticipate the conclusions from this investigation, evangelical statements of faith present a solid – even remarkably uniform – core of widely shared convictions. But they also present, as one might expect in light of great diversity within the tradition, an extraordinarily diverse range of differences on matters of faith and practice beyond that core.

The Organizations and Their Statements

The doctrinal statements employed for this chapter come from three of the largest American denominations within the evangelical tradition, six special-purpose or parachurch evangelical agencies, and one international evangelical movement in which Americans have played an important role.

The three denominations are the Southern Baptist Convention, the Church of God in Christ, and the Assemblies of God. With its approximately sixteen million members, the Southern Baptist Convention is the largest American denomination in the American evangelical mosaic. Its very size and dominance in the southern regions of the country does mean that Southern Baptists often do not describe themselves in generic or transdenominational terms as evangelicals, yet almost all surveys of American religion feature the Southern Baptists as a major descendant of the revival movements of the eighteenth and nineteenth centuries and the chief institutional promoter of their values in the United States today. The Southern Baptists' statement of doctrine (called Baptist Faith and Message) is an extensive seven-page document.[4] When its eighteenth chapter on the family was last revised in 1998, the Southern Baptists' effort at reinforcing traditional understandings of home and family became the source of considerable public comment.[5]

The Assemblies of God is the largest mostly white pentecostal denomination in the United States, while the Church of God in Christ (COGIC) is the largest mostly African-American pentecostal denomination. The two shared some personnel and many common interests in the early days of the twentieth century, but emerged as separate denominations in 1907 (COGIC) and 1914 (Assemblies). There are now nearly three million members of the Assemblies and over five million members of COGIC. The Assemblies' "Statement of Fundamental Truths" is a long document of eleven single-spaced pages, while COGIC defines its beliefs in a half-page summary statement followed by an expansion of that summary spread over six pages.[6]

The six evangelical parachurch groups selected for this survey usually employ the term "Statement of Faith" to identify their beliefs. They include three organizations for which Billy Graham has played a key role – the Billy Graham Evangelistic Association (BGEA) itself, the National Association of Evangelicals (NAE), and Christianity Today, Inc. (CTi, the publisher of *Christianity Today* and several other magazines). The doctrinal statements of two of the best known evangelical organizations aimed at working with college students are also included – Campus Crusade for Christ and InterVarsity Christian Fellowship. The sixth organization is Wheaton College, the alma mater of Graham and an institution that many visible evangelical leaders have attended.[7] The statements of faith for these groups are much shorter than for the denominations; they range in size from one-third of a page for InterVarsity to roughly two pages for Campus Crusade and Wheaton.

Finally, two important international documents are also part of this survey, the Lausanne Covenant of 1974 and the Manila Manifesto of 1989. These documents grew from the first and second "International Congresses on World Evangelization," meetings financed in large part by American evangelical organizations, including the Billy Graham Evangelistic Association, but also drawing participants from a very broad worldwide constituency. Individuals identified with evangelical movements from about 150 countries met at Lausanne and, among other activities, produced a six-page "covenant" of beliefs. Fifteen years later in Manila representatives came from even more countries and published a thirteen-page "manifesto" as an "elaboration" of the original Lausanne Covenant.[8]

When these statements of belief are read together, it is possible to identify where formal evangelical statements of belief converge, and also where they diverge. The convergence turns out to be surprisingly substantial.[9] In what follows the doctrines are taken up in the order in which they appear in most of the statements.

Convergence

Convergence in these evangelical statements of faith begins with the *Bible*. Eight of the ten begin with a statement on Scripture (for the other two – Wheaton and Lausanne – Scripture comes second). All of them speak in unison by affirming that the Bible is infallible (it does not let people down) and inspired (its writing reflects the direct influence of God). They are equally in agreement that Scripture is the ultimate authority for beliefs and practices. The InterVarsity statement puts it most economically in affirming belief in "the unique divine inspiration, entire trustworthiness and authority of the Bible." The Lausanne Covenant expands matters considerably, but much along the lines of the other statements: "We affirm the divine inspiration, truthfulness and authority of both Old and New Testament Scriptures in their entirety as the only written word of God, without error in all that it affirms, and the only infallible rule of faith and practice. We also affirm the power of God's word to accomplish his purpose of salvation. . . . Through it [Scripture] the Holy Spirit still speaks today. He illumines the minds of God's people in every culture to perceive its truth freshly through their own eyes and thus discloses to the whole Church ever more of the many-colored wisdom of God."

Not only do these evangelical statements begin with Scripture, but all of them make an effort to show how reliance on the Bible provides the content for everything else in the statements. That reliance is most obvious in the longer documents, with the Assemblies of God and COGIC providing explicit reference to individual biblical texts as the basis for their other doctrines, and with the Southern Baptist, Lausanne, and Manila statements employing even more extensive citations of texts. The Southern Baptists, for instance, cite 13 passages from the Old Testament and 16 from the New as support for their statement on the Bible, and another 42 scriptural references (28 Old Testament, 14 New) in support of their statement on the family.

The evangelical statements are just as unanimous on *God*, who is described as the only God and the creator of the universe.[10] Evangelical descent from classical Christian traditions is indicated by affirmation of the mystery of the Trinity, the ancient Christian conviction that the one God exists eternally in three persons, Father, Son, and Holy Spirit. The Southern Baptist statement expresses this consensus clearly: "There is one and only one living and true God. He is an intelligent, spiritual, and personal Being, the Creator, Redeemer, Preserver, and Ruler of the universe. God is infinite in holiness and all other perfections. To Him we owe the highest love, reverence, and obedience. The eternal God reveals Himself to us as Father, Son, and Holy Spirit, with distinct personal attributes, but without division of nature, essence, or being."

The statements are just as united in what they affirm about *Jesus Christ*. Jesus was born of a virgin without a human father through the miraculous agency of the Holy Spirit. (Four of the statements – BGEA, Southern Baptists, CTi, Wheaton – mention the Virgin Mary by name.) As at once both God and human, Jesus lived a sinless life. His death on a cross was substitutionary and a sufficient payment for the penalty owed to God by the sins of humanity. After Jesus rose bodily from the dead, he ascended into heaven where he now resides at the right hand of the Father. In heaven Jesus continues to serve humanity by acting as a mediator and advocate for sinners within the counsels of the Trinity. At the end of time, Jesus will return to the earth, and this Second Coming will mark the ultimate and visible triumph of God as well as the end of the world as we have known it.

The Assemblies of God self-consciously echo classical traditions on the nature of Christ: "The Lord Jesus Christ, as to His divine and eternal nature, is the proper and only Begotten of the Father, but as to His human nature, He is the proper Son of Man. He is therefore, acknowledged to be both God and man; who because He is God and man is 'Immanuel,' God with us." The BGEA, as befits its major interest in spreading the Christian message, affirms that "Jesus Christ was conceived by the Holy Spirit, born of the Virgin Mary. He led a sinless life, took on Himself all our sins, died and rose again, and is seated at the right hand of the Father as our mediator and advocate."

General unanimity also characterizes what is said about the person of the *Holy Spirit*, at least up to a point. There is broad agreement that the special function of the Spirit is to dwell in Christian believers and strengthen them for life and service. The two pentecostal denominations go on to say that the indwelling of the Holy Spirit manifests itself in speaking with tongues; the same two statements also refer to many other activities of the Holy Spirit that are not mentioned in the other documents. The Lausanne Covenant makes a special point of spelling out the work of the Spirit in preparing Christians for evangelization. And several statements speak explicitly of the Holy Spirit's important role in bearing witness to God's saving work in Christ. The NAE expresses a typical form of belief in the third person of the Trinity: "We believe that for the salvation of lost and sinful people, regeneration by the Holy Spirit is absolutely essential. . . . We believe in the present ministry of the Holy Spirit by whose indwelling the Christian is enabled to live a good life." COGIC's affirmation of the "Baptism of the Holy Ghost" shows how the pentecostal denominations extend the consensus teaching:

We believe that the Baptism of the Holy Ghost is an experience subsequent to conversion and sanctification and that tongue-speaking is the consequence of the baptism in the Holy Ghost with the manifestations of the fruit of the spirit (Galatians 5:22–23; Acts 10:46, 19:1–6). We believe that we are not baptized with the Holy Ghost in order to be saved (Acts 19:1–6; John 3:5). When one receives a baptismal Holy Ghost experience, we believe one will speak with a tongue unknown to oneself according to the sovereign will of Christ. To be filled with the Spirit means to be Spirit controlled as expressed by Paul in Ephesians 5:18–19. Since the charismatic demonstrations were necessary to help the early church to be successful in implementing the command of Christ, we therefore, believe that a Holy Ghost experience is mandatory for all men today.

Even with such important differences between pentecostal and non-pentecostal evangelicals on the subject of the Holy Spirit, there still is as much uniting these different parts of the movement as dividing them.

On *humanity* and *human nature*, the statements make common reference to a familiar biblical story: humans were created in the image of God for the purpose of enjoying his fellowship. But Adam and Eve disobeyed God and brought judgment down upon themselves and their progeny. As a result of sin (and the emphasis is on sins that people themselves commit more than on what is inherited from Adam and Eve), humans are separated from God and stand in need of salvation through Christ. In the ordering of evangelical doctrinal statements, these assertions about humankind often follow statements about the nature of Christ and precede declarations about the person and work of the Holy Spirit. The sections from Campus Crusade for Christ are entirely representative, even to using "man" as a generic term for all humans: "Man was originally created in the image of God. He sinned by disobeying God; thus, he was alienated from his Creator. That historic fall brought all mankind under divine condemnation. . . . Man's nature is corrupted, and he is thus totally unable to please God. Every man is in need of regeneration and renewal by the Holy Spirit."

Most of the statements also say similar things about *evangelization*, or the privilege and imperative of passing on the gospel ("good news") about salvation in Christ. COGIC includes its statement on bearing witness in its discussion of the Holy Spirit: "The Holy Ghost is a gift bestowed upon the believer for the purpose of equipping and empowering the believer, making him a more effective witness for service in the world. He teaches and guides one into all truth (John 16:13; Acts 1:8, 8:39)." Although COGIC's placement of this discussion is unusual, what its statement says is quite typical.

The various doctrinal standards also say much the same thing about *Christian living*. Terms, phraseology, and scriptural citations differ a great deal, but almost all the statements mention the importance of believers living a godly life. The Lausanne and Manila statement are especially strong in adding extensive consideration of social duties to their comments on Christian living, but most of the others refer to such matters at least indirectly. A long discussion from Manila on "the gospel and social responsibility" begins with this summary: "The authentic gospel must become visible in the transformed lives of men and women. As we proclaim the love of God we must be involved in loving service, as we preach the Kingdom of God we must be committed to its demands of justice and peace."

Finally, the statements say much of the same things about the *church*, the *final judgment*, and the *ordinances* of baptism and the Lord's Supper (or communion, Eucharist). All affirm the church as Christ's Body in the world. Several emphasize the importance of the church for world evangelization, several underscore its centrality for worship, and several stress its universal character. What the statements for the most part lack are strong affirmations about the institutional character of the church such as might be found among Roman Catholics, Lutherans, Episcopalians, or Presbyterians.

The reality of a final divine judgment also frequently appears. The BGEA, Lausanne, and COGIC statements do not mention a final judgment as such, though all imply that one will take place. The others affirm straightforwardly that at this last judgment the redeemed will remain forever with God while those who are not redeemed will be damned. Here is how Wheaton College puts it: "We believe in the blessed hope that Jesus Christ will soon return to this earth, personally, visibly, and unexpectedly, in power and great glory, to gather His elect, to raise the dead, to judge the nations, and to bring His Kingdom to fulfillment. We believe in the bodily resurrection of the just and unjust, the everlasting punishment of the lost, and the everlasting blessedness of the saved."

In its statements on ordinances, the Church of God in Christ adds foot-washing to baptism and the Lord's Supper. As could be expected, most of the parachurch groups do not mention the ordinances, whereas the denominations spend considerable time, with considerable reference to Scripture, in detailing their position on these rites. None of them uses the term "sacraments" for baptism and the Lord's Supper.

Divergence

The list of noticeable differences in the eleven statements of faith is considerable, though not, on balance, as striking as the extensive core of common affirmations. The most notable contrast is the more extensive treatment provided to the person and work of the Holy Spirit from the

pentecostal denominations. Included in those two statements are extensive comment on the divine healing applied by the Holy Spirit and made
possible by the way in which Christ's death on the cross conquered physical sickness as well as spiritual death. Other evangelicals may also believe
that God sometimes performs miraculous cures, but pentecostal groups
are usually the only ones to state such convictions as part of their doctrinal foundations.

Otherwise, the styles of presentation (from short, colloquial, and
without explicit scriptural documentation to long, formal, and with
extensive biblical citation) are more obviously distinctive than anything
they affirm. The Southern Baptists, for example, include extensive discussions of Sunday as the Lord's Day, peace and war, the proper way to
carry out education, and the requirements for a godly family. But what
is said in these discussions is quite similar to what many evangelicals
associated with the other groups would have written had they provided
an equally lengthy statement.

Other shades of difference also show up in the statements. The
Assemblies of God are unusual in stressing that the return of Christ will
be pre-millennial (that is, that it will occur before the thousand-year
reign of Christ mentioned in Revelation 20, a reign construed as
metaphorical by some other evangelicals). Wheaton refers to God's creation of Adam and Eve as "direct." COGIC specifically mentions angels
and demons, and Wheaton refers directly to Satan. Lausanne and Manila
(along with the Southern Baptists) have extensive discussion of religious
liberty. Lausanne and Manila also contain the most thorough affirmations about the need for Christian believers to be active socially, although
both Wheaton and the Southern Baptists sketch in brief what the two
worldwide statements expound upon at length.

Looking at formal doctrinal statements of officially established organizations is naturally not the same as finding out what the adherents to
these groups actually believe and practice. As suggested in chapter 12 of
this book, that search might be more productive from a study of hymns
than from a study of formal doctrinal statements. Yet paying attention
to these official statements of faith is beneficial. After reading them carefully, it would be difficult to accuse evangelicals (at least in formulating
official statements) of emoting off the cuff, for they all reflect the exercise of careful thought. The pay-off from that careful thought is a
genuine measure of clarity, useful for guiding evangelical adherents in
exploring the resources of the faith they say they affirm and also allow-

ing outsiders to describe accurately what evangelicals do (and do not) consider their most important beliefs.

Notes

1 Steve Bruce, *The Rise and Fall of the New Christian Right: Conservative Protestant Politics in America, 1978–1988* (Oxford: Oxford University Press, 1988), p. 20.

2 Nehemiah Curnock, ed., *The Journal of John Wesley*, 8 volumes (London: Epworth, 1909–16), *volume 5*, p. 61. This definition is included in a letter that Wesley wrote to clergymen connected to what he called the "great work in England" that God had begun, dated April 19, 1764. The letter itself does not contain the word "evangelical."

3 Timothy George, "If I'm an evangelical, what am I?" *Christianity Today*, August 9, 1999, p. 62.

4 Text from http://www.sbc.net/bfmreport.cfm (December 15, 1999). For the background of this statement in Baptist history, see Timothy George and Denise George, eds, *Baptist Confessions, Covenants, and Catechisms* (Nashville: Broadman & Holman, 1996).

5 For national attention to the statement, see *New York Times*, June 10, 1998, p. A1; and June 13, 1998, p. A11. The revised chapter 18 now includes these affirmations: "God has ordained the family as the foundational institution of human society. It is composed of persons related to one another by marriage, blood or adoption. . . . The husband and wife are of equal worth before God, since both are created in God's image. The marriage relationship models the way God relates to His people. A husband is to love his wife as Christ loved the church. He has the God-given responsibility to provide for, to protect, and to lead his family. A wife is to submit herself graciously to the servant leadership of her husband even as the church willingly submits to the headship of Christ. She, being in the image of God as is her husband and thus equal to him, has the God-given responsibility to respect her husband and to serve as his helper in managing the household and nurturing the next generation."

6 Statements from http://www.ag.org/top/about/truths.cfm (December 15, 1999); and http://www.cogic.org/Faith.html (December 15, 1999).

7 Statements from http://www.billygraham.org/faithstatement.asp (December 15, 1999); http://www.nae.net/about-mission.html (December 15, 1999); http://www.christianityonline.com/overview/faith.html (December 15, 1999); http://www.ccci.org/Faith.html (December 15, 1999); http://www1.gospelcom.net/iv/general/faq.html (December 15, 1999); and http://www.wheaton.edu/catalog/sof.html (December 15, 1999).

8   Statements from http://www.lausanne.org/statements/covenant.html
    (December 15, 1999); and http://www.lausanne.org/statements/manila.
    html (December 15, 1999).
9   Choice of other groups and statements would certainly result in alterations
    in emphasis, but it is doubtful if adding the formal belief statement of any
    group widely recognized as evangelical would materially alter the conclu-
    sions that follow. The only exception would be denominations derived
    from European movements of the Reformation period, where the state-
    ment of faith would reflect sixteenth- and seventeenth-century concerns
    more obviously than do modern statements.
10 The brief InterVarsity statement presupposes rather than affirms God; ref-
    erence to God as creator is omitted in four of the shorter statements.

5

Region, Class, Race

When in the *Washington Post* for February 1, 1993, writer Michael Weisskopf opined that evangelicals were "largely poor, uneducated, and easy to control," he was met with skepticism mingled with criticism. But if he had said that evangelicals were Southern, white, middle class, and female, he would have been on somewhat more solid ground – depending, of course, on which definition of evangelical was employed. Locating evangelicals by region, class, race, and gender is, at best, an inexact exercise since variety among evangelicals takes in a full range of demographic, social, economic, ethnic, and political differences, as well as differences on such religious matters as the gifts of the Holy Spirit, the extent of human free will, and details surrounding the Second Coming of Christ. This chapter and the next make a start on such questions of location with a brief review of historical developments and more extensive presentation of recent survey data. For issues of region, class, and race, the available information paints a fairly clear picture. Questions of gender prove more complicated both historically and for the present, and are addressed in the next chapter. The main conclusion to come from each of these demographic forays is caution. While definite patterns can be glimpsed among evangelicals, demographically as well as religiously, they are never so dominant or overwhelming as to allow the kind of blanket, unqualified ascriptions for which writer Weisskopf was justly chastised.

Region

Foreign visitors to the United States are regularly amazed at the great number of different churches they find, especially Protestant churches, often evangelical Protestant churches. Yet a few of the shrewdest visitors have also noticed that the variety of churches pertains to the nation as a whole, and not necessarily to each of its regions.[1] America's great cities do, in fact, usually provide a home for many varieties. But once outside the cities adherents to the various denominations tend to be clumped together fairly closely into strong regional concentrations. Thus it has always been. In the 1770s, for example, the largest denomination in the new United States was Congregationalism, whose churches were located almost exclusively in New England, and the second largest was Episcopalianism, which was concentrated overwhelmingly in the southern states. Soon the intensely evangelical Methodists and Baptists spread out over many parts of the new nation, but even they were more heavily concentrated in some areas than in others. Methodists predominated in the country's middle regions,[2] Baptists in the South.

Regional strength of the various denominations, which reflects also on the question of where evangelicals live, continues to be important. The Glenmary Research Center in Atlanta periodically prepares color-coded maps to plot the distribution of denominations.[3] In these maps each county is given a color for its most populous religious group. The color is dark if that denomination has over half the church adherents, light if it has 25 percent or more. With Catholics given the color blue, such maps show solid dark blue through New York and New England, around the shores of Lake Michigan, in the Southwest, and in the far southern portions of Texas, Louisiana, and Florida.

Baptists, one of the most consistently evangelical denominations, are assigned the color red. On all such maps, the South is a sea of red. In 1990, Baptists made up the largest sector of the churched population (including Catholics) in fourteen Southern and mid-South states (in eight of these states Baptists represented 50 percent or more of the church population, in six between 25 and 49 percent). Additionally, on maps showing just Protestants, Baptists appeared as the largest Protestant grouping in another six states of the Southwest and West. Outside of the broad southern third of the country, however, Baptists rarely constitute even the largest Protestant group in a county. Rather, in the Midwest the color turns to green, for the Lutherans, who are the largest Protestant body in all the states of the Upper Midwest (Wisconsin, Iowa, Minnesota, North Dakota, South Dakota, Nebraska, and Montana). Lutherans, it is well to remember, are often "evangelical" in the old-world sense of confessional Protestantism, and some Lutherans are

Table 5.1 Percentages of those who hold three or four of the evangelical convictions by US regions

	Northeast	*South*	*Midwest*	*West*	*Total*
US population	20	35	23	22	100
Evangelical beliefs	14	44	25	17	100

kindly disposed to the beliefs and practices associated with Anglo-American evangelicalism. But as a whole, students of contemporary religion who categorize Lutherans as mainline Protestants make a wise choice.[4] The Methodists, another mainline body with some evangelical representation, are especially strong in a band running from Delaware (the state with the highest concentration of Methodists in the country) through Nebraska. The main denominations of the Restorationist movement (Churches of Christ, Disciples of Christ, and Christian Churches), which have more ties to current self-defined evangelicals than either Lutherans as a whole or Methodists as a whole, are likewise strong in the lower Midwest and upper South. Scattered across the country are also many individual counties where for specific historical reasons individual evangelical groups predominate. For example, pentecostal churches make up the largest Protestant group in several counties in Washington, Oregon, and northern California; and there are a few counties in South Dakota where an evangelical variety of Episcopalianism predominates because of Episcopalian missions among the Dakota Indians. A realization that denominations reflect a varied presence in different regions is good preparation for realizing the same thing about evangelical beliefs and affiliation more generally.

The Angus Reid cross-border survey of 1996 spotlighted more particularly the geography of evangelicals, whether identified by their convictions or their church attachments. The regional distributions shown in tables 5.1 and 5.2 are for percentages of those who professed at least three of the four evangelical convictions that are discussed in chapter 2. The tables show that in Canada the distribution of those who held to the evangelical beliefs roughly approximates the distribution of the national population as a whole, while in the United States, by contrast, profession of the evangelical beliefs is overrepresented in the South and underrepresented in New England and the West. The American

Table 5.2 Percentages of those who hold three or four of the evangelical convictions by Canadian regions

	BC	Alberta	Sask./Man.	Ontario	Quebec	Atl. Prov.	Total
Canadian population	13	9	7	38	25	8	100
Evangelical beliefs	12	9	11	36	21	12	101

Table 5.3 Percentage of each religious tradition in different US regions

	Northeast	South	Midwest	West	Total
US population	20	35	23	22	100
Evangelical Protestant-hi	12	46	26	16	100
Mainline Protestant-hi	19	37	28	15	99
Black Protestant	18	54	19	9	100
Catholic-hi	28	20	29	23	100
Secular/nominal	22	28	21	29	100

Table 5.4 Percentage of each religious tradition in different Canadian regions

	BC	Alberta	Sask./Man.	Ontario	Quebec	Atl. Prov.	Total
Canadian population	13	9	7	38	25	8	100
Evangelical Protestant-hi	21	14	15	30	8	12	100
Mainline Protestant-hi	11	9	12	64	7	13	98
Catholic-hi	6	5	5	36	38	10	100
Secular/nominal	16	10	6	37	25	6	100

Midwest contains about the same percentage of the national population as the percentage of those who affirm at least three of the evangelical beliefs.

Tables 5.3 and 5.4 shift the focus to the denominational traditions that are historically identified with evangelicals. These tables also use one additional variable. Instead of counting all those as evangelicals who declared that they were, say, Baptists, these tables count only those who made such a profession and also said they practiced religion at least modestly. (Those who said they were Methodists, Catholic, Church of Christ, or the like, but did not pray, almost never went to church, and did not think religion was important in their lives were lumped together within the secular/nominal category.) This variable adds the label "hi" as an additional designation for the largest traditions: Roman Catholics, mainline Protestants, and evangelical Protestants.[5]

Tables 5.3 and 5.4 record that in the United States distribution by denominational tradition is as skewed as by evangelical beliefs, with once again evangelicals overrepresented in the South and underrepresented in the West and Northeast. The Canadian situation for denominational tradition is this time more like the American, for the traditional evangelical denominations are considerably overrepresented in Western Canada and the Atlantic provinces, slightly underrepresented in Ontario, and much underrepresented in Quebec.

Region, in other words, makes a difference in describing American evangelicals. There are more in the South, fewer in the Northeast and West. Since the nation's elite media and instructions of higher education are concentrated in the West and the Northeast, the underrepresentation of evangelicals in those areas probably leads to some misapprehensions in academic and journalistic sources. The other side of this skewed national distribution, however, is that especially in the South there remain enclaves where evangelicalism constitutes an informal state within the state.

Class

There does not appear to be as much that distinguishes American evangelicals by class as by region. In a rough assessment of the eighteenth- and nineteenth-century patterns, evangelicals seem to have been largely drawn from the middle and lower-middle classes, with significant numbers of adherents also attracted from elite and marginal groups as well.[6] The most obvious class factor in evangelical history is the recurring propensity of evangelical groups to start low and aim high – to begin, that is, as upstart movements of the marginalized but to move up the social and economic ladder fairly rapidly as these radical movements mature. This pattern has been visible among eighteenth-century evangelicals in England, among British and American Methodists in the

Table 5.5 Income and education for various religious traditions (1980–1990, percentages)

	At least some college education	Family income over $30,000
Evangelical Protestants	30	27
Mainline Protestants	46	41
Catholics	38	41
Jews	67	59
No religion	41	35

nineteenth century, with black Protestants since the early formation of African-American churches, and with pentecostal, holiness, and Southern Baptist groups in the twentieth century.[7]

Results from modern survey research verify these general conclusions. By aggregating information from six biennial surveys undertaken by the University of Michigan's Center for Political Studies from 1980 to 1990, a picture emerges of evangelical social location as it existed in the 1980s.[8] At first glance, table 5.5 indicates some support for Michael Weisskopf's assessment of evangelicals as relatively poor and uneducated. The data from these surveys as shown in table 5.5 defined evangelicals by belief in evangelical doctrines *and* by adherence to traditional evangelical denominations; they also include blacks and whites together.

But this table's picture of evangelicals as considerably less well educated and less affluent is deceptive. When additional items are assessed from these surveys, it becomes clear that evangelicals are overrepresented among the young, Southerners, and African Americans – historically groups that show less education and income in such surveys. Table 5.6 summarizes the demographic data. This table suggests that what look like markers of lower social class for evangelicals may be related as much to other factors as to religion. In passing, it is interesting to observe that these surveys from the 1980s disclosed even more overrepresentation of Southerners among evangelicals than did the Angus Reid 1996 poll.

More recent surveys show less differences in class markers between evangelicals and other Americans. The best survey on charitable giving within denominations has been done by John and Sylvia Ronsvalle.[9] They found from an extensive survey in 1994 that while giving among

Table 5.6 Age, residence, and racial identification for various religious traditions (1980–1990, percentages)

	Aged 30 or under	Live in South	African-American
Evangelical Protestants	20	54	26
Mainline Protestants	12	26	6
Catholics	17	15	4
Jews	12	18	1
No religion	37	22	10

members of eight denominations belonging to the National Association of Evangelicals was higher per capita than giving among members of eight denominations from the National Council of Churches ($630 per person annually versus $443), reported per capita income for the two groups was virtually identical (National Council of Churches $15,119; National Association of Evangelicals $15,144). Other research, including the 1996 Angus Reid cross-border survey, has found scant differences in education and wealth between evangelicals and other church adherents, although almost all such surveys have revealed somewhat higher levels of church commitment and giving among evangelicals than among other groups in the population.[10]

Class, in other words, cannot be ruled out entirely as an aspect of the history and current situation of American evangelical Christians. But it does not seem to be a major determinant now, and it appears only marginally important in the past.

Race

The situation could not be more different for race. Even though African-American Protestants began to practice forms of evangelical Christianity quite early, serious barriers have always separated blacks and whites. Historically the enslaved status of most African-Americans before the Civil War greatly affected the religious situation, but so also did the African origin of black Americans in contrast to the European roots of most white Americans.[11] The anomalous situation emerged rapidly in the early history of the United States, where black and white Christians often expressed similar beliefs and gathered for worship in churches with

Table 5.7 Black–white convergence in beliefs, but divergence in social attitudes (percentages)

	Evangelical	African-American	Mainline
Beliefs and religious practices			
Give a tithe or more to church	42	52	20
Believe Adam and Eve were real people	89	94	73
Believe in miracles today	80	86	79
Pray daily or more	77	83	64
Social and political attitudes			
Strongly agree that more should be spent to fight hunger	55	72	57
Strongly agree that defense spending should be cut	46	58	48
Strongly agree that an Equal Rights Amendment is needed	54	78	60

similar names (Methodist, Baptist), but where racial and social segregation led to separate attitudes, practices, and associations.[12]

That situation prevails to this day, where informal attitudes and ingrained community habits rather than laws continue to separate blacks and whites who share roughly the same evangelical beliefs.[13] To be sure, evangelicals have made some serious efforts to cross the racial divide, including efforts to create organizations for self-identified evangelical blacks, to link programs and conferences, to explore agencies for social outreach, and to cooperate on other kinds of projects.[14] But these efforts have only begun to bridge a chasm.

Indications of the dimension of that chasm are again suggested by the results of recent surveys. In 1992, a poll of 4,001 Americans conducted for the University of Akron asked a large number of specific questions about religious beliefs and practices, as well as attitudes toward public and social questions.[15] The survey's results reveal that white evangelicals (defined by both beliefs and adherence to traditional evangelical denominations) and black evangelicals were very close in their religious beliefs, but they were quite far apart in political attitudes. In table 5.7, white mainline Protestants are included for the sake of comparison.

The 1996 Angus Reid survey carried the same message. In response to questions about their religious beliefs and their social-political attitudes, white evangelicals and black Protestants responded in similar proportions on most religious matters and a few social-political ones. But for many social-political issues (and only a few religious ones) there were major differences.[16] As examples, reasonably similar proportions of white evangelicals and black Protestants responded that the Bible was inspired, that Scripture should be accepted literally word-for-word, that they had been converted, that they prayed daily, and that they read the Bible or religious literature at least weekly. Somewhat greater differences showed up in response to the question whether all religions were equally true (30 percent of white evangelicals said yes, 53 percent of black Protestants) and as to whether the world would end in a great battle of Armageddon (70 percent of the white evangelicals, 49 percent of the black Protestants). But the largest differences appeared on social-political issues. Do you have confidence in law enforcement? (white evangelicals 64 percent, black Protestants 39 percent). Do you think the government should spend more to alleviate poverty? (white evangelicals 48 percent, black Protestants 77 percent). Do you have confidence in the President [this was Bill Clinton before the Lewinski scandal]? (white evangelicals 38 percent, black Protestants 68 percent). In addition, as we will see in greater detail in chapter 9, white evangelicals Protestants have been the strongest segment in American society voting for Republican presidential candidates throughout the 1990s, while religiously active African-Americans constitute one of the most consistent voting blocks in favor of the Democratic candidates.

In one of the Angus Reid survey's most telling indications of separate religious worlds, the pollsters found that roughly the same proportion of white evangelicals and black Protestants called themselves "pentecostals" (white 21 percent, black 18 percent) and "charismatics" (white 23 percent, black 19 percent). Quite a few more white evangelicals called themselves "fundamentalists" than African-American Protestants did (white 43 percent, black 24 percent). But the differences were most pronounced when identifying as either "evangelical" (white 50 percent, black 17 percent) or "liberal-progressive" (white 32 percent, black 53 percent). Such comparisons underscore an enduring historical reality. American blacks and whites might share a heritage of evangelical beliefs and affiliation in roughly equal measure, but the historical similarities in religious background do not translate into shared religious associations or public attitudes.

A solid recent book by sociologists Michael Emerson and Christian Smith contains a sophisticated analysis of these historic standoffs. On the basis of extensive polling and field interviews, these researchers found that many white evangelicals would like to end racial divisions and inequality, but that their efforts to move in that direction are often counterproductive. Racial problems, in this reading, do not result from ignorance or prejudice. They arise instead because of "the ways in which culture, values, norms, and organizational features that are quintessentially evangelical and quintessentially American, despite having many positive qualities, paradoxically have negative effects on race relations." Among other factors, the sociologists highlight the entrepreneurial, individualistic quality of evangelical Protestant life. This religious style opens up great room for innovation and creativity, but it also is inherently conservative because it thrives on the ability to enlist audience support. Moving against the grain – in this case, by changing economic habits, rethinking what good housing should be, or questioning assumptions about racial stereotypes – requires the sort of top-down leadership authority that evangelicals have always mistrusted.[17]

Attempting to factor issues of region, class, and race into the identification of evangelicals clarifies much. It shows again how deceptive bare statements about "evangelical this" or "evangelical that" can be. It also shows, however, that making even modest attempts at discriminating within the large, but amorphous, group of those who are called evangelicals yields rich rewards of clarity, precision, and good sense. The same results also accompany care in assessing the question of evangelicals and gender.

Notes

1   For example, Steve Bruce, "Pluralism and Religious Vitality," in *Religion and Modernization: Sociologists and Historians Debate the Secularization Thesis*, ed. Steve Bruce (Oxford: Clarendon, 1992), pp. 170–94.
2   Martin Marty once suggested that the strength of Methodism was "the North of the South and the South of the North," in Jackson W. Carroll, Douglas W. Johnson, and Martin E. Marty, *Religion in America: 1950 to the Present* (San Francisco: Harper & Row, 1979), p. 87.
3   The detailed information on which the most recent set of maps was based is found in Martin B. Bradley et al., *Churches and Church Membership in the United States 1990: an Enumeration by Region, State and County Based*

on Data Reported by 133 Church Groupings (Atlanta: Glenmary Research Center, 1992).

4 As in, for example, Wade Clark Roof and William McKinney, *American Mainline Religion: Its Changing Shape and Future* (New Brunswick, NJ: Rutgers University Press, 1987).

5 Adding this variable expands the conclusions provided in chapter 2 about constituencies of evangelicals (and others) in the USA and Canada. With these additional categories, the Angus Reid survey found the following distribution for the United States: evangelical Protestant-hi 19.9 percent; evangelical Protestant-lo 6.2 percent; mainline Protestant-hi 9.5 percent; mainline Protestant-lo 5.2 percent; black Protestant 9.2 percent; Catholic-hi 12.9 percent; Catholic-lo 7.3 percent; secular/nominal 19.9 percent; other 9.8 percent. For Canada the distribution was as follows: evangelical Protestant-hi 7.1 percent; evangelical Protestant-lo 3.2 percent; mainline Protestant-hi 7.2 percent; mainline Protestant-lo 9.3 percent; Catholic-hi 13.4 percent; Catholic-lo 12.5 percent; secular/nominal 40.2 percent; other 7.2 percent.

6 Among the books that illuminate the complex issue of class among early evangelicals, see Rhys Isaac, *The Transformation of Virginia, 1740–1790* (Chapel Hill: University of North Carolina Press, 1982); David Bebbington, *Evangelicalism in Modern Britain: a History from the 1730s to the 1980s* (London: Unwin Hyman, 1989); John Wigger, *Taking Heaven by Storm: Methodism and the Rise of Popular Christianity in America* (New York: Oxford University Press, 1998); Christine Heyrman, *Southern Cross: the Beginnings of the Bible Belt* (New York: Knopf, 1997); Nathan Hatch, *The Democratization of American Christianity* (New Haven, CT: Yale University Press, 1989); and Jon Butler, *Awash in a Sea of Faith: Christianizing the American People* (Cambridge, MA: Harvard University Press, 1992).

7 Scholars differ dramatically on how they assess this process of evangelical betterment, but many testify to its occurrence; for examples only, see E. P. Thompson, *The Making of the English Working Class* (New York: Vintage, 1966); David Hempton, *Methodism and Politics in British Society, 1750–1850* (London: Hutchinson, 1984); Curtis Johnson, *Islands of Holiness: Rural Religion in Upstate New York, 1790–1860* (Ithaca, NY: Cornell University Press, 1989); Randolph Roth, *The Democratic Dilemma: Religion, Reform, and the Social Order in the Connecticut River Valley of Vermont, 1791–1850* (New York: Cambridge University Press, 1987); Kathryn Teresa Long, *The Revival of 1857–58* (New York: Oxford University Press, 1998); James T. Campbell, *Songs of Zion: the African Methodist Episcopal Church in the United States and South Africa* (Chapel Hill: University of

North Carolina Press, 1998); Clarence E. Walker, *A Rock in a Weary Land: the African Methodist Episcopal Church During the Civil War and Restoration* (Baton Rouge: Louisiana University Press, 1982); James Melvin Washington, *Frustrated Fellowships: the Black Baptist Quest for Social Power* (Macon, GA: Mercer University Press, 1986); Robert Mapes Anderson, *Vision of the Disinherited: the Making of American Pentecostalism* (New York: Oxford University Press, 1979); and Grant Wacker, *Heaven Below: Early Pentecostals and American Culture* (Cambridge, MA: Harvard University Press, 2001).

8   I am grateful to Lyman Kellstedt and Joan Blauwkamp for providing these data.

9   John L. Ronsvalle and Sylvia Ronsvalle, *The State of Church Giving through 1994* (Champaign, IL: empty tomb, inc., 1996), with numbers in next sentence from p. 32.

10   For indications of higher giving among Assemblies of God and Southern Baptists than among Lutherans, Presbyterians, or Catholics, see Dean R. Hoge and Fenggang Yang, "Determinations of religious giving in American denominations: data from two nationwide surveys," *Review of Religious Research*, 36 (December), 1994, pp. 123–48; and Dean R. Hoge, Charles Zech, Patrick McNamara, and Michael J. Donahue, *Money Matters: Personal Giving in American Churches* (Louisville, KY: Westminster John Knox, 1996). For a summary of the Angus Reid information on giving, see Dean R. Hoge and Mark A. Noll, "Levels of contributions and attitudes toward money among evangelicals and non-evangelicals in Canada and the US," in *More Money, More Ministry: Money and Evangelicals in Recent North American History*, eds Larry Eskridge and Noll (Grand Rapids, MI: Eerdmans, forthcoming).

11   See Section I, "The African heritage," in Albert J. Raboteau, *Slave Religion: the "Invisible Institution" in the Antebellum South* (New York: Oxford University Press, 1980).

12   As signal works describing this situation, see Eugene D. Genovese, *Roll, Jordan, Roll: the World the Slaves Made* (New York: Random House, 1974); Milton C. Sernett, *Black Religion and American Evangelicalism: White Protestantism, Plantation Missions, and the Flowering of Negro Christianity, 1783–1865* (Metuchen, NJ: Scarecrow, 1975); Mechal Sobel, *The World They Made Together: Black and White Values in Eighteenth Century Virginia* (Princeton, NJ: Princeton University Press, 1987); Margaret Washington Creel, *"A Peculiar People": Slave Religion and Community Culture among the Gullahs* (New York: New York University Press, 1988); and Sylvia R. Frey and Betty Wood, *Come Shouting to Zion: African American Protestants in the American South and Caribbean to 1830* (Chapel Hill: University of North Carolina Press, 1998).

13   For discussion of a similar situation with mainline Protestants, see David
     W. Wills, "An enduring distance: black Americans and the establishment,"
     in *Between the Times: the Travail of the Protestant Establishment in America,
     1900–1960*, ed. William R. Hutchison (New York: Cambridge University
     Press, 1990), pp. 168–92; and Randall K. Burkett and Richard Newman,
     eds, *Black Apostles: Afro-American Clergy Confront the Twentieth Century*
     (Boston: G. K. Hall, 1978).

14   As examples from a surprisingly large list, see Tom Skinner, *How Black Is
     the Gospel?* (Philadelphia: Lippincott, 1970), William H. Bentley, *The
     National Black Evangelical Association* (Chicago: W. H. Bentley, 1979);
     Raleigh Washington and Glen Kehrein, *Breaking Down Walls: a Model for
     Reconciliation in an Age of Racial Strife* (Chicago: Moody, 1993); John
     Perkins and Thomas A. Tarrants III, *He's My Brother: Former Racial Foes
     Offer Strategy for Reconciliation* (Grand Rapids, MI: Chosen Books, 1994);
     John M. Perkins, ed., *Restoring At-risk Communities: Doing It Together and
     Doing It Right* (Grand Rapids, MI: Baker, 1995); George A. Yancey, *Beyond
     Black and White: Reflections on Racial Reconciliation* (Grand Rapids, MI:
     Baker, 1996); and Dennis L. Okholm, ed., *The Gospel in Black and White:
     Theological Resources for Racial Reconciliation* (Downers Grove, IL: Inter-
     Varsity Press, 1997).

15   The survey was conducted by John Green, James Guth, Lyman Kellstedt,
     and Calvin Smidt; I am grateful to Lyman Kellstedt for sharing its results
     with me.

16   The comparisons spelled out in the next sentences contrast white evan-
     gelicals in the "high" category of religious participation with all black
     Protestants, which makes similarity in religious professions even more
     striking. For the purpose of this comparison, I considered proportions
     within 20 percent of each other as relatively close, but differences of over
     20 percent as indicating greater separation.

17   Such arguments, and many more, are worked out with a great deal of
     sophistication in Michael O. Emerson and Christian Smith, *Divided by
     Faith: Evangelical Religion and the Problem of Race in America* (New York:
     Oxford University Press, 2000), quotation on p. ix.

6

Gender

The complexity of gender issues among evangelicals is nicely illustrated by the experiences of two African-American exhorters of the nineteenth century. Jarena Lee (1783–1850) was converted to an evangelical form of Christianity through the ministry of Richard Allen, founder of the African Methodist Episcopal (AME) Church, while she was living in Philadelphia in 1804.[1] Soon thereafter she underwent the experience of sanctification, which Methodists taught was a second work of the Holy Spirit following conversion that cleansed believers for purer service to God. Soon after that experience she felt called to preach. Richard Allen responded that Lee was welcome to "exhort" – that is, to speak public words of encouragement or warning to believers and nonbelievers – but not to become a regular preacher. Lee soon married, bore several children, and moved around a bit. In 1818, after the death of her husband, she returned to Philadelphia and finally convinced Allen of the validity of her calling. For the next thirty years she was a vigorous itinerant who later also became active in support of the American Antislavery Society. In an autobiographical reflection, Lee explained the way in which evangelical commitments to Experience and Truth had competed for supremacy in her life:

> The Bishop was pleased to give me an appointment at Bethel Church, but a spirit of opposition arose among the people against the propriety of female preaching. My faith was tried – yet I felt my call to labor for souls none the less. "Shall the servant be above his Master?" The ministers of Jesus must expect persecution, if they would be faithful witnesses against sin and sinners – but shall they, "awed by a mortal's form, conceal the word of God?" Thou God knowest my heart, and that thy glory is all I have in view. Shall I cease from sounding the alarm to an ungodly world,

when the vengeance of offended heaven is about to be poured out, because my way is sometimes beset with scoffers, or those who lose sight of the great Object, and stop on the road to glory to contend about non-essentials? Rather let the messengers of God go on.[2]

The experiences of Julia A. J. Foote (1823–1900) were similar. After conversion and sanctification in an AME congregation in Albany, New York, she felt a call to preach but also encountered opposition, at first from her husband, but also from others who could not credit the validity of such a vocation. Eventually that opposition was overcome, and Foote became an itinerant for the African Methodist Episcopal Zion Church throughout upstate New York, Canada, Ohio, and Michigan. Toward the end of her life, her services were recognized when she was appointed as her denomination's first woman deacon (1894) and then ordained as its second female elder (1900). As with Jarena Lee, however, the reconciliation of evangelical experience pushing her to public activity and evangelical conventions reacting against that push resulted in considerable inner turmoil:

I had always been opposed to the preaching of women, and had spoken against it, though, I acknowledge, without foundation. . . .

The trouble my heavenly Father has had to keep me out of the fire that is never quenched, he alone knoweth. My husband and friends said I would die or go crazy if something favorable did not take place soon. I expected to die and be lost, knowing I had been enlightened and had tasted the heavenly gift. I read again and again the sixth chapter of Hebrews [which speaks of the impossibility of bringing back to repentance those who had tasted the heavenly gift and then fell away].

Nearly two months from the time I first saw the angel, I said that I would do anything or go anywhere for God, if it were made plain to me. He took me at my word, and sent the angel again with this message: "You have I chosen to go in my name and warn the people of their sins." I bowed my head and said, "I will go, Lord."[3]

Jarena Lee and Julia Foote were untypical only because African Americans have always been a minority within evangelical movements and because their Methodism represented a minority, albeit a substantial minority, of evangelical adherents. What was typical about their accounts was the confluence of important strands of evangelical belief and practice.

Those strands included a conservative approach to the doctrine of Scripture and conservative traditions of biblical interpretation. Respect for the Bible and traditional practices of interpretation, however, have worked several ways in evangelical history. Because evangelicals take the Bible seriously – even literally – they are always aware of passages like I Corinthians 14:34 ("Let your women keep silent in the churches"), I Timothy 2:12 ("I suffer not a woman to teach, nor to usurp authority over the man, but to be in silence"), or Ephesians 5:24 ("as the church is subject unto Christ, so let the wives be to their own husbands in every thing").[4] But because of the same conservative approach to Scripture, they have also always been alert to literal implications of passages like Acts 2:17 ("And it shall come to pass in the last days, saith God, I will pour out of my Spirit upon all flesh; and your sons and your daughters shall prophesy"), Galatians 3:28 ("there is neither Jew nor Greek, there is neither bond nor free, there is neither male nor female: for ye are all one in Christ Jesus"), or Ephesians 5:25 ("Husbands, love your wives, even as Christ also loved the church, and gave himself for it").[5]

Similar contrasting possibilities opened up when evangelical experiences of God's grace clashed with the social traditions of patriarchy. Evangelical belief in the reality and power of God's direct action upon individuals – an action respecting neither age nor wealth, neither social status nor gender – has worked time and again as a force liberating the silent and giving courage to the powerless. Direct contacts with angels such as Julia Foote experienced have not necessarily been the norm, but her sense of immediate connection to God is definitely representative. This evangelical tradition has undermined tight gender-role expectations and freed up women, African Americans, and lower-class men for self-confident Christian service. Yet in British and North American history, evangelicals have also been great defenders of propriety, eager to display the ennobling, purifying, stabilizing, and even pacifying effects of godliness. This latter evangelical tradition has often supported barriers between men and women, encouraged all sorts of people to "stay in their place," and nurtured passivity in the face of social wrongs.

At the end of the twentieth century, the rise of feminism in the universities and among the elite media (arenas already suspect to many evangelicals) has complicated the equation. Evangelicals are almost always defenders of the family, of sex within monogamous marriage, and of traditional attitudes toward homosexuality, abortion, and pornography. These stances have made some evangelical leaders prominent in the culture wars and enlisted many evangelical followers into the ranks of the Christian Coalition, the Concerned Women of America, and other politically conservative movements. Such right-wing mobilization, however, obscures historical evangelical attitudes toward gender, which were sometimes quite radical. It also obscures the surprising breadth of interest shared between at least some leading feminists and many rhetorically anti-feminist evangelicals.

Full attention to the subject of evangelicals and gender would require a book much longer than this entire volume. It would also demand serious probing of what evangelical beliefs and practices have meant for male self-concepts and images of ideal masculinity, subjects that are only just now beginning to receive serious study.[6] It would also, to speak frankly in the authorial first person, require more clarity on cultural and theological matters than I possess.

What is possible, however, is an interpretive survey of highlights from the significant literature on women in evangelical movements that has been pouring forth from a growing number of authors for more than two decades.[7] That literature is now highly nuanced in describing a complicated picture. It presents the sort of complexity about evangelicals and gender that neither cultural warriors nor quick-fix journalists appreciate. But trying to make some general sense of a stellar line-up of books and articles is the place where responsible attention to the subject must begin.

For the sake of convenience, the outstanding array of recent scholarship can be broken down into its treatments of eighteenth- and nineteenth-century developments, the twentieth-century history of women within fundamentalist and neo-evangelical groups, the twentieth-century record of women in pentecostal and other more radical forms of evangelicalism, and contemporary accounts of women's activities in self-consciously evangelical churches. For each era and subject, attention must be sketchy, but the notes should be sufficient for pointing to more thorough discussions.

Evangelical Origins and Nineteenth-century Developments

Among the other disruptions brought about by the evangelical revivals of the eighteenth century was a disruption of traditional gender roles.

When men and women were converted, often in life-shaking moments of great crisis, gender distinctions receded or were reversed. When individuals were born again – "swallowed up in God" or "wrapped up in God" were phrases used more than once – everything changed.[8] Those changes affected gender boundaries differently depending on who and where the born-again evangelicals were. Evangelical movements within the Church of England, Scottish or new-world Presbyterianism, and New England Congregationalism experienced a loosening of tight gender expectations – women might occasionally give voice in public to their experiences of grace, pastors paid more attention to what might be learned from women about the ways of God, and leaders encouraged household, private, and outside-of-church religious activities by both men and women. In his Congregational Church in Northampton, Massachusetts, for example, Jonathan Edwards regularly singled out women (and young girls) as offering models for the kind of spirituality he felt the Bible described. Occasional women of status and wealth, like the Countess of Huntingdon in England, could become powers behind the scenes. Yet within these formal, established churches longstanding traditions of Western Christendom prevailed where only men were ordained, men were the ones who defined theological boundaries, and women were expected to exert an influence mostly with the confines of the household. These conventional traditions would remain especially strong in the American South until the present.

It was a different situation among the evangelical groups that sprang up on the margins of polite society (Methodists) or that were dramatically energized by the currents of revival (Baptists). In groups like the Baptists, where congregational autonomy was an important principle, a powerful new sense of community encouraged converted women to speak, allowed for the participation of women in cases of church discipline, and featured a new concern for humble egalitarianism on the part of many men. Converted women found the agency that had hitherto been reserved for men; converted men found a depth of caring relationships that had previously been the preserve of women.[9]

Although the Methodists were led by the Tory Anglicans John and Charles Wesley, these leaders were also unusually attuned to the spiritual potential of ordinary people. Especially the Methodist class meeting opened up unusual new spiritual opportunities for women, and also for lower-class men, since these cell groups were lay-led, they encouraged all who attended to give verbal spiritual testimonies, and they asked each to sit in spiritual judgment on all the rest (though, of course, with as much humility as the sanctified saints could muster).[10] These encouragements led naturally to women speaking up in the larger public meetings of Methodists. Usually that public speaking took the form of exhortation rather than formal sermons. But the early Methodist movement and also the outworking of revival among Baptists and other anti-establishmentarian localists also opened at least some opportunities for women to expound the Scriptures more formally.[11]

The blurring of traditional gender roles receded as the heat of the early revivals cooled. At the time of the War for Independence, the opportunity for Baptist and other hitherto marginalized evangelical men to take part in the era's momentous political struggle seems to have reinforced a return to sex-segregated roles. For men to play a public political part meant to back away from the intense church communities that had bound the converted, both male and female, into intense spiritual fellowship.[12] In Britain, widespread reaction to the disruption of the French Revolution had a similar impact in reinforcing stronger distinctions between the roles of evangelical men and evangelical women.[13]

The democratization of American society that occurred in the 1790s and subsequent decades allowed some room for evangelical women of all sorts to expand the scope of their spiritual activity. Among anti-formal, anti-establishmentarian evangelicals there arose a surprising number of active women preachers. As described recently in rich detail by Catherine Brekus, during the first four decades of the new century more than a hundred Methodists, Free Will Baptists, Disciples of Christ, and Cumberland Presbyterian women – white and black – left solid documentary record of their service as itinerating preachers or pastors.[14] This activity faded away by the 1840s, sometimes helped along by increasingly formal attitudes of male leaders in the once radical denominations. But where this female preaching existed, it was a remarkable testimony to the ability of at least some evangelical groups to bend the boundaries of inherited expectations.

Among the middle- and upper-class women of the wealthier, more prestigious denominations, pressure for women to preach or to be ordained grew only gradually. But other avenues of public service opened very rapidly. Women, like the teacher of holiness, Phoebe Palmer of New York City, became popular writers on Christian subjects, and some of these writers, like Palmer herself, could be provoked into vigorous defense of such activity.[15] Other women of Palmer's class, education, and wealth exploited the United States' burgeoning network of voluntary societies to enter more directly into public life. Writers and speakers like the sisters Sarah and Angelina Grimké, though born in a conservative Southern milieu, became expert leaders of special-purpose religious and moral-reform societies once they absorbed the egalitarian implications of American republican ideology, found confirmation of that egalitarianism in the Scriptures, and moved North where unconventional public activity of respectable women was possible.[16]

In the South, evangelical women never were as visible in public or as active in the leadership of voluntary societies as their counterparts in the North. Yet once evangelical faith moved beyond the Baptists, Methodists, and Disciples, who were usually not slaveholders, into the elite levels of Southern society where Presbyterianism and Episcopalianism prevailed, women of the slave-holding classes joined their commoner peers in using evangelical Christianity to dignify their own lives and control their own surroundings. The defense of slavery fostered attention to traditional roles of all sort, but within those strictures evangelical women were more active than any other unorganized element in Southern society.[17]

Throughout the nineteenth century evangelical women also became more and more engaged in the various tasks of the missionary movement.[18] Women had been the well publicized partners of the United States' pioneering missionaries like Adoniram Judson. The dangers of mortality in missionary service, but also the opportunities for enhanced service, were sharply underscored in well received accounts of Judson's successive wives: Ann Hasseltine Judson, Sarah Boardman Judson, and Emily Chubbuck Judson.[19] Although these women did not enjoy long life, the record of their mission service established a powerful ideal. Later in the century, women in several denominations organized their own missionary societies, volunteered more frequently than men for service abroad, and brokered missionary service into lives of distinctive public service.[20] Female missionary activity was – and continues to be – especially vibrant among the Southern Baptists who otherwise presented a mostly conservative face to the broader world on issues of sex and gender.[21]

The first century and a half of modern evangelicalism, in short, illustrates the complex dynamics of the movement. Women were empowered and silenced. They volunteered in ever-increasing numbers for all kinds of religious and moral purpose, yet only rarely sought formal ordination to the ministry. They exploited expanded opportunities as missionaries abroad while most evangelical denominations at home remained content to have men monopolize public leadership. These complexities were heightened by currents that emerged toward the end of the nineteenth century and that continue to this day.

Fundamentalists and New-evangelicals

The fundamentalist and pentecostal movements of the early twentieth century brought significant changes to evangelicalism, though in different ways. Fundamentalism was a species of culture warfare that depended for its strength on standing up to selected trends in the wider society. Pentecostalism was a force of religious revitalization that flourished by neglecting the wider society. Both movements came out of the nineteenth century's biblical revivalism. Both movements consequently shared much with each other, a fact that has been increasingly recognized over the past fifty years as descendants of early fundamentalism and early pentecostalism find ever-increasing opportunities for cooperation in pan-evangelical activities. It is, therefore, an artificial division to treat gender questions among fundamentalists and pentecostals separately, but because the two movements nicely illustrate prominent themes in more general evangelical history, that artifice will be followed here.

A widely shared stereotype of early fundamentalism is of the brash and bold leader – Billy Sunday, say – lashing out at all manner of cultural degradation, including many sins committed primarily by women. These sins might include following the evil ways of the flappers, abandoning the proper tasks of motherhood to mix it up in the workplace, or insisting on bossing around men in the churches. While such a stereotype is not made up out of whole cloth, it is nonetheless a caricature. By following the best recent writing on the subject, it is possible to see that the fundamentalist movement did encourage a boisterous kind of militantly two-spheres religion, but also that its ideals of godliness opened up surprisingly wide avenues of public service, that these avenues allowed more fundamentalist women to take an active part in their churches than did women in mainline Protestant denominations, and that customs sometimes regarded as distinctly fundamentalist were in actual fact representative of general shifts in American popular culture.[22]

The rhetoric of fundamentalist leaders on women was not univocal, but it was often extreme. The flamboyant urban evangelist Billy Sunday, for instance, happened to be a champion of women's suffrage, but not because he believed strongly in women's rights. As he once put it with characteristic panache, "I never could understand laws that permit some beer-guzzling, whiskey-soaked ignorant product of the grog shop to vote and refuse that right to an intelligent, clean, upright Christian woman. . . . Opposition to women suffrage comes straight from the distillery or crank out of the brewery. It is enough for me to know what forces are against woman suffrage to line me up for it."[23]

On other questions, Sunday and early leading fundamentalists more closely fit the stereotype as ardent defenders of exclusively maternal, domestic roles for women. Yet there was an almost constant tension displayed by the prominent male leaders of fundamentalism.[24] Conservative leaders among the northern Presbyterians and Baptists saw themselves as competing for women members. As male liberal Protestant leaders tried to assuage females from whom they were in the process of taking control over women's missionary organizations, fundamentalists in these denominations feared the machiavellianism of power-hungry modernists. In this struggle, making any concessions to women or to feminine religious ideals looked like a tactical error. At the same time, some of the very denominational conservatives were glad to work with women from the Bible schools and other centers of "safe" religious activity. As both Presbyterian and Baptist conservatives tried to maintain their influence within their denominations, a certain pessimism about femininity could appear. Women were perceived as being easily led astray. John Roach Straton, a fundamentalist headliner in New York, complained that women were being used as naive tools of the modernists. At the same time, Straton and like-minded conservatives insisted on a treasured conviction of the nineteenth century: that the fate of society depended upon the godliness of its mothers.

In the 1930s, an even more pugnacious fundamentalist leader, John R. Rice, emerged as a strident opponent of gender blurring and liberal feminization. Like many fundamentalists of his generation, Rice equated active promotion of social service with modernism in Christian doctrine, and so was prone to greater suspicion of women as the ones who had always borne the brunt of such service. Rice, like Billy Sunday before him, was also determined to prove that Christianity was a religion for red-blooded American men. As he expressed it, "God intended every husband and father to know more Bible than his wife and children. Any man who does not has slacked; he has shirked; he has quit on God."[25]

The difficulty in trusting only to the rhetoric of such leaders is that fundamentalist practices tell a different story. For example, the same John R. Rice, who argued so strongly against women in ministry, also expressed the opinion that he would rather his own daughters devoted their lives to full-time Christian ministry than to marriage and family.[26] Even more consequentially, the fundamentalist conception of religion placed great stress on activity for God. In practice, this urgent fundamentalist spirituality motivated women – with the nearly unanimous concurrence of fundamentalist men – to many public activities like teaching Sunday School, raising support for missionary work, volunteering as missionaries, leading youth work, and engaging in active music ministry.

One of the most important pieces of evidence for public female activity was the Bible school, which as Virginia Brereton and others have demonstrated lay at the heart of the movement.[27] At Moody Bible Institute in Chicago, the West Point of northern fundamentalism, women constituted half the student body, and in many other Bible schools they made up a majority. The key point is that Bible schools regularly prodded, pushed, and trained all their students, men and women, to take on a wide variety of public activities. Women educated in Bible schools, as well as the wives of prominent fundamentalist men, were frequently asked to speak at summer Bible conferences, like Winona Lake in Indiana, which were important networking points for the entire movement. Many women also started special purpose organizations supporting Christian education in the churches. From the 1930s, the Christian Education department at Wheaton College was led by a quiet, but very determined, pair of sisters, Mary and Lois LeBar, who sent out hundreds of young men and women as active lay and clerical leaders into fundamentalist churches.[28] The same and more can be said about the innovative Christian Education programs mounted in Southern California from about the same time by Henrietta Mears, who, though she never sought ordination, was greatly esteemed as an effective Bible teacher and motivator of future pastors.[29] The popular currents driving such programs were well illustrated in the history of the Moody Bible

Institute. From late in the nineteenth century its publications regularly reported on the activities of Moody graduates, including hundreds of women serving as evangelists, rural pastors, co-pastors with husbands, Christian education directors, and in other public posts.[30] Self-identified fundamentalist women did not usually seek ordination and most leading fundamentalist organizations did not appoint women as directors or trustees, but these were about the only roles that fundamentalist women did not take on in some shape or form.

Again, it is important to stress that activity by fundamentalist women arose not primarily out of a feminist push for rights, but from fundamentalist ideals of religion. God wanted the converted to be active in nurturing, instructing, and converting others. Women were converted; women were active. In Michael Hamilton's apt phrase, "in addition to their respect for marriage, Fundamentalists placed a high value on a Protestant equivalent of celibate monastic preachers, and many women found this ideal attractive."[31] Indeed, the large numbers of unmarried fundamentalist women who volunteered for mission service are particularly eloquent testimony to the persuasive force of that logic. When statistics were gathered for the 1910 Edinburgh World Missionary Conference, researchers found that nearly 55 percent of the over 21,000 Western missionaries enumerated for this report were women.[32] This total is especially remarkable since, according to missionary-promoter and Bible-translator Helen Barrett Montgomery, there had been only fifty years earlier not even one unmarried American woman who was serving as a duly certified missionary.[33]

During the first half of the twentieth century, the non-ecclesiastical, market-driven, lay-oriented fundamentalist movement probably offered – whatever the rhetoric of leaders – more openings for women's service than did the mainline churches.[34] Within mainline Protestantism, the women's missionary groups that had been so active from the time of the Civil War were gradually taken over by the male leadership of denominations. In addition, formal appeals for ordination succeeded only partially, as when the Northern Presbyterians opened up the eldership to women in 1930 but chose not to go further to ordain women as ministers. Mainline Protestants did not indulge in as much flamboyant rhetoric as fundamentalists, and a few mainline boards added a few women as trustees. But women made up a far smaller percentage of students at mainline seminaries than women did at fundamentalist Bible schools, and the mainline conventions of formal worship and bureaucratic church organization offered less room for female activity than did many fundamentalist churches and denominations.

Rhetorical and pragmatic practices among fundamentalists become clearer when cast against the backdrop of larger social changes in North America.[35] In public pronouncements, fundamentalists did stress the virtues of female domesticity and they also became great public defenders of women's primary commitments to marriage and family. But from the 1890s to the 1950s, prominent voices and media in American polite culture also stressed these same things. The shift in general public attitudes was almost certainly more of a factor than the dynamics of fundamentalist religion in making certain kinds of public activity less attractive to women.

Historians describe things that really did happen when they find fundamentalist leaders of the early twentieth century ranting against women who broke with traditional gender roles. At the same time, it is a gross oversimplification to view fundamentalism monolithically as a traditionalist movement militantly arrayed against progressive, liberal individualism.[36] At least before the 1960s, fundamentalist and related evangelical Protestants may have shouted a little louder than their mainline contemporaries, but otherwise there was little difference. If difference existed, it was in how fundamentalist women exploited the entrepreneurial zeal of their movement in getting to work.

Through and after the Second World War, fundamentalist and the emerging neo-evangelical churches mostly maintained the older practices as well as the older rhetoric. John R. Rice's books on women continued to be reprinted; most fundamentalist and neo-evangelical women remained content not to seek ordination; many of the same women ran their churches' youth, music, and outreach programs; many of them volunteered for missionary service abroad; only a few felt stifled in these roles that they had mostly chosen for themselves; and, as ever, women made up a majority in the fundamentalist churches.

Female Leadership within Pentecostalism

The situation among pentecostal and the more self-consciously holiness groups was different because they were more directly the heirs of nineteenth-century traditions of radical evangelicalism.[37] The difference cannot lie in the realm of general attitudes, for pentecostal and radical

holiness groups reflected many of the same concerns as their fundamentalist peers. Nor does it lie in general relations to American society,
for, as we shall see, the same strengthened emphasis on marriage and
domesticity that influenced fundamentalists (and most other Americans)
also became stronger among the radical evangelicals over the first half of
the twentieth century.

The difference lies, rather, in the greater openness of these evangelicals to public recognition of women's leadership in the churches.
They were the ones, rather than fundamentalists and neo-evangelicals,
who sustained or revived the Wesleyan, Free Will Baptist, sectarian
impulses that had pushed women into visible religious leadership in
the wake of the earlier Great Awakenings. They were the ones among
whom ardent religious experience overrode the conventions of gender-
segregated practice and male-only leadership.

During and immediately following the outbreak of the Holy Spirit
gifts in the first decade of the twentieth century, pentecostals and their
near relations among the ardent holiness denominations offered multiple opportunities for women to exhort, preach, heal, organize, and
pastor. In the period 1890 to 1920, which Edith Blumhofer has labeled
an era of "Prophesying Daughters," pentecostal and holiness women of
almost all sorts freely participated in the ministries of the new movement, with the exception of only the most official actions of the most
formal organizations. This activity was driven by a literal appropriation
of biblical promises of God's spirit poured out on men and women alike
in the Last Days, on a strong belief that when the Holy Spirit anointed
someone to minister (male or female), it was good simply to step out of
the way, and on the widely shared belief that opened opportunities for
ministry were signs of the soon Return of Christ. With these convictions, women not only found a welcome home in the new pentecostal
denominations (with the ones for which records exist showing large
majorities of women members). They also took a lively part in public
ministry. The Assemblies of God, which immediately from its founding
in 1914 betrayed its Methodistic roots by careful diligence in record-
keeping, noted in 1918 that 21 percent of all ministers on its rolls were
women, while over half of its missionaries were likewise female.[38]

As with early pentecostal nonchalance about America's historic racial
divides, however, the indifference to gender did not last long.[39] Beginning in the 1920s and continuing through the Second World War, a
period that Blumhofer calls "reorienting the sphere," space for women's
public ministry gradually shriveled. Prominent women revivalists like

Uldine Utley and revivalist/organizers/empire-builders like Aimee Semple McPherson went on with their activities.[40] But public attention increasingly shifted away from the values of women's work to its limits. The same kind of anxiety about female contributions undercutting traditional Christian morality that inspired John R. Rice's outbursts worked more quietly in the Assemblies of God and other pentecostal denominations. The result was not a repudiation of women as ordained ministers but a steady elimination of women from places of public visibility. In 1931 the Assemblies of God voted to limit the ordination of women to the office of evangelist and decreed that women so ordained could not perform marriages, bury the dead, or administer the ordinances.[41] At least some of the largely African-American pentecostal and holiness churches did not follow this general trend, but most white and some black churches did.[42]

After the Second World War, as American society itself underwent significant practical changes – especially the entrance of middle-class women into the workplace – and when feminist voices pushed attitudes about gender to the forefront of public discussion, pentecostal and holiness evangelicals once again picked up the debate. Several of the major pentecostal denominations, like the Assemblies of God, continued to allow female ordination, but the numbers involved did not become large. In 1993, for instance, 15 percent of all credentialed ministers in the Assemblies were women, but only 7 percent of these ordained women were senior pastors of churches, fewer than 2 percent of the Assemblies' nearly 12,000 churches were pastored by women, and women were virtually absent on the District and General Councils.[43] The situation, in other words, resembles that found among Baptist, Methodist, and other radical evangelical movements after the revivals of the eighteenth and early nineteenth centuries. In both instances, disjunctions between male and female roles grew as the intensity of the early movement was replaced by institution-building.[44] The pentecostal and holiness strands of radical evangelicalism thus grew ever closer to the fundamentalist and neo-evangelical strands as the twentieth century progressed.

Contemporary Developments

It is far too early for a single historian to attempt nuanced analysis of the past several decades for the stories of women, men, and gender among

American evangelicals. Since the 1950s, evangelicals have paid heightened attention to the doctrine of biblical inerrancy, but they have also become more aware of complexities involved in interpreting the Bible. There has been new awareness of radical elements in earlier stages of evangelical sub-movements. Visible organizations, like the Concerned Women of America founded by Beverly LaHaye, have organized evangelical women for right-wing political causes. Small organizations like Christians for Biblical Equality have organized some evangelicals to promote egalitarian interpretations of marriage, ecclesiastical office, and social authority. A few feminists have attacked fundamentalists, evangelicals, and other religious conservatives for promoting false consciousness among women, or even fostering conditions for violence to women. The multiplying stresses of modern life – two-career families, escalating expectations for the nurture of children, ever-increasing demands of work and entertainment – have taken their toll on evangelicals as on all Americans. Evangelicals have joined with conservative Catholics, Mormons, and Orthodox Jews in opposing *Roe* v. *Wade*, in seeking legislation to end easy access to abortion, and in setting up homes for unwed mothers and their children. Evangelicals, again like all Americans, have experienced a much higher incidence of divorce than was the case before mid-century. A few evangelical, fundamentalist, and pentecostal movements have endured well publicized incidents of parental abuse of children. Several evangelical leaders have undergone well publicized sex scandals. New parachurch ministries like Promise Keepers have begun to address the spiritual needs of men. Dr James Dobson and his Focus on the Family ministries – books, radio, videotapes, public advocacy – have achieved a phenomenal popularity. Articulate evangelical women like Elisabeth Eliot have championed women's submission to men as rooted not in the Fall, but in creation itself, while articulate evangelical women like Mary Stewart Van Leeuwen have championed gender egalitarianism as a product of Christ's triumph over sin. In such a climate all unqualified, facile accounts of evangelicals and gender are immediately suspect.[45]

Thankfully, however, a growing number of scholars have begun to study selected questions relating to evangelicals and gender, and in so doing have provided several carefully researched angles of sight into this congeries of tumultuous activity. Although this scholarship has been produced for the most part by academics who are not themselves evangelicals, it presents contemporary currents among evangelical women with an appreciation for the ambiguities and complexities we have observed in the entire history of the movement.[46]

A pioneering investigation that featured empirical research at the local level instead of merely attention to the pronouncements of evangelical leaders was undertaken by sociologist Susan Rose in the years 1982–3.[47] Rose studied an independent charismatic fellowship in upstate New York, where she found what she expected with respect to the ideology of gender relations. This evangelical church upheld the principle of patriarchy for leadership in church, as well as in society. Practice, however, did not conform completely to principle. Rose found that the evangelical women of "Covenant Community" emphasized their traditional wifely submission in pretty active negotiations with the supposedly dominant male members of the community. Most community decisions, as a result, were actually taken after discussion in which women seemed to have as much influence as men. Rose did find that a few women of the community, including some who had forsaken feminist pasts for the attractions of this church, expressed disquiet with the ordering of gender they had embraced. For such ones, as well as for the women who accepted the ideology of patriarchy without reservation, prayer was a central spiritual practice. For them prayer was a way to exercise spiritual power and to influence the fellowship and their own families. Rose found that gathering for prayer also gave women a strong sense of communication with each other, as well as with God.

The theme of prayer is central to the breakthrough book on gender relations from the 1990s, Marie Griffith's study of the Women's Aglow Fellowship entitled *God's Daughters*.[48] For two years Griffith attended New England meetings of the Fellowship, founded in the late 1960s as an offshoot of the pentecostal Full Gospel Businessmen's Fellowship. Griffith's key findings were that prayer enabled Women's Aglow members to exercise considerable power in church and community, and that prayer in conjunction with practical activity positively reshaped the identities of women who took part. In its organization and actual dynamics, the Fellowship bore the marks of three sources: traditional evangelical teaching as expressed in modern charismatic terms, emphasis on the therapeutic culture that has become so strong in the United States since the 1960s, and selected themes of modern feminism. In the early years of the Fellowship, leaders stressed the need for wives to submit to their husbands, but in recent years the accent has shifted somewhat to the mutual submission of husbands and wives to each other. That shift in principle, however, has not been attended by large consequences, because of the abiding importance of prayer in the Fellowship's activities.

Prayer is the most important part of the Aglow meetings. Through prayer, women ask for God's help, especially in overcoming traumas of sexual abuse and restoring ruptured personal relationships. They also offer thanks for instances of God's gracious favor. Prayer also serves powerful descriptive and prescriptive functions, since it verbalizes crises in relationships and articulates ideal social roles. When women regard themselves as prayer warriors, they see themselves as playing a very important part in the spiritual struggle of contemporary times. By emphasizing the theme of spiritual warfare, participants in Women's Aglow exercise a spiritual authority that extends beyond the church, beyond questions of activism, and beyond mundane details of ordinary lives.

The women of this movement manage relationships with men carefully. Without challenging traditional principles of wifely submission, they nonetheless are expert in using the practice of submission to restrain the destructive behavior of husbands, to protect their children, and to reach goals of their own devising.

In sum, Griffith finds the Women's Aglow Fellowship not as different from organized modern feminism as she had imagined it would be. The two shared significant experiences of wounding by men, significant growth in shared female consciousness, and significant ability to control their own lives. Women's Aglow participants regularly criticize the women's movement for its secular humanism, but they share with the feminists they criticize a belief in the ability of women to accomplish great things in the world. Griffith herself summarizes the importance of her study for broader matters within evangelical history: "Far from being a fixed entity churning out traditional teachings on gender roles, evangelical ideology has always been varied, so that even a group as apparently conservative as Aglow contains a broad repertoire of choices and mutable scripts dealing with such ideals as female submission to male authority."[49]

Significant books by Brenda Brasher and Christel Manning that appeared soon after Griffith's *God's Daughters* reinforce the general picture she presented.[50] Over the course of a six-month ethnographic study, Brasher investigated the religious ideas and practices of fundamentalist/evangelical women from two large Southern California churches of several thousand members each. Both churches have large women's ministries (one with 300 attending the weekly women's Bible study), and young married couples predominate in both congregations. With Griffith, Brasher concludes that fundamentalism, despite its restrictive theology, actually improves the ability of these women to direct the course of their lives.

The two churches that Brasher studied have a virtually all-male leadership (one has a female designated as "women's pastor"). But the churches' women's ministries provide a welcome and supportive enclave. In practice, the dynamism of these enclaves undermines the patriarchal ideology of these churches. Yet since women's energies are directed into these enclaves, the male leaders do not feel threatened. For activities outside of the church, almost all of the women that Brasher interviewed supported the equality of men and women.

Some of the women Brasher observed upheld the traditional idea of wifely submission to husbands, but more spoke out in favor of mutual submission of spouses to each other. For both types, the women were assertive in holding men responsible for their actions with respect to their wives and children. On questions about the ordering of the family, Brasher discovered that unmarried women were quite a bit more rigid in upholding female submissiveness than were the married women. The clearest teaching these women received on traditional sex-role differences came from tapes and books made available in the church, and from church-approved attendance at seminars sponsored by groups like James Dobson's Focus on the Family. From their own pulpits they heard a somewhat gentler message, perhaps because both the senior pastors of the churches Brasher studied were themselves divorced.

As other researchers also conclude, Brasher found more in common between evangelical women and feminists than she had expected. Both regard equality in the workplace and in society as a positive good. Both favor passage of laws against abusive husbands. Both call for men to exercise more responsibility in all social and domestic relationships. Brasher's conclusion reflects the complexities of a long evangelical history: "Through involvement with overall congregational life, believing women acquiesce to a male-dominated religious world; but, in turn, they undercut their acquiescence by establishing and supporting intra-congregational female enclaves through their participation in women's ministries. Willing neither to walk away from the religious good nestled within a patriarchal schema nor overthrow its patriarchal leadership, the

. . . women I interviewed bargain with patriarchy to get what they want."[51]

Christel Manning's study focused on adult converts or returnees to conservative Christianity (Roman Catholic and evangelical/charismatic) and Orthodox Judaism in three Southern California congregations. Again, Manning found that conservative religious women are not opposed to many of the aims of feminism, even though they profess anti-feminist sentiments. In her own phrases, "While religious conservatives resist feminism, they cannot escape its influence. Though they officially condemn feminism as heretical – declaring it outside the boundaries of orthodoxy – many conservative religious leaders have begun to incorporate feminist language into their rhetoric, thus implicitly acknowledging its compatibility with conservative religion."[52]

As with the women in the congregations studied by Brasher, the women in Manning's research overwhelmingly affirm the equality of the sexes in the workplace and in society at large. For these women the historic Protestant idea of vocation is used to legitimate the actual choice to work outside the home or not. Evangelical women tend to express their decision not in terms of whether to work, but in terms of where work would be invested, in the home or outside.

Manning's subjects are most traditional when the focus is on religious life. They accept traditional male leadership within their congregations as ordained by God. They view their own contributions to religious life as important, but different from the contributions made by men. Many of Manning's women, particularly evangelicals and Jews, speak of the spiritual and moral superiority of women and so view male leadership as positive for the way it involves men in religious activities. In all three traditions women used popular psychology along with traditional religious teaching to justify separate religious spheres for men and women.

Within the family, evangelical and Jewish women stressed principles of submissiveness and cooperation, but they also articulated high expectations for their husbands in terms of performing household duties and nurturing children, including the raising of non-sexist sons. To Manning it was clear that submission is a bargain, a tool for avoiding conflict and divorce as well as for gaining what women want. The occasional instances where evangelical women justified non-submission to their husbands were defended not by pragmatic reasoning, but by appealing to the tradition of *sola scriptura* and the need to "obey God rather than men" (Acts 5:29 in both the King James Version and the New International Version, the two most popular evangelical translations of Scripture).

Manning several times poses the question as to why these conservative religious women profess anti-feminist sentiments, despite what Manning regarded as their support of what the feminist movement has sought. Her conclusion is that these women think modern feminists ignore the importance of children and family and are obsessed with forcing women to succeed by measures originally created for men. To these religious women, feminists are extremists and simply out of touch with their own day-to-day lives.

By way of summary, the studies by Rose, Griffith, Brasher, and Manning share several general conclusions. With a few qualifications having been made, they view the worlds of evangelical women as positive and not nearly as bleak as caricatures of patriarchal religion had led them to expect. They also find that contemporary evangelical women betray scant differences from American citizens more generally in their views on women in the workplace. They find that within the family the language of wifely submission is giving way to ideals of mutual submission. But whether in traditional or more modern forms, submission is a mark not of passivity, but of active interaction with ministers and especially husbands, whom they expect to participate in household activities and the raising of children. These women remain quite traditional in their general religious beliefs, including the conviction that women bear the greater responsibility for the moral tone of family, church, and society. These beliefs fit seamlessly alongside an acceptance of male-only church leadership. For the women researched for these studies, the practice of prayer was the primary vehicle for exerting control and finding coherence in their lives. The women's ministries in which they participated were welcome sources of healing and strength within a traditional evangelical framework. Brasher, a liberal Christian, and Rose are less convinced that the gender bargains struck by evangelical women are, in the end, genuinely advantageous to them or society more generally. By comparison, Griffith, a liberal Christian, and Manning, a secular feminist, are more sympathetic and find evangelical women reaching some of the same goals sought through other means by contemporary feminists.

Conclusion

A typology proposed by the Canadian evangelical theologian John Stackhouse nicely captures the spectrum of attitudes toward women and women's activities among evangelicals, both historically and in the present.[53] Stackhouse describes five general models. First is what he labels "speechless majority," a traditional situation where women, though they may contribute a majority of the adherents and provide much behind-the-scenes assistance to evangelical enterprises, simply do not appear, or desire to appear, in public. A second model Stackhouse calls "missionary exceptions." It is what looks to outsiders like the anomalous practice of allowing evangelical women to perform all sorts of public tasks in missionary settings while maintaining the "speechless majority" pattern in home congregations. The third model is "parachurch autonomy," where Stackhouse draws attention to the indubitable fact that much of the activity, energy, accomplishments, and public debate among evangelicals for nearly two hundred years has been carried out by and within special-purpose voluntary societies, where women have been more active than in formal churches and denominations. Next is the model of "activity 'under authority'." By this category Stackhouse designates the theologically conservative position that finds male headship taught in Scripture as a universal principle, but where as much space as possible is opened for women to teach, minister, direct, and nurture – just as long as a man or men are ultimately in charge. The last model is "equal partners in ministry," in which, backed by what supporters consider the impeccable exegesis of passages like Galatians 3:28 ("there is neither . . . male nor female"), evangelicals affirm the full participation of women in all religious duties and offices.

It would be nearly impossible to quantify the proportions of evangelicals fitting in these five models. The last, as the newest position, would probably contain the fewest. But the boundaries between precept and practice are so involved among evangelicals that one could predict very large numbers in each of the other four, as well as very substantial numbers who might say they fit into one model yet pursue other practices.

Outsiders to evangelicalism, as well as spokespersons for evangelical movements, will not adequately grasp the evangelical history of women, and also of men, through the trumpeting of simplifications. Evangelical views of Scripture do push evangelicals toward differentiated ideals for maleness and femaleness. But the same evangelical scripturalism also supports religious practices in which knowing the glory of God and experiencing the healing grace of God relativize that differentiation. The place of evangelicals as culturally adaptive biblical experientialists is nowhere more clearly seen than in evangelical histories of gender.

Notes

1 On Lee, see Catherine A. Brekus, *Strangers and Pilgrims: Female Preaching in America, 1740–1845* (Chapel Hill: University of North Carolina Press, 1998), pp. 171–2, 214–15, passim, and for a portrait, p. 259.

2 *Religious Experience and Religious Journal of Mrs Jarena Lee, Giving an Account of Her Call to Preach the Gospel* (Philadelphia: By the author, 1849), 32; as reprinted in *Spiritual Narratives*, ed. Sue E. Houchins (New York: Oxford University Press, 1988).

3 Julia A. J. Foote, *A Brand Plucked from the Fire: an Autobiographical Sketch* (Cleveland: Lauer & Yost, 1886), pp. 67–8; as reprinted in *Spiritual Narratives*.

4 These passages and the ones that follow are quoted from the Authorized, or King James, Version, since this was the Bible that was nearly universal among evangelicals, and almost all other Protestants, until the 1960s.

5 Debates over the meaning and application of such passages have been going strong for at least 150 years; for examples, out of countless possibilities, of biblical commentary from more traditional perspectives, see John Piper and Wayne Grudem, eds, *Recovering Biblical Manhood and Womanhood: a Response to Evangelical Feminists* (Wheaton, IL: Crossway, 1991); and likewise out of myriad possibilities, for commentary defending biblical egalitarianism, see Gilbert G. Bilezikian, *Beyond Sex Roles: What the Bible Says about a Woman's Place in Church and Family*, 2nd edn (Grand Rapids, MI: Baker, 1989).

6 For examples, Jack O. Balswick, *Men at the Crossroads: Beyond Traditional Roles and Modern Options* (Downers Grove, IL: InterVarsity Press, 1992); David G. Hackett, "Gender and religion in American culture, 1870–1930," *Religion and American Culture*, 5 (Summer), 1994, pp. 127–57; a series of essays by Mary Stewart van Leeuwen on the Promise Keepers movement, including "Promise Keepers and proof-text poker," *Sojourners*, January/February 1998, pp. 16–21; and Lisa Wilson, *Ye Heart of a Man: the Domestic Life of Men in Colonial New England* (New Haven, CT: Yale University Press, 1999).

7   My orientation to that literature has been provided primarily by Patricia Applebaum, "A bibliographic guide to contemporary sources," prepared for the project, "Women and Twentieth-century Protestantism," under the direction of Virginia Lieson Brereton and Margaret Lamberts Bendroth, and available from the Institute for the Study of American Evangelicals at Wheaton College. I would like to think Rachel Maxson and Joel Moore for indispensable assistance in working with the materials described in this bibliography.

8   For the use of these phrases, see George A. Rawlyk, *"Wrapped up in God": a Study of Several Canadian Revivals and Revivalists* (Burlington, Ont.: Welch, 1988); Susan Juster, *Disorderly Women: Sexual Politics and Evangelicalism in Revolutionary New England* (Ithaca, NY: Cornell University Press, 1994), pp. 57–62; and Brekus, *Strangers and Pilgrims*, op. cit., n. 1, p. 42.

9   This summary, as well as much else in my account of eighteenth-century matters is taken from Juster, *Disorderly Women*, op. cit., n. 8.

10 The best accounts of what it meant to be an early Methodist in England are found in the essays of John D. Walsh: for example, "Origins of the evangelical revival," in *Essays in Modern English Church History in Memory of Norman Sykes*, eds Gareth Bennett and John Walsh (New York: Oxford University Press, 1966), pp. 141–8; and "John Wesley and the community of goods," in *Protestant Evangelicalism: Britain, Ireland, Germany, and American, c.1750–c.1950*, ed. Keith Robbins (Oxford: Blackwell, 1990), pp. 25–50. For the American colonies, see the early sections of A. Gregory Schneider, *The Way of the Cross Leads Home: the Domestication of American Methodism* (Bloomington: Indiana University Press, 1993); in Schneider's usage, "domestication" refers to an evolution among Methodists that reasserted traditional gender roles and pushed women back more exclusively to the sphere of the household.

11 On such developments in the mid-eighteenth century, see the early sections of Deborah Valenze, *Prophetic Sons and Daughters: Female Preaching and Popular Religion in Industrial England* (Princeton, NJ: Princeton University Press, 1985); and of Brekus, *Strangers and Pilgrims*, op. cit., n. 1.

12 Juster, *Disorderly Women*, op. cit., n. 8, pp. 112–13 and passim.

13 For the general situation, without specific reference to evangelicals, see Linda Colley, *Britons: Forging the Nation, 1707–1837* (New Haven, CT: Yale University Press, 1992), pp. 250–72.

14 Brekus, *Strangers and Pilgrims*, op. cit., n. 1.

15 See Phoebe Palmer's defense of women speaking and writing, *The Promise of the Father: or, A Neglected Speciality of the Last Days* (New York: Foster & Palmer, 1859).

16 See, for example, Nancy A. Hardesty, *Women Called to Witness: Evangelical Feminism in the Nineteenth Century*, 2nd edn (Knoxville: University of Tennessee Press, 1999); Donald W. Dayton, *Discovering an Evangelical Heritage* (New York: Harper & Row, 1976); and Gerda Lerner, *The Grimké Sisters from South Carolina: Rebels Against Slavery* (Boston: Houghton Mifflin, 1967). On the timing and circumstances leading to the ordination of women in mainline Protestant denominations, see Virginia Lieson Brereton and Christa Ressmeyer Klein, "American women in ministry: a history of Protestant beginning points," in *Women of Spirit: Female Leadership in the Jewish and Christian Traditions*, eds Rosemary Ruether and Eleanor McLaughlin (New York: Simon & Schuster, 1979), pp. 301–32.

17 See especially Donald G. Mathews, *Religion in the Old South* (Chicago: University of Chicago Press, 1977), pp. 101–24; and Christine Leigh Heyrman, *Southern Cross: the Beginnings of the Bible Belt* (New York: Knopf, 1997), pp. 161–205.

18 For an outstanding account, see Dana Lee Robert, *American Women in Mission: a Social History of Their Thought and Practice* (Macon, GA: Mercer University Press, 1996).

19 See especially Joan Jacobs Brumberg, *Mission for Life: the Judson Family and American Evangelical Culture* (New York: New York University Press, 1980).

20 As examples of a growing literature, see Patricia Hill, *The World Their Household: the American Women's Foreign Mission Movement and Cultural Transformation, 1870–1922* (Ann Arbor: University of Michigan Press, 1985); and Sylvia M. Jacobs, *Black Americans and the Missionary Movement in Africa* (Westport, CT: Greenwood, 1982).

21 For orientation, see Carolyn DeArmond Blevins, "Patterns of ministry among Southern Baptist women," *Baptist History and Heritage* 22, 1987, pp. 41–9; and Karen E. Smith, "Beyond public and private spheres: another look at women in Baptist history and historiography," *Baptist Quarterly*, 34, 1991, pp. 79–87. For similar orientation on American (Northern) Baptists, see Evelyn Brooks Higginbotham, "En-gendering leadership in the Home Mission Schools," *American Baptist Quarterly*, 12, 1993, pp. 10–25; and James R. Lynch, "Baptist women in ministry through 1920," *American Baptist Quarterly*, 13, 1994, pp. 304–18. The article by Lynch contains a helpful appendix listing information on 319 women from different Baptist denominations who left record of service in public ministry from 1638 to 1920.

22 The following paragraphs draw especially on Michael Hamilton, "Women, public ministry, and American fundamentalism, 1920–1950," *Religion and*

American Culture, 3 (Summer), 1993, pp. 171–96; and on several works by
Margaret Lamberts Bendroth, including *Fundamentalism and Gender, 1875
to the Present* (New Haven, CT: Yale University Press, 1993); "The search
for 'women's role' in American evangelicalism, 1930–1980," in *Evangelicalism in Modern America*, ed. George M. Marsden (Grand Rapids, MI:
Eerdmans, 1984), pp. 122–34; and articles cited below. Another helpful
account, which stresses continuity in thinking about gender between early
twentieth-century fundamentalists and late twentieth-century evangelicals
is Betty A. DeBerg, *Ungodly Women: Gender and the First Wave of
American Fundamentalism* (Minneapolis: Fortress, 1990).

23 Sunday quoted in Marty Nesselbush Green, "From sainthood to submission: gender images in conservative protestantism, 1900–1940," *The Historian*, 58, 1996, pp. 539–56; this helpful article on fundamentalist rhetoric
lacks what Bendroth and Hamilton supply by examining fundamentalist
practice. On the interest with which one young woman heard Billy Sunday,
see William G. McLoughlin, "Billy Sunday and the working girl of 1915,"
Journal of Presbyterian History, 54, 1976, pp. 376–84; and on Sunday's
extensive reliance on his wife, "Ma" Sunday, in all aspects of his public
work, see Lyle W. Dorsett, *Billy Sunday and the Redemption of Urban
America* (Grand Rapids, MI: Eerdmans, 1991), pp. 100–7 and passim.

24 This paragraph follows Margaret Lamberts Bendroth, "Fundamentalism
and femininity: points of encounter between religious conservatives and
women, 1919–1935," *Church History*, 61, 1992, pp. 221–33.

25 Quoted in Bendroth, *Fundamentalism and Gender*, op. cit., n. 22, p. 103,
with discussion of Rice on pp. 103–4, 111–13, and passim. Rice's reputation on such themes was won (and often caricatured) by his publication in
1941 of *Bobbed Hair, Bossy Wives, and Women Preachers*.

26 Hamilton, "Women, public ministry, and fundamentalism," op. cit., n. 22,
p. 174.

27 See Virginia Lieson Brereton, *Training God's Army: the American Bible
School, 1880–1940* (Bloomington: University of Indiana Press, 1990).

28 Paul Heidebrecht, "The educational legacy of Lois and Mary LeBar,"
unpublished paper, catalogued in the Wheaton College Library archives.

29 Ethel May Baldwin and David B. Benson, *Henrietta Mears* (Glendale, CA:
Regal, 1966). Regal Press was one of the many institutions founded by
Henrietta Mears.

30 See Janette Hassey, *No Time for Silence: Evangelical Women in Public Ministry around the Turn of the Century* (Grand Rapids, MI: Zondervan, 1986).

31 Hamilton, "Women, Public Ministry, and Fundamentalism," op. cit., n.
22, p. 174.

32 James S. Dennis, Harlan P. Beach, and Charles H. Fahs, eds, *World Atlas
of Christian Missions* (New York: SVM, 1911), p. 83. These researchers

found that of the 21,307 missionaries they counted, 5,377 were unmarried women; the rest were married women, unmarried men (very few), married men whose wives were also considered missionaries, and married men whose wives were not so counted.

33 Quoted in Ruth A. Tucker, "Women in missions: reaching sisters in 'heathen darkness'," in *Earthen Vessels: American Evangelicals and Foreign Missions, 1880–1980*, eds Joel A. Carpenter and Wilbert R. Shenk (Grand Rapids, MI: Eerdmans, 1990), p. 259.

34 Compare Margaret Lamberts Bendroth, "Women and missions: conflict and changing roles in the Presbyterian Church in the United States of America, 1870–1935," *American Presbyterians*, 65, 1987, pp. 49–59, with Hamilton, "Women, public ministry, and fundamentalism," op. cit., n. 22, pp. 180–4. For a solid picture of the situation of women in mainline Protestant denominations during the first half of the century, see Virginia Lieson Brereton, "United and slighted: women as subordinated insiders," in *Between the Times: the Travail of the Protestant Establishment in America, 1900–1950*, ed. William R. Hutchison (New York: Cambridge University Press, 1989), pp. 143–67.

35 This paragraph follows Hamilton, "Women, public ministry, and fundamentalism," op. cit., n. 22, pp. 184–6.

36 That kind of oversimplification mars the otherwise helpful effort to trace parallels among Shi-ite Muslims, American fundamentalists, Latin American pentecostals, and the New Religions of Japan found in Helen Hardacre, "The impact of fundamentalisms on women, the family and interpersonal relations," in *Fundamentalists and Society: Reclaiming the Sciences, the Family, and Education*, eds Martin E. Marty and R. Scott Appleby (Chicago: University of Chicago Press, 1993), pp. 129–50.

37 This section depends especially on Edith L. Blumhofer, "A confused legacy: reflections of evangelical attitudes toward ministering women in the past century," *Fides et History*, 22, 1990, pp. 49–61; Blumhofer, ed., "Women and American Pentecostalism," *Pneuma*, 17 (Spring) 1995, pp. 19–87; followed by "Feedback: women and pentecostalism," *Pneuma*, 17 (Fall), 1995, pp. 229–52; and Charles H. Barfoot and Gerald T. Sheppard, "Prophetic vs. priestly religion: the changing role of women clergy in pentecostal churches," *Review of Religious Research* 22 (September), 1980, pp. 2–17.

38 These figures, as well as the summary of motives supporting public service for women, are from Barfoot and Sheppard, "Prophetic vs. priestly religion," op. cit., n. 37, pp. 4–10.

39 On the short-lived duration of indiscriminate black–white worship and on many other matters, definitive treatment is found in Grant Wacker, *Heaven Below: Early Pentecostals and American Culture* (Cambridge, MA: Harvard University Press, 2001).

40	See Edith Blumhofer, "'A child shall lead them': Uldine Utley," in *The Contentious Triangle*, eds Rodney Petersen and Calvin Pater (forthcoming); and on McPherson's extraordinary career as itinerant and then founder of the Church of the Foursquare Gospel, Blumhofer, *Aimee Semple McPherson: Everybody's Sister* (Grand Rapids, MI: Eerdmans, 1993).

41	Barfoot and Sheppard, "Prophetic vs. priestly religion," op. cit., n. 37, p. 14.

42	For exceptions, see Cheryl Townsend Gilkes, "'Together and in harness': women's traditions in the sanctified church," *Signs*, 10 (Summer), 1985, pp. 678–99; and Gilkes, "The role of women in the sanctified church," *Journal of Religious Thought*, 43 (Spring/Summer) 1986, pp. 24–41.

43	Deborah Gill, "The contemporary state of women in ministry in the Assemblies of God," *Pneuma*, 17 (Spring), 1995, pp. 33–6.

44	See the books by Susan Juster and Catherine Brekus, above, compared with Margaret Poloma, "Charisma, institutionalization and social change," *Pneuma*, 17 (Fall), 1995, pp. 245–52.

45	Evangelical efforts to sift through the tumult include Mary Stewart Van Leeuwen, ed., *After Eden: Facing the Challenge of Gender Reconciliation* (Grand Rapids, MI: Eerdmans, 1993); and Jack O. Balswick and Judith K. Balswick, *The Family: a Christian Perspective on the Contemporary Home*, 2nd edn (Grand Rapids, MI: Baker, 1999).

46	Mention should also be made of two articles by non-evangelical sociologists who discovered through careful research that evangelicals were not as stereotypically patriarchal as preconceptions suggested: Lori G. Beaman, "The paths between resistance and collaboration: evangelical women in Atlantic Canada," *Atlantis*, 1 (Fall), 1997, pp. 9–18; and John P. Bartkowski, "Debating patriarchy: discursive disputes over spousal authority among evangelical family commentators," *Journal for the Scientific Study of Religion*, 36 (September), 1997, pp. 393–410.

47	Susan D. Rose, "Women warriors: the negotiation of gender in a charismatic community," *Sociological Analysis*, 48, 1987, pp. 245–58.

48	R. Marie Griffith, *God's Daughters: Evangelical Women and the Power of Submission* (Berkeley: University of California Press, 1997); see also Griffith, "Submissive wives, wounded daughters, and female soldiers: prayer and christian womanhood in Women's Aglow Fellowship," in *Lived Religion in America*, ed. David D. Hall (Princeton, NJ: Princeton University Press, 1997), pp. 160–95.

49	Griffith, *God's Daughters*, op. cit., n. 48, pp. 178–9.

50	Brenda E. Brasher, *Godly Women: Fundamentalism and Female Power* (New Brunswick, NJ: Rutgers University Press, 1998); and Christel Manning, *God Gave Us the Right: Conservative Catholic, Evangelical Protestants, and Orthodox Jewish Women Grapple with Feminism* (New Brunswick, NJ:

Rutgers University Press, 1999). See also Brasher, "'My beloved is all radiant': two case studies of congregational-based fundamentalist enclaves and the religious experiences they cultivate among women," *Review of Religious Research*, 38 (March), 1997, pp. 231–46.

51 Brasher, *Godly Women*, op. cit., n. 50, p. 68.

52 Manning, *God Gave Us the Right*, op. cit., n. 50, p. 56.

53 John G. Stackhouse, Jr., "Women in public ministry in twentieth-century Canadian and American evangelicalism: five models," *Studies in Religion/Sciences Religieuses*, 17 (Fall), 1988, pp. 471–85.

Part II
Flashpoints

7

Roman Catholics

In late 1983, the conservative Anglican theologian J. I. Packer began a book review with a revealing bit of autobiography. Packer had been nurtured in his faith by the robust evangelicalism of the English Puritans; his published writings had gained him renown in Britain, Canada, and the United States as one of the most articulate modern advocates of thoughtful, Reformed evangelicalism.[1] Packer's remarks about the book, which was called *The Born-again Catholic*, spoke of a momentous alteration in a longstanding religious quarrel:

> If when I was a student you had told me that before old age struck I should be reviewing a popular Roman Catholic book on the new birth which used Campus Crusade material, carried an official *nihil obstat* and *imprimatur*, and was already in its fourth printing in three years, I doubt whether I would have believed you. But that is what I am doing now. Again, if at that time you had predicted that one day an Anglican bishop would tell me how the last Roman Catholic priest to whom he talked quizzed him hard as to whether Anglicans really preached the new birth as they should, I would probably have laughed in your face. But this month it happened. Things are not as they were![2]

As true as it was in 1983 that things were not as they once had been, so a decade and more later the publication of "Evangelicals and Catholics together: the Christian mission in the third millennium" (1994) and "Evangelicals and Catholics together II: the gift of salvation" (1997) is further indication of a sea-change in a once stormy relationship.[3] A summary historical sketch, written mostly as a report on evangelical attitudes toward Roman Catholics, cannot by itself evaluate the changes played out in recent decades. But it can show the dramatic nature of what has been taking place. In particular, such a sketch is useful for revealing the nature of the historic standoff between Catholics and Protestant evangelicals that existed, as if set in concrete, from the early days of the Reformation until well after the Second World War; for highlighting some of the dramatic changes that have occurred in relations between Protestants and Catholics over the past four decades; for showing how the Protestant perception of Catholicism's civil character – whether as threatening or supporting public moral order – has always played a large role in evangelical attitudes throughout American history; and by noting some earlier anticipations of modern changes that went largely unnoticed because of the war-time footing that existed between the two camps. The story of relations between Roman Catholics and Protestant evangelicals, in short, cannot provide infallible guidance for the future, but it can provide grist for historical and theological reflection bearing on the search for Christian allies in the modern world.[4]

Historic Standoff

Once upon a time – in fact, within the memory of many people who are still very much alive – Catholics and evangelical Protestants regarded each other with the gravest possible suspicion. That suspicion reflected a world of religious strife dramatically opposed to the situation described by J. I. Packer in 1983 or as outlined in the various projects of "evangelicals and Catholics together." While Roman Catholics and Protestant evangelicals still are divided by many important differences, the possibilities that now exist for inter-communication, theological and social cooperation, and mutual encouragement are so much greater than even a generation ago as to constitute a minor revolution. To illustrate how far the age of combat between Catholics and Protestants extended into the recent past, it is necessary only to observe the general situation in the United States during the years immediately following the Second World War. The standoff appeared fixed, seemingly in place forever.

By mid-century, grosser forms of religious hostility that had prevailed widely throughout much of American history were subsiding, but the change was a matter of degree not kind.[5] Two comments, two events, and two books suggest the extent of Protestant–Catholic disengagement that existed in the decade and a half after the Second World War.

In 1945 the Presbyterian fundamentalist Carl McIntyre, who was then more centrally located on the religious spectrum than he later became, assessed the world situation in terms that some other evangelicals would also have shared:

> As we enter the post-war world, without any doubt the greatest enemy of freedom and liberty that the world has to face today is the Roman Catholic system. Yes, we have Communism in Russia and all that is involved there, but if one had to choose between the two . . . one would be much better off in a communistic society than in a Roman Catholic Fascist set-up. . . . America has to face the Roman Catholic terror. The sooner the Christian people of America wake up to the danger the safer will be our land.[6]

Three years later, the Protestant church historian Wilhelm Pauck, who moved in more liberal orbits than McIntyre, took stock of the inter-religious situation and concluded that "the difference between Protestantism and Roman Catholicism is so profound that it seems almost impossible to recognize them as two forms of one Christianity."[7]

These evaluations reflected a more general climate characterized by considerable mutual suspicion. In 1946 President Truman's assignment of a formal representative to the Vatican was greeted with a frightening din from all along the Protestant spectrum. G. Bromley Oxnam, Bishop of the Methodist Church in New York and president of the Federal Council of Churches, criticized the move as "encouraging the un-American policy of a union of church and state" which the Catholic church pursued.[8] Nor was suspicion all on one side. When the second General Assembly of the World Council of Churches met at Evanston in 1954, Chicago's Cardinal Samuel Strich issued a pastoral letter forbidding priests to attend even as reporters and urging Catholics in general to stay far away.[9]

Even authors who attempted to write sympathetically about Catholic–Protestant differences could at best describe a cordial antagonism. When Jaroslav Pelikan published *The Riddle of Roman Catholicism* from a Protestant perspective in 1959, he admitted "that the prejudices and clichés of past generations continue to dominate the image of the Roman church current in America." His book, by contrast, was a charitable effort to dispel prejudice. Yet when Pelikan came to describe the current situation, he turned instinctively to metaphors of conflict – "unconditional surrender," "the great divide," "theological alienation." Neither did he hold out high hopes for an improvement in "what we have now . . . on both sides, a picture of the other side that is part photograph, part old daguerreotype, and part caricature."[10] For Catholics the Newman Press translated Louis Bouyer's *The Spirit and Forms of Protestantism* for American readers in 1956, the year of its original French publication. Like Pelikan, Bouyer was eager to replace prejudice with sympathy; and he was willing to concede a great deal to Protestantism. But also like Pelikan a point was soon reached where the language of antithesis took over, and Bouyer concluded that, while the religion of Luther, Calvin, and their theological descendants contained insights which the Catholic church needed, it was "compromised . . . irremediably" by its fatal attachment to sixteenth-century nominalism.[11] In sum, on the very eve of Pope John XXIII's pontificate and, one might add, of the American presidential election of 1960, there seemed no particular reason to expect a quantum leap in Protestant–Catholic goodwill.

Among Protestants, differences with Roman Catholics were perceived most strongly by those who were the most evangelical. After the war, evangelical publishing still maintained a steady beat of anti-Catholic polemic. New books appeared with titles like *A Priest Speaks His Mind: Why He Returned to the Protestant Faith of His Fathers* and *Catholicism under the Searchlight of the Scriptures*. Evangelical publishers also reissued classic anti-Catholic works from the previous century like Charles Chiniquy's *Fifty Years in the Church of Rome*.[12] In 1962, the Presbyterian author Loraine Boettner published his lengthy study *Roman Catholicism*, which came to be regarded by many evangelicals as a definitive exposition and rebuttal of the Roman Catholic faith. Boettner's conclusions summarized a very long history of evangelical complaint:

> That the Roman Church has within it much of truth is not to be denied. It teaches the inspiration of the Scriptures, the deity of Christ, the virgin birth, the miracles, the resurrection of the body, a future judgment, heaven and hell, and many other Scripture truths. In every instance, however, it nullifies these truths to a considerable extent by adding to or subtracting from what the Bible teaches. . . . The Roman Church thus has such serious inherent defects that over the broad course of history it cannot possibly emerge successful. Clearly it has lost its power to evangelize the world, and instead has become so confirmed in its present course that it cannot be reformed either from within or from without. In the main it is as antagonistic and as much an obstacle to evangelical Christianity as are the pagan religions. . . . Its interpretation of the Scriptures is so erroneous and its principles are so persistently unchristian that over

the long period of time its influence for good is outweighed by its influence for evil. *It must, therefore, as a system, be judged to be a false church.*[13]

Attitudes toward Catholicism that evangelicals maintained with something close to unanimity into the 1960s reached back to the middle decades of the sixteenth century. A combination of attacks on church abuses and fresh articulations of biblical truths – which constituted the negative and positive poles of the Protestant Reformation – long dominated evangelical attitudes toward Catholicism. It is possible to find slightly different points to mark the hardening of religious division – perhaps 1541 and the failure of face-to-face Protestant–Catholic negotiations at Regensburg (Ratisbon) in Germany, or, at the latest, the work of the Catholic Council of Trent (1546–63) and the full-scale responses it evoked from such Protestant luminaries as John Calvin or the Lutheran Martin Chemnitz. Exact dating, however, is immaterial, for Catholic–Protestant antagonism rapidly became a fixed planet in the Western religious sky. Already by the second half of the sixteenth century, efforts to speak sympathetically about Protestant–Catholic similarities was met with stern opposition from both sides. Church historians of the era who tried to write with some appreciation for the opposition – like the Lutheran John Sleidan or the Huguenot Lancelot du Voisin, sieur de la Popelinière – were blasted by both Catholics and Protestants.[14]

The Protestant brief against Catholicism was expressed in a Niagara of books, pamphlets, and sermons so voluminous that no one human could possibly take the measure of it all. But the main points of that brief can be summarized quite easily. Catholics, in the Protestant view,

- taught that people earned their salvation by doing good deeds;
- prevented common people from reading the Bible and from taking their guidance for life from the Scriptures;
- manufactured extra-biblical saints, festivals, and rites that substituted human imagination for biblical patterns of worship;
- took away glory from Christ by making Mary a co-author of salvation;
- wantonly corrupted Scripture by forcing new doctrines onto the people merely at the whim of popes and councils whose supposed authority was no more than the imperialistic expression of their own selfish ambition;

- promoted a corrupting hierarchy that stripped the faithful of their proper status as priests before God.

In their turn, Catholics gave as good as they got. Wherever Catholic communities were placed in physical or intellectual connection with Protestants, a literature sprouted that reversed the charges. Rather than rescuing Christianity from corruption, Protestantism was hastening it toward decay. In the Catholic view, Protestants

- offered a "salvation" by faith that denied the need for holiness before God;
- abandoned the Bible to the interpretation of every Tom, Dick, and Mary (no matter how bizarre those interpretations might be) and so effectively stripped the Bible of normative, authoritative meaning;
- denied the ability of the Holy Spirit to work through ongoing teaching officers in the church as the Spirit had early worked in bringing the church into existence;
- scandalously neglected God's gracious help provided to humanity in the person of the Blessed Virgin Mary and the exemplary saints;
- rejected the apostolic authority of bishops, councils, and popes and so abetted the rising Western tide of rationalism, secularism, and moral anarchy;
- forsook genuine ecclesiastical leadership in favor of a political free-for-all where authority was reduced to merely the power of manipulation.

These polemics, which have echoed around the world since the mid-sixteenth century, also arrived early in the colonies that became the United States. Although the number of Catholics in the thirteen colonies was small (only 25,000 by 1790), Protestant anti-Romanism was a staple of the American theological world. It was fueled especially by the background of Catholic–Protestant strife in the English Reformation. That antagonism was enshrined for English-speaking readers everywhere in the pages of John Foxe's *Book of Martyrs*, which added Catholic persecution of Protestants to a long line of sufferings endured by true servants of Christ. As merely one instance of the antagonism as it came to America, it is helpful to note the language used when the Massachusetts Judge Paul Dudley in 1750 left a legacy to Harvard College for the purpose of establishing a series of theological lectures. The third of the lectures in a rotating cycle was to be devoted to "the detecting & convicting & exposing the Idolatry of the Romish Church, Their Tyranny, Usurpations, damnable Heresies, fatal Errors, abominable Superstitions, and other crying Wickednesses in their high Places; and Finally that the Church of Rome is that mystical Babylon, That Man of Sin, That apostate Church spoken of, in the New-Testament."[15] By the time Catholic immigration on a major scale began in the nineteenth century, anti-Catholic literature was a well entrenched theological genre. Ray Allen Billington's study of the six antebellum decades included a bibliography of nearly forty pages devoted exclusively to anti-Catholic periodicals, books, and pamphlets.[16]

An incident from the mid-1840s illustrates how difficult it had become to maintain even the most vestigial respect across the Catholic–evangelical divide. With the growing numbers of Catholics in the country and the conversion of some of them to Protestantism, evangelical denominations that practiced infant baptism were faced with the question of how to regard the status of Catholic baptism. It was a poignant sign of the current state of affairs when the conservative Presbyterian theologian, Charles Hodge, called down great wrath upon his head for defending the validity of Catholic baptism, even though that defense fully maintained Protestant arguments about the deviance of Rome. Hodge was far from a crypto-Catholic, since throughout his long career he regularly chastised Catholicism for what he thought were its manifest theological perversions. At the same time, however, Hodge held that proper discriminations had to be made. His reasoning against the action of the Old School General Assembly in 1845, which denied the validity of Catholic baptism, is worth quoting at length, both to show the normal terms that evangelicals used in talking about Catholics and to indicate how difficult it was for even a well respected evangelical leader to gain a hearing for even the most modest gesture of respect toward Rome:

Baptism therefore, not being an ordinance of any particular church, but of the church catholic, and every man who professes saving truth being a member of that church, Romish baptism if administered by a man professing such truth, is Christian baptism. . . . We maintain therefore Romish baptism to be valid; that is, that it avails to make the recipient a member of the church catholic, because it is a washing with water, in the name of the Trinity, with the design to signify, seal and apply the

benefits of the covenant of grace. . . . If the church of Rome is antichrist,
a synagogue of Satan, how can its ordinances be Christian sacraments?
This we doubt not is the difficulty which weighs most with those who
reject Romish baptisms as invalid. We would ask such persons, whether
they admit that a Roman Catholic can be a child of God? If he can, how
can a man be a member of the synagogue of Satan and of the body of
Christ at the same time? Is there no inconsistency here? If not, then there
is no inconsistency in declaring that the Romish system, so far as it is distinguished from that of evangelical churches, is antichristian, and yet that
those who are groaning under that system are in the visible church. The
terms antichrist, synagogue of Satan, etc., refer not to the mass of the
people, nor to the presbyters of that communion, nor the word of God,
nor the saving truths which they profess, but to the Popish hierarchy and
its corruptions. That hierarchy with its usurpations and errors, is the
mystery of iniquity, the man of sin, which in the church catholic, the
temple of God, exalts itself above all that is called God or that is wor-
shipped. If Roman Catholics are no part of the visible church, then the
Romish hierarchy is not "the man of sin" spoken of by the apostle, for
he was to rise and rule in the church. It is, therefore, one thing to
denounce the Roman system, and another to say that Romanists are no
part of the church catholic. And if they are in the church, their baptism
being a washing with water in the name of the Trinity, is Christian
baptism; just as the word of God, when read or preached by them, is still
his word, and is to be received and obeyed as such.[17]

The attitudes that Hodge both reflected and combated remained particularly strong among evangelicals. Even after the momentous shifts of
recent decades had begun, observers noted that conservative Protestant
positions were the most resistant to change. In 1978, the ethicist James
Gustafson wrote that a wide range of Protestant–Catholic dialogue was
then under way in the United States, with the exception that "the most
conservative Catholic and Protestant theologians do not relate to each
other at all."[18] Gustafson may have been overstating things a little, but
he was correct in concluding that many among the firmer sort of Protestants still retained much of their tradition's hereditary anti-Catholicism.

Religious Standoff, Civil Mistrust

As steadily as American Protestants maintained anti-Catholicism for
theological reasons, almost from the start of European settlement in the

New World they were nearly as concerned about Catholicism's civil tendencies. The reputation of Catholicism as a promoter of tyranny contributed fully to the first stages of the American love affair with liberty that began in earnest with the eighteenth-century colonial wars. When warfare between France and England swept up the colonies, colonial Protestants immediately made fateful rhetorical connections. As propounded from countless colonial pulpits during the mid-eighteenth century, Protestants proclaimed that they were fighting for the glories of Britain against the depredations of France, the truth of Protestantism against the lies of Catholicism, and the blessings of freedom against the perils of tyranny.

Two citations, from hundreds that could be quoted, show how, even before there was a United States, American republican commitments functioned as an ally of Protestantism and an enemy of Catholicism. George Whitefield, the great evangelist, was in Philadelphia in August 1746 when news arrived that "Bonnie Prince Charles," the Jacobite (and Catholic) pretender to the British throne, had been decisively defeated at the battle of Culloden. Whitefield immediately preached a sermon to thank God for rescuing the British from the multiplied woes of a Catholic monarchy: "How soon would our pulpits every where have been filled with these old antichristian doctrines, free-will, meriting by works, transubstantiation, purgatory, works of supererogation, passive-obedience, non-resistance, and all the other abominations of the whore of Babylon?"[19] Ten years later, the president of Princeton College in New Jersey, Aaron Burr, Sr, rallied his evangelical audience at the start of the French and Indian Wars with a frightful vision of France's Catholic religion: "We have heard of the Policy and Perfidy of France, of her arbitrary Power, Popish tyranny and Bigotry. . . . If we view our Enemies, in a religious, as well as political Light, we shall see the Necessity of guarding against them with all possible care. Their established religion is Popery; which, beside all its other Corruptions, disposes them from Principle, to be cruel to Protestants."[20] Only two decades later, American colonists found proof positive in Britain's tyranny when they saw the British extend civil rights and historic privileges to the Catholic church in Quebec. New England ministers saw the Act not as an overdue recognition of human rights but as an effort "to cut off all the liberties of the colonies."[21]

After the American War for Independence – and the social revolution arising from the Revolution that made liberty the center of the

American ideology – evangelical anti-Catholicism was given new life by the rising current of Catholic immigration into the United States. Protestant writing against Catholicism retained the historic theological animus, but it was almost always a political expression as well.

One of the main engines of the reform movements that galvanized American Protestants in the antebellum period was anti-Catholicism, sometimes of the rabid variety. Lyman Beecher, the whirlwind Congregationalist and Presbyterian who, in a long career, spearheaded Protestant outreach in rural Connecticut, Boston, and Cincinnati, often warned Americans about the threat from the Catholic church. Historian Sydney Ahlstrom summarized a major section of one of Beecher's most influential books, his *Plea for the West* (1834), as "a 140-page tirade which depicts the pope and Europe's reactionary kings, with the Austrian emperor at their head and Catholic immigrants for agents, as engaged in an organized conspiracy to take over the Mississippi Valley."[22] When ideological controversy increased between North and South over the issue of slavery, Northern Protestants knew how to put to use their long habit of linking Rome to tyranny. In the mid-1850s a broadside from the American (or Know-Nothing) Party tried to enlist anti-Catholic sentiment itself in the struggle against slavery: "Whereas, Roman Catholicism and slavery being alike founded and supported on the basis of ignorance and tyranny; and being, therefore, natural allies in every warfare against liberty and enlightenment; therefore, be it Resolved, That there can exist no real hostility to Roman Catholicism which does not embrace slavery, its natural co-worker in opposition to freedom and republican institutions."[23] In the two decades before the Civil War, anti-Catholicism was a political staple in shaping the political actions of many Protestants in the North as well as some in the South.[24] In the post-war period of renewed Protestant enthusiasm for the future of the country, Protestants were again quick to paint Catholics as anti-democratic and anti-republican. One of the most popular works of this type, which described both the day's moral crisis as well as hope for the future, was written by the midwestern Congregationalist Josiah Strong. The fifth chapter of Strong's *Our Country* was entitled "Conflict of Romanism with the fundamental principle of our government."[25]

A sampling of Protestant book titles can also show how central the civic qualities of Catholicism were to evangelical polemical literature: again, from a plethora of examples, N. L. Rice, *Romanism not Christianity: a Series of Lectures in which Popery and Protestantism are Contrasted,*

Showing the Incompatibility of the Former with Freedom and Free Institutions (Cincinnati, 1847); Thomas Bayne, *Popery Subversive of American Institutions* (Pittsburgh, 1856); Joseph Smith Van Dyke, *Popery: the Foe of the Church and of the Republic* (Philadelphia, 1871); and Jeremiah J. Crowley, *Romanism: a Menace to the Nation; Together with My Former Book, The Parochial School, a Curse to the Church, a Menace to the Nation* (Wheaton, IL, 1912), which was dedicated to "the lovers of liberty, enlightenment and progress throughout the world."

White evangelical Protestants almost universally felt that Catholics threatened the biblically based character of American civilization. Thus, the nineteenth-century's active anti-Catholicism was sparked especially by the belief that the Catholic hierarchy discouraged, or even prohibited, the use of Scripture among the laity. This belief, in turn, led to the conclusion that Catholicism was inimical to the American way of life, a conclusion set out with disarming frankness by an attorney arguing in 1887 to preserve the right of a Wisconsin school board to continue daily readings from the King James Version: "The decrees of the councils, the encyclicals of the Popes, the pastoral and other letters of the Archbishops and Bishops, and the writings of learned Catholics furnish abundant evidence that the Catholic church is opposed to popular government, that it is opposed to liberty of conscience, and of worship, and that it is opposed to our public school system."[26]

It only added fuel to Protestant fires when a few well known descendants of American Protestantism actually joined the Catholic church. Outrage at such actions was mitigated by the observation that some of the converts – like Mrs Sophia Ripley and Orestes Brownson – had already been tainted by their earlier association with the suspect Transcendentalist movement.[27]

In the twentieth century, specifically evangelical Protestants maintained the charge that Catholicism entailed a threat to American freedoms. *The Fundamentals* of 1910–15 included several stringent attacks on Rome, of which Bostonian J. M. Foster's was typical. His complaint was as much social and political as theological:

[The Catholic church is] the essential and deadly foe of civil and religious liberty. . . . The Roman hierarchy owns $300,000,000 in America. They have a parochial school system and clamorously demand a share in the public school fund. Their policy is the refinement of duplicity. They join the Jews, infidels and skeptics in driving the Bible from our public schools, on the ground that the State is only a secular corporation and has no right to teach morals and religion. . . . The answer which the organic people should return is: "This is a Christian State; the public school system is its agency for building up a Christian citizenship; morals and religion, so far as they are essential for discharging the functions of Christian citizenship, shall be taught in our public schools; and the school funds shall not be divided."[28]

The charge that Catholics could not be fully American, because of their allegiance to the pope and their promotion of religious error, played a large part in shaping Protestant voting during the presidential elections of 1928 and 1960, when Catholic candidates Al Smith and John F. Kennedy ran for the Democrats.[29] Just after the 1960 election, Loraine Boettner's evangelical attack on Catholicism featured the charge that "Roman Catholicism [is] a poor defense against communism." Very near the conclusion of his book, Boettner repeated the stock evangelical assertion that "in general it [the Catholic church] has sought to weaken or destroy free governments."[30]

In sum, the fixed Protestant opinion was that Catholicism was such a flawed version of Christianity as to be hardly Christian at all. In the United States, moreover, evangelical Protestants were leaders in arguing that Catholicism was not only a religious threat, but also that it subverted the free political institutions of the United States. Well after the Second World War, the anti-Catholic polemic went on. Into the late 1950s almost no one could have predicted that change was in the air.

Dramatic Change

That was then. Only short decades later, the situation has become very different. Four major factors help to explain why the Catholic–evangelical climate has changed and why that change has been so dramatic. First was a one-time political occurrence, second a far more important series of developments within the Catholic church, third a political reorientation among evangelicals, and fourth a theological breakthrough. Even a sketchy account of these factors can show that, while there remains much to discuss between evangelicals and Catholics, the basis for that discussion is dramatically different than it has ever been in American history.

(1)   The most visible public signal of a shift in the United States was the election of a Catholic as president in 1960. John F. Kennedy's victory was itself a milestone for overcoming Protestant bias and fulfilling earlier Catholic efforts at public service. It marked the culmination of a long process begun during the Revolutionary period by the participation of the Maryland Catholic, Charles Carrol, in the Continental Congress as well as by George Washington's proclamation suppressing traditional anti-papal demonstrations on November 5 (Guy Fawke's or Pope's Day). Kennedy's election was also the culmination of more than a century and a half of intensive Catholic involvement in grass-roots politics.[31] The circumstances of the 1960 campaign added even greater symbolic importance to Kennedy's election. His famous campaign speech before Protestant ministers in Houston seemed to convince them, and many others, that a Catholic president would not imperil national integrity. Kennedy's scrupulous record on church–state matters, particularly his opposition to government aid for parochial schools, silenced many critics who feared that Catholics did not have proper national priorities. On this issue Billy Graham spoke for others by bestowing the indelicate praise that Kennedy had "turned out to be a Baptist President."[32] Moreover, the apotheosis which occurred after Kennedy's assassination left him, a Catholic, one of the most popular American presidents among the public at large. The "religious issue" in American politics, though not yet dead, had suffered a crushing blow. Even Kennedy's misdeeds have helped to defuse inter-religious antagonisms, for his womanizing and power-grabbing were "ecumenical" in resembling the misdeeds of politicians who happened to be Protestant.

(2)   The Kennedy phenomenon was less significant for long-term improvement in Protestant–Catholic relations than the more strictly religious events which, after having been set in motion in Rome, led to great changes in America. The new situation between Catholics and evangelicals is a subset of a much larger reorientation of Catholic and Protestant relations more generally. Ripple effects from Pope John XXIII's ecumenical spirit were not long in coming. Even before he convened the Second Vatican Council (1962–5), the pope had sent Catholic observers to the 1960 assembly of the World Council of Churches in New Delhi and had established a Secretariat for Promoting Christian Unity in the Vatican. In the wake of the Council's Decree on Ecumenism, which "commends this work to the bishops everywhere in the world for their

Flashpoints

diligent and prudent guidance," the Conference of American Bishops in November 1964 set up its own Ecumenical Commission. This agency sponsored subcommissions which very soon were deep in discussion with the Orthodox church in the United States and with several of the major Protestant traditions.[33] Of these meetings, that between Lutherans and Catholics has produced the richest fruit, with a series of agreements on the Nicene Creed, baptism, the Eucharist, and, most importantly, justification by faith.[34] Catholic entrance into ecumenical activity has continued on a broad level. Although the church does not belong to either the National Council or World Council of Churches, it takes an active observer's role in the deliberations of these bodies. Moreover, it has become a member of the National Council's Commission on Faith and Order, an agency whose staff now regularly includes Catholics.[35] Catholic–Protestant discussions, instructions, debates, and dialogue are now a regular feature at nearly all the major inter-faith forums on almost every imaginable issue.

(3)   In light of how important the civic sphere has always been for Catholic–evangelical relations, it is not surprising that an alteration in political perception contributed greatly to the changes of recent decades. Several developments since the 1960s have conspired to extinguish (or at least greatly diminish) the evangelical fear of Catholicism as a civil threat. Some of these developments have been literary and theoretical. On the home front, American Catholics were among the leaders at the Second Vatican Council in securing strong statements on behalf of civil liberty. Although American evangelicals did not read widely in John Courtney Murray and other such American Catholic proponents of civil liberty, their work nonetheless undermined historic evangelical fears of Catholic tyranny.[36] In the international arena, even more damage was done to Protestant notions of Catholic tyranny by the contribution of the Catholic church to the Solidarity movement in Poland, the public leadership of Pope John Paul II in combating communism in Europe, and the pope's temperate statements on explosive political situations in Latin America, Africa, and Asia.[37] These political actions did not address doctrinal issues directly, but they did strip away much of the civil anxiety with which American Protestants had always looked upon Roman Catholics.

The practicalities of local political action have also done much to open doorways. Over the past several decades, contemporary political affairs have become so passionately tangled that Christian faiths and public stances on moral issues now collide in nearly every conceivable combination. The crucible effect wrought by this situation explains why many Catholic–evangelical barriers have fallen: committed toilers in the public vineyard have glanced up in surprise to find previously despised Catholics or evangelicals laboring right alongside.

The complex controversies surrounding three of America's fundamental social concerns – sex, national self-defense, and the economy – have contributed a great deal to the withering of old inter-religious antagonisms. Political debates on these issues, particularly controversy on how moral beliefs are to shape education, regularly reflect the passionate commitments of Americans from all points on the religious compass. Religiously infused arguments – especially on abortion, but also on other issues including health care reform, the justice or injustice of specific military actions, the merits of United States foreign policy, or the character of candidates for public office – fill the air. The significant fact for contemporary inter-religious relations is that allegiance to a general Protestantism or Catholicism is no longer a reliable indicator of commitments on public policy. Both theoretical questions and practical dilemmas, both theological applications and religious reflexes, are so diverse that whatever systematic differences still separate Catholics and Protestants are regularly lost in the public shuffle. In this new situation, Catholics and evangelicals often find themselves arguing the same or similar positions on public issues.[38]

(4) On specific theological issues, the ecumenical dialogues promoted by the Second Vatican Council have gone a considerable distance toward clarifying the difference between mistaken religious stereotypes and genuine theological disagreement. All of the Catholic dialogues with different Protestant groups have highlighted areas of continuing disagreement. But those same dialogues have also cast some historic standoffs into a startlingly new light. While American evangelicals, with their twentieth-century suspicion of ecumenical activity, have usually not kept abreast of the various Catholic–Protestant dialogues, their contents make fascinating reading for anyone with even a little knowledge of the historic standoff between Catholics and evangelicals.

Of many examples that could be cited, the US Lutheran–Roman Catholic dialogue on justification by faith, published in 1983, was the most remarkable. The promulgation of a joint statement was the product of extensive discussion over a period of several years. This complex, heavily footnoted document demands careful reading, yet its main points spoke directly to major sources of historic Catholic–Protestant antagonism. In particular, the document contended that much of the disagreement on this issue between Protestants (or, here, Lutherans) and Catholics was based on conditions that no longer prevailed. Specifically, both sides had been guilty of reading the Bible polemically in an effort to buttress their own positions, many "non-theological sources of division" that once separated Christians were now passé (like state-separated ecclesiastical establishments), and both Catholics and Lutherans should repent for the verbal abuse they had been hurling at each other for over 400 years. The document spoke not of "uniformity" on the substance of the doctrine of justification, but about "a convergence" on the meaning of the doctrine. Most importantly, the elements of "material convergence" began with the assertion that "Christ and his gospel are the source, center and norm of Christian life, individual and corporate, in church and world. Christians have no other basis for eternal life and hope of final salvation than God's free gift in Jesus Christ, extended to them in the Holy Spirit." The shapers of the document concluded by saying that they could agree on "a fundamental affirmation. . . . *Our entire hope of justification and salvation rests on Christ Jesus and on the gospel whereby the good news of God's merciful action in Christ is made known; we do not place our ultimate trust in anything other than God's promise and saving work in Christ.*"[39] Further sections of the document hedged this statement around with carefully chosen words to qualify matters from both Lutheran and Catholic directions. The qualifications, however, did not undermine the manifest implication of the words that were used.

The significance of these American discussions was heightened many times over when on October 31, 1999 – Reformation Sunday – representatives of the Vatican and the Lutheran World Federation signed a document affirming at that much broader level a mostly common understanding of justification by faith. This signing, which took place in Martin Luther's Germany, represented the last stage in a long, sometimes rocky, series of negotiations. Its basic affirmation, constructed without the assistance of American evangelicals, nonetheless had major implications for those evangelicals. That central affirmation signaled unprecedented progress in addressing the disputes of the Reformation: "Together we confess: By grace alone, in faith in Christ's saving work and not because of any merit on our part, we are accepted by God and receive the Holy Spirit, who renews our hearts while equipping and calling us to do good works."[40]

These documents on justification are the kind of evidence J. I. Packer had in mind when he said he had not anticipated he would ever live to see such signs of "evangelicalism" within the Catholic church. These are statements that, by recording a new willingness among at least many Catholics and Protestants to rethink old standoffs, herald a new day of inter-Christian fellowship and activity.

Re-engagement

Several signs of the recent Catholic–Protestant re-engagement have special bearing for evangelical Protestants. The experience of many individuals has paralleled that of the fundamentalist leader Carl McIntyre. Where McIntyre in 1945 claimed that he would rather be ruled by communists than Catholics, by 1969 his message had changed, at least a little. By the latter date McIntyre averred, "I'm much closer to the Catholics in my belief in the Virgin Birth than I am to liberal Protestants who deny it."[41] Protestants who started out more flexible than McIntyre have moved a proportionately greater distance, but McIntyre's general observation – that on some matters, some Protestants stand fairly close to some Catholics – has proven true for many individuals.

More generally, the spread of the charismatic movement (and then of songs, prayers, and worship styles going well beyond officially charismatic circles) has done a great deal to reduce the once-lofty barriers between Catholics and evangelicals.[42] Public taste in spiritual literature shows the same lack of respect for the great divide of the sixteenth century, with evangelicals buying the books of Catholics Thomas Merton and Henri Nouwen, Catholics reading evangelicals Richard Foster and Richard Lovelace, and American Christians of all sorts devouring the books from Britain's C. S. Lewis and G. K. Chesterton without caring a great deal that the former grew up in an evangelical ethos before finding "mere Christianity," while the latter moved from Anglicanism to Catholicism without ever embracing evangelicalism. American publishers have encouraged the growing traffic between the traditions by bringing out numerous books that treat inter-confessional differences far more relatively than authors in the 1950s could have imagined. To sample almost randomly, it is possible to point to popular titles like Boudreau's *The Born-again Catholic* (1980) from Living Flame Press, and more serious studies, such as George H. Tavard's *Justification* (1983) from Paulist Press, which argues that Luther's construction of this key doctrine is compatible with the theology of Trent, or T. F. Torrance's *Theology in Reconciliation: Essays towards Evangelical–Catholic Unity in East and West* (1976), published in the USA by Wm B. Eerdmans.

Even on matters concerning the Bible, always a sensitive barometer of public sentiment in America, the recent decades have witnessed a series of marvels. From rioting over Catholic desires to read the Douay-Rheims Bible in public school during the nineteenth century, to the creation of mutually exclusive networks of professional Bible scholars in the first half of the twentieth, the study and reading of Scripture has now become a non-sectarian free-for-all.[43] Catholics currently may read the Living Bible and the Good News Bible, both produced under Protestant auspices, with the *imprimatur* and *nihil obstat*. Catholic scholars sit on the revision committee of the Revised Standard Version, and Protestant purchasers swell the sales of the Catholic Jerusalem Bible. Official delegates were exchanged between the Catholic Biblical Association and the Society of Biblical Literature (SBL) for the first time only in 1959, yet by 1966 a Catholic had been elected president of the SBL.[44] So unpredictable had the times become that it was a Catholic group which set records in the distribution of Scripture, with the Sacred Heart League placing record orders from the American Bible Society for 775,000 New Testaments in 1979 and 800,000 in 1983.[45]

The recent careers of two stars in the religious media further suggest how much and how rapidly things have changed. Billy Graham, of Southern fundamentalist extraction and nativist evangelical education, enjoyed less than cordial relations with Catholics early in his evangelistic career. During the 1950s Catholic officials in South America and the Philippines forbade their co-religionists to attend his meetings; in the same years local priests and bishops in the United States also often discouraged attendance at Graham crusades. During the presidential election of 1960, Graham only just succeeded in muting his enthusiasm for Richard Nixon and, again just barely, in hiding his apprehensions about a Democratic regime that would include not only a Catholic president, but also a Catholic Majority Leader in the Senate (Mike Mansfield) and a Catholic Speaker of the House (John McCormack). Very soon thereafter, however, Graham began to work at improved relations with Catholics. His efforts were unusually successful. Catholics now make up a considerable portion of those who attend his meetings, record decisions for Christ, and watch the crusades on television. Tangible evidence of Graham's transcendence of inter-confessional antagonisms multiplied rapidly from the late 1960s. In 1977 he was granted permission to hold a crusade in one of American Catholicism's most hallowed locations, the football stadium at the University of Notre Dame. In 1978 he became the first Protestant leader to be entertained by the abbot of the shrine of the Black Madonna in Czestochowa, Poland. In 1981 he sought and was granted an audience at the Vatican by Pope John Paul II, who years before as Cardinal Karol Wojtyla had made it possible for Graham to preach in Catholic churches during his evangelistic tour of Poland.[46]

If Billy Graham's growing friendliness with Catholics is remarkable, what may be said about the Catholic *volte-face* on Martin Luther? Although the antagonisms of centuries had cooled somewhat by the 1950s, Luther was still treated harshly or ignored entirely by the Catholic populace at large. Only two of thirty American Catholic periodicals in one survey provided reviews of Roland Bainton's life of Luther, the most compelling modern study, when it appeared in 1950.[47] Catholic reaction to the Martin Luther movie of 1953 was also decidedly unfavorable. One commentator in *The Priest* summed up his judgment by calling Luther "a lewd satyr whose glandular demands were the ultimate cause of his break with the Christian Church."[48]

In the wake of the Second Vatican Council, however, an altogether different attitude filtered down rapidly into popular levels. By 1965, the pages of *The Priest* reflected a different picture. According to one writer, "We'd feel quite silly today declaiming against Luther in the intemperate words of yesterday."[49] Scholarly and popular reassessment of Luther went on apace until 1980 when a series of meetings to celebrate the 450th anniversary of the Lutherans' Augsburg Confession heard from many Catholics about the usefulness of that confession for their own tradition.[50] The re-evaluation reached a grand climax in 1983, during the celebrations marking the 500th anniversary of Luther's birth. Local Catholic officials, anticipating the pope's own appearance in Rome's Evangelical-Lutheran Christ Church on December 11, 1983, accepted invitations to preach in Protestant services.[51] In that year, conciliatory Protestant titles like *Martin Luther: Prophet to the Catholic Church* were echoed by Catholic books of similar spirit like *Luther: a Reformer for the Church*.[52] It encapsulates the startling changes wrought by the passage of only a few years to note that in the mid-1950s Chicago Catholics fought to keep the Luther film off local television, while in 1983 the Notre Dame alumni magazine devoted much of one issue, including an attractive cover portrait, to a discussion of "What Martin Luther means to us."[53] Only two years before there had been a similar chorus of Protestant and Catholic voices to mark the 800th anniversary of the birth of St Francis. But especially the dramatically altered position of Martin Luther in Catholic–Protestant relations testified eloquently to an unprecedented improvement in inter-confessional attitudes.

Outside the United States, similar signs point in the direction of the same altered conditions. To take only one of many possible examples, members of an interest group within Ireland's Catholic Church call themselves "Evangelical Catholics" and publish material hard to distinguish from standard issue evangelical sources.[54]

The most dramatic sign of improved Catholic–evangelical relations appeared with the promulgation of a document in May 1994 called "Evangelicals and Catholics Together" (ECT).[55] Under the leadership of the Catholic Richard Neuhaus and the evangelical Charles Colson, a small group of leaders formulated, and a somewhat larger group signed, this widely publicized appeal for dialogue and cooperation. The document's drafters made clear that this was an unofficial, non-ecclesiastical statement written by individuals. But their belief that the ancient Catholic–Protestant standoff needed to be overcome was unmistakable: "We are Evangelical Protestants and Roman Catholics who have been led through prayer, study, and discussion to common convictions about Christian faith and mission. . . . The love of Christ compels us and we are therefore resolved to avoid such conflict between our communities and, where such conflict exists, to do what we can to reduce and eliminate it. Beyond that, we are called and we are therefore resolved to explore patterns of working and witnessing together in order to advance the one mission of Christ." The document did not pretend that all historic differences were now passé – on, for example, the nature of baptism or the structure of authority. But the list of common affirmations was remarkably extensive – for example, on belief in the lordship of Christ, the divine inspiration of Scripture, the enduring validity of the Apostles' Creed, and the reality of salvation through justification by faith. The signers also pledged themselves to work together for morality in public life, for the free exercise of religion and home and abroad, for legal protection of the unborn, and for parental choice in education.

Publication of ECT was greeted by both jeers and cheers. The jeers came from evangelicals who felt that modern Roman Catholics could not both maintain their faith's own heritage and affirm what they were affirming in ECT.[56] The cheers, though often expressed with caution, were from evangelicals who found substantial areas of doctrinal and practical solidarity with at least some Catholics.[57] It is a sign of how large the two traditions loom for each other that commentary, pro and con, was much more extensive from evangelicals than from Catholics.[58]

The ECT initiative has continued with the publication in December 1997 of a joint statement called "Evangelicals and Catholics Together II – The Gift of Salvation."[59] This statement was, among other things, a response to criticism of the first document, especially criticism that questioned the sincerity of the signers in affirming a common picture of Christian salvation. A central paragraph of the new document expanded upon the core of theological agreement that the ECT process had defined:

> Justification is central to the scriptural account of salvation, and its meaning has been much debated between Protestants and Catholics. We agree that justification is not earned by any good works or merits of our own; it is entirely God's gift, conferred through the Father's sheer graciousness, out of the love that he bears us in his Son, who suffered on our behalf and rose from the dead for our justification. Jesus was "put to death for our trespasses and raised for our justification" (Romans 4:25). In justification, God, on the basis of Christ's righteousness alone, declares us to be no longer his rebellious enemies but his forgiven friends, and by virtue of his declaration it is so.

Again, the composers and signers of this second ECT document went out of their way to underscore its informal, voluntary character. And again there was an outcry from a few Protestant quarters.[60] But the salient fact of the ECT process remains that, however imperfect its promulgations and however limited the number of evangelicals and Catholics it might speak for, such cooperation on questions of doctrine and social practice was simply unimaginable less than a generation ago.[61]

The past several decades, in sum, have witnessed a major reorientation in relations between Protestant evangelicals and Roman Catholics.

To be sure, echoes of old antagonisms still remain. A residual anti-Catholicism lives on in some areas of American civil life, but that anti-Catholicism is not usually a direct product of Protestant evangelical concerns. More specific religious hostility lingers among a few Protestant fundamentalists and evangelicals. In the early 1980s, a California publisher issued two comic books, *Alberto* and *The Double Cross*, which illustrated the lingering force of that hostility. The books purported to tell the story of a former Spanish Jesuit, who was trained to subvert Protestantism through a number of ingenious schemes, and of his sister, who endured the terrors of Maria Monk in an English convent. They used a language every bit as unreserved as the harshest polemics of the sixteenth or the nineteenth centuries. The fairly wide sale of the comic books suggests that latent antagonisms remain in Protestant circles which the well publicized Catholic–Protestant re-engagements of recent years have not affected. As an indication of changing times, however, evangelicals joined other kinds of Protestants to denounce the books; the Christian Booksellers Association, which represents largely a conservative Protestant constituency, expressed its regret over the publications; and evangelical journalists contributed much of the hard information which exposed the comic books as fraudulent.[62] The hostilities that Jack Chick markets would have been well at home in the 1840s or 1890s. Then they were in the mainstream. Now they are on the margin.

Hints of Peace During Times of War

Before we pause for brief reflection on the meaning of the recent changes, it is helpful to take one more look into the past. Strife, in fact, was never the only reality in Catholic–Protestant exchange, even though it certainly was predominant. Simply to note that, even in the centuries of intense controversy, an occasional Catholic could commend an occasional Protestant, and vice versa, is to catch hints as to why Catholic–evangelical communication could blossom so rapidly since the 1960s. The key seems to have been that when "the other" manifested something self-evidently Christian (though not necessarily in the shape prescribed by either of the warring parties), then polemics could give way to dialogue. Enough of these moments existed to suggest that a dedicated search for Catholic–Protestant engagement, even in the darkest years of strife, might yield more edifying instances than the image of total war indicates. Before they broke up over the issue of ecclesiastical authority, Catholics and Protestants at the Council of Regensburg in 1541, for example, could agree that God's grace was entirely free in the salvation of sinners, and that it was wrong to separate faith and love. Not all on both sides thought this was a breakthrough, but John Calvin (though expressing what had already become a standard anti-Catholic attitude) could yet point out that something significant had occurred:

> You will marvel [Calvin wrote to William Farel] when you read the copy [of the article on justification] . . . that our adversaries have conceded so much. For they have committed themselves to the essentials of what is our true teaching. Nothing is to be found in it which does not stand in our writings. I know that you would prefer a more explicit exposition and in this you are at one with myself. But if you consider with what sort of men we have to deal, you will acknowledge that a great deal has been achieved.[63]

Moreover, even when the early Protestants were engaged in their most brutal debate with Catholic opponents, leaders of both sides continued to draw on the Christian insight of exemplary theologians from the Catholic middle ages, like Bernard of Clairvaux, Thomas à Kempis, and, above all, Augustine.[64]

Somewhat later, a long line of Protestants found inspiration in the bracing Christian vision of Blaise Pascal, who was treasured both for his attacks on the Jesuits and for his positive Christian exposition. Evangelicals perhaps avoided parts of Pascal's writings where he expressed his Roman convictions, but he remained a favorite of many, including the seventeenth-century Puritan Theophilus Gale, and the eighteenth-century awakeners George Whitefield, John Newton, Jonathan Edwards, and the Wesleys.[65] In 1739, when Charles Wesley was taken to task by his fellow Protestant, Dean Conybeare of Christ Church, Oxford, he urged the dean to read the Catholic Pascal, among other authors, as a means for understanding "justification by faith" and "vital religion."[66] The dean resisted, but did agree to read Pascal, at Wesley's urgings. For his part, John Wesley, who associated Pascal with the emphases in Henry Scougall's Scottish devotional classic *The Life of God in the Soul of Man*,

was on occasion remarkably sanguine about Catholicism. Less than a
year before his death, he wrote in 1790 to a nephew who had become a
Catholic, but who was now slipping away from all religion. To Wesley,
the brand name was far less important than that the nephew practice
the faith: "What do you want? Not clothes or books or money. If
you did, I should soon supply you. But I fear you want (what you
least of all suspect), the greatest thing of all – religion. I do not mean
external religion, but the religion of the heart; the religion which
Kempis, Pascal, Fénelon enjoyed: that life of God in the soul of man,
the walking with God and having fellowship with the Father and the
Son."[67]

A similar account can be given about Protestant affection for the
Catholic mystical tradition of François Fénelon and Madame Guyon.
When the Holiness preacher Thomas Upham published a life of
Madame Guyon in the mid-nineteenth century, denomination was
far less important to him than that Fénelon and Guyon had rightly
proclaimed "the doctrine of pure or unselfish love, in the experience
of which . . . the sanctification of the heart essentially consists."[68]
Throughout the twentieth century, even in decades of intense inter-
religious strife, evangelical Protestant publishers more than any other
kept the works of these Catholic mystics alive.[69]

Finally, it is appropriate to note that, in more reflective moments, even
battered veterans of the Catholic–Protestant wars could view the struggle above the battle lines. So it was with John Henry Newman, who had
been raised an evangelical Anglican but who became the most famous
English convert to Catholicism in the nineteenth century. Late in his life,
after decades of sometimes sharpest polemic with Protestants, an
acquaintance from deep in his past, the evangelical Edward Bickersteth,
sent Newman the copy of a poem he had written on the last judgment.
Newman's reply spoke for a reality that may have been more common
than antagonists were prepared to acknowledge: "I can but bow before
the great mystery that those are divided here and look for the means of
grace and glory in such different directions, who have so much in
common in faith and hope."[70]

Beyond question, disengagement and polemic were the prevailing
moods of evangelical–Catholic engagement in the four centuries before
1960. It may just be, however, that beneath the alarums of battle, even
in the days of war, there existed voices which, could they only have been
heard, heralded the reality that has now come to pass.

Reflections, Historical, and Theological

Several observations are possible after a historical review of evangelical–Catholic encounters. The most necessary concern the use of "Catholic" and "evangelical" without qualification. The time is long past when responsible analysts could speak of Catholics and evangelicals as homogeneous units. An awareness of pluralism has been a truism in the discussion of American Protestants since the end of the nineteenth century, but only in recent decades have historians taken seriously the near impossibility of lumping together (as only a partial list) Protestant mainliners, fundamentalists, liberals, Lutherans, pentecostals, Disciples, Plymouth Brethren, and a thousand and one other variations.

The larger Protestant reality obtains also for evangelicals. With no formal structure uniting those who share evangelical faith, with evangelicals strewn across multitudes of denominations, with no institutional voice presuming to speak for or to all evangelical Protestants, with deep theological, ecclesiastical, and social differences dividing evangelicals from each other, and with especially the racial divide in American history posing nearly insurmountable obstacles between white evangelicals and black evangelicals – it is presumptuous ever to speak casually about a common evangelical attitude to Catholics or to anything else. From the Protestant side, therefore, it is necessary to speak with extreme care about the often diverse elements that fit under the category "evangelical."

It has become almost equally true from the other side as well. Despite persisting tendencies to speak of a unified Catholic movement, such efforts are now nearly as indefensible as similar generalities applied to Protestants. Catholics do retain a structural unity symbolized by the pope and the church's hierarchy, but it would be wise for Protestants to let Catholics say what that structure means. Speaking as a Catholic theologian, Richard McBrien can say of the current scene "that there are sometimes sharper divisions *within* the Roman Catholic Church than there are between certain Catholics and certain Protestants."[71] As a sociologist, Andrew Greeley (who is also a Catholic priest) has made the same point: "Every generalization about values that begins with the word 'Catholic' is likely to be misleading, if not erroneous, precisely because the generalization will mask substantial differences in values that exist among the Catholic subpopulations."[72] Given the situation of religious pluralism *within* the Christian families, there is much more opportunity now than even fifty years ago to find meaningful fellowship across, as well as significant strife within, traditional evangelical and Catholic communities.

At least two results flow from this new situation. First, after windows have been opened even a little between evangelicals and Catholics, there are not only more opportunities for mutual encouragement, but also more opportunities for underscoring tensions among Protestants or Roman Catholics. To look at matters from just the one side, different groups within the evangelical mosaic find significant differences in those aspects of Catholicism to which they are attracted. Pentecostal evangelicals, for example, may appreciate Catholic openness to the subjective working of the Spirit but continue to dislike formal Catholic hierarchy; Confessional Reformed evangelicals may appreciate Catholic objectivity about the sacraments but dislike Catholic ways of expressing the way that faith should be active in love; the new wave of academic evangelical philosophers may appreciate the tough-minded tradition of Catholic philosophical reflection but shy away from the way that this sort of philosophy has been used to define expressly Catholic dogma; Anabaptist evangelicals may appreciate the dedication of the Catholic monastic tradition but worry about the application of Catholic just-war teaching to modern international conflict; and Arminian evangelicals may appreciate the space that Catholics preserve for the exercise of free will but continue to express reservations about the primacy of the papacy. The opening of Catholic–evangelical dialogue means, in short, that many discussions among Protestants are also under way.

The pluralism within Catholic and evangelical communities also poses genuine problems for the practice of evangelism. Most responsible Catholics and evangelicals recognize that it is at best dubious, and at worse simply wrong, for Catholics and evangelicals to proselytize across the Catholic–Protestant border in situations where believers are coming close to the finest standards of either faith. Most also agree that nominal religious adherence – whether Catholic or evangelical – establishes a different problem. Where Catholics and evangelicals will continue to differ among themselves (as well as, to some extent, from each other) is on the question of what counts as genuine faithfulness as opposed to nominal practice. The difficulties in such discussions are greatest where manifestations of either faith (such as evangelicalism in some areas of the American South or Catholicism in many areas of Latin America) have enjoyed a cultural hegemony, for that is the very circumstance that historically called forth efforts to reform the church.[73] To recognize pluralism within evangelicalism and Catholicism does not by itself solve delicate questions of proselytization, but it is a precondition for discerning understanding of local conditions.

The current situation in the United States poses unusual opportunities as well as unusual perils for evangelical–Catholic discussion. Again, to look at matters from the angle of evangelical Protestants, we can describe a curious situation. The formalism, the anthropocentric worship, the power-mongering, and the egotism – which Protestants saw so clearly in Roman Catholicism for so many centuries – now flourish on every hand within Protestant evangelicalism.[74] At the same time, an exaltation of divine grace, a concern for disciplined holiness, an expression of service to the poor in the name of Jesus, and an ability to apply the depths of Scripture to the complicated ethical questions of modern existence – which Protestantism came into existence in order to recover – now exist manifestly in one form or another throughout Roman Catholicism. Evangelicals who cherish the Reformation heritage face especially poignant issues in the modern climate. They are the ones who hold most tenaciously to the reformers' teachings about the radical sinfulness and irremediable finitude of human existence. But with fresh eyes to see, they can now observe these human traits as readily in the churches descended from the Reformation (and perhaps even in themselves) as in Catholicism. They are also able to see traits approved by historic Protestantism in the most luminous expressions of modern Catholicism, such as the ethical *gravitas* of Pope John Paul II, the moving writing of G. K. Chesterton, J. R. R. Tolkien, Evelyn Waugh, and Malcolm Muggeridge, or the "works" of a different kind from Mother Teresa, Henri Nouwen, and the L'Arche community founded by Jean Venier.[75] However such observations might disconcert evangelical descendants of the Reformation, they can take heart from the reformers' teachings about the incredible fecundity of divine grace, and so perhaps turn toward Roman Catholics with as much charitable expectancy as fearful dread.

Contemporary pluralism may also enhance the ability to make discriminations. If relatively important theological differences still divide Catholics and evangelicals, it is also the case that the contemporary world needs to hear more about what Catholics and evangelicals share in common than about their legitimate disagreements. J. I. Packer has spotlighted this issue well by pointing to "the currently urgent task of upholding faith in the Trinity, the Incarnation, the inerrancy of Scripture, and the primacy of the evangelistic and pastoral imperative according to Scripture, against the secularist, relativist and antinomian onslaught to which these things are being subjected in our time both without and within the churches." As Packer and many others, who have striven for perspective on the modern condition, conclude, "the cobelligerence of Catholics and Protestants fighting together for the basics of the creed is nowadays more important [than discussion of individual doctrines], if only because until the cancerous spread of theological pluralism on both sides of the Reformation divide is stopped, any talk of our having achieved unity of faith will be so irrelevant to the real situation as to be both comic and pathetic."[76]

Finally, if the historic shift recorded in this chapter – from all-out Catholic–evangelical antagonism to modest Catholic–evangelical engagement – marks a genuine moment of grace in the long history of the church, the way to exploit that grace will certainly not be simply to ignore the past, but to find a middle way of hope. In recent years, a number of significant voices have shown what that middle way of realistic, historically informed hope might look like. These voices usually come from those who know the past history very well, but who think that the impasses of history are the result of human rather than divine purpose.

From the Catholic side, such a message was voiced by Pope John Paul II when he spoke to the Lutherans in Rome at the observation of Martin Luther's 500th birthday.

> So we see ourselves in the midst of all the evident separations that still exist in teaching and life deeply linked in the solidarity of all the Christians of Advent. . . . We believe, in the year of remembrance of the birthday of Martin Luther five centuries ago, that we see as if in a distance the dawning of the advent of a reconstruction of our unity and community. This unity is a fruit of the daily renewal, conversion and penitence of all Christians in the light of the eternal word of God. It is at the same time the best preparation for the coming of God in our world.
>
> Let us follow the great figure of the time of Advent, let us follow the example of John the Baptist, the voice of the caller in the desert:
> "Make straight the way of the Lord" (John 1:23). Let us follow the invitation to reconciliation with God and among ourselves. Christ, the

ruler of all, is not only above us but also in our midst as the Lord who was, who is and who will be in eternity.[77]

A similar voice of realistic hope came as the result of a significant series of modern discussions in Europe. The book in which those discussions were summarized was entitled *The Condemnations of the Reformation Era: Do They Still Divide?* The answer was measured, but hopeful:

> Today it is possible to say the following: Far-reaching agreement in the interpretation of Holy Scripture, clearer insights about the historical contingency of traditional doctrinal formulations, and the new spirit of ecumenical dialogue, in awareness of the ties linking Christians of different denominational traditions through their faith in the one Lord, have all contributed essentially to the achievement of a large measure of mutual understanding. This understanding is not confined to the fundamental acknowledgment of the one Lord Jesus Christ. It applies also to central themes of Christian doctrine.[78]

The European Catholics and Protestants who published this book concluded that the condemnations of the Reformation were based on misconceptions, were aimed at extreme positions on the other side, and no longer apply to today's situations. While genuine differences remained, those differences did not appear as universal as once they seemed.

Of most relevance to American evangelicals are words written by George Carey when he was principal of Trinity Theological College in England. Since he wrote them, Carey has become the Archbishop of Canterbury where, in one of the unlikeliest surprises of recent history, he uses that ancient Anglican office to promote a program at once evangelical and catholic. Before going to Canterbury, Carey outlined his hope for the evangelical–Catholic future:

> How can Protestants with their faith anchored in the New Testament have unity with Catholics, whose official teachings include doctrines they cannot accept? The question is reciprocated from the Catholic side. How can the historical faith of the church be reconciled with the somewhat reduced faith of the Protestants? . . . There is, I believe, a way through this dilemma. The Second Vatican Council, in fact, opened new possibilities through a statement in the Decree on Ecumenism. The decree suggested that closer agreement among Christians is possible if we think

in terms of a hierarchy of truths. What the decree is getting at is this: unity is often barred by the attention given to our differences, but not all doctrines have the same importance for faith. Could we arrive at an understanding of the common core of the faith we share while allowing freedom with respect to other teachings less essential? This looks like a promising way forward. It is biblically true that not all the doctrines of the Christian faith have the same value for *saving faith* even if they are regarded as important in their own right.[79]

The voices of John Paul II, of the European Catholics and Protestants who are setting aside the anathemas of the sixteenth century, and of Archbishop Carey do not speak with American accents. Since they do not, for example, reflect the American way of intermingling religious and public life, they are not as alert as Americans themselves to the historic role that political values have played in American inter-confessional attitudes. In the end, the exhortations of outsiders require American confirmation. It remains for Americans, both evangelicals and Roman Catholics – and, even more, for divine grace – to determine whether they too can find together a middle way of historical realism and hope for the future.

Notes

1   On Packer's own influential career as an evangelical spokesman, see Mark A. Noll, "J. I. Packer and the shaping of American evangelicalism," in *Doing Theology for the People of God: Studies in Honor of J. I. Packer*, eds Donald Lewis and Alister McGrath (Downers Grove, IL: InterVarsity Press, 1996), pp. 191–206.
2   J. I. Packer, review of *The Born-again Catholic*, *Eternity*, December 1983, p. 92.
3   The first document and extensive contextual discussion is found in Charles Colson and Richard John Neuhaus, eds, *Evangelicals and Catholics Together: Toward a Common Mission* (Dallas: Word, 1995); the second document was printed in *Christianity Today*, December 8, 1997, pp. 35–8.
4   In the paragraphs below, I make use of historical material employed for different purposes in my essay, "The eclipse of old hostilities *between* and the potential for new strife *among* Catholics and Protestants since Vatican II," in *Uncivil Religion: Interreligious Hostility in America*, eds Robert N. Bellah and Frederick E. Greenspahn (New York: Crossroad, 1987), pp. 86–109.

5   In the literature on Catholic–Protestant hostility, one of the earliest books is still nearly the best: Ray Allen Billington, *The Protestant Crusade, 1800–1860* (New York: Macmillan, 1938). Other helpful discussions are found in John J. Kane, *Catholic–Protestant Conflicts in America* (Chicago: Regnery, 1955); David Brion Davis, "Some themes of countersubversion: an analysis of anti-Masonic, anti-Catholic and anti-Mormon literature," *Mississippi Valley Historical Review*, 47, 1960, pp. 205–24; John Higham, *Strangers in the Land: Patterns of American Nativism, 1860–1925* (Westport, CT: Greenwood, 1980; orig. 1963); Richard Hofstadter, *The Paranoid Style in American Politics* (New York: Knopf, 1965); James H. Smylie, "Phases in Protestant anti-Roman Catholic relations in the United States: monologue, debate, and dialogue," *Religion in Life*, 34 (Spring) 1965, pp. 285–9; Jay P. Dolan, "Catholic attitudes toward Protestants," in *Uncivil Religion*, op. cit., n. 4, pp. 72–85; Barbara Welter, "From Maria Monk to Paul Blanshard: a century of Protestant anti-Catholicism," in *Uncivil Religion*, pp. 43–71 (Welter's essay includes especially helpful bibliographical notes); and, for a trans-Atlantic perspective, John Wolffe, *The Protestant Crusade in Great Britain, 1829–1860* (Oxford: Clarendon Press, 1991).

6   Quoted in James Morris, *The Preachers* (New York: St Martins, 1973), p. 199.

7   Wilhelm Pauck, "The Roman Catholic critique of Protestantism," originally published in *Theology Today* (1948), in Pauck's *The Heritage of the Reformation* (New York: Oxford, 1968), p. 231.

8   Quotation from "Controversies aroused in US by Taylor mission to Vatican," *US News and World Report*, June 28, 1946, p. 21.

9   John B. Sheerin, CSP, "American Catholics and ecumenism," in *Contemporary Catholicism in the United States*, ed. Philip Gleason (Notre Dame, IN: University of Notre Dame Press, 1969), p. 75.

10 Jaroslav Pelikan, *The Riddle of Roman Catholicism* (New York: Abingdon, 1959), pp. 12, 176, 189, 219, 201.

11 Louis Bouyer, *The Spirit and Forms of Protestantism*, trans. A. V. Littledale (Westminster, MD: Newman, 1956), p. 223.

12 W. E. R. O'Gorman, *A Priest Speaks His Mind: Why He Returned to the Protestant Faith of His Fathers* (Glendale, CA: by the author, 1954); John Carrara, *Catholicism under the Searchlight of the Scriptures* (Grand Rapids, MI: Zondervan, orig. 1943, 6th printing 1951); Charles Chiniquy, *Fifty Years in the Church of Rome* (Grand Rapids, MI: Baker, printings in 1958, 1960, 1961, orig. 1886).

13 Loraine Boettner, *Roman Catholicism* (Philadelphia: Presbyterian and Reformed, 1962), pp. 455, 459.

14 G. Dickens and John M. Tonkin, *The Reformation in Historical Thought* (Cambridge, MA: Harvard University Press, 1985), pp. 16, 84.

15 Quoted in Sister Mary Augustina (Ray), BVM, *American Opinion of Roman Catholicism in the Eighteenth Century* (New York: Columbia University Press, 1936), p. 128.

16 Billington, *The Protestant Crusade*, op. cit., n. 5, pp. 445–82.

17 Charles Hodge, "The General Assembly," *Princeton Review*, 17 (July), 1845, pp. 469–71. For a full statement, see Hodge, "Is the church of Rome a part of the visible church?" *Princeton Review*, 18 (April), 1846, pp. 320–44.

18 James M. Gustafson, *Protestant and Roman Catholic Ethics: Prospects for Rapprochement* (Chicago: University of Chicago Press, 1978), p. 30.

19 George Whitefield, "Britain's mercies, and Britain's duty, preached at Philadelphia, on Sunday, August 24, 1746, and occasioned by the suppression of the late unnatural rebellion," in Whitefield, *Sermons on Important Subjects* (London: William Baynes, 1825), p. 56.

20 Aaron Burr, *A Discourse delivered at New-Ark, in New-Jersey, January 1, 1755. Being a Day set apart for solemn Fasting and Prayer, on Account of the late Encroachments of the French, and their Designs against the British Colonies in America* (New York: Hugh Gaine, 1755), pp. 16, 19.

21 John Lathrop, as quoted in Nathan O. Hatch, *The Sacred Cause of Liberty: Republican Thought and the Millennium in Revolutionary New England* (New Haven, CT: Yale University Press, 1977), p. 75.

22 Sydney E. Ahlstrom, *A Religious History of the American People* (New Haven, CT: Yale University Press, 1972), p. 561.

23 Quoted in Billington, *The Protestant Crusade*, op. cit., n. 5, p. 425.

24 See especially Richard J. Carwardine, *Evangelicals and Politics in Antebellum America* (New Haven, CT: Yale University Press, 1993), pp. 80–4, 199–203.

25 Josiah Strong, *Our Country: Its Possible Future and Its Present Crisis* (New York: American Home Missionary Society, 1885).

26 Quoted in John O. Geiger, "The Edgerton Bible Case: Humphrey Desmond's political education of Wisconsin Catholics," *Journal of Church and State*, 20 (Winter), 1978, p. 25. For Catholic efforts to promote Bible-reading in the nineteenth century that Protestants almost never noticed, see Gerald P. Fogarty, SJ, "The quest for a Catholic vernacular Bible in America," in *The Bible in America*, eds Nathan O. Hatch and Mark A. Noll (New York: Oxford University Press, 1982), pp. 164–9.

27 A good study of these Catholic converts is Jenny Franchot, *Roads to Rome: the Antebellum Protestant Encounter with Catholicism* (Berkeley: University of California Press, 1994).

28 J. M. Foster, "Rome: the antagonist of the nation," *The Fundamentals: a Testimony to the Truth*, 4 volumes (Grand Rapids, MI: Baker, 1972; orig. 1910–15), *volume 3*, pp. 301, 313–14.

29 In the 1960 election, anti-Protestant voting against Kennedy was at least partially compensated for by the extra measure of support Kennedy won from Catholics. See Lyman A. Kellstedt and Mark A. Noll, "Religion, voting for President, and party identification, 1948–1984," in *Religion and American Politics*, ed. Mark A. Noll (New York: Oxford University Press, 1990), pp. 361–2, 374–5.

30 Boettner, *Roman Catholicism*, op. cit., n. 13, pp. 7, 459.

31 The historical background is well illustrated in John Tracy Ellis, ed., *Documents of American Catholic History*, 2nd edn (Milwaukee: Bruce, 1962); and well told in James Hennesey, SJ, *American Catholics: a History of the Roman Catholic Community in the United States* (New York: Oxford University Press, 1981); and Jay P. Dolan, *The American Catholic Experience* (Garden City, NY: Doubleday, 1985).

32 Theodore C. Sorensen, *Kennedy* (New York: Harper & Row, 1965), pp. 188–95, 357–65. Marshall Frady, *Billy Graham: a Parable of American Righteousness* (Boston: Little, Brown, 1979), 446.

33 Sheerin, "American Catholics and ecumenism," in *Contemporary Catholicism*, op. cit., n. 9, pp. 75–8. Some of the texts from these discussions from the 1970s and early 1980s are collected in Harding Meyer and Lukas Vischer, eds, *Growth in Agreement: Reports and Agreed Statements of Ecumenical Conversations on a World Level* (New York: Paulist, 1984).

34 Completed "Dialogues," as published by Augsburg Press in Minneapolis, include *The Status of the Nicene Creed as Dogma of the Church* (1965), *One Baptism for the Remission of Sins* (1966), *The Eucharist as Sacrifice* (1967), *Eucharist and Ministry* (1970), *Papal Primacy and the Universal Church* (1974), *Teaching Authority and Infallibility in the Church* (1980), and *The One Mediator, the Saints, and Mary* (1992). The report on justification is discussed below at n. 37.

35 "Faith and order USA," pamphlet from The National Council of the Churches of Christ in the USA (n.d.).

36 See especially John Courtney Murray, *We Hold These Truths: Catholic Reflections on the American Proposition* (New York: Sheed and Ward, 1960).

37 A good treatment of the role of Catholicism in the fall of communism in Poland and Czechoslovakia is George Weigel, *The Final Revolution: the Resistance Church and the Collapse of Communism* (New York: Oxford University Press, 1992); for a responsible effort at biography, see Wiegel's *Witness to Hope: the Biography of Pope John Paul II* (New York: HarperCollins, 1999).

38 Those arguments are frequently found in the pages of *First Things*, a periodical edited by the Catholic priest, Richard Neuhaus, who was once a Lutheran, and the still-Lutheran James Nuechterlein.

39 "US Lutheran–Roman Catholic dialogue: justification by faith," *Origins: NC Documentary Service*, October 6, 1983, pp. 277–304 (with quotations, pp. 297–8).

40 Quoted in *Christian Century*, June 30 to July 7, 1999, p. 670. For cautious analysis by an American evangelical, see Douglas A. Sweeney, "Taming the Reformation," *Christianity Today*, January 10, 2000, pp. 63–5.

41 McIntyre quoted in Morris, *The Preachers*, op. cit., n. 6, p. 200.

42 For a brief survey of the results which the charismatic movement has had on Catholic–evangelical connections, see Donald Bloesch, *The Future of Evangelical Christianity: a Call for Unity Amid Diversity* (New York: Doubleday, 1983), pp. 38–42.

43 For background, see Hatch and Noll, eds, *The Bible in America*, op. cit., n. 26, pp. 4, 8, 16n36, 17n43, and 165–6.

44 Ernest W. Saunders, *Searching the Scriptures: a History of the Society of Biblical Literature, 1880–1980* (Chico, CA: Scholars Press, 1982), p. 84.

45 As reported in *The Presbyterian Journal*, July 6, 1983, p. 3.

46 William Martin, *A Prophet with Honor: the Billy Graham Story* (New York: William Morrow, 1991), pp. 278–80, 488–91; Frady, *Billy Graham*, op. cit., n. 32, pp. 326, 441–6; John Pollock, *Billy Graham: the Authorized Biography* (New York: McGraw-Hill, 1966), pp. 218–20; Pollock, *Billy Graham: Evangelist to the World* (San Francisco: Harper & Row, 1979), pp. 129–30, 290–1, 307–10; and Richard V. Pierard, "From evangelical exclusivism to ecumenical openness: Billy Graham and sociopolitical issues," *Journal of Ecumenical Studies*, 20, 1983, p. 428.

47 Survey conducted by Cy Hulse, "Luther's changing image among Catholics," prepared for a course at Trinity Evangelical Divinity School, *c*.1978. This fine paper is also the source for the quotations from *The Priest* below.

48 "Should we speak or hold our tongue?" *The Priest*, 12 (February), 1956, p. 134.

49 Perplexus (pseudonym), "The charm of melody," *The Priest*, 21 (July), 1965, p. 585.

50 For a review of this discussion, see Avery Dulles, SJ, "The Catholicity of the Augsburg Confession," *Journal of Religion*, 63 (October), 1983, pp. 337–54.

51 *New York Times*, December 12, 1983, pp. 1, 4.

52 James Atkinson, *Martin Luther: Prophet to the Catholic Church* (Grand Rapids, MI: Eerdmans, 1983); Mark Edwards and George H. Tavard, *Luther: a Reformer for the Churches* (Ramsay, NJ: Paulist, 1983).

53 Pelikan, *Riddle of Roman Catholicism*, op. cit., n. 10, p. 219. Kenneth L. Woodward, "Luther in excelsis," *Notre Dame Magazine*, October 1983, pp. 11–15.

54 For example, the pamphlet, "What is an evangelical Catholic?" (June 1992).

55 First published as "Evangelicals and Catholics together: the Christian mission in the third millennium," *First Things*, May 1994, pp. 15–22. Quotations are from this text.

56 For example, R. C. Sproul, *Faith Alone: the Evangelical Doctrine of Justification* (Grand Rapids, MI: Baker, 1995); James R. White, *Roman Catholic Controversy: What Draws and Divides Evangelicals* (Minneapolis: Bethany House Publishers, 1996); and press releases from ExCatholics for Christ. Responses from conservative evangelicals that explore the ambiguities of Catholic–evangelical interaction more extensively included John Armstrong, ed., *Roman Catholicism: Evangelical Protestants Analyze What Divides and Unites Us* (Chicago: Moody, 1994); and the best overall treatment from evangelicals in recent years, Norman L. Geisler and Ralph E. Mackenzie, *Roman Catholics and Evangelicals: Agreements and Disagreements* (Grand Rapids, MI: Baker, 1995). For summaries of evangelical responses, see J. Daryl Charles, "Evangelicals and Catholics together: one year later," *Pro Ecclesia*, 5 (Winter), 1996, pp. 73–90; and Jennifer V. Suvada, "A study of the evangelical Protestant reception of the document, *Evangelicals and Catholics Together*, from its release in March 1994 through December 1996, including a case study of the Southern Baptist Convention" (MA thesis, Trinity Evangelical Divinity School, 1997).

57 For example, J. I. Packer, "Why I signed it," *Christianity Today*, December 12, 1994, pp. 34–6; and the evangelical authors in the volume that Colson and Neuhaus edited around ECT, *Evangelicals and Catholics Together*. My own sympathies are revealed by the fact that I contributed a chapter to this book and have been a signatory to both ECT statements.

58 On this particular document as well as on Catholic attitudes toward modern evangelicals generally, the key authorities are Brother Jeffrey Gros, FSC of the Secretariat for Ecumenical and Interreligious Affairs of the National Conference of Catholic Bishops (see, for example, Gros, "Evangelical relations: a differentiated Catholic response," *Ecumeniccal Trends*, January 2000, pp. 1–9); and William Shea, author of a forthcoming book entitled *The Lion and the Lamb: Evangelicals, Catholics, and Modernity*.

59 "The gift of salvation," *Christianity Today*, December 8, 1997, pp. 35–8, from which the quotation below is taken; along with Timothy George, "'The gift of salvation': an evangelical assessment," pp. 34–5.

60 For example, resolutions expressing opposition to this new statement passed by the General Association of Regular Baptists (June 30, 1998) and the annual meeting of the IFCA (Independent Fundamental Churches of America) International (August 1998).

61 Insightful general accounts of this nascent convergence include J. Daryl Charles, "Assessing recent pronouncements on justification: evidence from 'The gift of salvation' and the Catholic *catechism*," *Pro Ecclesia*, 8 (Fall), 1999, pp. 459–74; and with an emphasis on Canada, Harold Jantz, "Keeping Company with One Another: evangelicals and Catholics are connecting on many fronts but doctrine still divides," *Faith Today*, May/June 1999, pp. 20–31.

62 Gary Metz, "Jack Chick's anti-Catholic *Alberto* comic book is exposed as a fraud," *Christianity Today*, March 13, 1981, pp. 50–2. "Bookseller's group may expel Chick," *Christianity Today*, October 23, 1981, p. 62.

63 Calvin quoted in Peter Matheson, *Cardinal Contarini at Regensburg* (New York: Oxford University Press, 1972), p. 109.

64 John Calvin, for example, quoted (almost always favorably) from eleven different works by Bernard of Clairvaux in his *Institutes*. In the American Edition of Martin Luther's works there is generally positive use of twenty works by Bernard. John T. McNeill, ed., *Calvin: Institutes of the Christian Religion*, 2 volumes (Philadelphia: Westminster, 1960), *volume 1*, p. 1601; Joel W. Lundeen, ed., *Luther's Works, volume 55: Index* (Philadelphia: Fortress, 1986), pp. 27–8.

65 John Barker, *Strange Contrarieties: Pascal in England during the Age of Reason* (Montreal: McGill-Queen's University Press, 1975), pp. 17 (Gale), 186 (Whitefield), 191 (John Newton), 181–95 (the Wesleys). On Jonathan Edwards's reading of Pascal, see Norman Fiering, *Jonathan Edwards's Moral Thought and Its British Context* (Chapel Hill: University of North Carolina Press, 1981), pp. 176.

66 Barker, *Strange Contrarieties*, op. cit., n. 65, p. 185.

67 Ibid., p. 191.

68 Thomas C. Upham, *Life and Religious Opinions and Experience of Madame de la Mothe Guyon: Together with Some Account of the Personal History and Religious Opinions of Fenelon, Archbishop of Cambray* (New York: Harper & Brothers, 1846), p. vi.

69 See especially Patricia A. Ward, "Madame Guyon and experiential theology in America," *Church History*, 67 (September) 1998, pp. 484–98.

70 Quoted in Sheridan Gilley, *Newman and His Age* (Westminster, MD: Christian Classics, 1990), p. 372.

71 Richard P. McBrien, "Roman Catholicism: *E Pluribus Unum*," in *Religion and America: Spirituality in a Secular Age*, Mary Douglas and Steven M. Tipton, eds (Boston: Beacon, 1983), p. 181.

72 Andrew M. Greeley, *The American Catholic: a Social Portrait* (New York: Basic Books, 1977), p. 252.

73 Failure in the first ECT document to distinguish between the Roman Catholicism practiced by North Americans and the more syncretistic vari-

eties in Latin America was perceptively criticized by W. Harold Fuller, *People of the Mandate: the Story of the World Evangelical Fellowship* (Grand Rapids, MI: Baker, 1996), Appendix H, "The background to the ECT debate," pp. 188–93. In 1980, the World Evangelical Fellowship invited observers from the Vatican to its Seventh General Assembly. The sensitivity of such moves where memory of old patterns of Catholic religious-civil hegemony remained alive was indicated by the withdrawal from this international body by the Italian Evangelical Alliance and the Spanish Evangelical Alliance. See *A Contemporary Evangelical Perspective on Roman Catholicism* (Wheaton, IL: World Evangelical Fellowship, 1986), p. 7.

74 See David F. Wells, *No Place for Truth: or, Whatever Happened to Evangelical Theology* (Grand Rapids, MI: Eerdmans, 1993); and Michael Scott Horton, *Made in America: the Shaping of Modern American Evangelicalism* (Grand Rapids, MI: Baker, 1991).

75 L'Arche communities exist for the support of people with mental handicaps. On Venier's viewpoint, see his *Becoming Human* (Toronto: Anansi Press and the Canadian Broadcasting Corp. 1998).

76 J. I. Packer, "Foreword," to George Carey, *A Tale of Two Churches: Can Protestants and Catholics Get Together?* (Downers Grove, IL: InterVarsity Press, 1985), p. ii.

77 "Text of John Paul's sermon at a Lutheran church," *New York Times*, December 12, 1983, p. 4.

78 Karl Lehmann and Wolfhart Pannenberg, *The Condemnations of the Reformation Era: Do They Still Divide?*, trans. Margaret Kohl (Minneapolis: Fortress, 1990), p. 27.

79 Carey, *A Tale of Two Churches*, op. cit., n. 76, p. 160, with Carey's own list of six "central points" that he regards as essential to Christian communion on pp. 161–2.

8

Science

Consideration of evangelicals and science, especially during the twentieth century, depends upon much broader developments in cultural and
intellectual history. For that larger picture, recent events and circumstances at the intersection of Christianity and science have provided
ample occasions for both hope and despair. The reasons for hope are primarily intellectual and historiographical. The reasons for despair are primarily cultural. An understanding of why hope mingles so thoroughly
with despair prepares the way for a better grasp of the way evangelicals
have wrestled with science over the past 250 years.

Science and Christianity at the Start of the
Twenty-first Century

In the realm of ideas, signs of hope in religion and science arise from at
least five types of inquiry. First is renewed consideration of the foundations of Western science. Now solidly established in a way that at the
start of the twentieth century seemed improbable is a secure historical
record of the important contributions that classical Christianity made to
the rise of modern Western science. At the beginning of the twentieth
century, works like John William Draper's *History of the Conflict between
Religion and Science* (1875) and Andrew Dickson White's *A History of
the Warfare of Science with Theology in Christendom* (1895) looked like the
historiographical last word. Their picture of intrepid lovers of pure scientific truth heroically overcoming the obstacles placed in their way by
dogmatic churchmen seemed secure. Now through the efforts of a
number of twentieth-century researchers on the fifteenth through seventeenth centuries – among others Michael Foster, Robert Merton,

Reijer Hooykaas, Alexander Koyré, Stanley Jaki, Francis Oakley, Charles Webster, Eugene Klaaren, Gary Deason, John Morgan, and Edward Davis – a much more complicated picture has emerged. If the strongest claims of some of these authors may be questioned – that Christianity was unquestionably the primary indispensable motive in the rise of Western science – they and others like them have nonetheless shown that Christian environments did much more to help, and far less to hinder, modern science than Draper or White could conceive.[1]

A second sign of hope is the wealth of fruitful proposals attempting to show how and why the study of nature and the study of God should be complementary rather than competitive. Such proposals come from many places on the theological landscape, they draw on many different intellectual traditions, and they are not necessarily compatible with each other. They include works by a number of consequential thinkers like Ian Barbour, Richard Bube, Langdon Gilkey, Charles Hummel, D. Gareth Jones, Donald Mackay, Nancy Murphy, A. R. Peacocke, John Polkinghorne, Del Ratzsch, Colin Russell, T. F. Torrance, and Howard J. Van Till. Yet whether from scientists concerned about theology, theologians concerned about science, or philosophers interested in both science and theology, the very diversity of these proposals suggests that a standoff between science and theology is simply unnecessary.[2]

A third sign of hope is the number of serious-minded Christian believers at work in scientific vocations who are willing to venture beyond the boundaries of their specialities to engage broader issues. An arena that has been fouled by people talking about a lot of stuff of which they are ignorant is being cleansed by people who are speaking up about matters on which they are qualified to give an opinion. The growing number of practicing Christian scientists is one of the main signs of hope for the future. In groups like the American Scientific Affiliation and the British Christians in Science, as also in publications like *Perspectives on Science and Christian Faith* and *Science and Christian Belief*, they are making a mark, and all for the good.[3]

A fourth sign of hope is the rising intellectual quality of specifically religious objections to the free ride of scientific naturalism. Here the work of a pugnacious legal scholar, Philip Johnson, a conscientious biochemist, Michael Behe, and a number of careful philosophers, like J. P. Moreland and William Dembski, is especially important. The promotion by such individuals of arguments for an Intelligent Designer of the universe may not persuade everyone. But they are certainly more

responsible than the nay-saying anti-evolutionism of previous generations. Even fellow-believers who disagree with their tactics or conclusions should recognize that these recent defenders of Intelligent Design
are moving in the right direction by foregrounding the philosophical and
theological issues that, left to lurk in the realm of assumption, have so
badly crippled serious discussion of issues in religion and science.[4]

With my own prejudices as a historian, I am inclined to think that
more general developments in the writing of scientific history constitute
the most important sign of hope. In the last quarter of the twentieth
century, a stunning, nearly incredible outpouring of historical works in
the history of science (and scientists) has greatly altered understanding
of relations between science, faith, personal conviction, and social location. Again, the perspectives informing these works are not necessarily
compatible; their authors include Christian believers, unbelievers, and
some in between; they do not present a coherent resolution to knotty
religious-scientific questions; and they often exasperate scientists,
philosophers, and theologians who want to cut through ambiguity to
hard and fast certainties. Yet together they have succeeded in showing
as clearly as humanly possible that no capital-S science and no capital-
R religion exist beyond the bounds of space and time or the boundaries
of personal and community circumstances. They have demonstrated
that no simple formula can adequately describe the rich, thickly tex-
tured, and complex relation between Christianity and Western science.
They have underscored the many kinds of complexity, ambiguity, and
irony that attend Christian-scientific issues in Western history, but also
the fact that "warfare" is one of the least fruitful metaphors for describing that relation. In particular, they have usefully highlighted the
context-dependent character of science-religion work of all sorts. Sometimes that highlighting is welcome – for example, to learn how John
William Draper projected a visceral anti-Catholicism onto his screen of
the past or to discern how A. D. White brokered a conflict model into
more self-control over the emerging institutions of American higher
learning like his Cornell University. Such historical positioning counteracts much of the sting that might be left in the poison of these once-
influential authors. But sometimes the highlighting of historical
background can be highly discomfiting for believers – for example, to
understand how all scientific conclusions are in some sense ideology
takes some of the fun out of discovering that Kepler or Boyle or Kelvin
went to church.

Among the early accessible statements of what might be called the new social history of science and religion was an impressive essay in 1978 from Frank Turner that pictured that conflict as a struggle between rival claimants for intellectual authority in nineteenth-century Britain.[5] An equally impressive essay in the following year from James Moore dealt a particularly stout blow to simplistic conflict models of religion and science. It was a historiographical tour de force, "Historians and historiography," which introduced Moore's *The Post-Darwinian Controversies*.[6] The years following have witnessed a number of exemplary works underscoring the relation of scientific practice to culture. Some showed how many unexpected historical dimensions attended supposedly simple struggles between science and religion (e.g. David Lindberg and Ronald Numbers, eds, *God and Nature: Historical Essays on the Encounter between Christianity and Science*, 1986; David N. Livingstone, *Darwin's Forgotten Defenders: the Encounter Between Evangelical Theology and Evolutionary Thought*, 1987; James R. Moore, ed., *History, Humanity, and Evolution: Essays for John C. Greene*, 1989; John Hedley Brooke, *Science and Religion: Some Historical Perspectives*, 1991). Others revealed more generally how deeply imbedded scientific practice has always been in the lived human realities of scientists and those who put the conclusions of scientists to use (e.g. John C. Greene, *Science, Ideology, and World View*, 1981; Adrian Desmond and James Moore, *Darwin: the Life of a Tormented Evolutionist*, 1991; Steven Shapin, *A Social History of Truth: Civility and Science in Seventeenth-century England*, 1994; Shapin, *The Scientific Revolution*, 1996). Although the virtues of ideological self-consciousness that these works illustrate on nearly every page have not been universally accepted, the newer history of science makes the practice of ideologically unselfconscious science inexcusable.

The great problem that looms over all such signs of hope, however, is the widespread, continued appeal to Science as an impersonal, abstract arbiter of political, social, or moral questions. A significant proportion of well known intellectuals from the academy, as well as a large proportion of evangelical Christians interested in such matters, continue to assert the simple objectivity of scientific conclusions and obscure the ineluctably human dimensions of scientific practice. And so the battles between militant "creationists" and militant "anti-creationists" go on. Something G. K. Chesterton wrote in 1933 to describe a past era remains, unfortunately, all too characteristic of the present: "Private theories about what the Bible ought to mean, and premature theories about what the world ought to mean, have met in loud and widely advertised controversy, especially in the Victorian time; and this clumsy collision of two very impatient forms of ignorance was known as the quarrel of Science and Religion."[7]

The "quarrel" Chesterton described survives only because combatants willfully turn from the lessons inculcated by the hopeful intellectual breakthroughs:

- that the contingencies of the physical world require careful experiments unencumbered, as far as it is possible to be unencumbered, by ideology;
- that all scientific practice is done by human beings for human ends in human circumstances;
- that many different kinds of compatibility have been found between the domains of theology and science;
- and that, however impossible it may be to divide questions of fact and value, or the internal and external aspects of scientific practice, it still is possible to distinguish between different usages of "science," such as the question of how to verify standards of accuracy for dating the deterioration of radioactive isotopes versus the question of how to provide an ultimate explanation for what appear to be breaks in evolutionary sequence.

This chapter provides material from evangelical history to show how this mingled situation of hope and despair came about.[8]

Since the rise of modern evangelicalism in the mid-eighteenth century, evangelical Protestants have been deeply engaged with the practice of science. Even more than engaging science narrowly conceived, however, evangelicals have been even more deeply involved in political and cultural contests over the role of science in public life. Because evangelicalism itself was a product of the early modern consciousness that arose in part from an exalted respect for "science," it should not be surprising that evangelical traditions have nearly everywhere been preoccupied with scientific questions. In order to assess the nature of that engagement, it is useful to address (a) problems of definition, (b) evangelical reliance on science, (c) the record of evangelical scientists, (d) attempts at narrowly evangelical science, (e) evangelical concern for Larger Meanings of science, (f) the Scopes Trial, and (g) modern "scientific creationism."

Definitions

"Science" has always been an ambiguous, negotiated term in the history of evangelicalism since, in the domains of popular culture where evangelicals flourish, the term is used with multiple (often inconsistent) meanings. In an infinite variety of actual practices, evangelicals have embraced, disdained, ignored, or equivocated upon these meanings: "science" as a methodological commitment to observation, induction, rigorous principles of falsification, and a scorn for speculative hypotheses (e.g. "Scientists deal with knowledge of the world derived from testable empirical hypotheses"); "science" as shorthand for generalizations about the natural world (or the human person and human society) that are thought to have been established by experts (e.g. "Scientists have shown that the Grand Canyon was formed over millions of years"); and "science" as a principle of reasoning amounting to an autonomous source of social, moral, or even political authority (e.g. "Science holds our greatest hope for the future"). Flexibility in the use of the term "science" by evangelicals, as well as by the general public, accounts for considerable intellectual confusion.

It is probably the case that the American evangelical engagement with science more properly belongs to the domain of social history than to the domains of intellectual history. Certain evangelicals at certain times have indeed worked diligently on *intrinsic* connections between science and theology, but that work has regularly been subordinated to *extrinsic* connections between science and society.[9] In other words, evangelicals have rarely queried the ordinary practices of science, but they have regularly disputed the implications that scientific work is alleged to entail for large philosophical or social questions. American society as a whole shares with evangelicals this tendency to talk about science while thinking about something else. In fact, one of the reasons why broader cultural matters have so thoroughly dominated the evangelical engagement with science in America is that broader cultural appropriations have loomed so large for American science in general.

At the start of the twentieth century, for example, it is little wonder that scientific questions became for evangelicals even more thoroughly political than before, since that was the era when post-Protestant denizens of America's new universities were making their most extravagant claims for the extrinsic social and metaphysical achievements of "science." In Bruce Kuklick's fine summary, "Dewey, Royce, Charles Peirce, and others . . . urged that loyalty to science would enable human beings to achieve existential integration most adequately. Mankind would make its greatest advance when the scientific method was applied to questions of ethics. Control would grow ever more rich and complex. The quality of human experience would change for the better and, consequently, human selves also."[10] For evangelicals to respond in kind to the cosmological claims put forth under the name of science by leaders of the new university was simply to refurbish a long tradition. A science put to use in shaping or promoting large-scale interpretations of the world, rather than for focusing study on the material world, was a science as old as American evangelicalism itself.[11]

Finally, the relationship between evangelicals, on the one side, and "science," on the other, is multifaceted in the extreme. The subject can refer to practicing scientists who are evangelicals (but where religious principles in the practice of science may not be distinct), to the stances of popular evangelical leaders on scientific matters like evolution (but where engagement with actual research results may be nil), to forms of anti-establishment science promoted by ardent Bible-believers (but where other evangelicals repudiate their conclusions as violating the true meaning of Scripture), and to many other possibilities. Ambiguity of definition, in sum, means that this chapter can only sample the extraordinarily diverse facets of a protean subject.

Evangelical Reliance on Science

Evangelical preference for what is learned from the Book of Scripture over what is learned from the Book of Nature, as well as fundamentalist willingness to contest the authority of mainstream science, loom large in the history of these groups. Yet because evangelicalism came into existence, at least in part, because of its ability to exploit emphases in the eighteenth-century world, evangelicalism from the start made full use of that century's devotion to scientific language, procedures, and warrants. The Puritan minister Cotton Mather of Boston may be said to have established the evangelical tradition of this usage with his publication in 1721 of *The Christian Philosopher*, a formidable volume of physico-theological erudition filled with scientific detail. Mather, for example, employed meteorological observations from learned European observers about snow in order to highlight another European's explanation for why humans needed to have their sins washed white as snow. Mather's volume aimed not simply, and not even primarily, at the practice of science, narrowly conceived, but rather at the meaning of science in very grand terms. Mather saw science as "a mighty and wondrous *Incentive to Religion*."[12]

Other early evangelicals like John Wesley and George Whitefield shared much, at least formally, with the era's promoters of science – including an exploitation of sense experiences (in order to encourage what they called "experimental" Christianity) and an anti-traditionalist reliance on empirical experience. By the end of the eighteenth century, evangelicals in both Great Britain and the United States had also committed themselves fully to apologetical natural theology – the effort to demonstrate the truthfulness of Christianity by appealing in a scientific manner to facts of nature and the human personality.[13]

For this enterprise, evangelical spokesmen in the United States enlisted scientific concepts to contend against the irreligion and disorder of the post-Revolutionary period. The Scottish immigrant John Witherspoon, president of the College of New Jersey (later Princeton University), led the way with a variation of philosophical common-sense realism, which he had brought from Scotland. This view, with its confidence in finding truth through careful observation and inductive reasoning, appealed to American evangelicals as well as to Americans as a whole. It provided an intellectually respectable way to secure a stable intellectual world where in the American setting so much effort was going into creating government and society from scratch. In such an environment the legs on which virtue and truth traditionally rested – tradition itself, divine revelation, history, social hierarchy, inherited government, and the authority of religious denominations – were all highly suspect. Norman Fiering has described the "new moral philosophy" of the eighteenth-century Scottish Enlightenment as "uniquely suited to the needs of an era still committed to traditional religious values and yet searching for alternative modes of justification for these values."[14] The only two authorities escaping the stigma of tyranny attached to the traditional intellectual authority of Europe were science and the Bible. These were the authorities that leaders like Witherspoon put eagerly to use.[15]

American evangelicals were thus trying to meet challenges from deism, radical democracy, and the disorderliness of the frontier with an appeal to universal standards of science and a vigorous application of Scripture. In the 1790s and for several decades thereafter evangelicals on both sides of the Atlantic recommended the natural theology of William Paley, even though they were often uneasy with Paley's utilitarian ethics and the ease with which he accounted for apparent waste and violence in nature.[16]

Later, as evangelicals in America began to write their own apologetical textbooks, they drew ever more directly on methods of science. When Timothy Dwight became president of Yale in 1795, he used arguments from natural theology to confront undergraduate doubts about the veracity of the Bible.[17] Scientific arguments of one sort or another were also a staple in the lengthy battles between the Unitarians and Trinitarians of New England. Widespread as the recourse to scientific demonstration was among the Congregationalists, it was the Presbyterians who excelled at what T. D. Bozeman has called a "Baconian" approach to the faith.[18] In divinity, rigorous empiricism became the standard for justifying belief in God, revelation, and the trinity. In the moral sciences, it marked out the royal road to ethical certainty. It also provided a key for using physical science itself as a demonstration of religious truths. In each case, the appeal was, as the successor of Witherspoon at Princeton, Samuel Stanhope Smith, put it, "to the evidence of facts, and to conclusions resulting from these facts which . . . every genuine disciple of nature will acknowledge to be legitimately drawn from her own fountain."[19] Among both Congregationalists and Presbyterians, the most theologically articulate evangelicals in the early republic, this approach predominated in rebuttals to Tom Paine's *Age of Reason* in the 1790s, and to other infidels thereafter. Their kind of "supernatural rationalism" was also useful for counteracting the impious use of science, by making possible the harmonization of first the Bible and astronomy, and then Scripture and geology.[20]

Revivalism, perhaps the least likely feature of antebellum evangelical life to reflect the influence of a scientific worldview, nonetheless took a new shape because of that influence. Charles G. Finney, the great evangelist of the antebellum period and one of the most influential Americans of his generation, did not by any means speak for all evangelicals. But his vocabulary in a widely read book, *Lectures on Revivals of Religion* (1835), showed how useful scientific language had become. If God established reliable laws in the natural world, so he had done in the spiritual world. To activate the proper causes for revivals was to produce the proper effect. In Finney's words, "The connection between the right use of means for a revival and a revival is as philosophically [i.e. scientifically] sure as between the right use of means to raise grain and a crop of wheat. I believe, in fact, it is more certain, and there are fewer instances of failure."[21] Because the world spiritual was analogous to the world natural, observable cause and effect must work in religion as well as in physics.

Nowhere did the language of evangelical Protestantism and the inductive ideals of modern science merge more thoroughly than in American evangelical appropriation of the Bible. The orthodox Congregationalist, Leonard Woods, Jr, wrote in 1822, for example, that the best method of Bible study was "that which is pursued in the science of physics," regulated "by the maxims of Bacon and Newton." Newtonian method, Woods said, "is as applicable in theology as in physics, although in theology we have an extra-aid, the revelation of the Bible. But in each science reasoning is the same – we inquire for facts and from them arrive at general truths."[22] Many others from north, south, east, and west said the same. The best known statement of scientific biblicism appeared after the Civil War in Charles Hodge's *Systematic Theology*, but it was a position that he with others had been asserting for over fifty years: "The Bible is to the theologian what nature is to the man of science. It is his store-house of facts; and his method of ascertaining what the Bible teaches, is the same as that which the natural philosopher adopts to ascertain what nature teaches. . . . The duty of the Christian theologian is to ascertain, collect, and combine all the facts which God has revealed concerning himself and our relation to him. These facts are all in the Bible."[23]

Such attitudes were by no means limited to the established denominations with reputations to protect. To cite just one of many other possible examples, Alexander Campbell led the Restorationist movement – which eventuated in the Disciples of Christ, the Churches of Christ, and the Christian Churches – in using scientific language as a principle of biblical interpretation. In self-conscious imitation of Francis Bacon, one of Campbell's successors, James S. Lamar, published in 1859 his *Organon of Scripture: Or, the Inductive Method of Biblical Interpretation*, in which deference to scientific thinking was unmistakable: "The Scriptures admit of being studied and expounded upon the principles of the inductive method; and . . . when thus interpreted they speak to us in a voice as certain and unmistakable as the language of nature heard in the experiments and observations of science."[24]

Later in the nineteenth century, when new higher critical views of Scripture came to the United States from Europe, evangelicals resisted by appealing directly to scientific principles. As they did so, an irony emerged, for America's new research universities, where higher critical views prevailed, also prided themselves on being scientific. In the 1870s and 1880s, graduate study on the European model began to be offered at older universities like Harvard and newer ones like Johns Hopkins. At such centers objectivist science was exalted as the royal road to truth, and the new professional academics reacted scornfully to what they perceived as parochial, uninformed, and outmoded scholarship. All fields, including the study of the Bible, were to be unfettered for free inquiry. The sticking point with evangelicals was that university scholarship, in keeping with newer intellectual fashions, relied heavily upon evolutionary notions; in this new understanding, ideas, dogmas, practices, and society all evolved over time, as did religious consciousness itself. Evangelicals were also troubled by the agnostic conclusions promoted by popularizers of the new science and by the efforts of scientific professionals to replace religious professionals as society's key arbiters of truth. Andrew Dickson White, president of Cornell University, typified those whom evangelicals fought against in his claims that his school would "afford an asylum for Science [note capitalization] – where truth shall be sought for truth's sake, where it shall not be the main purpose of the Faculty to stretch or cut sciences exactly to fit 'Revealed Religion'."[25] Thus was battle joined not only on the meaning of the Bible, but on proper uses of science.

The inaugural public discussion of the new views occurred between Presbyterian conservatives and moderates from 1881 to 1883 in the pages of the *Presbyterian Review*. Both sides, as would almost all who followed in their train, tried as if by instinct to secure for themselves the high ground of scientific credibility. At stake was not just religion, but the cultural authority that evangelical Protestants had exercised in American society. The moderates, led by Charles A. Briggs, were committed to "the principles of Scientific Induction." Since Old Testament studies had "been greatly enlarged by the advances in linguistic and historical science which marks our century," it was only proper to take this new evidence into account.[26] The conservatives were just as determined to enlist science on their side. William Henry Green, for example, chose not to examine W. Robertson Smith's "presumptions" that led him to adopt critical views of the Old Testament, but rather chose the way of induction: "We shall concern ourselves simply with duly certified facts."[27]

Once the terms of the debate were set in this scientific form, the evangelicals defended their position tenaciously. One of D. L. Moody's colleagues, R. A. Torrey – no slouch in science himself, after studying geology at Yale – published in 1898 a book entitled *What the Bible Teaches*. Its method was "rigidly inductive," where "the methods of modern science are applied to Bible study – thorough analysis followed by careful synthesis." The result was "a careful, unbiased, systematic, thorough-going, *inductive* study and statement of Bible truth."[28]

Almost since their emergence as a distinct form of Protestantism, evangelicals adopted, promoted, and exploited the language of science as their own language. In recent decades, many evangelical and fundamentalist enterprises – including the widely used apologetic manuals of the popular evangelist, Josh McDowell, and the myriad presentations promoting creation science – have maintained this reliance on early-modern scientific demonstration. The fact that such full efforts to exploit the prestige of early-modern science have accompanied evangelical resistance to certain conclusions of modern scientific effort means that simple statements about evangelicals and science are almost always wrong.

Evangelical Scientists

The evangelical engagement with science includes also the professional scientific labors of self-confessed evangelicals. This activity adds further complexity to the story. In both Britain and North America, evangelical scientists were especially prominent during the nineteenth century. After Darwinism and other potentially naturalistic explanations began to dominate professional science from the last third of that century, the presence of evangelicals has not been as obvious, but the numbers have always been greater than the stereotype of evangelical–scientific strife would suggest.

In Britain, a lengthy roster of evangelicals enjoyed considerable scientific repute for well over a century.[29] Among these were a trio of evangelical Anglicans – Isaac Milner (1750–1820), Francis Wollaston (1762–1823), and William Farish (1759–1837) – who occupied in succession the Jacksonian Chair of Natural and Experimental Philosophy at Cambridge. Michael Faraday (1791–1867), the renowned pioneer of electromagnetism, was the member of a small evangelical sect, the Sandemanians or Glasites (after founder John Glas and major promoter Robert Sandeman) who zealously practiced their unusual modification of traditional Calvinism. For later evangelicals, the Victoria Institute provided an ongoing base for evangelicals who wanted to use respectful science in harmony with, rather than in opposition to, the faith.

In Scotland the combination of Presbyterian seriousness about learning and the empirical bent of the Scottish Enlightenment produced several notable evangelical scientists. Sir David Brewster (1781–1878), after training for the ministry, became a specialist in optics, especially the polarization of light. Eventually he served as Principal of the University of Edinburgh. The Rev. John Fleming (1785–1857) was Professor of Natural History at King's College, Aberdeen, and the leading Scottish zoologist of his day. Hugh Miller (1802–56), a well known geologist, opposed evolution but not the idea that the earth could be very old. His pioneering work included investigations of fossilized fish. Until his death in 1847, the leading Scottish minister of his age, Thomas Chalmers, not only supported his friends Brewster, Fleming, and Miller, but also himself gave popular lectures on astronomy and offered other encouragements in scientific matters.[30] The theological college of the Scottish Free Church, founded under Chalmers's leadership in 1843, maintained a chair of natural science whose incumbents included noteworthy theologian-scientists like John Duns. A final notable among Scottish evangelicals was William Thomson, Lord Kelvin (1824–1907), who as professor of natural philosophy at the University of Glasgow for over fifty years was perhaps the most respected mathematician and physicist of his day.

In North America, a similar roster of evangelicals gained similar scientific eminence.[31] Joseph Henry (1797–1878), student of electromagnetism, diligent meteorologist, and first director of the Smithsonian Institution, was a long-time Presbyterian who, during his years as a professor at the College of New Jersey, regularly joined his friends at Princeton Theological Seminary to discuss issues at the intersection of theology and science. Asa Gray (1810–88), a botanist and taxonomist of extraordinary energy, became Charles Darwin's most active disciple in the United States, but without giving up his beliefs as an active Congregationalist in historic Christianity or his efforts to convince Darwin that natural selection could be construed as a teleological system. James Dwight Dana (1813–95) eventually accepted a form of evolution in the last edition of his influential *Manual of Geology*, but (with Gray) only in a teleological sense. The Canadian geologist and paleobotanist John William Dawson (1820–99) won his reputation through fieldwork in Nova Scotia, eventually became Principal of McGill University, remained a dedicated Presbyterian, and participated actively in meetings and publications of the international Evangelical Alliance. George Frederick Wright (1838–1921) was a minister and a geologist who published important papers on the effects of glaciers on North American terrain and who encouraged Asa Gray to write essays promoting a Christianized form of Darwinism. Wright lived long enough to become disillusioned about developments in evolutionary theory, but he never lost his earlier confidence that science, properly carried out, would reinforce Christian theology, properly conceived.[32] Just about the same could be said for several important evangelical geologist-educators of the nineteenth century, including Benjamin Silliman, Edward Hitchcock, Arnold Guyot, and Alexander Winchell.

These nineteenth-century scientists were supported by some prominent members of the evangelical community, a support that is exemplified by the theologians of Princeton Theological Seminary. As these theologians primarily sought a way to shore up reliance on biblical inspiration, they also contended for a much more frankly empirical approach to the natural world. The same Charles Hodge who supported scientific biblicism asked to have Darwin's *Voyage of the Beagle* re-read to him in the last weeks of his life,[33] and initiated this push toward empiricism with his attitude toward the historic "two books" of Scripture and nature. As early as 1863, Hodge offered a forthright defense of the rights of empirical science in response to criticism of his *Biblical Repertory and Princeton Review*. When the editor of a religious newspaper criticized an article in the *Review* for giving up the Bible too easily when new scientific results contradicted traditional biblical interpretations, Hodge leapt to the challenge. Even as he reaffirmed a full doctrine of biblical infallibility, he also affirmed in sharpest terms the need for unfettered empirical practice in the investigation of nature:

The proposition that the Bible must be interpreted by science is all but self-evident. Nature is as truly a revelation of God as the Bible; and we only interpret the Word of God by the Word of God when we interpret the Bible by science. . . . There is a two-fold evil on this subject against which it would be well for Christians to guard. There are some good men who are much too ready to adopt the opinions and theories of scientific men, and to adopt forced and unnatural interpretations of the Bible, to bring it to accord with those opinions. There are others, who not only refuse to admit the opinions of men, but science itself, to have any voice in the interpretation of Scripture. Both of these errors should be avoided. Let Christians calmly wait until facts are indubitably established, so established that they command universal consent among competent men, and then they will find that the Bible accords with those facts. In the meantime, men must be allowed to ascertain and authenticate scientific facts in their own way, just as Galileo determined the true theory of the heavens. All opposition to this course must be not only ineffectual, but injurious to religion.[34]

Hodge would later become better known for attacking the underlying philosophical basis of Darwin's evolution. But even in the last stage of his career, when he made his strongest assault on what he regarded as Darwin's ateleological philosophical atheism, Hodge continued to argue that Christians should give the fullest possible scope to the independent empirical inquires of scientists.[35]

B. B. Warfield, who became Hodge's successor as Princeton's major theologian and who formulated the modern statement upholding biblical inerrancy, maintained Hodge's position to the end of his lifelong interest in science. To Warfield, who read with close attention much of the best general literature on science for over forty years, the question of science and religion came down not to metaphysics, but to facts. In 1895, he wrote that "The really pressing question with regard to the doctrine of evolution is not . . . whether the old faith can live with this new doctrine. . . . We may be sure that the old faith will be able not merely to live with, but to assimilate to itself all facts. . . . The only living question with regard to the doctrine of evolution still is whether it is true." By "true" Warfield did not have in mind a question of scriptural exegesis but a question of empirical science: whether "(1) we may deduce from the terms of the theory all the known facts, and thus, as it were, prove its truth; and (2) deduce also new facts, not hitherto known, by which it becomes predictive and the instrument of the discovery of new facts, which are sought for and observed only on the expectation roused by the theory."[36]

With their relative naiveté about bare approaches to questions of fact, Hodge and Warfield bore the marks of the nineteenth-century Baconian realism in which they had both been reared. Since they could not benefit from the kind of analysis that has been illustrated so ably in recent years by, for example, Adrian Desmond and James Moore, or Steven Shapin, they were not as aware as they would have been that empirical experience can provide only a certain level of verification or falsification for only a certain level of middle range hypotheses, or that it is necessary to pay closer attention to encompassing worldviews in order to ascertain the deeper social axioms that function like necessary hypotheses for the doing of science.[37] But such adjustments having been made, we still see in Hodge and Warfield a theological commitment to the virtues of empirical investigation that opened the possibility of a new direction for American evangelicals.

In the twentieth century, professional scientists with evangelical convictions have found a home in Britain with the Victoria Institute (founded 1865) and in the United States with the American Scientific Affiliation (founded 1941). Both groups have received the unwelcome compliment of being criticized by the scientific establishment as too religious and by their fellow evangelicals as too naturalistic.[38]

Other evangelicals beyond Princeton also continued their support for empirical investigation of natural phenomena, as illustrated by essays that appeared in *The Fundamentals* (1910–15). In that series, which sought to confirm traditional faith, at least two of the authors attempted to differentiate between the intrinsic and extrinsic aspects of scientific problems such as evolution. Thus, James Orr, once he had made what seemed to him necessary emendations of Darwin's ideas, felt free to say that "'Evolution' . . . is coming to be recognized as but a new name for 'creation,' only that the creative power now works from *within*, instead of, as in the old conception, in an *external*, plastic fashion. It is, however, creation none the less."[39] Similarly, G. F. Wright felt confident enough in factuality (although still of the nineteenth-century sort) to say that "The worst foes of Christianity are not physicists but metaphysicians. . . . Christianity, being a religion of fact and history, is a free-born son in the family of the inductive sciences, and is not specially hampered by the paradoxes inevitably connected with all attempts to give expression to ultimate conceptions of truth."[40] For Orr and Wright, in other words, the meaning of science depended upon the proper prosecution of science.

During the nineteenth century, most self-identified evangelical scientists looked upon their research as a way of confirming Design in the universe. Twentieth-century evangelical scientists usually speak with greater restraint about the apologetical value of natural theology, but they join their predecessors in viewing scientific investigation as a way of glorifying God as creator and sustainer of the natural world. As mentioned above, the end of the twentieth century witnessed a much more sophisticated effort at Design Theology that does not feature concern for defending a literal interpretation of early Genesis.[41] What remains to be investigated is whether specifically evangelical beliefs or practices, as distinguished from more general Christian convictions shared with Roman Catholics and Protestants who are not evangelicals, have shaped the actual practices of active scientists.

A similar question remains unanswered for the significant number of major scientific figures who were raised in evangelical environments and whose work, or work habits, may have continued to reflect earlier evangelical influences. Such ones include: the paleontologist William Berryman Scott (1858–1947), grandson of Charles Hodge, who influenced several generations of younger investigators from his post at Princeton University; John Wesley Powell (1834–1902), the son of a Methodist parsonage and recipient of a Wesleyan education who later adopted social Darwinist views during his explorations of the West and service as director of both the United States Bureau of Ethnology and the United States Geological Survey; and the contemporary socio-biologist Edward O. Wilson.[42]

Narrowly Evangelical Science

In the popular stereotype, evangelicals are better known as promoters of alternative scientific visions than as participants in the scientific mainstream. There is reasonably good cause for such a stereotype. The modern proponents of what is variously called flood geology, biblical creationism, or creation science – that is, a science at odds with the mainstream academy – are in fact carrying on an evangelical tradition almost as old as the tradition of evangelical professional science.

Among the early evangelicals of the eighteenth century were some who found congenial the anti-Newtonian science of John Hutchinson. Hutchinson (1674–1737) developed his views of the material world in direct opposition to what he held to be materialistic implications of Newton's gravitational mechanics.[43] If in the Newtonian world objects could attract each other at a distance with no need for an intervening medium, Hutchinson concluded that Newton was setting up the material world as self-existent and hence in no need of God. From a painstakingly detailed study of the linguistic roots, without vowel points, of Old Testament Hebrew, Hutchinson thought he had discovered an alternative Bible-based science. The key was the Hebrew identity of the roots for "glory" and "weight," which led Hutchinson to see God actively maintaining the attraction of physical objects to each other through an invisible ether. By analogous reasoning from the New Testament's full development of the Trinity, it was evident to Hutchinson that a three-fold reality of fire, air, and light offered a better explanation for the constituency of the material world than did modern atomism.

Hutchinson's ideas were promoted by a series of dons and fellows at Oxford and by several highly placed bishops in the Church of England, but despite their appeal to the Bible as sole authority, they never received much allegiance from evangelicals. To be sure, in Britain, several early evangelicals, including John Wesley, felt the tug of Hutchinsonianism, and William Romaine (1714–95), a leading evangelical Anglican preacher in London, held something like Hutchinsonian views.[44] In America there were similar indications of interest, including a respectful mention by Archibald Alexander in 1812 during his inaugural sermon as first professor at the Princeton Theological Seminary.[45] Yet Hutchinsonianism no more caught on among American evangelicals than it did among their British colleagues.

The reason probably rests in the commitments that evangelicals had made to Baconian–Newtonian ideals and to a distaste for the high church environments in which Hutchinsonianism flourished. The fact that the most visible Hutchinsonians in both Britain and North America were Tories, high church Anglicans, and students of the Bible in Hebrew and Greek conveyed an elitist, authoritarian ethos at odds with the populist, self-taught, and voluntaristic character of the evangelical movement.[46]

Other forms of Bible-only science gained somewhat more allegiance among evangelicals during the course of the nineteenth century.[47] In

Britain a school of "scriptural geology," advanced by a book with that title by George Bugg in 1826, gained some public credibility early in the century. This effort drew conclusions about the history of the earth directly from Scripture. Bible-only approaches to science were advanced unsystematically during the 1820s and 1830s by Edward Irving, leading figure of the Catholic Apostolic Church and promoter of an intensely supernaturalistic, romantic evangelicalism. Irving and his associates tended to devalue the results of natural investigation while exalting their own interpretations of Scripture as a source of knowledge opposed to other forms of human learning. The result was a heightened super-naturalism affecting doctrines of the Bible, the Second Coming of Christ, and the special presence of the Holy Spirit, as well as heightened supernaturalism concerning the operation of the physical world. Similar opinions were also at work in North America at just about the same time.

Irving's biblicism was far different from that promoted by Philip Gosse (1810–88), a naturalist of wide experience in Canada, the United States, and Jamaica, as well as England. Gosse was a well respected student of marine invertebrates who came to oppose what he thought were the anti-biblical implications of evolutionary theory. His response, given fullest airing in *Omphalos* (1857), tried to retain both a literal inter-pretation of early Genesis and his own life's work as an observer of nature. To gain this end, Gosse proposed that evidence for the ancient age of the earth might be the result of God's deliberate creation of the world with the marks of apparent age.

Significantly, these varieties of Bible-only or Bible-dependent science enjoyed only modest acceptance among American evangelicals. One of the few who accepted Gosse's views on the apparent age of the earth was the Southern Presbyterian theologian Robert L. Dabney; apparently, American evangelicals who practiced science did not accept Gosse's theory.[48] Evangelicals were much more likely to seek accommodating adjustments between biblical authority and new scientific findings. Most prominent were efforts to finesse earlier allegiance to a literal interpre-tation of the early chapters of Genesis. By the start of the twentieth century, the most popular of these accommodations were the "gap theory" (where a vast expanse of time was postulated between God's original creation of the world and the specific creative acts specified in Genesis 1:3 and following) and the "day-age" theory (where the days of creation in Genesis chapter 1 were interpreted as standing for lengthy geological eras). At least into the twentieth century, even in debates over evolutionary theories – which began well before Darwin published his *Origin of Species* in 1859 and which always involved much more than Darwin's own notions of development through natural selection – evangelicals were as likely to propose accommodations between biblical revelation and scientific conclusions as they were to set the Bible over against science.

Unlike Hutchinsonianism and, to a certain extent, earlier forms of Bible-derived science, flood geology or creation science has been able, since especially the 1960s, to exploit alienation from the centers of learning and to make its case in democratic, populist, and voluntarist forms that accentuate, rather than contradict, major themes in the evangelical tradition. The long history of evangelical engagements with science, however, suggests that the antagonisms promoted by creation science owe at least as much to recent developments as to historic patterns among either evangelicals or scientists.

Larger Meanings of Science

Public debates over evolution and creation science highlight the fact that evangelical engagement with science has regularly focused on grand metaphysical implications rather than on minute particulars.

In the first century after the awakenings of the 1730s and 1740s, when many evangelicals became ardent promoters of the age's new science, a few of their peers occasionally complained that too much authority was being given to natural theology at the expense of simple preaching or simple trust in Scripture. But more common were attitudes like those of Scotland's Thomas Chalmers. Chalmers did lecture and publish widely on themes from natural theology, but he also paused regularly to show the limited value of those arguments. In a work published in 1836, Chalmers wrote,

> It is well to evince, not the success only, but the shortcomings of Natural Theology; and thus to make palpable at the same time both her helplessness and her usefulness – helpless if trusted to as a guide or an informer on the way to heaven; but most useful if, under a sense of her felt deficiency, we seek for a place of enlargement and are led onward to the higher manifestations of Christianity.[49]

Evangelical apologists in the United States were more inclined to
wager higher stakes on the results of natural theology. Archibald Alexander of Princeton Theological Seminary provides an example of those
higher stakes. He wrote in the 1830s.

> In receiving . . . the most mysterious doctrines of revelation, the ultimate
> appeal is to reason: not to determine whether she could have discovered
> these truths; not to declare whether considered in themselves they appear
> probable; but to decide whether it is not more reasonable to believe what
> God speaks, than to confide in our own crude and feeble conceptions.
> . . . There is no just cause for apprehending that we shall be misled by
> the proper exercise of reason on any subject which may be proposed for
> our consideration. . . . But what if the plain sense of Scripture be
> absolutely repugnant to the first principles of reason? Let that be demon-
> strated and the effect will be rather to overthrow the Scriptures, than to
> favour such a method of forming a theory from them. But no such thing
> can be demonstrated.[50]

Alexander, in other words, was fully committed to the extrinsic implications of his era's scientific reasoning.

The Canadian situation supplies an interesting contrast. Evangelical
intellectuals in nineteenth-century Canada prosecuted natural theology
and explained the harmonies of mental and physical science with as
much vigor as their peers in the United States. But the Canadians never
regarded their efforts with quite the deadly seriousness found in the
United States. As therefore could be expected, the Canadians experienced a good deal less trauma in the early years of the twentieth century
in adjusting to new scientific ideals and practices.[51] The difference on
how seriously to treat scientific natural theology may be one of the
reasons why later clashes between fundamentalists and modernists
(involving great strife over the question of who was using the proper
form of scientific procedure) were sharper in the United States than in
either Canada or the United Kingdom, where natural theology was
usually promoted in Chalmers's spirit.

As long as evangelicals took a substantial part in mainstream professional research, contrarian views of science never enjoyed more than
local popularity. Thus, the alternative science of flood geology only
gained ground in the 1920s when society-wide tension was emerging
between evangelicals and proponents of university-certified specialized
scientific knowledge. Opinions in the *Princeton Theological Review* illus-

trate this shift from an evangelical world in which intrinsic competed against extrinsic implications of science to one in which the extrinsic prevailed over all. In 1901, for instance, an author in the conservative publication could treat the question of whether the human body descended from animal ancestors as an open issue to be adjudicated by research: "The difference between his [the human's] physical structure, with his erect posture, his greater weight of brain, etc., and that of the other primates is indeed striking, but does not exclude the hypothesis of common origin. In many of his mental characteristics again man shows a kinship with the brutes." The reason the author could countenance such a question as a proper subject for research was the distinction between science as empirical research and science as metaphysical statement. "Darwinism," he concluded, "has made men think. . . . The outcome of forty years of scientific investigation and apologetic discussion is, however, the growing conviction both among scientists and theologians that evolution as a scientific theory and theology have very little to do with each other, and that evolution neither increases materially the theologian's difficulties, nor helps him to solve them."[52]

Within twenty years the tone of the *Princeton Theological Review* had changed to stress the extrinsic character of scientific work. Thus, in a series of articles from the early 1920s, Princeton conservative evangelical assessment of modern science came to focus on broader concerns. In 1922, one author contended that the "world-view" of evolution "because of its monism, is both at first so attractive and afterwards so compelling that, if yielded to, it must at last revolutionize civilization."[53] In 1924 another contributor discussed speciation as a matter of ultimate concern: "The other adequate explanation of this similarity [of features in different species] is found in the assumption of a creation of each species by a personal God. On independent grounds the theist reaches the conclusion that a personal God exists. If this conclusion is correct, and if God is the actual ground for the existence of the universe and of matter and if even on an evolutionary hypothesis the only adequate explanation of the existence of the first living cell is to suppose that God created it, there is no presumption against the possibility of his having created each species. If he *did* create each species, then the similarity between the species would be adequately accounted for by the fact that the different species were created on a similar plan by the same Great Architect."[54] In 1925, a biblical doctrine of "a completed Creation" was posed against what the author calls "this essentially pagan or atheistic theory" of evolution.[55]

These accounts in the *Princeton Theological Review* from the mid-1920s show several things: that the empirical approach that earlier Princeton theologians like Charles Hodge and B. B. Warfield had tried to champion was now failing; that the effort to differentiate intrinsic from extrinsic scientific concerns had become passé; and that evangelicals were ready for the Scopes Trial. As was the case in the first half of the nineteenth century, so also now in the third decade of the twentieth: much more was at stake for American evangelicals in the cosmological meaning of science, much less in the actual doing of science.

The Scopes Trial

The celebrated Scopes Trial of 1925 had almost nothing to do with the history of science considered as the testing of hypotheses about the nature of the physical world. To be sure, in the far distant background was the emergence of the neo-Darwinian synthesis and a decline in the number of scientists who interpreted evolution as fitting in with God's design of the world. Yet even such questions were submerged far beneath the waves of publicity generated by the event. In the ocean of symbol, myth, legend, and moralistic shorthand associated with the trial in the popular mind since 1925, science *per se* has been almost entirely lost.

The Scopes Trial, rather, continues to have everything to do with the history of science considered as the struggle for intellectual hegemony in the broader American society. A recent Pulitzer Prize winning book by lawyer-historian Edward Larson provides a welcome antidote to simplistic treatment of the highly publicized battle between William Jennings Bryan and Clarence Darrow in Dayton, Tennessee.[56]

Larson's book shows, for example, how little the American Civil Liberties Union (ACLU), which defended science teacher John Scopes as one of its first ambitious cases, was concerned with evolution as such. The ACLU's interest was instead in protecting the rights of minorities at the time of the Red Scare. Such information makes it entirely clear why William Jennings Bryan remained a respected figure for several of the individuals who stage managed the ACLU's defense of Scopes. For his part, Bryan supported Tennessee's anti-evolution law not primarily because he wanted to promote outmoded biblical interpretations, but because of his lifelong desire to defend America's humbler citizens – workers, farmers, women, children, and the poor.

Larson's greatest contribution is to show how easily the public disputants over evolution in 1925 and since could slide from considering natural phenomena to making grandiose statements about The Nature of Things. For the anti-evolutionists the move was from evolution to a plot to "rob [society of its moral] compass" and so "endanger" humanity.[57] From the other side the move was equally intuitive from evolution to "the progress of the world" or the struggle between American "liberty" and "narrow, mean, intolerant and brainless prejudice of soulless religio-maniacs."[58] With the Scopes Trial so firmly fixed in the national consciousness, and with the trial continuing to inspire such a pall of logical nonsense, Edward Larson has provided skillful, but also dismaying, evidence to explain why discussion of evolution and related matters in both religion or science suffers so badly in American public discourse.

Modern "Scientific Creationism"

Despite widespread impressions to the contrary, "creationism" was not a traditional belief of nineteenth-century conservative Protestants or even of early twentieth-century fundamentalists.[59] At least until the 1960s only a tiny minority of American evangelicals, or even self-confessed fundamentalists, believed what are now common features of "creationism" or "creation science," like the conviction that the earth is only 6,000–10,000 years old or that the universal flood of Noah was responsible for the fossil record. As we have seen, most conservative Protestants before the 1930s believed that the "days" of the first chapter of Genesis stood for long ages of geological development or that a lengthy gap existed between the initial creation of the world (Genesis 1:1) and a series of more recent creative acts (Genesis 1:2ff) during which the fossils were deposited. In fact, so widespread among fundamentalists were the "day–age" theory and the "gap" theory that R. A. Torrey, one of the editors of *The Fundamentals* (1910–15), could suggest as late as 1925 that a person could "believe thoroughly in the absolute infallibility of the Bible and still be an evolutionist of a certain type."[60] James Orr of Scotland and B. B. Warfield of Princeton Theological Seminary were far from the only conservative evangelicals to regard evolution from one or only a few original life forms as possibly God's way of creating plants, animals, and even the human body.[61] (Their position came close to official Roman Catholic teachings on the subject.) Popular opponents of evolution in the 1920s, like William Jennings Bryan, had no difficulty accepting an ancient earth. Bryan, with an acuity that his patronizers rarely perceive, argued that the great problem with evolution was not the practice of science but the metaphysical naturalism and consequent social Darwinism that scientific evolution was called upon to justify.

Modern "creationism" arose, by contrast, from the efforts of earnest Seventh-day Adventists who wanted to show that the sacred writings of Adventist founder Ellen G. White (who made much of a recent earth and the Noachian deluge) could provide a framework for studying the history of the earth.[62] Especially important for this purpose was the Adventist theorist George McCready Price (1870–1963), who published a string of "creationist" works highlighted in 1923 by *The New Geology*. That book argued that a "simple" or "literal" reading of early Genesis showed that God had created the world six to eight thousand years ago and had used the Flood to construct the planet's geological past. Price, an armchair geologist with little formal training and almost no field experience, demonstrated how a person with such a belief could reconstruct natural history in order to question traditional understandings of the geological column and apparent indications for an ancient earth.

The gist of Price's argument was eventually embraced by other doctrinal conservatives – especially the Presbyterian itinerant Harry Rimmer (1890–1952), the Baptist patriarch of Minneapolis William Bell Riley (1861–1947), and a few conservative Lutherans and Dutch Reformed – even if none of the other early "creationists" were quite so rigid as Price (and "creationists" after 1960) in rejecting the main conclusions of academic geology. Such speakers (their writings almost always retained the style of public address) kept alive Price's general approach to geology and evolution, but shifted its basis from the dictates of Ellen White to a literal interpretation of the early chapters of Genesis. That strategic adjustment, in turn, paved the way for the remarkable worldwide surge of "creationism" over the past forty years.

When a rising corps of university-trained conservative evangelical scientists founded the American Scientific Affiliation (ASA) in 1941, "creationist" flood geologists thought this society would provide a receptive forum for their conclusions. It did not. Although leaders of the ASA maintained high views of biblical authority and defended the sovereignty of God over the natural world, almost all of them held to the older day–age or gap theories. Some of them even felt that divine revelation in Genesis and natural revelation from empirical investigation did not need to be harmonized in the ways that had been repeatedly tried, revised, and tried again since the early nineteenth century. Extensive debate within the ASA over many issues related to themes of God and creation reveal an internal evangelical diversity rarely noticed by outside observers.[63]

The rise of modern "creation science" began in 1961 with the publication of an influential book. John C. Whitcomb, Jr (b. 1924), a theologian at Grace Theological Seminary (Winona Lake, Indiana) of the Grace Brethren denomination, and Henry M. Morris (b. 1918), a hydraulic engineer of Southern Baptist background, had each been moving in a "creationist" direction for quite a while before finding confirmation in Price's work. Each was also disturbed by a book published in 1954 by the evangelical Baptist theologian Bernard Ramm, *The Christian View of Science and Scripture*, which had delighted most members of the ASA by proposing a much more flexible approach to reconciling evidence from nature interpretation of the Bible. Soon after Whitcomb and Morris met they published *The Genesis Flood*, an updating of Price's work, but one that, because of Whitcomb's theological contribution and Morris's scientific expertise, made Price's points more persuasively.

The Genesis Flood became an immediate bestseller. Its vision of "creationism" has been popularized in millions of copies of other books, articles, pamphlets, and Sunday School lessons. It sparked the entrance of "creationism" into Britain (where conservative anti-evolutionists had almost never promoted the idea of a young earth). It lay behind the desire of a growing number of "biblical creationists" to seek equal time for "creation science" in public school instruction. It helped to recruit a number of capable public speakers to promote the "creationist" viewpoint in highly publicized public debates with evolutionists. It led eventually to a few university-trained geologists advocating the "creationist" viewpoint. Prosecution of these arguments has led to wounded reactions from the scientific establishment and intense battles in many towns and cities over how evolution was or was not taught in the schools. In sum, since 1960 "creationism" has done more than any other issue, except abortion, to inflame the cultural warfare in American public life.

Several aspects of the new "creationism" deserve special mention. First, it is important to acknowledge that the appeal of "creationism" accords well with the great respect for Scripture that continues to define modern evangelical movements. In the words of one commentator, whom Numbers quotes, "Tens of thousands of Christians have been convinced by Morris & Whitcomb's books because *they made sense of the Bible*."[64]

Second, it is worth observing that "creationism" has risen alongside a resurgence of apocalyptic speculations based on the same kind of biblical literalism underlying creation science. "For Christians expecting the end of the age," as Numbers puts it, "Whitcomb and Morris offered a compelling view of earth history framed by symmetrical catastrophic events and connected by a common hermeneutic."[65]

Third, "creationism" should also be considered a political movement reacting to the great expansion of national government authority that has taken place since the 1930s. Especially the intrusion of the national government into local educational concerns has politicized all topics on the borders between science and religion.[66] After *Sputnik*, the United States poured unprecedented amounts of money into a frenzied effort aimed at reinvigorating the teaching of science in American schools. One of the by-products of this effort was the production of influential biology textbooks that not only introduced major contemporary findings, but also propounded grandly phrased metaphysical claims about the evolutionary character of the cosmos. Such hegemonic governmental intrusions have regularly produced intense localist reactions. "Creationism" has been one of the most intense.

Fourth, "creationists" also deploy some resentment against America's self-appointed knowledge elites. As such, they are part of a natural reaction to the intellectual imperialism so regularly practiced by at least some of the scholars at the nation's best known universities. A world in which a physicist like Cornell's Carl Sagan becomes a guru concerning All Things, or a paleontologist like Harvard's Stephen Jay Gould presumes to define the theoretical limits of "science," is a world primed for an ancient languages expert like Whitcomb and an engineer like Morris to offer their own counter-pontifications about how The World Is.

"Creationism," it is clear, does not primarily concern empirical observation of the natural world. It is instead the deductive extrapolation of a particular pre-understanding of how the Bible should be read onto the metaphysical issues posed by modern theories of evolution. The actual looking at the earth or the carrying out of experiments has been relatively unimportant for "creationists." Research does take place, and experiments occur, but often because "creationists" are checking out something they discovered in scientific literature that seems to pose problems for large-scale evolutionary theories. "Creationism," at root, is religion. It has become politics because of the overweening metaphysical pretentions of elitist pundits exploiting the prestige of "science."

The activity of "creationists" should be welcomed by all who regret the mindless ease with which, since at least the mid-nineteenth century, public pundits have transformed the carefully qualified observations of working scientists into grandiose cosmological claims about the Nature of Things. "Creationist" literature is filled with oceans of nonsense, but probably has never descended to the level of obfuscating banality found in the anti-"creationist" pamphlet published in 1984 under the pretentious title, *Science and Creationism: a View from the National Academy of Sciences*. In this glossy booklet distributed widely in American schools are found choice bits of purest scientism, like the following, which Numbers quotes: "In a nation whose people depend on scientific progress for their health, economic gains, and national security, it is of utmost importance that our students understand science as a system of study, so that by building on past achievements they can maintain the pace of scientific progress and ensure the continued emergence of results that can benefit mankind."[67] "Creationists" have every right to be infuriated by such hokum, where "science" takes over for God.

But if "creationists" are justified in attacking the pretentious use of "science" to perform tasks once reserved for the deity, their own strategies nonetheless pose grave difficulties for the ongoing discussions at the intersection of Christianity (which has always made important claims to the reality of empirically observable events) and empirical science (which has always proceeded within the context of religious-like assumptions about the world).

The only major analogy to the naive positivism of the "creationists" with respect to biblical texts is the naive positivism with respect to natural observations that lingers among some who worship at the shrine of modern "science." It solves none of the weighty issues involved in the subject to observe that *persons* read texts and that *persons* make observations of the natural world. But that observation, rather than positivistic naiveté, is the place to begin.

By adding their weight to the politicizing of science, "creationists" make it harder, rather than easier, to isolate the critical issues at the intersection of religion and science. The roar of battle between "creationists" and their "scientific" opponents drowns out more patient, more careful voices. Both those who want actually to look at nature as a way of understanding nature and those who want actually to look at themselves as a way of understanding how cosmological explanations are formed get shouted down.

Conclusion

Modern contentions over evolution, fomented by fundamentalists and some evangelicals, regularly begin as debates over scientific results, procedures, and verifications. But almost invariably they move on rapidly to arguments over issues only remotely related to what practicing scientists do in their laboratories or in the field. From the defenders of modern scientific procedures come protests about professional expertise, qualifications, and decorum. From fundamentalists and evangelicals come protests about the decline of Western morality. In moving so rapidly to great moral questions, evangelicals only follow a longstanding tradition, which had been expressed with great clarity by William Jennings Bryan. For Bryan, it was necessary to oppose evolution, not because evolution imperiled traditional interpretations of Genesis 1, or because it sabotaged empirical investigations, but because evolution was a threat to a treasured social ideal. As Bryan put it in 1925, the year of his appearance at the Scopes Trial, evolution is "an insult to reason and shocks the heart. That doctrine is as deadly as leprosy; . . . it would, if generally adopted, destroy all sense of responsibility and menace the morals of the world."[68] In making this assertion, Bryan upheld a long evangelical tradition that subsumed the narrowly, research-oriented aspects of science to its broad, social implications.

The irony of evangelical antagonism toward conclusions of modern evolutionary science is that evangelicalism itself emerged as a potent religious force in part by exploiting the prestige of science that was so important for Anglo-North American culture of the eighteenth and nineteenth centuries. Yet descendants of this earlier evangelicalism, especially in fundamentalist forms, now view recent forms of science as a grave threat to what Christians value most. That irony, however, is also eloquent testimony to the depth and persistence of evangelical engagement with science, an engagement that has always been more complicated than either the champions of, or detractors from, evangelicalism have been willing to concede.

From the angle of deeply held views on the extrinsic meanings of science, the evangelical engagement had been persistent, profound, sometimes savvy, and regularly alert to the political implications of intellectual discourse. From the angle of science as an intrinsic exercise, evangelical engagement has been more ambiguous. Although many evangelicals have contributed to the practices of intrinsic science, the face of evangelicalism as a movement has turned so consistently to extrinsic matters that the bearing of evangelical faith on the intrinsic practices of science remains a mystery, largely undefined by practitioners and mostly undisturbed by later historians of their work.

Notes

1 For outstanding historiographical summaries, see the editors' introduction to David C. Lindberg and Ronald L. Numbers, *God and Nature: Historical Essays on the Encounter between Christianity and Science* (Berkeley: University of California Press, 1986), pp. 1–18; and John Hedley Brooke, *Science and Religion: Some Historical Perspectives* (New York: Cambridge University Press, 1991).

2 Outstanding examples include J. C. Polkinghorne, *Belief in God in an Age of Science* (New Haven, CT: Yale University Press, 1998); and Robert John Russell et al., eds, *Chaos and Complexity: Scientific Perspectives on Divine Action*, 2nd edn (Berkeley, CA: Center for Theology and the Natural Sciences, 1997).

3 For especially careful documentation, see Mark Alan Kalthoff, "The new evangelical engagement with science: the American Scientific Affiliation, origin to 1963" (PhD dissertation, Indiana University, 1998).

4 For a popular statement, see Phillip E. Johnson, *Darwin on Trial* (Chicago: Regnery, 1991); and for more academic treatment, William A. Dembski, *The Design Inference: Eliminating Chance through Small Probabilities* (New York: Cambridge University Press, 1998).

5 Frank M. Turner, "The Victorian conflict between science and religion: a professional dimension," *Isis*, 69, 1978, pp. 356–76.

6 James R. Moore, *The Post-Darwinian Controversies: A Study of the Protestant Struggle to Come to Terms with Darwin in Great Britain and America, 1870–1900* (New York: Cambridge University Press, 1979), pp. 17–122.

7 G. K. Chesterton, *Saint Thomas Aquinas: "The Dumb Ox"* (New York: Doubleday, 1956, orig. 1933), p. 88.

8 As such, it draws on some material I published before in chapter 7, "Thinking about science," in *The Scandal of the Evangelical Mind* (Grand Rapids, MI: Eerdmans, 1994); and in "Science, theology, and society in America: from Cotton Mather to William Jennings Bryan," in *Evangelicals and Science in Historical Perspective*, eds David Livingstone, D. G. Hart, and Mark A. Noll (Oxford: Oxford University Press, 1999).

9 Especially due to conversations with James Moore and David Livingstone over many years, I am aware of the artificial character of this intrinsic–extrinisic distinction. "Intrinsic" science cannot be simply considered as objective, neutral, and free of social influences, for all science is done by humans, within human social settings, and for human purposes. Nevertheless, it does seem self-evident that "intrinsic" questions like "what am I seeing through this microscope now?" are influenced by ideology and social setting in different, less extreme, ways than "extrinsic" questions like "what do someone else's conclusions about variations in a pigeon population suggest about the presence or absence of design in the universe?"

10 Bruce Kuklick, *Churchmen and Philosophers from Jonathan Edwards to John Dewey* (New Haven, CT: Yale University Press, 1985), p. 202.

11 In this American situation I am talking about something different than Steven Shapin describes in *A Social History of Truth: Civility and Science in Seventeenth-century England* (Chicago: University of Chicago Press, 1994), where broad, underlying, all-but-invisible cultural assumptions are described as shaping, or determining, the credibility of scientific conclusions. Rather, I am describing a situation where political, ideological, cosmological, and metaphysical matters have been self-consciously at work in relation to the practice and place of science in American society.

12 Cotton Mather, *The Christian Philosopher: a Collection of the Best Discoveries in Nature, with Religious Improvement* (London: E. Mathews, 1721), p. 1. For learned discussion and a reliable modern edition, see Winton U. Solberg, ed., *Cotton Mather, the Christian Philosopher* (Champaign: University of Illinois Press, 1994).

13 See especially Jonathan R. Topham, "Science, natural theology, and evangelicalism in early nineteenth-century Scotland: Thomas Chalmers and the *evidence* controversy," and Allen C. Guelzo, "'The science of duty': moral philosophy and the epistemology of science in nineteenth-century America," both in *Evangelicals and Science in Historical Perspective*, op. cit., n. 8.

14 Norman Fiering, *Moral Philosophy at Seventeenth-century Harvard: a Discipline in Transition* (Chapel Hill: University of North Carolina Press, 1981), p. 300.

15 For extensive discussion, see Mark A. Noll, *Princeton and the Republic, 1768–1822: the Search for a Christian Enlightenment in the Era of Samuel Stanhope Smith* (Princeton, NJ: Princeton University Press, 1989).

16 See William Smith, "William Paley's theological utilitarianism in America," *William and Mary Quarterly*, 11, 1954, pp. 402–24.

17 See John R. Fitzmier, *New England's Moral Legislator: Timothy Dwight, 1752–1817* (Bloomington: Indiana University Press, 1998).

18 See especially T. D. Bozeman, *Protestants and the Age of Science: the Baconian Ideal and Antebellum American Religious Thought* (Chapel Hill: University of North Carolina Press, 1977).

19 Samuel Stanhope Smith, *An Essay on the Causes of the Variety of Complexion and Figure in the Human Species* (Philadelphia: Robert Aitken, 1789), p. 3.

20 The phrase "supernatural rationalism" is from E. Brooks Holifield, *The Gentlemen Theologians: American Theology in Southern Culture, 1795–1860* (Durham, NC: Duke University Press, 1978).

21 Charles G. Finney, *Lectures on Revivals of Religion*, ed. W. G. McLoughlin (1835, reprinted Cambridge, MA: Harvard University Press, 1960), p. 33.

22 Quoted in Herbert Hovenkamp, *Science and Religion in America, 1800–1860* (Philadelphia: University of Pennsylvania Press, 1978), p. 3.

23 Charles Hodge, *Systematic Theology*, 3 volumes (1872–3, reprinted Grand Rapids, MI: Eerdmans, n.d.), *volume 1*, pp. 10–11.

24 Quoted in Richard L. Hughes and C. Leonard Allen, *Illusions of Innocence: Protestant Primitivism in America, 1630–1875* (Chicago: University of Chicago Press, 1988), p. 156.

25 Quoted in Henry Warner Bowden, *Church History in the Age of Science: Historiographical Patterns in the United States, 1876–1918* (Chapel Hill: University of North Carolina Press, 1971), p. 7.

26 Charles A. Briggs, "Critical theories of sacred scripture," *Presbyterian Review*, 2 (July), 1881, p. 558.

27 William Henry Green, "Professor W. Robertson Smith on the Pentateuch," *Presbyterian Review*, 2 (January), 1882, pp. 108–56.

28 R. A. Torrey, *What the Bible Teaches* (Chicago: Fleming H. Revell, 1898), p. 1.

29 The next two paragraphs follow David W. Bebbington, "Science and evangelical theology in Britain from Wesley to Orr," in *Evangelicals and Science in Historical Perspective*, op. cit., n. 8, pp. 120–41.

30 See the essay by Jonathan Topham cited in n. 11 above.

31 Many of the individuals mentioned in this paragraph are sketched in David N. Livingstone, *Darwin's Forgotten Defenders: the Encounter Between Evangelical Theology and Evolutionary Thought* (Grand Rapids, MI: Eerdmans, 1987).

32 Excellent on Wright is Ronald L. Numbers, "George Frederick Wright: from Christian Darwinism to fundamentalist," *Isis*, 79, 1988, pp. 624–45.

33 William Berryman Scott, *Some Memories of a Palaeontologist* (Princeton, NJ: Princeton University Press, 1939), p. 75, which reports the title as *Voyage of a Naturalist*.

34 Charles Hodge, letter to the *New York Observer*, March 26, 1863, pp. 98–9; with discussion in Charles Hodge, *What Is Darwinism?*, eds Mark A. Noll and David N. Livingstone (Grand Rapids, MI: Baker, 1994, orig. 1874), pp. 51–6. For fuller context, see Bradley John Gundlach, "The evolution question at Princeton, 1845–1929" (PhD dissertation, University of Rochester, 1995).

35 For attacks on ateleology (or the assertion that the universe does *not* exhibit design), see Hodge, *What Is Darwinism?*, op. cit., n. 34, and Hodge, *Systematic Theology*, 3 volumes (New York: Charles Scribner's Sons, 1872–3), *volume 1*, pp. 550–74, *volume 2*, pp. 3–41. For a repetition of his convictions on the rights of an independent science, see *Systematic Theology*, *volume 1*, pp. 59, 170–1, and 573–4 (reprinted and annotated in *What Is Darwinism?*, pp. 56–9).

36 Benjamin B. Warfield, "The present status of the doctrine of evolution," *The Presbyterian Messenger*, 3(10), December 5, 1895, pp. 7–8.

37 Adrian Desmond and James Moore, *Darwin: the Life of a Tormented Evolutionist* (London: Michael Joseph, 1991); Shapin, *A Social History of Truth*, op. cit., n. 11.

38 On the Victoria Institute, see Moore, *The Post-Darwinian Controversies*, op. cit., n. 6, pp. 84–5 and passim; on the ASA, see Kalthoff, n. 3 above.

39 James Orr, "Science and Christian faith," in *The Fundamentals*, 4 volumes (Grand Rapids, MI: Baker, 1972, orig. 1917), *volume 1*, p. 346.

40 George Frederick Wright, "The passing of evolution," in *The Fundamentals*, op. cit., n. 39, *volume 4*, p. 87.

41 See above, n. 4.

42 Edward O. Wilson, *Naturalist* (New York: Warner, 1994).

43 For orientation on Hutchinson, see Albert J. Kuhn, "Glory or gravity: Hutchinson vs. Newton," *Journal of the History of Ideas* 22, 1961, pp. 303–22; and Brooke, *Science and Religion*, op. cit., n. 1, p. 190.

44 David Bebbington, *Evangelicalism in Modern Britain: a History from the 1730s to the 1980s* (London: Unwin Hyman, 1989), p. 57.

45 *The Sermon, Delivered at the Inauguration of the Rev. Archibald Alexander, D.D., as Professor of Didactic and Polemic Theology, in the Theological Seminary of the Presbyterian Church, in the United States of America . . .* (New York: J. Seymour, 1812), p. 77.

46 This thesis is developed by J. C. D. Clark, *English Society, 1688–1832* (New York: Cambridge University Press, 1985), pp. 218–19.

47 Bebbington, "Science and evangelical theology in Britain," op. cit., n. 29, p. 177.
48 Robert L. Dabney, "Geology and the Bible" (orig. July 1861), in *Discussions by Robert L. Dabney, volume 3: Philosophical*, ed. C. R. Vaughan (Richmond, VA: Whittet & Shepperson, 1892), p. 95; "A caution against anti-Christian science" (orig. 1871), in ibid., p. 131; "The caution against anti-Christian science criticized by Dr Woodrow" (orig. 1873), in ibid., pp. 169–70.
49 Thomas Chalmers, *On Natural Theology* (Edinburgh, 1836; reprinted, New York: Robert Carter, 1844), p. xiv.
50 Archibald Alexander, *Evidences of the Authenticity, Inspiration, and Canonical Authority of the Holy Scriptures* (Philadelphia: Presbyterian Board, 1836), pp. 10, 15.
51 See especially Michael Gauvreau, *The Evangelical Century: College and Creed in English Canada from the Great Revival to the Great Depression* (Montreal and Kingston: McGill-Queen's University Press, 1991).
52 William Hallock Johnson, "Evolution and theology today," *Princeton Theological Review*, 1, 1903, pp. 417, 422.
53 William Brenton Greene, Jr, "Yet another criticism of the theory of evolution," *Princeton Theological Review*, 20 (October), 1922, p. 537.
54 Floyd E. Hamilton, "The evolutionary hypothesis in the light of modern science," *Princeton Theological Review*, 22, 1924, p. 422.
55 George McCready Price, "Modern botany and the theory of organic evolution," *Princeton Theological Review*, 23, 1925, p. 65.
56 Edward J. Larson, *Summer for the Gods: the Scopes Trial and America's Continuing Debate over Science and Religion* (New York: Basic Books, 1997). Larson's book points out once again, as several judicious commentors had done before, that the popular play and movie *Inherit the Wind* is useless for historical information concerning what actually happened at the Dayton trial in July 1925. Larson also describes clearly how much the image of the Scopes Trial, though hardly its historical reality, remains alive to shape contemporary debates between creationists and their opponents aimed at controlling publicly financed scientific education.
57 Bryan quoted in Larson, *Summer of the Gods*, op. cit., n. 56, p. 198.
58 Hunter's *Civic Biology* pre-trial edition and Clarence Darrow quoted in Larson, *Summer of the Gods*, op. cit., n. 56, pp. 23, 146.
59 This section on "creationism" draws heavily from the fullest, most judicious modern account, Ronald L. Numbers, *The Creationists: the Evolution of Scientific Creationism* (New York: Knopf, 1992). Quotation marks around the word "creationism" are intended as a protest against the hijacking of a word. "Creationism," by rights, should define all who discern a divine mind at work in, with, or under the phenomena of the natural world,

even though that term has come to denote the view that God created the world ten thousand or fewer years ago and that God used a worldwide flood in the days of Noah to form the geological evidence that most modern scientists think reveals an ancient earth with evolutionary changes over great expanses of time.

60 Quoted in Ronald L. Numbers, ed., *Antievolution before World War I* (New York: Garland, 1995), p. xv.

61 For more on such figures, see Livingstone, *Darwin's Forgotten Defenders*, op. cit., n. 31.

62 The Adventists' interest in such matters has had the subsidiary benefit of providing some of the best modern historians of anti-evolutionism. For a moving account of Ronald Numbers's personal pilgrimage out of Adventist and "creationist" circles, see the introduction by Jonathan M. Butler to Numbers's *Prophetess of Health: Ellen G. White and the Origins of Seventh-Day Adventist Health Reform*, 2nd edn (Knoxville: University of Tennessee Press, 1992).

63 See essays on the history of the ASA in *Perspectives on Science and Christian Faith*, 43 (December), 1991, pp. 238–79; and 44 (March), 1992, pp. 2–24.

64 Numbers, *Creationists*, op. cit., n. 59, p. 338.

65 Ibid., p. 339.

66 Robert Wuthnow, *The Restructuring of American Religion* (Princeton, NJ: Princeton University Press, 1988).

67 Quoted in Numbers, *Creationists*, op. cit., n. 59, p. 321.

68 William Jennings Bryan, *The Last Message of William Jennings Bryan* (New York: Fleming H. Revell, 1925), p. 51.

9

Politics

As the story goes, the Constitutional Convention was deadlocked and rapidly approaching a point of no return. It was Thursday, June 28, 1787. Small states refusing to give way on the principle of one state–one vote and large states refusing to give way on the principle of representation apportioned by population were at loggerheads. At this critical juncture, Benjamin Franklin, aged 82 and mostly silent to that point, rose to speak. Franklin's brief address implored the delegates to find a compromise and then asked why it was that "this Assembly, groping as it were in the dark . . . [has] not hitherto once thought of humbly applying to the Father of lights to illuminate our understandings?" He reminded the delegates that during the contest with Great Britain the Continental Congress had daily prayed "in this room for divine protection" and that "all of us who were engaged in the struggle must have observed frequent instances of a superintending providence in our favor." Franklin told the assembly that "the longer I live, the more convincing proofs I see of this truth – *that God Governs in the affairs of men*," and he reminded them of the assurance "in the sacred writings" that "except the Lord build the House they labour in vain that build it." And so he moved that the assembly institute "prayers imploring the assistance of heaven, and its blessings on our deliberations, [to] be held in this Assembly every morning before we proceed to business."[1]

The motion was immediately seconded by Roger Sherman, a cagey veteran of Connecticut politics who was also a strong alley of his minister at the Second Congregational Church in New Haven, the Rev. Jonathan Edwards, Jr.[2]

Thus far, this account is recorded in James Madison's *Notes* on the Constitutional Convention. Now, however, the story takes on an interesting twist as recorded in two books by Peter Marshall and David

Manuel which in various editions have sold over 850,000 copies in the past twenty years and which have become mainstays in the historical consciousness of many evangelical Protestants. Their titles are *The Light and the Glory: Discovering God's Plan for America from Christopher Columbus to George Washington* and *From Sea to Shining Sea: Discovering God's Plan for America in Her First Half-century of Independence, 1787–1837.*

Franklin's appeal for prayer "marked the turning point." It was

> clearly the most extraordinary speech anyone had delivered in the entire three months the delegates had been meeting. . . . They immediately declared three days of prayer and fasting, to seek God's help in breaking the deadlock among them. At the end of that time, all the resentment and wrangling were gone. . . . Why does [the Constitution] work so well? One reason is that it was divinely inspired. A second is that it was the completion of nearly two hundred years of Puritan political thought. Those early church covenants recognized the sinfulness of man. They anticipated the possibility of human wrong. The Constitution does exactly the same thing. In effect, it documents the Covenant Way on national paper.[3]

Much of the force as well as much of the confusion in and about evangelical political mobilization in the United States in the years toward the end of the twentieth century is illustrated by the farrago of fact and fantasy surrounding Franklin's appeal for prayer at the 1787 convention. The facts, as provided by the manuscript sources closest to the incident and clarified by careful historians, are these:

1 Franklin did make such a motion.
2 This same Franklin only a short time later wrote at some length to the Rev. Ezra Stiles concerning his objection to traditional Christian beliefs. Franklin believed in God but concerning "Jesus of Nazareth," he had, "with most of the present Dissenters in England . . . some Doubts as to his Divinity."[4]
3 Franklin's motion was not approved but tabled; there was no three-day recess; and the Convention never did begin its sessions with prayer.
4 The story that the Convention acted positively on Franklin's motion, that it recessed to fast, and that it was miraculously guided in writing the Constitution was first published in the mid-1820s. Only in 1833, in a tract by Thomas S. Grimké, did this account begin to

figure in broader assessments of the American funding. But that tract was explicitly repudiated by James Madison, by then one of the few surviving members of the Constitutional Convention, who told Grimké with great assurance that Franklin's motion had never been enacted.[5]

The matters that are pertinent for a consideration of evangelical political mobilization in modern America are the relative absence of an explicitly evangelical discourse in the founding era itself and the emergence of an evangelical discourse about the sacred character of the founding only in the 1830s. In order to link this early American history to contemporary concerns, however, it is necessary to revisit critical definitions. After briefly discussing terminology and after briefly summarizing the major features of evangelical political mobilization today, this chapter returns to the first century of the United States' history in order to make several points. First, although Christian faith of a generally Protestant variety played a large part in the founding era of the United States, this form of Christianity was not primarily what is usually meant today by the term "evangelical." Second, evangelical Christianity became important in the early United States only after 1800 and only in national situations quite different from those prevailing during the founding period. Third, attention to the historical circumstances in which Protestant evangelicals became active in American politics during the period 1815–60 offers more insight concerning evangelical political mobilization today than does attention to the evangelical stake in the American founding.

The Contemporary Situation

Dwelling on questions of definition, though only a preliminary exercise, is important because of the appalling lack of precision in much contemporary discussion of religion and politics. For the word "evangelical," the most important discrimination is whether it is being applied as a term in the history of Christianity or as a term in the assessment of modern political life.

As we have seen, the most serviceable general definition of "evangelical" for the purposes of the history of Christianity has been provided by the British historian David Bebbington, who highlights four key defining characteristics: biblicism, conversionism, activism, and cruci-centrism.[6] But as we have also seen, attachment to at least some of these convictions is widespread in North American societies. They are of course held by most adherents to evangelical Protestant denominations, but they are also widely spread among mainline Protestants and Roman Catholics.[7]

Of much more interest for concerns of religion and politics are the denominational traditions explained in chapter 2 as catalogued by the political scientists Green, Guth, Kellstedt, and Smidt. These are the designations evangelical Protestants, mainline Protestants, black Protestants, Roman Catholics, secular/nominal, and other. The additional discrimination provided by these scholars was the difference between those who regularly practice their religion ("high") and those who do so only rarely ("low").

With religion and United States politics in view, these distinctions among religious traditions and between high and low levels of religious participation take on a striking partisan significance. At least in recent American politics, evangelical beliefs and practices do not by themselves mean nearly as much as adherence to specific church traditions.

To show the importance of such distinctions, it is possible to compare (a) political connections to beliefs and (b) political connections to beliefs as well as affiliations. As shown in tables 9.1 and 9.2, with results again taken from the October 1996 Angus Reid cross-border poll, the differences are striking.

The Angus Reid survey, thus, showed a clearer political payoff from religious traditions than from religious beliefs. To drive home the difference that affiliation makes, it is useful to present one more table from a different poll. Green, Guth, Kellstedt, and Smidt carried out their own survey of American voters in 1996. In this poll, the designations "traditionalist" and modernist" spoke for matters of religious belief and practice. By using a scale measuring religious adherence, as well as style of religion, they found even higher levels of support for Republican candidates among traditional conservative Protestants.[8] These results are presented in table 9.3.

Tables 9.1, 9.2, and 9.3 allow for the following conclusion: narrowly considered in strictly religious terms, evangelicalism turns out to have an interesting, but not overwhelming, connection with political choice (table 9.1). By contrast, evangelical convictions that take shape in a conservative Protestant environment have a much stronger political con-

Table 9.1 Percentages of support for presidential candidates (October 1996) divided by numbers of evangelical beliefs affirmed

	Clinton	Dole	Perot
All four beliefs	48	46	6
Three	62	30	8
Two	63	28	9
One	63	28	9
Zero	68	22	10

Table 9.2 Percentages of support for presidential candidates (October 1996) divided by religious traditions

	Clinton	Dole	Perot
Conservative Protestant-hi	37	57	6
Conservative Protestant-lo	48	41	11
Mainline Protestant-hi	46	47	11
Mainline Protestant-lo	57	34	9
Black Protestant	96	1	3
Catholic-hi	60	33	7
Catholic-lo	63	26	7
Secular/nominal	68	22	10
Other	63	27	9

nection (tables 9.2 and 9.3). This connection has led in recent years to solid evangelical support for Republican political candidates. But as tables 9.2 and 9.3 also show, African-American Protestants, who share many of the evangelical beliefs, have opted overwhelmingly for Democratic candidates.

The conclusion to be drawn from such tables is that when people speak of the evangelical political mobilization of the past quarter-century, the discussion almost always concerns not just evangelical beliefs and practices *per se*, but evangelical beliefs and practices combined with adherence to conservative Protestant denominational groups.

Have we labored like an elephant to bring forth only a mouse of a distinction? No. For an accounting of religion, it is important to see that

Table 9.3 Percentages of support for presidential and House vote (1996) divided by religious groups and loyalty to religious traditions

	(% of popn)	*Clinton*	*Dole*	*Perot*	*House GOP*
White Conservative Protestant-trad	(12)	22	74	4	79
White Conservative Protestant-mod	(10)	42	48	10	60
White Mainline Protestant-trad	(6)	31	63	6	79
White Mainline Protestant-mod	(7)	54	42	4	60
White Catholic-trad	(8)	39	52	9	63
White Catholic-mod	(7)	57	31	12	37
Black Protestant	(9)	95	5	1	13
Secular/nominal	(28)	56	29	16	36

Note: trad, traditional; mod, modern.

belief in the Bible as authoritative divine revelation or belief in the need to be converted to Christ cannot in fact be as easily clustered with a particular political movement as the bare use of the term "evangelical" often implies. Even when considering evangelicals in conservative Protestant denominations, it is necessary to remember that a substantial minority oppose the main political drift of their fellow conservative Protestants.

Nonetheless, among white evangelical adherents of conservative Protestant denominations there has decidedly occurred a political mobilization during the past quarter-century. That mobilization is most easily seen in the extraordinarily high electoral support provided to Republican candidates at the state and federal levels. Less obviously, the mobilization is noticeable in a series of changes that have taken place since 1950 among white conservative Protestant evangelicals:

1   There has been a notable politicization of subject matter in evangelical periodicals.[9] More articles address politics and more of these articles do so with engaged or adversarial language.
2   Entire religious families that were once largely apolitical have entered into political activity. Pentecostal denominations like the Assemblies of God are the most prominent examples, but within many other

Holiness, Baptist, or even Anabaptist denominations there is now a degree of political activity that was unknown two generations ago.

3 Conservative Protestants follow a new set of leaders who have embraced political partisanship. In the early 1950s Billy Graham's sermons fully exploited the rhetoric of the Cold War, but he remained mostly non-partisan in his domestic politics (Graham's closest presidential friends were the Democrat Lyndon Johnson and the Republican Richard Nixon).[10] No widely known evangelical in the 1950s addressed political issues and named political names with the frankness exhibited by James Dobson, Jerry Falwell, and Pat Robertson during the past twenty years.

4 Political changes in the South, the region with the most white evangelicals, have affected evangelical politics. The movement of the South from a mainstay of the Democratic party to an active shaper of the Republican party – and during a period when the largest conservative Protestant denomination in the South, the Southern Baptist Convention, has witnessed a successful effort by self-styled conservatives to control their denomination – has contributed greatly to evangelical political mobilization in the nation as a whole.

The political mobilization of evangelical conservative Protestants is evident on every hand. Almost as evident are the basic reasons for that mobilization. Even after well publicized debacles like the Scopes Trial of 1925 or setbacks about the same time in Northern Protestant denominations like the Presbyterians and the Baptists, Protestant conservatives did not vanish as some notable commentators at the time asserted. Rather, conservative Protestant efforts were turned to local situations and the effort to preserve their own churches and voluntary agencies.[11] The British sociologist Steve Bruce, one of the shrewdest observers of such matters, has put his finger on the key factor that transformed these local actions into national mobilization. Conservative Protestants, Bruce writes, "were working to create social institutions which would permit them to reproduce their own culture sheltered from modernizing influences. The problem was that such boundary-maintaining activity depended on a weak (or benign) federal government which would permit the regions (and pockets of fundamentalists more centrally located) to go their own way."[12]

As others, like Robert Wuthnow, have also noted, the mobilization of evangelical Protestant conservatives coincides with the expansion of federal authority and the consequent resentment of the conservatives at the imposition of what are in effect national standards of moral practice.[13] The issues at stake are various – racial desegregation of the schools, destruction of racial barriers to the franchise, national funding for science education, discovery of a right to abortion in the right to privacy, elimination of prayers in public schools, judicial erection of a wall of separation between religion and society, mandates for equality between men and women in higher education, and assertions of civil protection for non-traditional sexual preferences – but the result is the same. Local situations where it had once been possible to work at (or neglect) solutions to morally charged issues locally were now being addressed by federal actions. National efforts to legislate morality struck many conservative Protestants as so instinctively wrong-headed as to justify their own counter-attempts at legislating an alternative morality.

We will note a historical irony to that resentment shortly, but here it is important to record two aspects of evangelical political mobilization that are securely rooted in American history. First was the application of the Manichean vocabulary of revival to the political arena. Conservative Protestants had grown accustomed over the preceding two centuries to preaching in apocalyptic terms about the battle between God and Satan for the souls of human beings.[14] It was, thus, only second nature to enter politics with a similar vocabulary in which apocalyptic rhetoric was applied to the struggle between godliness and the evil forces of big government, secular humanism, the Supreme Court, the National Education Association, or the Democratic Party.

The second characteristic was a sense of historical violation. Part of the animus behind evangelical political mobilization is the deep conviction that the United States was once a Christian country in a meaningful, if non-establishmentarian, sense of the term, which in the fairly recent past has been hijacked by secularists in a great conspiracy to negate that historical reality. The widespread historical grievance that energizes the labors of Marshall and Manuel, David Barton, Tim LaHaye, Francis Schaeffer, and John Whitehead[15] – to mention only some of the bestselling authors who share this historical opinion – can be summarized as a paraphrase of the words of Mary Magdalene from the twentieth chapter of the Gospel of John: they have taken away my country and we do not know where they have laid it.

Rethinking the Past

At this point, it is appropriate to return to the past that conservative Protestants think has been stolen from them. A clearer, non-mythological picture of evangelical involvement in the early period of American history will, in the first instance, clarify a picture regularly misconstrued by partisans of the New Christian Right – and also, it must be said, by partisan opponents of the New Christian Right, as in the provocative recent polemic, *The Godless Constitution*, by R. Laurence Moore and Isaac Kramnick.[16]

In the second instance, a clearer picture of the evangelical place in early America will make it possible to understand current evangelical attitudes as a complex continuation of historic positions and by so doing may promote a clearer assessment of religion and politics more generally in American society today.

The central historical points concern the role of evangelicals in the founding period, the rise of evangelicalism only after 1800, the appropriation by evangelicals of the founders' expectations for church–state interaction, and the fragmented character of evangelical politics in the early United States.

(1)   Evangelicalism as defined by its conservative Protestant exponents today played at best a negligible role in the founding era of the 1770s and 1780s. Almost all the leading Protestants who were politically active in the period of the Declaration of Independence, the Revolutionary War, and the Constitutional Convention differed substantially from modern evangelical conservative Protestants. Several of the leaders whose beliefs came closest to the modern meaning of evangelical, like John Witherspoon of New Jersey and Patrick Henry of Virginia, were advocates of religious establishments who thought that state support of the churches was essential for their health and the health of society. Others, like the Episcopalians Madison, Washington, and James Wilson, were office-holders in Protestant churches but either so reticent about their own religious convictions or so obviously deistic in their beliefs as

to represent a kind of Enlightenment religion. Still other Protestants of a traditional European sort were sincere supporters of their churches but innocent of the stress on conversion or the practices of pietism that distinguish modern evangelicals. Historian John Murrin may overstate matters, but only slightly, when he claims that

> the Federal Constitution was, in short, the eighteenth-century equivalent of a secular humanist text. The delegates were not a very orthodox group of men in any doctrinal sense. The only born-again Christian among them was probably Richard Bassett of Delaware, a Methodist who generously supported the labors of Francis Asbury and other missionaries but who said nothing at the convention. One cliché often applied to the Constitution is not correct in any literal sense – that at least the Founders, unlike the wildly optimistic French, believed in original sin and its implications for government and politics. Quite possibly not a single delegate accepted Calvinist orthodoxy on original sin.[17]

In light of what happened later in the United States, where Methodists and Baptists supplied a very high proportion of the great army of evangelical activists, it is significant that the Constitutional Convention of 55 delegates included only two Methodists and not a single Baptist.[18]

To assert rather than to argue carefully through a complicated historiographical thicket, it is also possible to suggest that the public discourse on display in the Declaration of Independence, the Articles of Confederation, and the Constitution, while respectful of the deity in general, was hardly evangelical in any specific sense of the term. The most careful studies of religion in the founding era make strong claims for the presence of Protestant elements in the politics of the Revolutionary period, but none claims an overwhelmingly Protestant ethos, and none claims for the founding a specifically evangelical influence.[19] The well documented debates on the ratification of the Constitution were not entirely devoid of interest in religion, since those debates included concern for protecting religious liberty as later specified in the First Amendment. But the overwhelmingly this-worldly character of those debates reveals no preoccupation with explicitly Christian, much less explicitly evangelical, concerns.[20]

Americans during the 1780s and 1790s continued to herald the divine blessing on the United States, but they did so with at least as much attention to an Enlightenment deity as to an explicitly evangelical God. In a word, the political discourse of the founders was not atheistic, but neither did it represent a repristination of vigorous Puritan Calvinism or an anticipation of activistic Protestant evangelicalism.

(2)   One of the reasons why the evangelical engagement with politics in the founding era was so slight is that American evangelicalism was in a parlous state of transition precisely in the half-century surrounding 1776. In that period most forms of Protestantism in North America were undergoing a momentous shift. They were moving beyond a territorial Protestantism dominated by establishmentarian Congregationalists, Episcopalians, and Presbyterians where evangelical impulses and sectarian forms of church organization were distinctly at the margin. They were evolving toward a distinctly evangelical Protestantism dominated by Methodists and Baptists that used sectarian modes of church organization and voluntary organization outside the churches to accomplish their spiritual and social mission.

The Great Awakening of the 1740s had injected an evangelical element into the American churches and had shaken up inherited European patterns of church establishment, but it had not succeeded in transforming American Protestantism into a thoroughly evangelical religion. It was more successful at ending Puritanism than inaugurating evangelicalism. The magnitude of the change under way in the later Revolutionary era is suggested by shifting ecclesiastical demography. In 1776, fully 55 percent of all adherents to churches in the United States were Congregationalists, Presbyterians, and Episcopalians, almost all of whom continued to favor church–state establishments and of whom only a minority would have identified with the newer evangelical impulses. By 1850, these three groups made up fewer than 19 percent of all church adherents while the proportion of Methodists and Baptists had risen from virtually nowhere to constitute about 55 percent of the churched population.[21]

During the 1770s and 1780s, the newer configuration of overtly evangelical, sectarian, and voluntaristic American Protestantism could be glimpsed in a wide range of frontier revivals and also in the beginnings of systematic Methodist organization.[22] But the flourishing of evangelical Protestantism did not occur until after the turn of the new century.

One of the reasons for that later flourishing, however, is relevant to politics. It was in part by adapting to the American political environment as shaped by the Revolution that the largely European Protestantism of the colonial period evolved into the evangelicalism of the national period. Perceptive historians like Nathan Hatch and Russell Richey have shown that the evangelicalization of Protestantism in the new United States is the story of how American Protestantism came to embrace the democratic, republican, commonsensical, liberal, and providential conceptions by which the founders had defined America in the 1770s and 1780s.[23]

The links between internal developments within Protestantism and Protestant investment in the new American values are numerous. For instance, English–language Protestants moved away from Calvinist notions of God (which had been the dominant view in the colonial period) at the same time that they joined the American outrage against arbitrary imperial authority. Protestants likewise moved rapidly away from established churches exercising authority by inherited right to voluntary churches exercising authority through the charisma of individual leadership at the same time that they embraced the new principles of American democracy. Similarly, the shift from reliance on the Bible as interpreted by learned, properly educated authorities to reliance on the Bible as interpreted by individuals exercising their democratic rights coincided with the spread of American notions of self-reliance.

These changes in Protestantism led to two important results. First, evangelicalism, in part because it knew how to exploit the new American vocabulary, emerged as the overwhelmingly dominant form of religion in the national period. Second, evangelical Protestantism, exploiting both its internal religious energies and its synergistic adaptation to the new American values, grew like wildfire. Absolute church statistics are a problem in the national period, since membership requirements were stiff and churches enrolled far fewer formal members than the much larger number affected by their work. But absolute numbers are not the key thing about antebellum American Protestantism. Rather, the key is that in comparative terms the United States possessed no alternative ideology that came anywhere close to the influence of evangelical Protestantism from the early years of the nineteenth century through the Civil War.[24]

The important chronological point is that a form of evangelical Protestantism reasonably similar to what is known as evangelical Protestantism today did not emerge in the United States until a generation or more after the founding period. This Protestantism combined a radical religious individualism (especially in notions of conversion) with a strong communal sense expressed through voluntary organization of churches and parachurch special-purpose agencies. It tended to stress the family as a sacred space insulated from the hustling confusions of the marketplace, but nonetheless participated vigorously and with discipline in that marketplace. This singular form of what might be called proprietary sectarianism was the immediate ancestor of contemporary evangelicalism.

(3)   To note the timing of the evangelical surge is to realize that as expansionary-minded evangelicals went about the conversion of both Americans and American society in the early national period, they did so within a framework for religion and society handed down from the founding generation. This point is worth repeating: Protestants similar to today's evangelicals came into existence only in the early nineteenth century. By that time, the basic guidelines for church–state, religious–social interaction had been set by the founding generation to which evangelicalism as we know it had contributed very little. But since wholehearted accommodation to public values propounded by the founders was one of the means by which evangelicalism surged on many fronts in the early nineteenth century, evangelicals were also quick to baptize the founders' framework for religious–political interaction as their own. Evangelical attachment to the Constitution was, therefore, by adoption rather than by natural birth. This sequence explains why it was not until the 1820s and the 1830s that evangelicals began to construct, with the aid of Benjamin Franklin (a very strange ally), a distinctly evangelical account of the Constitutional Convention.

But since evangelicals did come to embrace fully the founders' framework as their own, it is important to review the nature of that framework. To do so, the arguments of a fine recent book by John G. West, *The Politics of Revelation and Reason: Religion and Civic Life in the New Nation*, are especially valuable.[25]

The major founding fathers, though they differed among themselves on many questions of religion as well as politics, did come to a basic agreement on the place of religion in society. West, for example, documents a wide range of agreement on such questions among John Jay and John Witherspoon, who were evangelicals in something like the modern sense of the term; James Wilson and Alexander Hamilton, whose attachment to Christian orthodoxy varied throughout their lives; George Washington and James Madison, who shared devotion to the republic and an extreme reticence about declaring their personal faith; and Benjamin Franklin, John Adams, and Thomas Jefferson, deists or Unitarians who, if only for pragmatic reasons, did not rule out public activities by more traditional believers. All nine of these founders wanted the new United States to promote religious liberty and none wanted the national government to dictate religious beliefs or practices to its citizens. The surprising degree of agreement among those whose own religious convictions differed so considerably rested on two shared assumptions: that the moral goods promoted by the churches largely coincided with the moral goods promoted by the government, and that the churches had a role to play in making the moral calculus of republicanism actually work.

This moral calculus of republicanism was, and remains, an extraordinarily significant assumption for many Americans, including evangelicals. As the calculus was expressed in the first century of the United States, it embraced two separate convictions: that morality was necessary to create the virtuous citizens without which a republic could not survive, and that the churches should contribute to the promotion of that morality. The practical challenge inherited from the founding era was how a new-fangled kind of church, which had given up the rights of establishment, might insert itself as a promoter of morality into a public sphere from which the founders' commitment to religious freedom had excluded the old style of established churches.

Evangelical Protestants responded to that challenge vigorously. To be sure, the first explicitly evangelical political engagement – an attack on Jefferson as a dangerous infidel in the run-up to the election of 1800 – was a flop.[26] This first evangelical mobilization failed in part because Jefferson turned out to be a moral president and even supported a wide range of religious practices, like attending Sunday services of Christian worship in the Capitol building and authorizing federal support for military chaplains and Christian missions to the Indians. The attack on Jefferson also failed because evangelicals seem instinctively to have grasped that they were treating Jefferson as a monarch who might set up an alternative state religion rather than what he really was, a democratically elected official whose job was to preside over free, competitive public space.

Evangelicals hit their stride after about 1812 by turning to voluntary societies as the way of promoting public morality. Petition drives against Sunday mails and missionary mobilization against Cherokee removal were two of the earliest efforts.[27] In these efforts, the main evangelical groups were largely successful in meeting the challenge posed by the founders by aiming not at establishment, but at provision of private moral capital to sustain the republic.

The fact that evangelicals failed in their efforts to stop the transport of mail on Sunday and to halt the removal of the Cherokee from Georgia does not negate the conclusion that these campaigns illustrated successful evangelical adaptation to a non-establishmentarian, yet still vigorously religious, effort to provide the morality without which a republic would collapse.

The proof that they had learned how to function as openly Christian advocates in a republic defined by Constitutional freedom of religion is found in the extraordinary role that evangelicals played in the sectional antagonism leading to the Civil War. That role has recently been documented in a magisterial book by Richard J. Carwardine, *Evangelicals and Politics in Antebellum America*.[28] The point that it makes, along with many other outstanding recent studies, is that, as powerful as evangelical public influence was in the full generation before Fort Sumter, it was of course an influence divided starkly by the Mason and Dixon Line.

(4) The final historical point, therefore, is that evangelical politics in the first century of the United States was in fact never unitary. While virtually all evangelicals and all organized forms of evangelicalism embraced the founders' framework for religion and politics, deep internal fissures divided evangelicals from one another with respect to how, where, and with what means public action should proceed within those guidelines. A solid recent survey of antebellum evangelicalism by Curtis D. Johnson provides a vocabulary for summarizing those differences.[29]

In Johnson's picture, antebellum evangelicals were divided into three distinct groups, formalists, anti-formalists, and African-Americans. Formalists – mostly Congregationalists and Presbyterians, with some Episcopalians and Reformed – flavored their evangelical convictions with a dose of establishmentarian principle. These formalists were the key agents in establishing the most visible voluntary societies. They were central in high profile religious events like the Businessman's Revival of 1857–8.[30] They were also the ones who enjoyed the highest profiles in national leadership: for example, the preacher-reformer Lyman Beecher; Beecher's children the golden-throated Henry Ward and the bestselling author Harriet; Theodore Frelinghuysen, the "Christian Statesman" who ran as the vice presidential candidate on Henry Clay's 1844 Whig ticket; and the abolitionist Theodore Dwight Weld, who was a protégé of the revivalist Charles Grandison Finney. Formalist evangelicals were concentrated in Northern towns and cities. They were natural allies of the Federalist, Whig, and Republican parties. From among them came many leading abolitionists as well as most of the public voices for moderation on the questions of slavery and states' rights. The irony of the formalists' contribution to American evangelicalism is that they favored the kind of active, moralistic government that most white evangelicals after the Second World War have denounced.

Another three-fifths of American evangelicals were what Johnson calls anti-formalists, generally Methodists, Baptists, and adherents of the new-minted American restorationist denominations, "Christians," Disciples, and Churches of Christ.[31] They tended to come from middle and lower classes, to be stronger in the West and South, and to live in small towns and rural areas. Anti-formalist religion was frankly sectarian, emotional, apocalyptic, and determinedly conversionist. Leading figures were the Baptist preacher John Leland, who was as fervent in his support for Jefferson as he was faithful as an itinerant revivalist; Alexander Campbell, the dominant force in the Restorationist movement; and the Methodist Nathan Bangs (in the earlier, revivalist stage of his career). Anti-formalists were marked by great solicitude for spiritual liberty, and so they were often in the forefront of opposition to the formalists' national plans for promoting education, distributing the Bible, and encouraging social reforms. They tended to be anti-Yankee, anti-Whig, and anti-Republican, and thus Democrats (except in regions where strife with other anti-formalist Democrats pushed some into the arms of Whigs or Republicans). This group is less well studied than the formalists but quite significant. From it came also a number of evangelical anti-abolitionists who held with ever-increasing determination that the Bible sanctioned the black chattel slavery of the Southern states.

Johnson suggests that African-Americans made up about one-fifth of the total evangelical population in the antebellum period. African-Americans were primarily Methodists and Baptists who shared most of the evangelical convictions and many evangelical habits of piety. The politics of African-Americans were of course severely restricted. The evangelicalism of African-Americans was the faith of the disinherited and so very different from either of the two main white segments.

The rest of the Protestants in antebellum America probably did not total as many as the African-Americans. Yet some of them, especially from among the Lutherans but also from smaller German groups of Pietists, were also being pulled into the orbit of formalist evangelicals. Mostly, however, these other Protestants remained isolated by language and their distinctive religious practices. (By 1850, the Roman Catholic church was growing rapidly, but it still counted fewer adherents than either the Methodists or the Baptists, and it was still decades away from exerting a national political influence.)

The crucial historical point is that evangelicals in the national and antebellum periods overwhelmingly accepted the founders' guidelines for religious–political interaction, but differed considerably among themselves as to how best to act within those guidelines. To be sure, a movement did arise toward mid-century promoting the passage of a "Christian Amendment" to the Constitution in order to rectify what especially Presbyterians with strong Scottish connections thought was a mistake in the original in not acknowledging God's sovereignty over the United States. But support for this amendment never caught on.

If most evangelicals agreed that the founders had acted wisely in the Constitution, they nonetheless failed to rally around a single strategy. Internal differences were sharpest on questions pitting local and individual values against national and communal values. For example, every presidential election from the early 1830s featured an effort to portray the candidates as godly individuals. While this effort was more of a challenge for some candidates than for others, the remarkable thing is that Whigs, Republicans, Democrats, Free Soilers, and Know Nothings all were eager for religious, often specifically evangelical, sanction for their contrasting policies. Formalist evangelicals organized massive voluntary activity aimed at rectification of social wrongs, especially intemperance and slavery. But many of these campaigns for social reform were themselves contentious, with anti-formalists resisting the national programs of the formalists. Further disagreement arose when some of the formalists sought government action against intemperance and slavery. The most dramatic illustration of evangelical divisions was the aggressive evangelical support for both Northern Unionism and the Southern Confederacy. Evangelical certainty about the virtue of the North, or of the South, was one of the prime factors making resort to arms such a fearful step.

A summary is now in order to clarify several matters concerning the past which contemporary evangelical Protestant conservatives think has been stolen:

- Evangelicals are mistaken in thinking of the founding period as strongly influenced by the kind of religion that they hold dear.
- Evangelicalism began to exert a large presence in America, in fact, only a generation or more after the founding.
- But the voluntaristic, non- or anti-establishmentarian forms of evangelicalism that came to prevail widely in the nineteenth century were closely bound to the ideals of the founders about the relationship of religion and society.
- That commitment to the founders' guidelines, which very early on, as in the story of Benjamin Franklin at the Constitutional Convention, became a distinctly religious commitment, did not yield a unified evangelical approach to public life. Regional, class, hermeneutical, and intra-evangelical denominational differences created several opposing evangelical political tendencies in the antebellum period.

Back to the Present

If these historical conclusions are even approximately correct, they bear in several ways on the recent political mobilization of evangelical conservative Protestants. First, for analysis of the Constitutional warrants often applied to public disagreements today, better history shows how much it complicates issues to view the founders in their own historical context. The founders' guidelines for religion and society came out of a situation that was much more theistic than some modern liberals admit, but also out of a situation that was much less explicitly Christian than modern evangelicals wish it had been. The founders wanted much less specific religious influence on politics than contemporary evangelical conservative Protestants seek, but they looked to religion for much more support for republican morality than opponents of contemporary evangelicals can tolerate.

While giving due weight to the normative character of the Constitution's reasoning on religion and society, historically informed exegesis of the Constitution requires great finesse. The founders' guidelines for religion and society were written in a situation where it was assumed that denominations in the European fashion wanted a formal stake in ordering government, where religious activity was organized primarily through the churches, where very few institutions of national government touched the daily lives of ordinary citizens, and where almost all varieties of religion in America were either Protestant or Enlightenment modifications of Protestantism. Now we live in a situation where no denominations seek establishment, where tremendous amounts of religious activity are organized outside the churches, where institutions of national government regularly touch day-to-day life in many ways, and where the range of Christian varieties, of other religions, and of no religion is much broader than in the founding period.

These historical realities mean that there is no Constitutional silver bullet to be fired by evangelical conservative Protestants, or by anyone else, for questions of religion and public life. Romantic evangelical recreations of a godly Constitutional elysium undercut honest political debate as much as do procedural libertarian dismissals of the founders' presuppositional theism. To the extent that evangelical political mobilization, or mobilization by any other interest, rests on fraudulent views of real historical situations, responsible political debate is compromised.

A second conclusion concerns evangelicalism more directly. For analysis of the evangelical conservative Protestantism that has mobilized so vigorously over the last generation, better history shows how this mobilization is both traditional and novel. It is traditional for American evangelicals to mobilize for political action. It is novel to synthesize antiformalist and formalist impulses. In the early nineteenth century, formalist and anti-formalist evangelicals opposed each other and so defused the impact of evangelical political energy. Over the past several decades, however, formalist and anti-formalist evangelical tendencies have united. The result is a more concentrated political vision among evangelicals than ever existed in the national or antebellum periods. Contemporary evangelical mobilization is, therefore, fueled by both proprietary and sectarian concerns. The proprietary concern seeks means to coerce Americans to do good. The sectarian concern wants Americans to be left alone. These two impulses are both historically evangelical, but in the early period they often canceled each other out. Today they are joined and so create a movement with a confused political philosophy, but also with an unusual potential for concentrated action.

Third, for analysis of evangelicalism as a religious expression, better history shows how dangerous political involvement can be. It would be especially useful for contemporary evangelical conservative Protestants to realize that evangelical political activity in an earlier United States peaked in the 1850s. In the words of Richard Carwardine: "When during the climax of the campaigns of 1856 and 1860 ministers officiated with equal enthusiasm at revival meetings and at Republican rallies, it was clear that religion and politics had fused more completely than ever before in the American republic."[32] In other words, evangelical religion provided much of the impetus that led to the Civil War.

The trauma of that war leaves much for all Americans to contemplate, but especially evangelical Protestants. In its wake, and in large measure as a result of the energies that had led to the war, evangelicals were not only sundered North and South but also pathetically weakened as a spiritual force in both regions. In the North, varieties of formalist evangelicalism soon fell apart into quarreling factions of fundamentalists and modernists, both of which regained only portions of earlier evangelical vigor. In the South, with largely anti-formalist types of evangelicalism prevailing, there was no inner motivation to confront the sin of racism until forced to do so by a singular combination of African-American evangelical prophecy and Big Government national intervention. In other words, the evangelical energies that led, again in Richard Carwardine's words, to "the cultivation of regional demonologies" were energies that in the end severely compromised the character of evangelicalism itself.[33] A better grasp of history would help modern evangelical conservative Protestants to realize that their predecessors met the challenge of the founders' political guidelines so well that, as a result of fifty years of political action climaxing in the 1860s, evangelicals came close to winning all of America, but only at the cost of nearly losing their own souls.

Finally, for analysis of the political situation more generally, better history shows how thoroughly evangelical political mobilization has been embedded in the founders' solution for religion and politics. In particular, the burden of evangelical politics is to recall the moral calculations of the founders. Evangelical conservative Protestants have played fast and loose with the historical record, but they have gotten one thing right. Even if the founders did not operate from the evangelical assumptions they embrace, the founders did indeed rest their hopes for the future of the United States on the proper functioning of the republican moral calculus. In those terms, evangelical political mobilization today poses a challenge to all Americans that is, in fact, well rooted in what actually did take place. Evangelical conservative Protestants often frame political issues bumptuously, but some of their questions are well grounded in the true history of the American founding. For example, can a republic survive where the virtue of its citizens is no longer a widespread concern? Or is there any agency that has ever proven more effective than the churches at promoting the virtue of citizens? It is clear that evangelicals make a mistake in claiming the founders as their own. It is not clear that they make a mistake in thinking that abandoning the founders' formula for the well-being of a republic would bring the American nation into serious peril.

Notes

1   *Notes of Debates in the Federal Convention of 1787 Reported by James Madison*, Bicentennial Edition (New York: Norton, 1987, orig. 1966), pp. 209–10.

2   Christopher Collier, *Roger Sherman's Connecticut: Yankee Politics and the American Revolution* (Middletown, CT: Wesleyan University Press, 1971), p. 327.

3   Marshall and Manuel, with Anna Wilson Fishel, *From Sea to Shining Sea for Children* (Grand Rapids, MI: Fleming H. Revell, 1993), pp. 18–19; Marshall and Manuel, with Anna Wilson Fishel, *The Light and the Glory for Children* (Tarrytown, NY: Fleming H. Revell, 1992), p. 156.

4   Franklin to Stiles, March 9, 1790, *Benjamin Franklin: Representative Selections*, rev. edn, eds Chester E. Jorgenson and Frank Luther Mott (New York: Hill & Wang, 1962), p. 508.

5   For the first printing of the story, see *The Records of the Federal Convention of 1787*, 3 volumes, ed. Max Farrand (New Haven, CT: Yale University Press, 1911), *volume 3*, p. 471; and for the disavowals, Madison to Jared Sparks, April 8, 1831, and Madison to Thomas S. Grimké, January 6, 1834, in ibid., pp. 499–500, 531.

6   David W. Bebbington, *Evangelicalism in Modern Britain: a History from the 1730s to the 1980s* (London: Unwin Hyman, 1989), pp. 2–17.

7   See above, chapter 2.

8   Table 9.3 is adapted from John Green, Lyman Kellstedt, James Guth, and Corwin Smidt, "Who elected Clinton: a collision of values," *First Things*, August/September 1997, pp. 35–40, esp. p. 37.

9   I owe this information to a dissertation in progress at the University of Chicago Divinity School by Kristen Burroughs Kraakevik.

10   See, most recently, Billy Graham, *Just As I Am: the Autobiography of Billy Graham* (San Francisco: HarperCollins, 1997), chapters 22 and 24.

11   See especially Joel A. Carpenter, *Revive Us Again: the Reawakening of American Fundamentalism* (New York: Oxford University Press, 1997).

12   Steve Bruce, *The Rise and Fall of the New Christian Right: Conservative Protestant Politics in America, 1978–1988* (Oxford: Clarendon Press, 1988), p. 30.

13   Robert Wuthnow, *The Restructuring of American Religion: Society and Faith Since World War II* (Princeton, NJ: Princeton University Press, 1988).

14   On how these religious habits influenced politics, see especially Leonard I. Sweet, "Nineteenth-century evangelicalism," in *Encyclopedia of the American Religious Experience*, 3 volumes, eds Charles Lippy and Peter Williams (New York: Charles Scribner's, 1988), *volume 2*, pp. 875–99.

15   For example, David Barton, *Spirit of the American Revolution* (Aledo, TX: Wallbuilders, 1994), and *Original Intent in the Courts, the Constitution and Religion* (Aledo, TX: Wallbuilders); Tim F. LaHaye, *The Battle for the Mind* (Old Tappan, NJ: Revell, 1980) and *The Battle for the Family* (Old Tappan, NJ: Revell, 1982); Francis A. Schaeffer, *A Christian Manifesto* (Westchester, IL: Crossway, 1981); and John Whitehead, *The Second American Revolution* (Elgin, IL: David C. Cook, 1982).

16   Moore and Kramnick, *The Godless Constitution: the Case Against Religious Correctness* (New York: Norton, 1996), is the work of sophisticated scholars but displays so much exasperation at the populist historical simplicities of evangelical Protestant authors as to commit simplicities of liberal individualism in rebuttal.

17   John M. Murrin, "Religion and politics in America from the first settlements to the Civil War," in *Religion and American Politics*, ed. Mark A. Noll (New York: Oxford University Press, 1990), p. 31.

18   Capsule biographies, with denominational affiliations, are found in M. E. Bradford, *A Worthy Company: the Dramatic Story of the Men Who Founded Our Country* (Westchester, IL: Crossway, 1988).

19   The strongest argument for a Protestant presence are Alan Heimert, *Religion and the American Mind from the Great Awakening to the Revolution* (Cambridge, MA: Harvard University Press, 1966), and Barry Alan Shain, *The Myth of American Individualism: the Protestant Origins of American Political Thought* (Princeton, NJ: Princeton University Press, 1994), but both Heimert and Shain recognize other influences as well. Solid treatments suggesting even more intermingling of sacred and secular categories are Nathan O. Hatch, *The Sacred Cause of Liberty: Republican Thought and the Millennium in Revolutionary New England* (New Haven, CT: Yale Uni-

versity Press, 1977); Patricia U. Bonomi, *Under the Cope of Heaven: Religion, Society, and Politics in Colonial America* (New York: Oxford University Press, 1986); Ellis Sandoz, *A Government of Laws: Political Theory, Religion, and the American Founding* (Baton Rouge: Louisiana State University Press, 1990); Ronald J. Hoffman and Peter J. Albert, eds, *Religion in a Revolutionary Age* (Charlottesville: University Press of Virginia, 1994); and Dale S. Kuehne, *The Design of Heaven; Massachusetts Congregationalist Political Thought, 1760–1790* (Columbia: University of Missouri Press, 1996). For a popular text arguing for much more explicitly Christian influence on the founding documents, see Gary Amos and Richard Gardiner, *Never Before in History: America's Inspired Birth* (Dallas, TX: Haughton, 1998).

20   Bernard Bailyn, ed., *The Debate on the Constitution*, 2 volumes (New York: Library of America, 1993).
21   Roger Finke and Rodney Start, "How the upstart sects won America, 1776–1850," *Journal for the Scientific Study of Religion*, 18, 1989, pp. 27–44.
22   Stephen Marini, "The government of God: religion in revolutionary America," unpublished MS; Russell E. Richey, Kenneth E. Rowe, and Jean Miller Schmidt, eds, *Perspectives on American Methodism* (Nashville, TN: Kingswood, 1993), section 1, "The founding period."
23   Nathan O. Hatch, *The Democratization of American Christianity* (New Haven, CT: Yale University Press, 1989); Russell E. Richey, *Early American Methodism* (Bloomington: Indiana University Press, 1991).
24   For a survey, see Sydney E. Ahlstrom, *A Religious History of the American People* (New Haven, CT: Yale University Press, 1972), part IV, "The golden day of democratic evangelicalism."
25   West, *The Politics of Revelation and Reason: Religion and Civic Life in the New Nation* (Lawrence: University Press of Kansas, 1996). West expands upon solid accounts by, among others, Thomas J. Curry, *The First Freedoms: Church and State in America to the Passage of the First Amendment* (New York: Oxford University Press, 1986), pp. 193–222; and John F. Wilson, "Religion, government, and power in the new American nation," in *Religion and American Politics*, op. cit., n. 17, pp. 77–91.
26   See Mark A. Noll, *One Nation Under God? Christian Faith and Political Action in America* (San Francisco: Harper & Row, 1988), chapter 5, "The campaign of 1800: fire without light."
27   See Richard R. John, *Spreading the News: the American Postal System from Franklin to Morse* (Cambridge, MA: Harvard University Press, 1995), pp. 169–205; William G. McLoughlin, *Cherokees and Missionaries, 1789–1839* (New Haven, CT: Yale University Press, 1984).
28   Richard J. Carwardine, *Evangelicals and Politics in Antebellum America* (New Haven, CT: Yale University Press, 1993).

29 Curtis D. Johnson, *Redeeming America: Evangelicals and the Road to Civil War* (Chicago: Ivan R. Dee, 1993).
30 See Kathryn Teresa Long, *The Revival of 1857–58* (New York: Oxford University Press, 1998).
31 The key account of antiformalist religion in the early United States is Nathan O. Hatch, *The Democratization of American Christianity* (New Haven, CT: Yale University Press, 1989).
32 Carwardine, *Evangelicals and Politics in Antebellum America*, op. cit., n. 28, p. 322.
33 Ibid., p. 452.

Part III
Opinion

10

Evangelical Politics: a Better Way

Is there diadem as Monarch,
That his brow adorns?
Yea, a crown, in very surety,
but of thorns.
　　　John Mason Neale (1862)

With the last three chapters of the book, we move further away from simply describing evangelicalism to my own evangelical interpretations of that phenomenon. The first of these chapters has been set up by the analysis of chapter 9, where I try to show why modern evangelical political mobilization both makes a great deal of sense and causes so many problems. In this chapter, I explore the difference it could make for evangelical Christians to base their politics on evangelical theology, specifically on what they regularly teach about the person and work of Christ.

Self-consciously Christian efforts in political thought and practice have historically featured biblical themes of divine creation, human fallenness, God-given human capacity, the kingly rule of Christ, and the restoration of creation. Such efforts have often been extraordinarily beneficial; I do not think they should be replaced. But perhaps they can be supplemented, deepened, and broadened by specific attention to a theme central in evangelical history, namely the redemptive work of Christ. Because God is integral and because every aspect of God's revelation to humanity flows from divine integrity, Christian dogma should also be integral – its various pieces should depend upon each other. Christian soteriology traditionally has featured human sinfulness, the work of Christ on the cross, and the saving ministry of the Holy Spirit. But in order to grasp the significance of these realities, it is necessary also to see them in relationship to general considerations of creation, the church, divinely ordained ideals for social relationships, and the kingly rule of Christ. In the same way, when seeking to formulate principles for Christian politics, it is entirely appropriate to feature considerations of humanity in general as created by God and ruled by God, but these matters also deserve to be considered in light of how God provides special redemption for Christian believers.

At this point it is necessary to proceed cautiously. In speaking of Christ and his work, it is important not to identify "Christ" only with the cross, the resurrection, and the redemption of God's people. Jesus Christ is the redeemer, but the same Jesus Christ is also the incarnate Son of God, the second person of the Trinity, through whom and for whom all things were created in the beginning and in whom all things will at the last day be offered humbly to the Father. The point in urging fuller consideration of the specifically soteriological aspects of Christ and his work is not to contrast a suffering and redeeming Christ with an otherwise natural order of reason, natural revelation, and the general providence of God the Father. Rather, the point is to underscore the ineluctably organic harmony among creation, judgment, redemption, and eschatological fulfillment. A plea to focus attention on the redeeming Christ is not, therefore, an appeal to neglect or deny the creating Christ, the ruling Christ, or the eschatological Christ. It is, rather, an appeal to seek the resplendent plentitude of Christ and his work, and so to err on the side of neither a world-denying pietism nor a redemption-denying immanentism.[1]

Those Christians who confess that Christ and his work must have a this-worldly significance along with its other-worldly significance are precisely the believers best situated to consider Christian soteriology in connection with politics, since they will not be tempted to swing to the extreme of an other-worldly pietism. At the same time, however, it is important for Christians of whatever sort to consider the ways that soteriology is foundational to human relations with God. In order to be more faithful to the character of Christianity itself, in other words, efforts to formulate a Christian politics may well need to supplement consideration of God as creator with consideration of God as trinitarian redeemer. To images of the believer as saint ruling alongside Christ must be added images of the believer as sinner redeemed solely by the grace of God in Christ. Alongside the general principles of God's written word, a Christian politics should also heed closely what is written about the Word made flesh. In other words, when thinking about politics, it is worth considering what the leaven of Lutheran cross-centeredness can add to an already nutritious lump of Calvinist kingly rule.[2] Put most simply, I want to explore the difference it might make if Christian politics featured Christ.

The effort to think like a Christian about politics is a worthy task for believers in all times and places, but it is an especially important task today. The United States is witnessing a resurgence of evangelical polit-ical action unlike anything seen since the years before the Civil War when several political parties with distinct evangelical aspirations made their mark on the national scene. Whether groups like the Christian Coalition live up to their name as "Christian" is, of course, an important ques-tion,[3] but no one can deny the importance of the Coalition, or of other centers of Christian political involvement found among Catholics, Protestants, and in alliances transcending even the historic division between Catholics and Protestants.[4] In Canada the Reform Party – which burst onto the national scene with surprising success in that country's next-to-last federal election – features a more explicit link to specifically Christian concerns than has any Canadian political body since the rise of Social Credit and the Cooperative Commonwealth Federation over fifty years ago.[5] Elsewhere around the world Christian concerns are now more visible than anyone could ever have thought possible even a decade ago. Whether one thinks of the political awakening of the huge Zionist churches in South Africa, behind-the-scenes efforts to bridge Catholic–Protestant divisions in Northern Ireland, the apocalyptic fears of Norwegian pietists concerning the European Union, the reawaken-ing of Orthodox political aspirations in Eastern Europe and the former Soviet Union, the political role of pentecostals in selected Latin American countries, the influence of a reforming Catholicism in other Latin regions, the surprising contribution of Christians to the struggle for Palestinian liberation, or the lucid assessments of political realities from Pope John Paul II – the world is witnessing a remarkable resur-gence of Christian political activity. At such a moment, an effort to think about the significance for politics of the person and work of Christ is as timely as it is important.

The chapter begins with a general argument, that apprehension of the person and work of Christ, within the context of the Trinity, should be the starting point for all Christian reflection, including reflection on politics by evangelical Christians. It then goes on to suggest that, for

neglecting the bearing of Christology on politics, the evangelical practice of politics in America (and elsewhere) has often fallen short of
Christian ideals. It closes with suggestions for how concentration on a
fuller range of Christological realities, especially the meaning of the
Incarnation, may improve both attitudes in political situations and
theorizing about the nature of politics.

The Christian Starting Point

Apprehension of the person and work of Christ, within the context of
the Trinity, should be the starting point for all Christian reflection,
including Christian reflection on politics.

In the eye of God, creation comes first, then fall, then redemption,
then at the end the restoration of all things. Christian politics is often,
and profitably, constructed by following reality as God experiences
reality. So perceived, the creation of humanity includes a potential for
political life which, if pursued faithfully and if the effects of the fall are
checked, contributes to human flourishing. In these terms, the potential
for a just political order is one of the many gifts of God bestowed upon
all humanity in the creation. The Christian's task is to follow the trajec-
tory of creation and work toward a fulfillment of the political good
that God originally formed and continues, by his providence, to make
possible. In this picture, sin and its effects, as well as grace and its effects,
can be taken quite seriously, for sin counteracts the potential for good
that God made possible in creation, while grace enables the repentant
sinner to promote political justice as one way of serving God. In this
view, Christian politics is primarily an effort to realize the potential built
into the creation and to serve God by doing his will in the political
sphere.

The great virtues of this approach have been exemplified in various
ways by the Thomistic tradition, by John Calvin, John Knox and the
Scottish reformers, by the English and American Puritans, by the Dutch
Calvinist tradition culminating in the work of Abraham Kuyper
(1837–1920), and by modern neo-Thomists. What these people and
movements share is a desire to employ God's own vision as displayed in
a perfect creation and in what God has revealed about the eschatological restoration of that creation, in order to forge an understanding
of politics and to shape an agenda for political practice. The virtues

inherent in this approach have been most apparent when its proponents practice politics as part of what the Heidelberg Catechism calls the "gratitude I owe to God for . . . redemption."

I find no problem with this general approach as such, if only those who formulate a Christian politics on the basis of creation and the restoration of creation remember who they are. Christians, that is, should never forget that they are not God. Rather, it is a central teaching of their religion to remember that they are sinners saved by grace. Moreover, they are saved by God's grace as fully displayed in the Incarnate Christ. And the Incarnate Christ, in the classic formula of the Chalcedonian Definition (AD 451) is at once fully God and fully human – "this one and the same Christ . . . made known in two natures." Each of these realities is directly or indirectly an aspect of Christology. Each is also big with implications for the understanding and practice of politics.

Believers know that they are not God. Nowhere is this knowledge sharper than when Christians are measured against the command of Christ to be perfect as the Father in heaven is perfect (Matt. 5:48). Believers realize most concretely their separateness from God, that is, when they see themselves most clearly as sinners and realize most keenly their need of the Savior. In fact, it is a distinctly evangelical assertion that until individuals see themselves as sinners in need of a savior, they do not see anything clearly at all. Philosophers and theologians debate the noetic effects of the fall – the toll that a fallen condition takes on the human ability to see selves, the world, and God clearly.[6] And well they should, for the persistent tendency of unbelief is to treat the self (or sometimes one's group) as if it were God and thereby to lose perspective on all things – on God, on self, on our group, and on the world besides. To be a Christian is to confess, joyfully, that God is God and I am not.

The leaven that this soteriological reality adds to the political lump is the reminder that, however much God may have made possible the good potential for politics before humanity fell into sin, all humans experience the creation from their position as those who are alienated by sin from God. The implication must be that, when Christians define the potential for politics as rooted in divine creation and pointed toward eschatological fulfillment, they do so with the awareness that their grasp of politics remains the grasp of a creature graciously granted partial insight into the purposes of God. Human knowledge, even redeemed human knowledge, can never be divine in its fullness, its purity, and its perfection. Accordingly, for Christians who know that they are saved by grace, there will be no political judgments rendered as if from Mt Sinai, there will be no pronouncement of doom on political opponents, and there will be no promise of paradise for choosing a particular political path – since judgments of Sinai, pronouncements of doom, and promises of paradise are powers reserved to God alone.

A similar benefit arises for evangelicals when they continually remind themselves of the keystone of their religion – not only are humans not God, but Christian believers are also sinners saved by grace. The category distinction is simple, but profound in its effects. At the start, in the middle, and at the end of a Christian's pilgrimage, evangelicals assert that the Christian is reconciled to God and the purposes of God by God alone and never because of his or her own perfection. The implications for politics of this realism – this recognition that perfection awaits the life to come – are as simple as they are elusive. A properly Christian politics will display humility, a willingness to question one's own motives, and the expectation that reform of political vision will always be needed because even Christian politics is carried out by individuals who know they are still sinners, however glad they are to be sinners saved by grace.

It makes a more subtle, but no less important, political difference to realize that the means of redemption – the reason why Christians know that they are not God and that they are sinners saved by grace – is the Incarnation of God the Son. If the believer's entire apprehension of the world is shaped by the need for a savior, and if God offers himself as that savior, then the means by which God offers the savior should affect apprehension of the entire world, including the world of politics. For the purposes of political reflection, one of the most striking Christian affirmations about the Incarnation is its miraculous combination of the particular and the universal. The nature of that miraculous combination – as well as hints about the political implications of that combination – have been put well by the Scottish missiologist Andrew Walls:

> Christ took flesh and was made man in a particular time and place, family, nationality, tradition and customs and sanctified them, while still being for all men in every time and place. Wherever he is taken by the people of any day, time and place, he sanctifies that culture – he is living in it.

And no other group of Christians has any right to impose in his name a set of assumptions about life determined by another time and place. But to acknowledge this is not to forget that there is another, and equally important, force at work among us. Not only does God in His mercy take people as they are: He takes them to transform them into what He wants them to be.[7]

To extrapolate Walls's insight more specifically for political purposes, the nature of the Incarnation suggests that a fully Christian politics will incorporate the full weight of contingent circumstances, developments, and events in particular cultures as well as the general truths of the Christian revelation.

Believers who see the way in which the Incarnation both dignifies particular cultures and brings a universal saving truth may expect, for example, that political justice in the new Republic of South Africa will incorporate aspects of traditional tribal hierarchialism as well as aspects of Western democratic capitalism. Those who promote the spread of justice in relations between church and state for the rapidly changing nations of Eastern Europe might expect to find aspects of the region's historic link between religion and the state functioning with, instead of simply in opposition to, properly universal ideals of religious liberty. Americans concerned about opportunities for Christian values in public life may well be able to learn a lesson from Canadian experience where, for at least much of the twentieth century and at least in comparison with the United States, citizens have been less preoccupied with grand national strategies and more concerned about working out procedures for education, health care, and labor legislation at provincial and local levels. The result is much less uniformity in Canadian public life as a whole – Newfoundland, for example, has until recently funded its primary and secondary public education through a system of church-sponsored schools, while some western provinces provide tuition payment but not capital investment to church schools. But also by comparison with the United States, the Canadian situation provides a better balance between local circumstances and broad national standards. It is too crass to say that the Canadian pattern embodies Christological realities where the United States does not, but not extreme to say that, in this one instance, the structure of Canadian political life tends more in the direction of the combination of particular and universal embodied in the Incarnation than does American political life.

If it is valuable to let the Incarnation's combination of local reality and universal truth shape Christian political expectation, so too might it be possible to allow reflection on the very character of the Incarnation to influence thinking about politics. Such reflection, however, can be disconcerting, for it features the well known doubleness of classical Christological dogma: that Jesus Christ was fully God, fully human, and – though fully human and divine – one integral human being. The reality of this dogma as well as the difficulty in relating its tension has been well sketched recently by the theologian Gabriel Fackre who, in recommending the work of Kierkegaard, Sergius Bulgakov, and Donald Baillie, suggests that their writing "pointed to antinomies all over scripture and Christian teaching, paradigmatically in the doctrine of the incarnation, and it noted that the assertion of mutually exclusive propositions – humanity and divinity in one person – never satisfies human reason, which is always interested in relaxing the tension in one direction or the other."[8]

The political point from such realizations – that a fully orthodox view of Christ affirms a doubleness with which human reason has been historically uncomfortable – is that believers should not be surprised to find a corresponding doubleness in political life. If, that is, the Incarnation stands at the heart of reality – or at least reality as it can only be perceived by sinners saved by grace – then perhaps political reality may display a doubleness hard to fathom by conventional human categories.

For example, Christians might conclude, with an eye toward the Incarnate Christ positioned at the very heart of the universe, that many political judgments should be as complex as they possibly can be – as a possible instance, that for preserving a constitutional system through the great depression and the Second World War, Franklin D. Roosevelt was one of the United States' greatest presidents, but also for expanding nearly without limit the power of government over against other God-given spheres of authority, FDR was at exactly the same time one of the worst presidents.

Or, again with an eye toward the Incarnate Christ positioned at the heart of the universe, it may be true that Christian parents have every right to work for justice with respect to the use of public funds in the education of their children, but also true that Christian parents have no unalienable rights whatsoever for themselves or their children.

I do not want to dwell on these examples. I do want to make the point that if the heart of the Christian religion affirms the cosmic significance of a single person who is fully divine and fully human, and if believers affirm that this religion shapes an entire view of the world, then such odd conjunctions of apparently contradictory realities can only be expected in politics as in other spheres of life.

In summary to this point, I am suggesting that the human need for salvation is central to all lives, and because it is central to all lives, so too should it be central to the human perception of the world, including the political world. Since Christians claim the means of redemption is an Incarnation that legitimates both cultural particularity and universal absolutes, so ought a Christian politics to make room for local particularities alongside universal absolutes. Finally, since the Incarnate Christ stands at the center of existence as humans must perceive that existence, since the Incarnate Christ is central for the life of every Christian, and since the Incarnation embodies the miraculous fact of divine and human natures joined in one person "without confusion, without change, without division, and without separation," so might we expect in every human sphere – including politics – to confront situations where two apparently different (or even contradictory) things are present indissolvably in one actual reality.

Reflection on creation and the restoration of creation has been a rich source for the construction of Christian political thought and action. In proposing to enlist Christology directly for politics, I do not see the need to abandon any of the achievements gained by concentrating on creation and its restoration. It may be, however, that those who quite properly exploit the God-given realities of created political potential will do so even more fully – and with more occasion to praise the name of God – by seasoning images of Christ ruling at the head of the saints over a restored creation with images of Christ suffering for the saints on the cross.

Evangelical Politics Has Neglected Christology to Its Peril

For neglecting the bearing of Christology on politics, the evangelical practice of politics in America (and elsewhere) has often been anti-Christian.

The practical importance of the cross for politics can be illustrated in the history of almost any place on the globe where Christians have constituted a large enough interest group to exert real political influence. Believers who constitute distinct minorities in their nations or cultures have not needed to be instructed about the importance of the cross. Theocracy is usually not an option where no opportunity exists to exercise power. By contrast, in those situations where Christians either have exercised power or have had a history of exercising power, the implications for a politics of the cross are often set aside in favor of a vision of a restored creation ruled over by Christ and the saints. Consequently, the importance of the cross may be greatest precisely in those times and places where believers have had the most chance to exercise power. Such chances have included many venues in the Christian middle ages, many situations in the Orthodox regions of Central and Eastern Europe, most of the European nations in the immediate wake of the Reformation and the Counter-Reformation, and much of the history played out over the past few centuries in the United States and Canada.

What these situations reveal is a conundrum. Christian life focused around the cross is a motive force that propels churches and their adherents into dominant political positions. Yet once in dominant positions, "Christian politics" usually features themes of righteousness, holiness, and commandment-keeping more closely associated with doctrines of a restored creation rather than the themes of humility, self-abasement, and repentance associated with the cross. To put complicated historical situations much too crudely, there would have been no opportunity for the political influence of the Roman state in the church during the fourth century if there had not existed remarkable success in proclaiming the new message of a crucified God throughout the Mediterranean world of the second and third centuries. There would have been no rise of an imperial papacy in the twelfth and thirteenth centuries if there had not been a movement of monastic renewal energized by thoughts like Bernard of Clairvaux's on the sacred head of Christ now wounded. There would have been no Protestant regimes in sixteenth-century Europe if it had not been for the effective proclamation to unworthy sinners of justification by free grace. Later in European history there would have been in the Netherlands no neo-Calvinist Christian Democratic movement seeking political power if leaders like Abraham Kuyper had not been overwhelmed by experiences of God's grace. Coming closer to North American experience, there would have been no thought of setting up the kingly rule of Christ in Scotland had not John Knox and his colleagues so effectively proclaimed the authority of the crucified Christ. There would have been no attempt at Puritan hegemony under Oliver Cromwell in England and no successful establishment of a Puritan way of life in New England if there had not been several generations of effective Puritan preachers who knew how to call wounded consciences to the Great Shepherd. There would have been no effort in nineteenth-century Protestant America to protect the nation from Roman Catholics, Southern Europeans, Asians, and other "aliens" if earnest evangelical preachers had not so successfully proclaimed in towns, villages, and fields the message of a merciful savior. There would have been no biblical defense of a "Southern way of life" in the decades before the Civil War if multitudes of Southerners had not found forgiveness for their sin through the biblical message of Christ. Nineteenth-century Canada never could have aspired to the status of "His Dominion from sea to sea" had not several generations of Canadian evangelists called their fellows to the self-denial of conversion. And, one presumes, there would be no Christian Coalition today if masses of ordinary Americans had not experienced what the pollsters call a "born-again experience" or an "intense religious experience focused on the person of Jesus Christ." Historically considered, the effort to mount an effective Christian politics – the effort to guide society in the kingly name of Christ – has been unthinkable without a prior commitment to the work of Christ on the cross.

Yet once aspiring to make a difference in the political sphere – once set on a course of defending or propagating a vision of reality generated by an experience of the suffering Christ – believers regularly push to the side memory of Christ's two natures, of his suffering, and of his redeeming work. Righteousness rather than forgiveness, duty rather than repentance, become the watchwords. To be sure, this situation is not entirely misguided. It is a political analogy to the pilgrimage of the individual believer from regeneration and conversion through sanctification toward glorification. Yet just as the redeeming work of Christ remains important for the proper outworking of sanctification, so too the cross of Christ should remain important for the ones who, having been redeemed, make an attempt to rule in Christ's name.

Unfortunately, the memory of realities associated with the cross has usually faded rapidly in American experience once evangelical believers turn their direct attention from what constitutes them as Christians to what needs to be done politically. So it certainly was in the decades before the Civil War with the Anti-Masonic, Liberty, and American (or Know Nothing) political parties. Christian belief and energy contributed substantially to the creation of each of these parties. Christian zeal was responsible for the remarkable, if short-lived, success each of them enjoyed. The organizers of these Christian political parties had grasped firmly the intensity of the mandate to make the kingdoms of this world into the kingdom of our Lord and of his Christ. Unfortunately, however, they missed the reality that they were themselves redeemed by the Lord of creation, that the political opponents whom they demonized were individuals for whom Christ died, and that none of the defining issues around which they organized were as straightforwardly simple as they thought. Evaluated in Christian terms that embrace both cross and crown, those Christian political parties were half right, and therefore doubly dangerous. They took seriously the need to exalt Christian standards in the political world, but they erred grievously (and in so doing may have damaged the cause of Christianity itself) by assuming that they had moved beyond the need of the cross.

Christological themes have regularly played a major role in the mainstream of American political life. In fact, two of the most dramatic pronouncements in all American political rhetoric exploited powerful references to Christ. When William Jennings Bryan addressed the Democratic National Convention in Chicago during its platform debate in 1896, he was still a political stripling who had not lost any of his idealism by serving in Congress or as a newspaper editor in Omaha. His rousing address attacked efforts to keep gold as the only support of United States currency even as it urged, as a way of helping debtor farmers and small-scale entrepreneurs, the free coinage of silver. Bryan's reference to christological realities in the peroration of his speech was as dramatic as it could be: "If they dare to come out in the open field and defend the gold standard as a good thing, we will fight them to the uttermost. Having behind us the producing masses of this nation and the world, supported by the commercial interests, the laboring interests, and the toilers everywhere, we will answer their demand for a gold standard by saying to them: You shall not press down upon the brow of labor this crown of thorns, you shall not crucify mankind upon a cross of gold."[9]

Only sixteen years later, in 1912, again in Chicago, another crusading idealist also enlisted a christological image as the concluding metaphor for a powerful political oration. On June 17, the very day that the Republican National Convention choose William Howard Taft as its presidential nominee over Theodore Roosevelt, Roosevelt responded with a stem-winding speech to his supporters. In this address Roosevelt pledged himself to fight a no holds barred battle against the knavery of political bosses and the corruption of crooked businessmen. He ended with these words: "We fight in honorable fashion for the good of mankind; fearless of the future; unheeding of our individual fates; with unflinching hearts and undimmed eyes; we stand at Armageddon, and we battle for the Lord."[10]

A comparison between these two speeches is instructive. Theodore Roosevelt employed the language of the ruling Christ leading his faithful followers into battle against a well defined foe. Unlike Roosevelt, Bryan employed the language of the cross. But like Roosevelt, Bryan was using Christological language to inspire supporters for a fight against hosts of wickedness that threatened Bryan and his fellow saints from without.

Bryan's use of cross-language in the same militant manner that Roosevelt used crown-language is far from uncommon in Western history. The most important precedent was the Crusades, where believers "took the cross" as a symbol of their desire to push Islam out of the Holy Land. For our purposes, it is important to note that Bryan's use of the cross as a symbol inspiring a crusade against an external foe is by no means rare in specifically evangelical experience.

The two best known hymns surviving from the era of the Civil War, for example, both employ christology to these ends. The Presbyterian minister George Duffield wrote "Stand up, stand up for Jesus! Ye soldiers of the cross" in the heat of revival in 1858, but it became a much beloved hymn in the Union army.[11] The best known anthem of the Civil War itself, "The Battle Hymn of the Republic," written by Unitarian Julia Ward Howe, raised the employment of gospel- or cross-focused language to a high art. The hymn not only linked Christ's birth "in the beauty of the lilies" with the need for dying "to make men free." It also jumbled gospel and self-exertion, grace and works, spiritual tyranny and temporal tyranny, with breath-taking abandon, as well illustrated in one of the hymn's later verses:

I have read a fiery gospel writ in burnish'd rows of steel;
"As ye deal with my condemners, so with you my grace shall deal!"

Let the hero, born of women, crush the serpent with his heal,
Since God is marching on.

One contemporary reference can illustrate the way that Christology continues to be put to use in this combative style. Following the defeat in November 1994 of a Florida referendum that would have expanded casino gambling in that state, a leader of the anti-gambling forces was quoted as saying that, when it comes to gambling, "the ballot box is like the cross to Dracula."[12]

These Christological references share a common form. The one who employs the image is beset by sinister foes. Images from the story of Jesus are presumed to resonate with sacred power. The speaker identifies himself or herself with Christ's own struggle against the hosts of evil. Christological images link the speaker's viewpoint with the righteousness of Christ. So connected, the speaker and the speaker's cause share, at least rhetorically, the supreme sacred power evoked by the Christological image.

Regarded theologically, the use of these images is problematic. In classical theology, Christ does manifest great power – defeating sin, death, and the devil, while establishing the church as an institution secure eternally against its raging foes. But it is the means by which Christ exercises his power that makes Christological rhetoric a curious motif in American political battles. In the gospels, Jesus says that "the Son of Man came . . . to give his life" (Matt. 20:28). He said that God the Son had no place by night to lay his head (Matt. 8:20). In the climactic hour of his earthly existence, Jesus rebuked those who would fight on his behalf. In the great hymn found in the second chapter of Philippians, Christ at his incarnation gives up the prerogatives of deity and assumes the inauspicious form of an ordinary servant. In the New Testament, as opposed to American political rhetoric, Jesus *accepts* a crown of thorns and also *welcomes* the agonizing shame of the cross. Christ indeed promises to appear in the last day with power and great glory, but only in the last day. In the interim – in anticipation of that last day – the ones who would be Christians are urged to take up their cross and follow Jesus – not to victory, but to the denial of their own selves. If, therefore, the Christological metaphor put to use by Protestants in American politics is followed back to their source, if in particular the cross is valued as it is valued in Scripture, it is hard to recognize the combative American Christology as anything but a perversion.

My point is not a radical one. I do not hold that all believers must imitate literally the self-abnegating Christ or so concentrate on the passive repentance required to find justifying grace as to abandon the political sphere. Such radicalism flows from an artificial pietism that seriously unbalances the biblical account of Jesus and his work. The suffering Savior is, in fact, also the Ruling Son. The kingdom that must be entered as a child offers full and satisfying work for adults. The point, rather, is that the sort of Christian politics seen so often in America, but not only in America, should more accurately be styled "so-called Christian politics." A Christian politics that forgets the cross, a Christian politics that neglects the realities of redemption, a Christian politics that assumes a God-like stance toward the world – is a Christian politics that has abandoned Christ.

Implications

What would a Christian politics look like that remembered Christ, that recalled the cross with the crown, that kept in mind the realities of justification while going on to the tasks of sanctification? I suspect that, from the outside, a politics that is Christian in this sense would not look too different from responsible political action advanced by, say, Catholics, Calvinists, Anabaptists, or many kinds of evangelicals. It would be a politics attempting to discover, for any specific problem or in any general situation, the path of justice and the appropriately just means to advance the cause of justice.

To be sure, a Christ-centered politics would feature the themes that loom large in the Scriptures that Christ taught, recommended, and embodied. Themes like the necessity for rulers to act fairly or like the need to protect those who cannot protect themselves are so richly displayed in the entirety of Scripture as in the work of Christ himself that it is reasonable to expect these themes to dominate any truly Christian politics. By the same standard of biblical norms, a truly Christian politics will also tend to concentrate much more diligently on the rights of others than on one's own rights.[13] But within such basic biblical guidelines, the practicalities of a Christian politics alert to the cross may not differ all that much from a Christian politics inspired by the vision of the ruling Christ.

Where awareness of the cross, and the circle of redemptive realities for which it stands, may make more of a difference, however, is in *attitudes* carried into the political fray and in *perspectives* on the nature of politics itself.

Attitudes

Attitudes – mental and emotional expectations, levels and qualities of commitments, judgments of self and others – must, by the nature of the case, be strongly influenced by one's view of Christ. To put the historical situation in very general terms, Christian approaches to politics within four of the most important Christian traditions can be said to be marked by relatively straightforward attitudes. In their own way, Orthodox, Roman Catholic, Calvinist, and Anabaptist politics have involved relatively straightforward efforts to define, and then to preserve, as under God, the political good. Orthodox, Roman Catholics, Calvinists, and Anabaptists have, of course, differed with each other and among themselves as to what political goals are most important and how they should be preserved. But they have resembled each other in the forthright, clear, and often courageous way they have defined and pursued, as Christians, the political ends that their visions of the faith spell out.

A Lutheran perspective has, at least on occasions, been different. The Lutheran perspective is marked, as historian and editor James Nuechterlein recently put it, by its "dialectic theological framework." As Nuechterlein explains what he means by Lutheran dialectics, we begin to see why a Lutheran perspective cannot foster the straightforward approaches to political matters that, by contrast, are more commonly found among Orthodox, Roman Catholics, Calvinists, and Anabaptists, and also why that perspective might assist American evangelicals. "The Lutheran dialectic," according to Nuechterlein, "takes a variety of forms: the emphasis on the Law/Gospel distinction as hermeneutical principle and theological guide; the understanding of social ethics and responsibilities according to the doctrine of the Two Kingdoms; the conception of the human condition as essentially *Simul* – we are at once, Luther insisted, sinners and saints, enemies of God and yet fully redeemed participants in His eternal glory." Not everyone will agree with Nuechterlein that "these distinctly Lutheran perspectives . . . command attention because they conform to the reality of our lives."

Yet within other major Christian traditions, believers are aware of how difficult it can be to systematize the different aspects of biblical revelation and how much inner conflict can arise in living out the various dimensions of Christ-centered faith. And so, even if others cannot agree with Nuechterlein's value judgment about the Lutheran theological difference, they know what experiences he is talking about when he claims that the Lutheran dialectics

> fit the rough contrariness of our experience; they are at once contradictory and true. We yearn to be followers of God even as we rebel against His injunctions. The Lutheran *Simul* captures our reality better than do visions of perfection or divinization or anticipation of the eschaton. Lutheranism engages us in our doubled condition and reminds us of its founder's central insight, confessed as he died, that we are all beggars before God. . . . [I]t is within the Lutheran tradition that the antinomies of the faith have been most vibrantly kept alive."[14]

Again, my concern is not with an evaluation of Lutheranism *per se* as it is with the great value a Lutheran leaven might bring to political reasoning rooted in other Christian traditions. Indeed, political history since the sixteenth-century Reformation suggests that, if left to itself, the Lutheran leaven can sometimes decay into political passivity or encourage an other-worldly pietism that makes very little contribution to living out the gospel in the world.[15] The point, rather, is to suggest that other Christian traditions which encourage a more straightforward, conclusive political thinking and more self-confidently direct political action would benefit from *adding* an element of Lutheran dialectic to the politics derived from their own theologies.

Here are two examples of how Lutheran leaven, proceeding from a concentrated focus on the person and work of Christ, might refine the attitudes of Christians active in politics.

(1)   Luther taught that the essence of the church was to proclaim in word, sacrament, and other visible signs the free grace of God communicated through Jesus Christ. This conviction drove his criticism of the Roman Catholic church of his day, because he thought that the papal system was concentrating on itself instead of pursuing its proper "work," which was to convey the message of the forgiveness of sin. Luther's view of the church is similar to that which grounds the

assertion of the non-Lutheran New Testament scholar, C. K. Barrett, that "the church had and has an impossible task, for it can affirm itself only at the cost of denying its own proper being."[16] That is, for the church to defend itself, however legitimately, is to threaten to turn attention away from its most basic role of proclaiming Christ and the free offer of the gospel. More specifically, for American evangelicals to fight for their rights in the political sphere undercuts their ability to promote the evangelical message of the cross.

Now consider the debate which might someday rise over whether to continue income tax deductions for contributions to churches and other charities. I happen to think that there are sound reasons for maintaining these deductions – for example, that they play an important role in promoting social justice and the general stability of the body politic – and I hope my opinions find effective advocates if and when the debate over tax-deductible contributions begins. But I also happen to think that a Christian who remembers the potential danger to the gospel when churches begin to assert their own rights will mount a defense of the deduction with a different attitude toward the issue itself and toward those who argue on the other side than a Christian who forgets this foundational Christological conviction about the church.

(2) One of Luther's most enduring contributions in general was his obsessive focus on justification by faith. Regardless of how other believers evaluate his final conclusions on this doctrine, it is possible for all Christians to benefit from Luther's probing of the disguises assumed by efforts at self-salvation disguised as deference to God. He is also worth heeding when he describes the multifaceted temptations to self-justification found in human history. Even those who reject Luther's formulation of *sola fide* are better off in the exposition of their own faith for having followed Luther in exposing the multitudinous ways in which humans attempt to save themselves.[17]

Now consider the fight against abortion on demand. I happen to consider this fight the noblest cause of the New Christian Right and the feature of contemporary "Christian politics" that comes closest to fulfilling the biblical mandate to care for the powerless. While I do not agree with every tactical move or intellectual argument of the most visible pro-life leaders, I commend their work in general and often ask myself why I am not more active on behalf of expectant mothers and their children *in utero*. But I also happen to think that, as vitally important as the pro-life cause is, it is possible that those who sin in promoting abortion may yet be saved by God's free grace in Christ, and that it is possible for pro-life advocates so thoroughly to commit themselves to their cause that they run the risk of trusting in their own pro-life advocacy as the *sine qua non* of their acceptance before God. I hope a fervent pro-life advocacy that deals justly with both mothers- and children-to-be will flourish, but I also hold that the political attitudes of those who think as I do will be more thoroughly Christian if we continue to remember that we are pro-life because we are Christians and not Christians because we are pro-life.

In general, the Lutheran leaven will have its greatest impact in moderating Christian political attitudes in situations of conflict. There are, and always will be, culture wars. There are, and always will be, saints defending the truth and scoffers assaulting the truth. But for one who truly knows Christ, the culture wars will always be recognized for what they are – as *relatively* important battles, as warfare fought with *relatively* secure knowledge of who the enemy is and what the issues at stake are. The reason why the Christian who remembers Christ knows that culture wars can never be fought with more than relative certainty is the reason Alexander Solzhenitsyn spelled out with piercing clarity in *The Gulag Archipelago*, when he wrote, "If only [the struggle between good and evil] were so simple! If only there were evil people somewhere insidiously committing evil deeds, and it were necessary only to separate them from the rest of us and destroy them. But the line dividing good and evil cuts through the heart of every human being. And who is willing to destroy a piece of his own heart?"[18] In a word, there is a field of combat even more fundamental than the arena of public culture. That more fundamental field is the human heart where for every person, believer and unbeliever alike, the battle between God and self, light and dark, righteousness and corruption, is fought every day and where there will be no absolute, complete, or perfect triumph until the end of time.

Lutherans are far from the only Christians who realize how much Christological realities should shape the attitudes, including the political attitudes, of believers. It is necessary to think only of St Patrick, Bernard of Clairvaux, Francis of Assisi, Pascal, John Newton, P. T. Forsyth, or John Stott, to name only a few non-Lutherans, who have broadcast this truth. At the same time, the striking community of witness that extends from Luther along different lines to Philip Jakob

Spener and Ludwig von Zinzendorf, to J. S. Bach, to Søren Kierkegaard, and to Dietrich Bonhoeffer is a community testifying eloquently to how a Christian perception of the world will be different, and different for the good, if the suffering, atoning Christ is kept in view.

Perspective

Much of the best Christian thinking over the centuries on the nature of politics has tended to be theoretical, doctrinal, and aprioristic rather than practical, historical, and contingent. It has arisen more from the universal, permanent relationships God established with the world through creation and by reference to the unchangeableness of his own character than from the contingent, particularized work of the Incarnation. Yet concentration on the Incarnate Christ shows clearly how vital it is to reason about both God's relationship to humanity and the hope for human salvation in terms of local conditions, contingent events, particular circumstances, and individual actions. The ways in which the particularities figure in the Incarnation have been well put by a number of contemporary voices. So Bonhoeffer, "Nicht von der Welt zu Gott, sondern von Gott zur Welt geht der Weg Jesus Christi (The way of Christ goes not from this world to God but from God to this world)."[19]

So the Southern Baptist educator, William Hull, "Flesh for God is not a mask, a disguise, or a subterfuge as the Gnostics supposed. Rather, it is a strategy, a witness, a vehicle for involvement. God's Son wants high visibility in order to be seen and heard and touched by others."[20]

And so with great force the Yale missiologist from Gambia, Lamin Sanneh: "The localization of Christianity is an essential part of the nature of the religion, and . . . without that concrete, historical grounding Christianity becomes nothing but a fragile, elusive abstraction, salt without its saltiness. This is the problem which dogs all attempts at defining the core of the gospel as pure dogmatic system without regard to the concrete lives of men and women who call themselves Christian. And it is precisely the historical concreteness of Christianity which makes cross-cultural mutuality possible and meaningful."[21]

If the catalogue of concrete realities displayed in the Incarnation is so important for humanity in general, certainly it must be important as well for Christian theorizing about politics. Yet much of the truly important Christian theorizing about politics has tended to be more general, abstract, and timeless, rather than particular, concrete, and contingent. Harro Höpfl, editor of a helpful anthology of political writing by Luther and Calvin, notes that although Luther actually propounded several different stances on how Christians should practice politics, each was "general and abstract in form."[22] Each, that is, formulated political advice for Christians from biblical texts, Christian dogmas, supposedly universal human situations, and the dictates of unvarying reason. (In this instance, at least, Luther himself failed to live up to the Christological insights I recommend in the previous section.) Luther worked out his politics in this relatively abstracted way, however, despite the fact that it is now transparently obvious that the contrasting political conclusions Luther drew at various stages of his career arose out of his own immediate political experience. That is, when the depredations of anti-Protestant rulers were foremost in his mind, Luther's politics moved toward Anabaptist separatism, but when positive support from pro-Protestant princes for reforming the church was before his eyes, Luther's politics accepted a full measure of church–state cooperation.[23] Regarded from the angle of Christ, who was incarnate in the specific circumstances of the rule in Judea of Pontius Pilate, the problem was not that Luther let local circumstances affect his thinking, but that he did not realize how important it was for his own political theorizing to take into account the contingencies of his own situation.

A similar problem obtains for the various changes made by John Calvin in the sections on civil government in Book IV, chapter 20, of *The Institutes of the Christian Religion*.[24] In early editions, when the activities of the Catholic king of France against the Protestants and the vacillation of Geneva's councils were uppermost in his mind, the *Institutes* stressed the negative functions of government – the role of the state in restraining evil and allowing space for the church to carry out its own activities. By contrast, in the 1559 edition, when Calvin, after prolonged struggle, had come to enjoy nearly unanimous support for his church reform from the Geneva councils, he assigned government a much more positive role in supporting not only a truly reformed church, but the first table of the Decalogue as well. Significantly, however, as in Luther's case, Calvin consistently reasoned, in 1536 as well as in 1559, from general, abstract, and universal biblical, theological, and philosophical principles, and he did so despite what now seem to be transparent connections between the contingencies of his own circumstances and his conclusions about the nature of Christian political duty. The notion that full, self-conscious attention to shifting political events and circumstances should figure in the formulation of Christian political principles or duties was as absent from Calvin as from Luther.

A similar mode of reasoning prevailed in the creation of neo-Calvinist political thought in the Netherlands during the second half of the nineteenth century. That thinking was principial from beginning to end. It focused on universal, cosmological realities. So it was, for example, that Groen van Prinsterer, in his seminal lectures that gave rise to political neo-Calvinism, could attack "republicanism" as if it were a universal solvent of godly order that always operated in a uniform pattern with a uniform set of baneful consequences. Or as he put the matter from another angle, "Calvinism assuredly never led to any sort of republicanism."[25] Yet from the perspectives of British or American history, it is clear that when Groen thought about "republicanism," he was thinking about a form of political philosophy that had developed in eighteenth-century France and that came in nineteenth-century Europe to be closely linked with anti-clerical secularism. The notion that in other places and in different circumstances – for example, in seventeenth-century Britain or eighteenth-century America – some forms of Calvinism did lead to some forms of republicanism could not fit into the vision of first principles that Groen articulated.[26]

Just about the same comment can be made about the even greater contribution of Abraham Kuyper, who capped his career as Calvinist politician by serving as Prime Minister of the Netherlands from 1901 to 1905. At least for Kuyper as politician, Christianity was supremely a life-system, a world-and-life view. As James Skillen has summarized the matter, "Kuyper emphasized the need for a comprehensive Christian worldview that would allow for an 'architectonic' or structural critique of the creation's disorder and lead to a multidimensional approach of human service to God and neighbors in all spheres of life. Each human responsibility has its own God-given characteristics and responsibilities."[27] Kuyper himself stated his preference for Calvin over Luther in similar terms by emphasizing the way in which Calvin's theology led naturally to constructing overarching principles for conduct in politics: "Luther as well as Calvin contended for a direct fellowship with God, but Luther took it up from its subjective, anthropological side, and not from its objective, cosmological side as Calvin did. Luther's starting point was the special-soteriological principle of a justifying faith; while

Calvin's, extending far wider, lay in the general cosmological principle of the sovereignty of God."[28]

Yet to an outside observer, it seems transparent that specifically Dutch conditions – for example, a tradition of close links between the throne and certain religious advisors – shaped the formulation of Kuyper's political theory. Even more obvious is the way that local conditions channeled the outworking of Kuyper's Christian political theory once he became Prime Minister of the Netherlands. During his tenure, Kuyper's firm grasp of neo-Calvinist, anti-revolutionary political principle certainly shaped his exercise of political power, but so did his decidedly situated actions in cooperating with Roman Catholic political leaders, in urging Britain to moderate its positions during the Boer War, in responding to arguments from the organizers of railroad unions, and in handling the struggle for native rights in Holland's East Asian colonies.[29] I intend no criticism of what Kuyper taught about the nature of a proper Christian politics, but I do think his political practice would have been even more thoroughly Christian had Kuyper taken more self-consciously into account the contribution of local political conditions to the outworking of his Christian political theory. Perhaps if Kuyper, as a follower of the Christ incarnate at the time of Pontius Pilate in the period of late-temple Judaism, had acknowledged that his Christian politics were being shaped in part by local conditions in the Netherlands, they would have been less easily misapplied elsewhere. I am thinking specifically of South Africa, where for one subgroup in one Dutch Reformed church Kuyper's political principles became a constituent part of a program of apartheid in a local context marked by very different circumstances than prevailed in the Netherlands.[30] Had Kuyper been able to see how some of his Christian principles were directly (and properly) the result of local Dutch conditions, his principles would have been less easily applied where the local context differed so dramatically from his own.

In sum, attention to a trinitarian doctrine of Incarnation, as also to the place of that doctrine in the scheme of the universe, might suggest that Luther, Calvin, Groen van Prinsterer, and Kuyper were being too fastidious. Because of the Incarnation, in other words, it would have assisted their political reflection to countenance fully their particular circumstances in formulating Christian advice on politics, rather than pretend that they were drawing that advice from Scripture and universal reasoning without the mediation of their own circumstances.

The lesson must surely be that evangelicals who seek a truly Christian politics must be alert to the circumstances of local situations as well as to the universal norms of the gospel. Christian political principles from the past are necessary for contemporary Christian politics, but they are not sufficient. None of the great mentors of classical Christian theology did their work in a political situation like ours – not Augustine, not Thomas Aquinas, not Luther, not Calvin, not Abraham Kuyper – that is, where women and the propertyless vote, where popular media have become the forum for promoting political ideas, or where local economies are tied into worldwide economic connections. To think politically as a Christian today it is necessary to take these realities into account – to heed the multiple meanings of the particulars of human experience – as well as to heed general Christian principles about human nature, the divine economy, and the unchangeable law of God. This counsel for shaping political perspective arises not from pragmatism, but from a sense of how important the particularities of the Incarnation were and are to its meaning.

Ideas certainly do have consequences. The appearance of God the Son in human flesh means also that consequences breed ideas.

Conclusion

As an example of how attitudes and perspective shaped by Christology can affect political reasoning, it is possible to quote the last words of a recent essay by Michael Novak in which he examined the ways in which Christianity shaped the Western political economy. Novak develops his argument in considerable detail – he provides readers a full opportunity to assess whether he is interpreting correctly the divinely created realities affecting human nature, the character of freedom, the nature of economic activity, and so forth. But he is also aware that underneath the meaning of Jesus for questions of political economy is the meaning of Jesus for everything. The conclusion to his essay shows how one can give questions in the realm of political economy their due while still remembering the suffering, atoning savior. I am not necessarily recommending Novak's conclusions about political economy, although they deserve serious attention, but I do think that he has expressed the connections of the realms of Christological reality just about as well as they can be expressed: "Better than the philosophers, Jesus Christ is the teacher of many lessons indispensable for the working of the free society. . . . But that alone would be as nothing, of course, if we did not learn from Jesus that we, all of us, participate in His life, and in living with Him, live in, with and through the Father and the Holy Spirit in a glorious community of love. For what would it profit us, if we gained the whole world, and all the free institutions that flourish with it, and lost our own souls."[31]

The message – which is a very evangelical message – is worth the attention of all American evangelicals. In recent years, one of the most bracing encouragements to think and act like Christians in the political sphere has been to hear contemporary neo-Calvinists of various sorts – like Richard Mouw, James Skillen, or Nicholas Wolterstorff – quote the spine-tingling tocsin that Kuyper first declaimed 115 years ago at the opening of the Free University of Amsterdam. "There is not an inch," he roared, "not an inch in the entire domain of our human life of which Christ, who is sovereign of all, does not proclaim 'Mine'."[32]

Politically considered, no truer words could ever be spoken. They convey the dramatic picture of Christ transfigured in glory, hand out-stretched, finger extended in commanding power, standing over the halls of Congress, the White House, the United Nations, the state legislature, the local school board, the tax assessor's office, the weary citizen sitting at home and reading the front page of the local newspaper, and declar-ing with full, yet winsome authority, "This too is mine!" Yet it may be that this picture is not quite complete, for the footprints of the Jesus who points to every one of our political institutions, to every one of our polit-ical practices, to every one of our political theories, and claims each one as his very own, are footprints spattered with blood. And the hand that points is marked with a wound. Evangelical politics will be a Christian politics, if we evangelicals follow the commanding Christ as he takes pos-session of the world, but it will be a fully Christian politics only if my fellow evangelicals and I recall the road to Calvary that the Lord Jesus took to win his place of command and never forget that the robes of the saints shine white only because they are washed in the blood of the Lamb.

Notes

1   I am grateful to James Skillen for some of the wording in this paragraph, and also for many years of patient tutelage on connections between Christianity and politics.

2   I am pleased to acknowledge inspiration from Robert Benne and Christa Klein as American Lutherans who are trying to express a distinctly Lutheran outlook on questions of public life; see, for example, Benne, *The Paradoxical Vision: a Public Theology for the Twenty-first Century* (Minneapolis: Fortress, 1995). A sensitive discussion of some of the themes from the angle of Calvinism influenced by the great Dutch Calvinist leader Abraham Kuyper, as addressed from the framework of Kuyperian theology, is John Bolt, "Creation and cross: the tension in reformed ethics," in Bolt, *Christian and Reformed Today* (Jordan Station, Ontario: Paideia, 1984).

3   For a probing of this question, see, for example, James W. Skillen, "The political confusion of the Christian Coalition," *Christian Century*, August 30 to September 6, 1995, pp. 816–22.

4   See chapter 7 above.

5   The periodical *Christian Week* out of Winnipeg is an outstanding source of news and reflection on the religious dimensions of recent Canadian politics.

6   Of the vast amount of writing on such themes, one of the most pertinent essays is Merold Westphal, "A reader's guide to 'reformed epistemology'," *Perspectives*, November 1992, pp. 10–13.

7   Andrew Walls, "Africa and Christian identity," in *Mission Focus: Current Issues*, ed. Wilbert R. Shenk (Scottdale, PA: Herald, 1980), p. 217.

8   Gabriel Fackre, "An evangelical megashift?" *Christian Century*, May 3, 1995, p. 485.

9   William Jennings Bryan, "Speech concluding debate on the Chicago platform," in *The First Battle: the Story of the Campaign of 1896* (Chicago: W. B. Conkey, 1896), p. 206.

10 John Milton Cooper, Jr, *The Warrior and the Priest: Woodrow Wilson and Theodore Roosevelt* (Cambridge, MA: Harvard University Press), p. 161.

11 George M. Marsden, *New School Presbyterians and the American Evangelical Mind* (New Haven, CT: Yale University Press, 1970), pp. 182–4.

12 *The Economist*, March 18, 1995, p. 27.

13 I have expanded on such themes in the chapter, "The Bible in politics," in *One Nation under God? Christian Faith and Political Action in America* (San Francisco: Harper & Row, 1988).

14 James Nuechterlein, "Lutheran blues," *First Things*, April 1995, p. 12.

15 For a haunting account of the political dead-ends of a thoroughly Lutheran piety, see Ruth Rehmann, *Der Mann auf der Kanzel: Fragen an einen Vater* (Munich: Carl Hansler Verlag, 1979), a daughter's narrative of a pious Lutheran pastor's political immobilization in the crucible of modern German affairs.

16 C. K. Barrett, *Church, Ministry, and Sacraments in the New Testament* (Grand Rapids, MI: Eerdmans, 1985), p. 78.

17 Philip S. Watson, *Let God Be God! An Interpretation of the Theology of Martin Luther* (Philadelphia: Fortress, 1970, orig. 1947), remains a powerful summary of Luther's Christ-centered theology of redemption.

18 Alexander Solzhenitsyn, *The Gulag Archipelago, 1918–1956* (New York: Harper & Row, 1974), p. 168.

19 Quoted in John Lukacs, *Confessions of an Original Sinner* (New York: Ticknor and Fields, 1990), p. 32n.

20 William E. Hull, "We would see Jesus" [sermon on John 12:21], Occasional Papers of the Provost, Samford University (February 12, 1995), p. 10.

21 Lamin Sanneh, "Gospel and culture: ramifying effects of scriptural translation," in *Bible Translation and the Spread of the Church: the Last 200 Years*, ed. Philip C. Stine (Leiden: E. J. Brill, 1990), pp. 10–11.

22 Harro Höpfl, ed., *Luther and Calvin on Secular Authority* (New York: Cambridge University Press, 1991), p. x.

23 See Lewis W. Spitz, "Luther's ecclesiology and his concept of the prince as *Notbischof*," *Church History*, 22, 1953, pp. 113–41.

24 The meticulous notation by John T. McNeill of the editorial changes in the various versions of the Institutes makes this comparison possible; see *Calvin: Institutes of the Christian Religion*, 2 volumes, ed. John T. McNeill, trans. Ford Lewis Battles (Philadelphia: Westminster, 1960).

25 Groen van Prinsterer, *Lectures on Unbelief and Revolution*, ed. Harry Van Dyke (Jordan Station, Ontario: Wedge, 1989), para. 149.

26 On the positive connection between republicanism and Christianity in the American setting, see Barry Alan Shain, *The Myth of American Individualism: the Protestant Origins of American Political Thought* (Princeton, NJ: Princeton University Press, 1994).

27 James W. Skillen, "The Kuyper lecture" pamphlet from the Center for Public Justice (1995), p. 8.

28 Abraham Kuyper, *Lectures on Calvinism* (Grand Rapids, MI: Eerdmans, 1931), p. 22, as quoted in Richard J. Mouw, "Lutherans from a Reformed Perspective," *Word & World*, 11 (Summer), 1991, p. 301. Mouw's essay is superb on indicating how Lutheran and Calvinist strengths may be combined.

29 Frank Vandenberg, *Abraham Kuyper* (St Catharines, Ontario: Paidia, 1978), pp. 193–232, is not analytical about Kuyper's tenure as Prime Minister, but does provide an outline of its course.

30 See the carefully qualified discussion in André du Toit, "Puritans in Africa? Afrikaner 'Calvinism' and Kuyperian neo-Calvinism in late nineteenth-century South Africa," *Comparative Studies in Society and History*, 27, 1985, pp. 227–30; and du Toit, "The construction of Afrikaner

chosenness," in *Many Are Chosen: Divine Election and Western National-ism*, eds William R. Hutchison and Hartmut Lehmann (Minneapolis: Fortress, 1994), pp. 126–9.

31 Michael Novak, "A new vision of man: how Christianity has changed polit-ical economy," *Imprimis* [Hillsdale College], May 1995, p. 7.

32 Abraham Kuyper, *Souvereiniteit in Eigen Kring (Sovereignty in Its Own Sphere)*, trans. Wayne A. Kobes (Amsterdam: J. H. Kruyt, 1880), p. 35. As different examples, see Richard J. Mouw, *Pluralisms and Horizons: an Essay in Christian Public Philosophy* (Grand Rapids, MI: Eerdmans, 1993); James W. Skillen, *Recharging the American Experiment: Principled Pluralism for Genuine Civic Community* (Grand Rapids, MI: Baker, 1994); and Nicholas Wolterstorff, *Until Justice and Peace Embrace* (Grand Rapids, MI: Eerd-mans, 1983).

11

Learning a Lesson from Canada

Trying to learn things from Canada is not a very American thing to do. Yet for American evangelicals to make such an effort would be worth their while. Chapter 2 revealed some of the similarities and differences among evangelical constituencies in the United States and Canada. This chapter moves beyond questions of quantity to issues of quality in bringing "the True North Strong and Free" into the American picture.

Two widely separated incidents can serve to introduce a portrait of evangelicalism in Canada as it looks from the United States. The first, which is reported by William Westfall and John Webster Grant, concerns two of Ontario's great religious leaders of the nineteenth century – the Methodist Egerton Ryerson (1803–82) and the Anglican John Strachan (1778–1867).[1] Strachan, who eventually became the Bishop of Toronto, was Ontario's most active proponent of an Anglican establishment as the necessary vehicle for creating a Christian civilization in the Canadian wilderness. Ryerson came to public attention in 1826 when he published a fierce rebuttal to a statement of such principles from Strachan. During a funeral address for the first Anglican bishop of Quebec, Strachan had denounced the Methodists. In his opinion they were "uneducated itinerant preachers, who leaving their steady employment, betake themselves to preaching the Gospel from idleness, or a zeal without knowledge, by which they are induced without any preparation, to teach what they do not know, and which from pride, they disdain to learn." Ryerson responded immediately and stressed what was wrong with Strachan's idea of religion. "Our savior," wrote Ryerson, "never intimated the union of his church with the civil polity of any country." Anglican ritual, to Ryerson, was "all pompous panegyric." What Canadians needed was passionate "preaching the gospel" for repentance and conversion. To Strachan the establishment of religion was the secret to creating a Christian society, to Ryerson it was the camp meeting. From a modern angle, Strachan was a representative of mainline Protestantism, Ryerson was an evangelical of the evangelicals.

Yet between the mid-1820s and the incident I describe in the early 1840s significant shifts took place in Upper Canadian religion. As the Methodists grew by leaps and bounds and as a never-ending series of complications impeded Strachan's push for an Anglican establishment, tempers cooled and former antagonists began to drift closer to each other. This confluence of Methodist and Anglican interests set the stage for the first face-to-face meeting between Strachan the mainliner and Ryerson the evangelical. It took place in February 1842 when Ryerson, returning from Kingston to Coburg, found himself unexpectedly thrown together in a coach with Bishop Strachan. As Ryerson and Strachan chatted during their long ride, they were surprised to discover how well they got along. The Methodists, under Ryerson's leadership, had just obtained provincial approval for transforming their denominational academy into Victoria College. During the journey, Strachan offered Ryerson some advice on how to tap proceeds from the Clergy Reserves to fund the Methodists' new college. Neither Strachan nor Ryerson wanted to give up the distinctive contribution of their respective traditions, but each found it relatively easy to integrate his own concerns with those of a former opponent, while together promoting the place of religion in Ontario society.

For one who studies evangelical history in the United States, several things are striking about this Canadian incident from 1842.

First, and most obviously, is how easily the antagonisms of the 1820s were set aside for the common Protestant purposes of the 1840s. Especially the way in which Ryerson's spikey evangelicalism mellowed illustrated an evolutionary, pacific, ameliorative response to challenges in church and society that stands in contrast to the polemical, sectarian, and all-or-nothing tendencies that have often characterized evangelicalism in the United States.

Second, from an American angle, it is notable that Strachan and Ryerson even met at all. Though Canada is geographically larger than the United States, its inhabited zone and the size of the population in that zone have always been much smaller. Thus, it is not too surprising that, somewhere in the course of their long lives, the Canadian evangelical leaders would encounter the leaders of establishment Protestantism. In the United States, such face-to-face meetings of key leaders of various church factions have always been less frequent. To the best of my knowledge, for example, I do not think that Francis Asbury (the dynamic leader of evangelical Methodism early in the nineteenth century) ever met face-to-face with his contemporary John Henry Hobart (the leader of American high-church Anglicanism).

Third, even when American church leaders did meet face-to-face, they have almost never – at least since the early nineteenth century – spent even a single moment discussing how to use government money for the support of their distinctly religious enterprises. Yet that is the very subject that Strachan and Ryerson talked about in 1842, and it is a subject that still engages various sorts of Canadian evangelicals to this very day.

The second incident is much more recent and much less historically important. In the fall of 1994 I was asked to take part in the taping of a television program west of Toronto near Burlington. The program was *Cross Currents*, hosted by Brian Stiller (then the executive director of the Evangelical Fellowship of Canada (EFC)) and sponsored by the EFC. Evangelical television efforts are by no means uncommon in the United States, but this Canadian venture seemed different. It was, for example, immediately obvious from the informal gatherings on the evening before the taping that Stiller (who is a Pentecostal minister) was being assisted – in chatting up the guests as well as in planning the general direction of the interviews – by Gerald Vanderzande, at that time Public Affairs Director of Citizens for Public Justice, a political interest group with roots in the Christian Reformed community. Such cooperation between two of the more widely separated branches on the Protestant tree is not unprecedented in American evangelical history. It took place to some degree, for example, in the preparation of the New International Version of the Bible, and it sometimes occurs in connection with Billy Graham's activities. Nonetheless, it has not been all that common.

For another thing, the various interview segments that I witnessed on the day of the taping were reasonably intelligent, and "intelligent evangelical television" are three words that one does not get to put together too often in the United States.

Yet a third observation concerns the relative casualness about boundary-marking that characterized the programs. Stiller and many of his evangelical guests made no effort to hide their own religious convictions, but the shows also included several guests from non-evangelical Christian traditions, and at least a few who made no religious profession at all.

For my program, Stiller had enlisted two other historians and myself to talk about whether religion in Canada was more than an export from the United States. The other two guests were a professor who studies the United Church and a historian who happens to be a socialist Baptist. Quite apart from the fact that there are not too many socialist Baptists of any sort in the United States, the panel's make-up was simply far too careless about theological and ecclesiastical boundaries to have been sponsored by most national evangelical bodies in the United States.

Finally, a comparison with the National Association of Evangelicals (NAE), which is the rough American equivalent to the Evangelical Fellowship of Canada, is in order. The NAE is now over fifty years old, and was in fact a kind of inspiration for the founding of the EFC. As explained in John Stackhouse's recent survey of twentieth-century Canadian evangelicalism, the EFC is a much more recent effort. It was founded only in 1964, and did not become a significant force until the early 1980s. But here is the contrast: even though the EFC is a considerably younger organization than the NAE, its television program has reached a level of sophistication and attained a degree of what can only be called theological-intellectual self-confidence unlike any similar activity that has ever been promoted by the NAE in the United States.[2]

To generalize from these two incidents – the one of historical significance from 1842 and my appearance on a television program sponsored by the EFC (which will not go down in history) – spotlights several differences between the nature of evangelicalism in Canada and in the United States, which may be summarized as follows:

- Canadian evangelicals inhabit a much smaller world with respect to each other than do American evangelicals.
- Canadian evangelicals have experienced a different set of expectations for relations between church and state, especially with respect to education, than have American evangelicals.
- Whether or not Canadian evangelicals have self-consciously focused more on intra-evangelical cooperation, they nonetheless seem to manifest more of that cooperation than have American evangelicals.
- Canadian evangelicals may not be more intelligent than American evangelicals, but they seem to have succeeded at providing better forums for displaying whatever intelligence they do possess than have American evangelicals.

- Finally, Canadian evangelicals seem at least slightly less concerned about ideological boundary-marking than do American evangelicals.

Qualifications

It is, of course, dangerous in the extreme to move from a pair of isolated incidents to large-scale generalizations about themes as broad as "American evangelicalism" and "Canadian evangelicalism." In the first place, categories like "America," "Canada," and "evangelicalism" invite the paralysis of essentialism, the danger of abstractions taking over from careful attention to particulars. It is a particular mistake when speaking of Canada and the United States to forget how very important regional differences are. It is, in fact, possible to draw some meaningful regional comparisons – the Maritimes, for example, function for the history of Canadian religion somewhat as the South does for the history of American religion; the Canadian-American "left coast" that stretches from San Diego to far north of Vancouver is certainly a distinct region very different from the mountain and prairie communities to the east. But to generalize even about *the* Maritimes, *the* South, or the peculiarities of *the* West Coast is a very risky enterprise indeed.[3]

It is just as risky to forget the meaningful differences within the general evangelical network. In the United States, for example, evangelicals in the Southern Baptist Convention and in the Wisconsin Lutheran Synod differ significantly in theological accent, attitudes toward the sacraments, styles of preaching, expectations for Christian engagement with culture, and many other matters.[4] So it is as well in Canada when comparing evangelicals within the United Church with Christian and Missionary Alliance evangelicals, Anglican evangelicals, Presbyterian evangelicals, Reformed evangelicals, Pentecostal evangelicals, Mennonite evangelicals, and so on.[5] So significant is intra-evangelical diversity that it would be difficult to identify even a single characteristic supposedly unique to Canadian evangelicalism that would *not* apply to some Canadian evangelicals, but that *would* characterize at least some American evangelicals. The same could be said for any conclusion supposedly identifying a unique quality of American evangelicalism.

Historiographical problems also beset the effort to interpret the evangelical presence in both countries. Methodism, for example, was immensely influential in setting the tone for nineteenth-century evangelical spirituality throughout all of North America, and it played a significant role as well in evangelical thought, social action, and worship. Yet for different reasons, at the end of the twentieth century historical attention to Methodism makes up only a small fraction of the research now being lavished on other evangelical groups. In the United States, Methodist historiography has been hampered by internal theological changes, which effectively alienate the present from the past, and by divisions between a Methodist mainline and sectarian holiness bodies. In Canada the absorption of Methodism into the United Church has left it without a visible constituency. In both cases the result is the same: for lack of a vibrant historiography during the past forty years, when history-writing for other evangelical traditions has flourished, Methodism remains the unknown X-factor in general assessments of North American evangelicalism.[6]

Another conceptual danger for a Canadian–American comparison is the tendency to downplay significant commonalities that have always bound Canadian and American churches together. Scholars like George Rawlyk and Nancy Christie have shown how significant were the religious border crossings in the eighteenth and early nineteenth centuries.[7] Other scholars – among them, Phyllis Airhart, Edith Blumhofer, Robert Burkinshaw, David Elliott, Ian Rennie, and William Westfall – have done the same service for the religious history of the twentieth century.[8] If so many religious figures – like Henry Alline, A. B. Simpson, Aimee Semple McPherson, or Leighton Ford – and so much shared religious experience – as represented by hymns like Joseph Scriven's "What a Friend We Have in Jesus" and Margaret Clarkson's "We Come O Christ to Thee" – have moved so easily from Canada to the United States, and if an even larger number of persons and a larger amount of religious baggage have moved so effortlessly across the border from south to north, it should be obvious that a very great deal links the evangelical histories of the two nations.

Another significant difficulty in comparing American and Canadian evangelicalism is what might be called the grass-is-greener effect. Particularly Americans with easily jaded temperaments have been known to magnify the difficulties in their own country at the same time as they romanticize the virtues of Canada. Fred Matthews of York University expressed this danger trenchantly in a thoughtful review of Seymour Martin Lipset's recent book, *Continental Divide*. According to Matthews,

Lipset "overstates a familiar and cherished picture of Canada as benevo-
lent bourgeois 'Other,' orderly, peaceful, sharing, and caring – a morally
superior model for a United States seen as disorderly, violent, and selfish.
Canada, one might say, is Starbuck to the American Ahab."[9] As a
warning to what follows, let me say that this rosy-tinted view of Canada
is a vision to which I also fall prey.

Finally, there are significant problems in comparing Canadian and
American evangelicalism posed by the periodization of Canadian history.
In more general historical terms, Canada's economic modernization
lagged behind the United States'. Census figures for the two countries
show the population shifting from rural to urban only slightly faster
in the USA than in Canada, but the broad influence of Canadian industrial and urban development lags by perhaps a generation in comparison
with the United States. For religious history, this difference is important, because rural, small-town, pre- and early-industrial America was
where evangelicalism flourished. Similarly, the transition from rural to
urban and from early-industrial to fully industrial marks the crest of
evangelical self-confidence in American history. If, therefore, some
aspects of Canadian evangelicalism look more attractive than their
American counterparts, part of the reason may be that Canadian developments should really be compared to American circumstances of a
generation earlier rather than to American developments of the same
generation.

A different sort of problem posed by periodization concerns the
general question of American influence in Canada. A feature noted by
many observers is that Canada – at least from the early nineteenth
century through the mid-twentieth century – was oriented more toward
Britain (with different British regions exerting special influence in different Canadian locales) than toward the United States. American evangelical patterns profoundly influenced Canadian Protestant history in its
early decades, until, that is, the War of 1812 convinced most Canadians
that republicanism at the point of a gun was not for them.[10] Again, once
Canada was absorbed into the American economic and media worlds
(which took place in the twentieth century), evangelical influences from
the states have been very strong north of the border.[11] But in between –
from the early decades of the nineteenth century through the middle of
the twentieth century – British religious influences (as well as indigenous adaptations to the Canadian environment) seem to have been

stronger in Canada than were American influences. As late as the run-up to the Second World War, for example, it was a matter of instinct for a young Canadian scholar like George Parkin Grant to seek graduate education in Britain rather than the United States. And it is not coincidental that this instinct was nurtured by the fact that Grant's own grandfather had been charged with the task of setting up the Oxford scholarships funded by Cecil Rhodes.[12] Much Canadian literature of the post-Second World War period – for example, the narratives of Farley Mowat or the novels of Robertson Davies – continues to be written against the backdrop of British imperial influence, even though these authors realize that Canada has passed, in Davies's memorable phrase, from "the British connection . . . as the Brits grew weary under Imperial greatness," toward "the American connection . . . under the caress of the iron hand beneath the buckskin glove."[13]

As early as 1923, Canadian trade with the United States surpassed volume of trade with Britain, and already in the 1920s radio stations from the United States reached more listeners in Canada than did Canadian radio stations.[14] But this expansion of American economic and media influence northward was significantly checked by the traumas of the Second World War, which not only brought British refugees and tens of thousands of RAF personnel to Canada, but also refocused Canadian public opinion on its ties to the empire. The important chronological point is that Canadian Protestant life was more heavily influenced from Britain than from the United States for about the century and a half before 1950. What this means for a comparison of Canadian and American evangelicalism is that characteristics seeming to divide Canadian and American evangelicals may often reflect the historically stronger British influence in Canada. It also means that, if American–Canadian contrasts are in fact due to that British influence, we should assume that recent American and Canadian evangelicalisms will appear increasingly similar as British influences in trade, education, and the media fade away in favor of expanding American influence.

These are the matters – forgetting the danger of large-scale categories like Canada, America, and evangelicalism; underestimating internal variations related to region and denomination; allowing romantic visions of a True North Strong and Free to overwhelm careful research; and dismissing the important changes in Canada's relations to both the USA and Britain – that prevent easy comparisons between Canadian and American evangelicalism.

Comparisons

Despite problems, the attempt at comparison is still worth it.[15] Evangelicalism is an unusually adaptable form of Protestant pietism. Culturally adaptive biblical experientialism supports three of its most prominent characteristic. First is a bias – it could be a slight prejudice, it could be a massive rejection – against inherited institutions. Second, evangelicalism, as a matter of principle, though often inarticulate principle, is extraordinarily flexible in relation to theological, political, social, and economic ideas. Third, evangelicals practice "discipline," to borrow a well considered phrase from Daniel Walker Howe.[16] Their experiential biblicism might lead along many different paths to principles of conduct for self and others, but, however derived, those principles embody a common evangelical conviction that the gospel compels a search for social healing as well as personal holiness.

The key thing is that the basic thrust of evangelicalism – experiential biblicism pushing out against tradition, in myriad forms, and with discipline – has been chameleon-like in its ability to adapt. Thus, more than with many other Christian movements, to study the way that evangelicalism takes flesh in a particular culture reveals much about the character of that form of evangelicalism. The very plasticity of the pietist impulse means that, even as it gathers strength in a society, it is likely to take on coloring from that society. That process of taking on the coloring of the surrounding society in turn affects the internal quality of the experiential biblicism itself.

Nowhere is the environmentally shaped character of evangelicalism more obvious than in a comparison between black and white evangelicals in the United States.[17] As we saw in chapter 5, a large portion of white Protestants and an overwhelming majority of African-American Protestants share the four evangelical characteristics identified by David Bebbington – conversionism, biblicism, activism, and crucicentrism.[18] Yet in the United States it has mattered greatly whether these evangelical traits took root in black or white communities.

The relevance here is that to study the contexts of Canadian and American evangelicalism – to assess the respective evangelical interactions with history, culture, ideology – is to do more than simply find variations of one common story for an essentially identical evangelical faith. It is, rather, to see how the propensity of all pietist movements to adapt to local coloring actually creates somewhat different varieties of evangelicalism. Although Lamarkianism (the idea that changes made in an organism can be passed on to descendants) may not be in favor with biologists, it does seem to work historically where, in this case, the evolution of varieties of evangelicalism since the eighteenth century arises from the inheritance of characteristics acquired by different evangelical species in the course of their interaction with different environments.

If this reasoning about adaptation to environment is correct, then one way to discuss differences between Canadian and American evangelicalism is to ask: (a) what makes Canada different from the United States; and (b) do these Canadian–American differences play out in noticeable differences between Canadian and American evangelicalism? It would be wrong to forget the full measure of similarities between the two societies: the same European-based forms of Christianity facing many of the same perils and opportunities in an open new world; the same heritage of British political ideals; the same participation in revival; the same commitment to moralistic social reform; the same investment in doxological, Baconian science; and the same fear of Roman Catholicism. Yet that full range of shared historical circumstances is not complete. Canadian civilization has developed differently from American civilization in a number of particulars.

Where the United States' most serious social tension has involved blacks and whites, Canada's has been between speakers of French and speakers of English. Where the Catholic church was a late force in American development, it was there from the start in Canada. Most importantly, where Americans find social and political axioms in the principles of their revolutionary break with Britain, Canadians find social and political axioms in the practice of loyalty and a commitment to peaceful, evolutionary change. Differences like these, moreover, are played out on two very different landscapes. Canada remains, by the standards of Asia, Europe, or even the United States, a scarcely inhabited land. (Quebec, for instance, is bigger than Alaska, but even as Canada's second most numerous province, it has considerably fewer people than New Jersey. Seven Canadian provinces are larger than California, but the population of California is roughly equivalent to the population of all Canada.)

If, therefore, evangelicalism in the two nations has absorbed some of the cultural coloring of the respective areas, we could only expect that the forms of evangelicalism would have significant differences as well.

What are those differences?

Flexibility and rapid deployment

A first concerns the possibilities opened up by Canada's relatively small population. We have seen already how rapidly the EFC sprang from almost nowhere during the past fifteen years to become a significant force. It is hard to imagine anything so substantial taking place so rapidly in the United States. In this same regard, it is also worth noting that Brian Stiller's double marginalization – as a Pentecostal and as a native of Saskatchewan – did not keep him from making a major contribution to all Canadian evangelicals in the way that such double marginalization might have done in the United States.

Canadian evangelicals reap the same sort of benefit in other spheres as well. The Mennonite Brethren, at best a speck on the religious landscape of the United States, have greatly assisted evangelicalism in Canada as a whole, nowhere more noticeably than through the newspaper *Christian Week*, which the vision of only a small number of Mennonite Brethren has made into an extraordinary national religious paper.

Similarly, Canada now enjoys fuller polling and interview data on its evangelical population than does the United States, because one person, Professor George Rawlyk of Queen's University, was able to parlay a modest amount of grant money and his own personal connections with the Angus Reid Group into a major, ongoing effort in opinion research.

The opposite side of this same coin is also worth considering. If effective evangelical projects require less time and bureaucracy in Canada, Canadians often seem stubbornly unwilling to be impressed with anything happening in their own nation. William Westfall has observed that "The first canon of Canadian historiography may well be the doctrine that important things happen elsewhere, that Canada receives from Clio [the goddess of history] only those things that are dull and second hand."[19] Canada's relatively small population means that good things can happen among evangelicals in a hurry, but also that most Canadians may not be too impressed. As an example, Canadian assessment of "the Toronto Blessing" seems only to have gotten off the ground once stories about this phenomenon began to appear in the United Kingdom, the United States, and even Australia.

Myths of national origin

A second way in which differences between Canadian and American history are played out cuts closer to the heart of the Christian faith. When comparing the founding myths of the two societies, it is obvious that these have been powerful in the United States since its break from Britain, but quite feeble north of the border. Canada has always lacked the sort of compelling national mythology that fuels American ideology. South of the border we have a wealth of inspiring slogans like "Give me liberty or give me death" or "with malice toward none, with charity toward all." North of the border there have been no civil wars worthy of the name and certainly no violent political revolution (the few local skirmishes in 1837 that are sometimes styled "rebellions" are significant mostly for how thoroughly Canadian leaders repudiated the spirit that inspired them).[20] The mythic pull exerted by Canada's founding fathers – railroad magnates and hard-drinking politicians meeting behind closed doors in the wake of the American Civil War to wheedle a hasty piece of legislation from the British Parliament in order to keep their defenseless provinces from falling into the maw of the rising American empire – is not exactly overwhelming.

The contrasts resulting from this difference are probably less now than formerly. But at least to a historian, the kind of comparisons drawn by Seymour Martin Lipset's *Continental Divide* remain persuasive. Lipset's main argument is that Canadian society "has been and is a more class-aware, elitist, law-abiding, statist, collectivity-oriented, and . . . [group-oriented] society than the United States."[21] The anti-statism, individualism, populism, violence, and egalitarianism that characterize American history have been decidedly less prominent in Canada. Where Canada has stressed the state and community values, the United States has featured the individual and *laissez-faire*. In contrast to the United States' embrace of classical liberalism (in the nineteenth-century, individualistic sense of the term), Canada has fostered a public attitude stressing communalities, whether "Tory-statist" on the right or "social democratic" on the left. The reasons for these systematic differences are both geographical and historic. Canada's vast space and sparse population have required a more active government and have placed a premium upon cooperation. Historically, the rejection of the American Revolution, the presence of Quebec as a distinct community, the Loyalism strengthened by American invasions during the war of 1812, and the prosaic understatement of the Dominion's founding slogan ("peace, order, and good government") have all tended to enforce organic as opposed to individualistic arrangements in Canadian life.

Lipset does recognize that contemporary Canada has changed; he stresses the new "Charter of Rights" as a main vehicle accelerating the pace of change.[22] Yet developments in the 1980s did not shake Lipset from his basic conclusion. A preponderance of social indicators continued to convince him that the historic differences between Canadian and American society were still present. These differences include, for example, a far lower Canadian murder rate, fewer police per capita, a relative absence of civil disorder, a higher tolerance for taxes and government regulation, and a willingness to support tight gun control.

Subtle, but important, religious differences have arisen from the social and ideological contrasts Lipset outlines. In both the United States and Canada anti-Catholicism has been one of the most stable elements of Protestant self-definition. Yet American anti-Catholicism has often differed from Canadian anti-Catholicism precisely because of the settings in which attacks on Rome took place. In American Protestant history, anti-Catholicism was fueled by a distinct sense of American messianism. Lyman Beecher and countless other evangelical leaders of the nineteenth century, for example, attacked Roman Catholics because of their threat to America's rising role in the Kingdom of God.[23]

In Canada, by contrast, anti-Catholicism more directly replicates English, Scottish, or Ulster polemics. Many examples could be cited of Canada's virulent brand of British anti-Catholicism, but one of the most telling occurred at Bay Roberts on Conception Bay, Newfoundland, in 1883. A successful mission by Catholic Redemptorists inspired a Protestant reprisal that led to rioting, the death of five people, and an international incident eventually put to rest by the arrival of a British battleship. Significantly, the Protestant attacks had been spearheaded by the local chapter of the Orange Order, an Ulster-inspired fraternity that carried on in the New World where it had left off in the old.[24]

In more general terms, the widespread acceptance in the United States of the liberalism of the American Revolution led not only to institutional differences with Canada (like the rigid American separation of church and state) but to many differences in tone. The exalted role for the language of freedom in general, the tendency to equate tradition with corruption, the suspicion of inherited institutions, the confidence in entrepreneurial innovation – all are traits flowing from American liberalism of the late eighteenth and nineteenth centuries that have affected the churches as well as American society as a whole.[25] Canada – and the Canadian churches – have traditionally presented a contrast to these American ways, not by affirming absolute antitheses, but by moderating individualistic liberalism with various forms of traditionalism, corporatism, communalism, and deference to authority. If that resistance to American liberalism has faded in the decades since the Second World War, it still exists. At least it can still seem to be present from an American angle, even if important Canadian prophets like George Parkin Grant think that the historic cultural contrast has passed away altogether.[26]

Politics

Again in very general terms, the historical result of these contrasting ideals is that American evangelicals maybe have gotten more done, but at a cost. Political participation is a major case in point. Outstanding historians have recently spotlighted the contrasting ways in which evangelicals contributed to the political history of their respective countries in the mid-nineteenth century. Richard Carwardine, whose recent book, *Evangelicals and Politics in Antebellum America*, is the finest account ever written of its subject, uses a contrast with the British situation during the same period to summarize his research on the evangelical contribution to American politics:

> American evangelicals' optimistic postmillennialism, their Manichaean perception of the world as a battleground between good and evil, their moral absolutism, and their weak sense of institutional loyalty to political parties all acted to destabilize the American polity in the middle decades of the nineteenth century, at the very time that British evangelicals and their fellow citizens were entering an "age of equipoise," a period of mid-Victorian peace and good order for which evangelicals themselves have been given considerable credit. American evangelicals killed each other in a fight over slavery and the Union, while their British counterparts, deeply divided among themselves only over the more containable issue of disestablishment, sought as Christian soldiers to advance Christ's kingdom by less murderous means.[27]

If evangelical political behavior in America contrasts sharply with British evangelical politics, the contrast with Canada may be even stronger. See now a brief paragraph from Michael Gauvreau, who is currently doing some of the best work in all North America on nineteenth-century connections among theology, political theory, and practical political outcomes: the model of evangelical voluntarism

> was fundamental to the peculiar reconciliation of monarchy and republicanism which occurred in British North America after 1815, and . . . the notions of "responsible government" undergirding the political system and the competition of parties could not have been accepted without the evangelical notion of the "responsible" individual and the "voluntary" model of society. . . . [M]ore speculatively, . . . evangelicalism, by underpinning this common culture, and by polarizing the politics of the colonies around religious issues between 1850 and 1864, provided an essential stimulus to those movements of colonial union which culminated with the . . . Confederation of 1867, which rested upon a delicate balance of local and federal power.[28]

A similar contrast might be drawn concerning evangelical contributions to politics earlier in the twentieth century. In each nation evangelicals played major roles in shaping important political visions, in the United States especially for the populist Democrats led by William Jennings Bryan, and in Canada with several different political movements west of Ontario. For a complicated set of reasons, Bryan's vision of populist communalism faded rapidly in America, while the rightist Social Credit of fundamentalist preacher William Aberhart and the leftist Cooperative Commonwealth Federation (CCF) led by the ordained Baptist minister Tommy Douglas both survived with considerable effect.[29] Necessary questions may be asked about the continuation of Christian values in the later history of Aberhart's Social Credit as well as in the evolution of Douglas' CCF into the New Democratic Party. For the Canadian–American comparison, however, it is significant that political movements with evangelical inspiration lasted longer and exerted broader effect than comparable efforts in the United States.

Another contrast may be relevant even for the most recent national elections in the two countries. While we must recognize that polling information is not exactly equivalent for the two countries and realizing that party configurations are somewhat different as well, in both nations

Table 11.1 Percentages of support by Canadians for political parties (October 1996), arranged by numbers of evangelical beliefs they affirm

	Prog. Conserv.	*Liberal*	*NDP*	*Reform*	*Bloc Q.*
All four beliefs	13	32	4	20	2
Three	12	43	5	6	4
Two	13	43	2	8	5
One	10	47	5	7	6
Zero	10	40	9	8	7

Note: row totals do not equal 100 percent because many of those surveyed expressed no political opinion.

Table 11.2 Percentages of support by Canadians for political parties (October 1996), divided by religious traditions

	Prog. Conserv.	*Liberal*	*NDP*	*Reform*	*Bloc Q.*
Conservative Protestant-hi	13	32	3	25	1
Conservative Protestant-lo	10	33	7	24	2
Mainline Protestant-hi	21	44	7	8	0
Mainline Protestant-lo	17	49	5	12	1
Catholic-hi	8	47	3	6	7
Catholic-lo	12	41	2	4	14
Secular/nominal	10	40	8	8	6
Other	5	44	10	4	1

Note: row totals do not equal 100 percent because many of those surveyed expressed no political opinion.

a strong bond has been forged between evangelical or conservative Protestant churches, on the one hand, and, on the other hand, a political body – the American Republicans and the Canadian Reform – that came to be perceived as "God's party." The point of contrast is that American evangelical support for Republican presidential candidates has been considerably stronger than conservative Protestant support for Reform parliamentary candidates in Canada. The information in tables 11.1 and 11.2 does show a Reform–evangelical bond in Canada (regardless of how "evangelical" is defined), but it is considerably weaker than the bond we observed between American evangelicals and the Republican party in chapter 9 (tables 9.1, 9.2, and 9.3). In addition, there is also nothing in America to match Canadian evangelical support for the Liberal Party. These two tables show Canadian evangelical support for the Progressive Conservative Party (the closest equivalent to the older elite of the American Republican Party), the Liberal Party (the closest equivalent to the Democrats), the New Democratic Party (the socialist successor to the Cooperative Commonwealth Federation), the Reform Party (which is Western and conservative, but in a populist way), and the Bloc Québecois (which is the Quebec nationalist party located exclusively in that province).

In sum, where in Canada evangelical connections with politics have often moderated extremes, in the United States they have more regularly exacerbated political extremes.

Liberal evangelicalism

A final contrast concerns the relatively large place in Canadian Protestant history of what is often called "liberal evangelicalism" – although "mediating evangelicalism" may in fact be a better term. Instead of militant or combative forms of evangelicalism, which have flourished in the states, Canadian evangelicalism has featured somewhat less polemic and a somewhat more accommodating spirit. It is difficult to define this mediating evangelicalism specifically, even if it is a central feature in much of the great upsurge of scholarship on the Canadian churches that has appeared in the past decade.

Even a partial review of such work shows the central place of a mediating evangelical spirit. John Webster Grant's magisterial account of nineteenth-century Ontario highlights the ability of evangelical Protestants to harness both the social gospel and new intellectual forces while retaining the substance of historic evangelical convictions.[30] William Westfall's description of Methodist and Anglican culture in nineteenth-century Ontario finds both of them maintaining a full measure of evangelical conviction, along with a culture-embracing sense of social propriety.[31] Michael Gauvreau's history of nineteenth-century evangelical intellectual life depicts a relatively pacific accommodation between genuinely evangelical beliefs and some modern intellectual habits.[32] Richard Vaudry's account of the Presbyterian Free Church tradition in the nineteenth century stresses its irenic adjustment to both other Presbyterians and the realities of Canadian life.[33] Marguerite Van Die's intellectual biography of the nineteenth-century Methodist leader Nathanael

Burwash reveals him as both doctrinally conservative and unflustered by the great intellectual changes at the end of the nineteenth century.[34] Much the same can be said about the equipoise of other important evangelical theologians, like the Presbyterians George Monroe Grant and W. W. Bryden, or – from the conservative side of the spectrum – John McNichol, long-time head of the Toronto Bible College.[35] Phyllis Airhart's book on the evolution of the Methodists in the half-century before the creation of the United Church in 1925 notes that Methodist revivalism in Canada retained its vigor, and postponed compromise with modernism, at least for a generation longer than was the case in the United States.[36] Edith Blumhofer's biography of Aimee Semple McPherson shows how the influence of the Canadian Salvation Army kept her ministry much more positive and much less polemical than comparable ministries of early twentieth-century Pentecostal itinerants.[37] George Rawlyk's history of twentieth-century Maritime Baptists helps to explain why a divisive fundamentalist–modernist battle did not occur in that body despite the presence of many of the same ingredients that led to such a showdown in the states.[38] Robert Burkinshaw's descriptions of conservative evangelicals in Western Canada show why they merited the label fundamentalist in some particulars, yet avoided some of the most polemical excesses of their American colleagues.[39] And John Stackhouse's recent book is notable, from an American perspective, especially for his argument that the feistier sort of polemicists, like T. T. Shields, did not in fact define the central concerns of Canadian evangelicalism.[40]

Whether called "liberal" or "mediating," this form of evangelicalism has been much more important in Canada than in the states. By contrast to the Canadian situation, American evangelicals in the nineteenth century featured a great deal more enthusiasm for sectarian causes. In the early twentieth century, American evangelicalism divided much more clearly than its Canadian counterpart into a militant evangelical conservatism (i.e. fundamentalism) and an accommodating evangelical inclusivism (verging toward modernism). Precisely what differentiated Canadian liberal or mediating evangelicalism from American varieties (whether the Reformed-Baptist doctrinal variety, the Holiness-Pentecostal experiential type, or hybrids) was its resistance to nineteenth-century "liberalism." That is, against an unrestrained focus on the spiritual freedom and the moral prerogatives of the individual,

Canadians retained more respect for tradition, they did not divorce social concern quite so easily from the need for regeneration, and they were somewhat less prone to thinking of piety as an alternative to intellectual endeavor.[41]

Conclusion

Canadian evangelicalism, in sum, has differed from American evangelicalism because Canada differs from the United States. Geography matters, but differences in ideology, attitudes toward history, and conceptions of national culture matter even more.

In the perspective of this chapter and earlier accounts of politics in the United States, *the* American evangelical problem in comparison with Canadian evangelicals has been to believe the ideology that justified the American Revolution. *The* mistake of American evangelicals has been to let that ideology, and the practices flowing from it, exert so much force in shaping Christian faith and life. *The* distinction of Canadian evangelicalism has been the space it offered for less nationalistic renderings of Christianity to shape faith and life.

Of course, the comparison is much more complicated than that. Canadian evangelicals – even Canadian mediating evangelicals – have never attained perfection. To cite just one example showing that the effects of the Fall linger north of the border too, it is possible to find Protestant leaders early in the twentieth century falling prey to racial stereotyping almost as easily as religious leaders did in the United States. In 1910, S. D. Chown, later a General Superintendent of the Canadian Methodist Church, asked belligerently: "Shall the hordes of Southern Europe overrun our country as the Huns and Vandals did the Roman Empire?" His contemporary, the Rev. C. W. Gordon, who wrote immensely popular novels under the name Ralph Connor, pointedly compared the sober Anglo-Saxons of Winnipeg with the "steaming, swaying, roaring dancers . . . all reeking with sweat and garlic" at a Ukrainian wedding. And an assistant superintendent of the Baptist Home Mission Board of Ontario and Quebec wrote in 1913: "We must endeavour to assimilate the foreigner. If the mixing process fails we must strictly prohibit from entering our country all elements that are non-assimilable. It is contrary to the Creator's law for white, black or yellow races to mix together."[42] Such lapses could be cited nearly without end. If Canadian evangelicalism has been superior to American evangelicalism, the superiority has been relative.

But at their best, Canadian evangelicals have embodied qualities all too rare in the states. They have preferred a degree of ecumenicity to ecclesiastical polemics, they have highlighted the virtues of peace over war, they have taken pretensions (whether religious or national) with a grain of salt, and they have made more rather than less of the ways in which Canadian Christianity fits into broader world patterns of the faith.

A final question is by now inevitable: if Canadian evangelicalism can be compared favorably with American evangelicalism in so many ways, why is it that the American varieties now seem to be so much more vigorous than their Canadian counterparts. The answer – at least in the terms stressed in this chapter – may be simple. If standards for success are not sought from an expanding cultural liberalism, then it is possible that other criteria than simply size or rampant energy deserve more attention. Since for a Christian it is always appropriate to ask what the Scriptures teach, I have a suspicion that, once fundamentally biblical standards are applied, it may be asked if evangelicalism in the United States is really that much better off today than it is in Canada.

Notes

1 Quotations from Strachan and Ryerson in this paragraph are from William Westfall, *Two Worlds: the Protestant Culture of Nineteenth-century Ontario* (Kingston and Toronto: McGill-Queen's University Press, 1989), pp. 24–6. I am following Westfall also in the account of Anglican–Methodist convergence. On the coach ride, see John Webster Grant, *A Profusion of Spires: Religion in Nineteenth-century Ontario* (Toronto: University of Toronto Press, 1988), p. 93.

2 John G. Stackhouse, Jr, *Canadian Evangelicalism in the Twentieth Century* (Toronto: University of Toronto Press, 1993), pp. 165–73. See also John Stackhouse, "The National Association of Evangelicals, the Evangelical Fellowship of Canada, and the limits of evangelical cooperation," *Christian Scholar's Review*, 25 (December), 1995, pp. 157–79.

3 For assists to regional study, see Charles H. H. Scobie and John Webster Grant, eds, *The Contribution of Methodism to Atlantic Canada* (Kingston and Montreal: McGill-Queen's University Press, 1992); Charles H. H. Scobie and G. A. Rawlyk, eds, *The Contribution of Presbyterianism to the*

Maritime Provinces in Canada (Kingston and Montreal: McGill-Queen's University Press, 1997). Robert K. Burkinshaw, "Conservative evangelicalism in the twentieth-century 'West': British Columbia and the United States," in *Amazing Grace: Evangelicalism in Australia, Britain, Canada, and the United States*, eds George A. Rawlyk and Mark A. Noll (Grand Rapids, MI: Baker; Kingston and Montreal: McGill-Queen's University Press, 1994); and Burkinshaw, *Pilgrims in Lotus Land: Conservative Protestantism in British Columbia, 1917–1981* (Kingston and Montreal: McGill-Queen's University Press, 1995). There is also some attention to regional differences in George A. Rawlyk, ed., *The Canadian Protestant Experience, 1760–1990* (Burlington, Ontario: Welch, 1990); and in books by Reginald W. Bibby, *Fragmented Gods: the Poverty and Potential of Religion in Canada* (Toronto: Irwin, 1987); *Mosaic Madness: the Poverty and Potential of Life in Canada* (Toronto: Stoddart, 1990); and *Unknown Gods: the Ongoing Story of Religion in Canada* (Toronto: Stoddart, 1993). It is, however, hard to complain about lack of serious attention to Canada's regions when the much larger tribe of American religious historians pays almost no attention to the question, with the exception of a longstanding interest in "the South."

4   See especially Donald W. Dayton and Robert K. Johnston, *The Variety of American Evangelicalism* (Downers Grove, IL: InterVarsity Press; Knoxville: University of Tennessee Press, 1991).

5   For a start, see the essays on various denominational traditions in Robert E. VanderVennen, ed., *Church and Canadian Culture* (Lanham, MD: University Press of America, 1991), a book sponsored by the Evangelical Fellowship of Canada and the Institute for Christian Studies in Toronto.

6   Recent noteworthy works partially belying this analysis include John Wigger, *Taking Heaven by Storm: Methodism and the Rise of Popular Christianity in America* (New York: Oxford University Press, 1998); Cynthia Lynn Lyerly, *Methodism and the Southern Mind, 1770–1810* (New York: Oxford University Press, 1998); Russell E. Richey, *Early American Methodism* (Bloomington: Indiana University Press, 1991); and Neil Semple, *The Lord's Dominion: the History of Canadian Methodism* (Montreal and Kingston: McGill-Queen's University Press, 1996).

7   George A. Rawlyk, *The Canada Fire* (Kingston and Montreal: McGill-Queen's University Press, 1994); Nancy Christie, "'In these times of democratic rage and delusion': popular religion and the challenge to the established order, 1760–1815," in *The Canadian Protestant Experience*, op. cit., n. 3.

8   Phyllis D. Airhart, "'As Canadian as possible under the circumstances': reflections on the study of Protestantism in North America," in *New Perspectives in American Religious American History*, eds Harry S. Stout and

D. G. Hart (New York: Oxford University Press, 1997); Edith L. Blumhofer, "'Canada's gift to the Sawdust Trail': the Canadian face of Aimee Semple McPherson," in *Aspects of the Canadian Evangelical Experience*, ed. G. A. Rawlyk (Montreal and Kingston: McGill-Queen's University Press, 1997); Burkinshaw, *Pilgrims in Lotus Land*, op. cit., n. 3; David R. Elliott, "Knowing no borders: Canadian contributions to American fundamentalism," in *Amazing Grace*, op. cit., n. 3; Ian S. Rennie, "Fundamentalism and the varieties of North Atlantic evangelicalism," in *Evangelicalism: Comparative Studies . . . 1700–1990*, eds M. A. Noll, D. W. Bebbington, and G. A. Rawlyk (New York: Oxford University Press, 1994); and William Westfall, "Voices from the attic: the Canadian border and the writing of American religious history," in *Retelling US Religious History*, ed. Thomas A. Tweed (Berkeley: University of California Press, 1997).

9 Fred Matthews, review of Seymour Martin Lipset's *Continental Divide*, *Journal of Interdisciplinary History*, 21 (Spring), 1991, p. 720 (entire review, pp. 719–21). For a related but more pointed criticism, that Lipset overstates Anglican at the expense of evangelical experience in discussing Canadian religion, see George Rawlyk, "Religion in Canada: a historical overview," *Annals, AAPSS*, 538 (March), 1995, p. 142n24.

10 In addition to references in n. 6, see Jane Errington and G. A. Rawlyk, "Creating a British-American community: the federalist–loyalist alliance in upper Canada," in *Loyalists and Community in North America*, eds R. M. Calhoon, T. M. Barnes, and G. A. Rawlyk (Westport, CT: Greenwood, 1994).

11 For a recent survey, see *Christian Week*, January 31, 1995, pp. 10–12.

12 William Christian, *George Grant: a Biography* (Toronto: University of Toronto Press, 1994).

13 For example, Farley Mowat, *The Dog Who Wouldn't Be* (1957), on growing up in Saskatchewan, or *And No Birds Sang* (1979), on Canadian soldiers in the Italian campaign. Robertson Davies's three trilogies – Salterton, Deptford, and Cornish – are cosmopolitan, but the main external influences are British and European rather than American. His two most recent novels – *Murthering Spirits* and *The Cunning Man* – are even more British (Welsh, Irish, and Scottish, as well as English). The quotation is from *The Cunning Man* (New York: Viking, 1994), p. 468.

14 Michael Bliss, "Northern wealth: economic life in the 20th century," *The Beaver*, December 1994/January 1995 (75th anniversary issue), p. 9.

15 The pioneer and still most trenchant student of such comparisons is Robert T. Handy; see *A History of the Churches in the United States and Canada* (New York: Oxford University Press, 1977), and also a number of essays, including "Trends in Canadian and American theological education, 1880–1980," *Theological Education*, 28 (Spring), 1982, pp. 175–218.

16 Daniel Walker Howe, "Religion and politics in the antebellum North," in *Religion and American Politics from the Colonial Period to the 1980s*, ed. Mark A. Noll (New York: Oxford University Press, 1990).

17 Some black–white comparisons are well worked out in Albert J. Raboteau, *Slave Religion* (New York: Oxford University Press, 1978); Milton C. Sernett, *Black Religion and American Evangelicalism . . . 1787–1865* (Metuchen, NJ: Scarecrow, 1975); and Donald G. Mathews, *Religion in the Old South* (Chicago: University of Chicago Press, 1977). But there is far less for the post-bellum period.

18 David W. Bebbington, *Evangelism in Britain: a History from the 1730s to the 1980s* (London: Unwin Hyman, 1989), pp. 2–17.

19 Westfall, *Two Worlds*, op. cit., n. 1, p. 84.

20 Allan Greer, *The Patriots and the People: the Rebellion of 1837 in Rural Lower Canada* (Toronto: University of Toronto Press, 1993), revises existing historiography, but it does not have to contend with powerful regnant myths in the way that every new book on the American Revolution must.

21 Seymour Martin Lipset, *Continental Divide: the Values and Institutions of the United States and Canada* (New York: Routledge, 1990), p. 8.

22 Ibid., p. 116.

23 See the essays, with references, on Protestant–Catholic tensions by Barbara Welter, Jay Dolan, and Mark Noll, in *Uncivil Religion: Interreligious Hostility in America*, eds Robert N. Bellah and Frederick E. Greenspahn (New York: Crossroad, 1987).

24 Paul Laverdure, "The redemptorist mission in Canada, 1865–1885," in *Historical Papers 1993: Canadian Society of Church History*, ed. Bruce L. Gunther (Canadian Society of Church History, 1993), pp. 86–7.

25 The most powerful statement is Nathan O. Hatch, *The Democratization of American Christianity* (New Haven, CT: Yale University Press, 1989), but see also Robert H. Wiebe, *The Opening of American Society from the Adoption of the Constitution to the Era of Disunion* (New York: Knopf, 1984); and Gordon S. Wood, *The Radicalism of the American Revolution* (New York: Knopf, 1992).

26 George Parkin Grant, *Lament for a Nation: the Defeat of Canadian Nationalism* (Toronto: McClelland and Stewart, 1965).

27 See Richard Carwardine, *Evangelicals and Politics in Antebellum America* (New Haven, CT: Yale University Press, 1993). The quotation here is from Carwardine, "Evangelicals, politics, and the coming of the American Civil War: a Transatlantic perspective," in *Evangelicalism*, op. cit., n. 8, p. 212.

28 Michael Gauvreau, manuscript research proposal, "The voluntary empire: evangelicalism, liberalism, and the formation of colonial society in British North America, 1775–1870."

29   See David R. Elliott and Iris Miller, *Bible Bill: a Biography of William Aberhart* (Edmonton: Reidmore, 1987); and Doris French Shackleton, *Tommy Douglas* (Toronto: McClelland and Stewart, 1975).

30   Grant, *Profusion of Spires*, op. cit., n. 1.

31   Westfall, *Two Worlds*, op. cit., n. 1.

32   Michael Gauvreau, *The Evangelical Century: College and Creed in English Canada from the Great Revival to the Great Depression* (Kingston and Montreal: McGill-Queen's University Press, 1991).

33   Richard W. Vaudry, *The Free Church in Victorian Canada, 1844–1861* (Waterloo, Ontario: Wilfrid Laurier University Press, 1989).

34   Marguerite Van Die, *Nathanael Burwash and the Methodist Tradition in Canada, 1839–1918* (Kingston and Montreal: McGill-Queen's University Press, 1989).

35   Barry Mack, on Grant, "Of Canadian Presbyterians and guardian angels," in *Amazing Grace*, op. cit., n. 3; John A. Vissers, "Recovering the Reformation conception of revelation: the theological contribution of Walter Williamson Bryden to post-union Canadian Presbyterianism," in *The Burning Bush and a Few Acres of Snow: the Presbyterian Contribution to Canadian Life and Culture*, ed. William Klempa (Ottawa: Carleton University Press, 1994); and on McNichol, Stackhouse, *Canadian Evangelicalism*, op. cit., n. 2, pp. 56–67.

36   Phyllis D. Airhart, *Serving the Present Age: Revivalism, Progressivism, and the Methodist Tradition in Canada* (Kingston and Montreal: McGill-Queen's University Press, 1992).

37   Blumhofer, *Aimee Semple McPherson: Everybody's Sister* (Grand Rapids, MI: Eerdmans, 1993).

38   George A. Rawlyk, *Champions of the Truth: Fundamentalism, Modernism, and the Maritime Baptists* (Kingston and Montreal: McGill-Queen's University Press, 1990), chapter 3, "In search of T. T. Shields' impact on the Maritime Baptists in the 1920s and 1930s."

39   Burkinshaw, *Pilgrims in Lotus Land*, op. cit., n. 3.

40   Stackhouse, *Canadian Evangelicalism*, op. cit., n. 2.

41   Phyllis Airhart's suggestion – that the entrance of American evangelical patterns derailed a delicate balance between liberal and conservative forces within Ontario Methodism – probably needs to be set in a larger context (i.e. with respect to other factors in Canada and to influences from Britain), yet it is still a thought-provoking idea. See Airhart, *Serving the Present Age*, op. cit., n. 36; and also "'What must I do to be saved?' Two paths to evangelical conversion in late Victorian Canada," *Church History*, 59 (September), 1990, pp. 372–85.

42   All three quotations are from N. K. Clifford, "His dominion: a vision in crisis," *Sciences Religieuses/Studies in Religion*, 2, 1973, pp. 317, 319. The

quotations are put to use by Robert Choquette, "Christ and culture during 'Canada's century'," in *New Dimensions in American Religious History*, eds Jay P. Dolan and James P. Wind (Grand Rapids, MI: Eerdmans, 1993), p. 88, but Choquette draws much more drastic conclusions about the decrepit quality of Canadian Christianity than any observer from the United States could ever do.

12

Evangelicalism at Its Best

This last substantive chapter attempts to restate the message of evangelical Christianity positively, not this time from formal doctrinal statements as in chapter 3, but through the medium of hymns. It is not the way all books on American evangelical Christianity should end, but it is an appropriate way for an evangelical writing about evangelicalism to make a final statement.

Evangelicalism at its best is the religion displayed in the classic evangelical hymns. The canon of evangelical hymnody is open, which means that before very long at least a few of the psalms, hymns, and spiritual songs being composed in such lively profusion in contemporary evangelical churches will be added to that canon. As they are added, they will take their place alongside three distinct layers of hymnody that, more than any other expression, define the modern evangelical movement at its best.

As we have seen, modern evangelicalism arose in the English-speaking world in the mid-eighteenth century with convenient markers commonly given as the beginning of Jonathan Edwards's preaching of justification by faith in his Northampton, Massachusetts, church in 1735; John Wesley's Aldersgate experience in May 1738; or George Whitefield's momentous preaching tour of New England in September 1740. But as an even better indication of fresh religious sensibility and an even better sense of things to come, it makes more sense to date the emergence of modern evangelicalism from an act of composition by Charles Wesley. The very week his brother John received an unusual manifestation of divine grace during a Moravian meeting at Aldersgate, Charles Wesley underwent a similar experience.[1]

Many know what John Wesley wrote in his journal after his experience: "About a quarter before nine, while [the speaker] was describing the change which God works in the heart through faith in Christ, I felt my heart strangely warmed. I felt I did trust in Christ, Christ alone, for my salvation; and an assurance was given me that He had taken away my sins, even mine, and saved me from the law of sin and death."[2] Many, many more have sung the words of the hymn that Charles composed and that he called "Christ the Friend of Sinners":

> Where shall my wond'ring soul begin? How shall I all to heaven aspire?
> A slave redeemed from death and sin, A brand plucked from eternal fire.
> How shall I equal triumphs raise, Or sing my great Deliverer's praise? . . .
> Come, O my guilty brethren, come, Groaning beneath your load of sin;
> His bleeding heart shall make you room, His open side shall take you in.
> He calls you now, invites you home – Come, O my guilty brethren, come.

If anyone doubts the weight of Charles Wesley's contribution to the emergence of modern evangelicalism, it is only necessary to ask how many words of Edwards, Whitefield, or John Wesley have been memorized by later evangelicals as compared to how many words of Charles Wesley have been stored away, not only in the mind, but also in the heart:[3]

> Hark, the herald angels sing, Glory to the new-born King. . . .
> Mild he lays his glory by, Born that man no more may die. . . .
> Jesu, Lover of my soul, Let me to thy bosom fly. . . .
> Arise, my soul, arise; shake off thy guilty fears;
> The bleeding Sacrifice in my behalf appears. . . .
> Love divine, all loves excelling, Joy of heaven to earth come down. . . .
> Come, Thou long-expected Jesus, Born to set Thy people free,
> From our fears and sins release us, Let us find our rest in Thee. . . .
> Ye servants of God, Your Master proclaim,
> And publish abroad His wonderful name:
> The name all-victorious of Jesus extol;
> His kingdom is glorious, And rules over all. . . .
> "Christ the Lord is risen today," Sons of men and angels say!
> Raise your joys and triumphs high: Sing, ye heavens; thou earth reply.

The hymns of Charles Wesley and of his contemporaries like John Newton, Anne Steele, William Cowper, and William Williams (Pantycelyn) mark the first great outpouring of evangelical hymnody.[4] The second appeared during the remarkable expansion of evangelicalism throughout Britain, Canada, and the United States during the first two-thirds of the nineteenth century.[5] Like the first wave, the classic hymns of the evangelical nineteenth century featured redemptive encounter with the living Christ described through images, tropes, metaphors, and quotations from the Bible. Evangelicalism always involved more than Christ-centered, biblically normed religious experience. But for leaders and followers alike, especially in day-to-day ordinary experience, that kind of piety remained the defining center of evangelical movements.

In the North Atlantic countries massive efforts in evangelism, voluntary social reform, and the refinement of taste led to something like an evangelical cultural hegemony. In the United States the sway of evangelicalism could be seen in the revivalistic tone of religious life present in both armies and on both home fronts during the Civil War and also by the way in which public political discourse developed along lines marked out by itinerating evangelical preachers and evangelical voluntary societies – in other words, by the features of American life that so impressed visitors like Alexis de Tocqueville. But a more intimate and quotidian measure of nineteenth-century evangelical cultural influence is found in the incredible popularity of the hymns of Fanny Crosby of Brooklyn, New York. Among the approximately 8,500 hymns that this blind author wrote, dozens became defining emblems of evangelical experience:

> Tell me the story of Jesus, write on my heart every word; . . .
> All the way my Savior leads me; what have I to ask beside?
> Can I doubt his tender mercy, who through life has been my guide? . . .
> Blessed assurance, Jesus is mine! O what a foretaste of glory divine!
> Heir of salvation, purchase of God, born of his Spirit, washed in his
>   blood. . . .
> This is my story, this is my song, praising my Savior all the day long.

In an American world very different from the refinement of Brooklyn Heights, a similar process was at work among those whom an ethical malignancy had made into America's hewers of wood and drawers of water. The decades between the American War for Independence and the Civil War witnessed an accelerating evangelization of African Americans, both slave and free.[6] When allowed, churches were formed and blacks exerted great energy in learning to read the Bible. Where allowed or not allowed, African Americans sang of their faith. The most distinctive form of that singing was the spiritual. Although authorship, origin, and exact distribution of many spirituals lie beyond historical recovery, by mid-century the spiritual had become a sturdy anchor of African-American religion. The life course reflected in those spirituals was very different from the world in which Fanny Crosby lived. But one thing was similar, the use of biblical materials focused on the omnicompetence of Jesus Christ:

> What ship is this that's landed at the shore! Oh, glory halleluiah!
> It's the old ship of Zion, halleluiah! . . .
> What kind of Captain does she have on board? Oh, glory halleluiah!
> King Jesus is the Captain, halleluiah. . . .
> In that morning, true believers, In that morning,
> We will sit aside of Jesus, In that morning,
> If you should go fore I go, In that morning,
> You will side aside of Jesus, In that morning,
> True believers, where your tickets, In that morning,
> Master Jesus got your tickets, In that morning.

It was the same in Canada. If anything, Protestant evangelical influence exerted an even stronger influence throughout the Maritimes and Ontario than in the United States. Yet more than the shaping of churches, schools, and public discourse, evangelicalism in nineteenth-century Canada could be defined by the hymns it sang and produced. None of the latter touched more lives than a hymn written by Joseph Scriven, who in its words reflected on the dislocation and personal tragedies that had attended his migration from Ireland to Port Hope, Ontario:[7]

> What a Friend we have in Jesus, All our sins and griefs to bear!
> What a privilege to carry Everything to God in prayer! . . .
> Are we weak and heavy-laden, Cumbered with a load of care?
> Precious Savior, still our refuge – Take it to the Lord in prayer.
> Do thy friends despise, forsake thee? Take it to the Lord in prayer.
> In his arms He'll take and shield thee – Thou wilt find a solace there.

Nineteenth-century Britain was an arena in which evangelicalism interacted deeply with conceptions of political economy, where different kinds of evangelical faith virtually monopolized the dissenting churches and also exerted a powerful influence in the Church of England, the Church of Ireland, and the Church of Scotland, and where evangelicals probably contributed more than any other group to the constitution of Victorian sensibility. In such a venue of multivalent evangelical activity, nothing spoke more directly of the spirituality that undergirded evangelical public life than the hymn. Horatius Bonar, who in 1843 gave up his pulpit in the Church of Scotland to join the Scottish Free Church, was one of the most eminent of those hymn writers, and most of his best known hymns reiterated for a new era what were already classical evangelical themes:

> Not what these hands have done can save this guilty soul;
> not what this toiling flesh has borne can make my spirit whole. . . .
> Thy work alone, O Christ, can ease this weight of sin;
> thy blood alone, O Lamb of God, can give me peace within. . . .
> Thy grace alone, O God, to me can pardon speak;
> thy power alone, O Son of God, can this sore bondage break.

Yet none of Bonar's hymns, popular as they are, has spoken to and for so many evangelicals as words written in the early 1830s by Charlotte Elliott (1789–1871), sister of an evangelical clergymen in the Church of England, cousin of the missionary activist Henry Venn, and friend of the Geneva evangelical leader H. A. César Malan:[8]

> Just as I am, without one plea, But that Thy Blood was shed for me,
> And that Thou bidst me come to Thee, O Lamb of God, I come.

Elliott's hymn has been used so widely – including by Billy Graham – because it so aptly summarized so many evangelical attitudes, especially as they took shape in the first two-thirds of the nineteenth century.

The same ability of hymns to express deep evangelical sentiments characterized the third wave of classic evangelical hymnody that produced the gospel song around the turn of the twentieth century. For white evangelicals, Ira Sankey led the way.[9] As D. L. Moody's song leader, Sankey was an indispensable contributor to Moody's phenomenal success in England, Scotland, Canada, and the United States. But much more than anything Moody ever wrote, Sankey's songs long continued to speak of powerful evangelical sentiments:

There were ninety and nine that safely lay In the shelter of the fold,
But one was out on the hills away, Far off from the gates of gold. . . .
None of the ransomed ever knew How deep were the waters crossed;
Nor how dark was the night that the Lord passed through
Ere he found his sheep that was lost.

The black counterpart to Ira Sankey was Charles A. Tindley, who through patience, persistence, and tireless promotion convinced large numbers of African-American churches to enrich their singing with new hymns adjusted to a new era. Tindley is best known for a song published in 1916 that was later amalgamated with the spiritual "I'll Be All Right," and sung to the tune of the latter spiritual as an anthem of the civil rights movement in the 1960s and 1970s. In its original version, the hymn's most telling effect was to demonstrate continuity with the Christ-centered emphases of earlier evangelicalism:

This world is one great battlefield, With forces all arrayed;
If in my heart I do not yield I'll overcome some day. . . .
Tho' many a times no signs appear Of answer when I pray,
My Jesus says I need not fear, He'll make it plain some day.
I'll be like Him some day, I'll be like Him some day.

As is clear from even the few hymns quoted here from the three great eras of evangelical hymnody, these classics defined, with an unusual degree of unanimity, the essence of evangelicalism. Whatever their many differences of theology, ethnicity, denomination, class, taste, politics, or churchmanship – and in these areas divisions existed beyond number – evangelical hymn-writers and hymn-singers pointed to a relatively cohesive religious vision.

Driving that vision was a peculiarly evangelical understanding of the Trinity. The holiness of God provided occasion for worship, but even more a standard that revealed human sinfulness, human guilt, and human need for a Savior. At the heart of the evangelical hymnody was Jesus Christ, whose love offered to sinners mercy, forgiveness, and reconciliation with God. In this Savior redeemed sinners found new life in the Holy Spirit, as well as encouragement in that same Spirit to endure the brokenness, relieve the pain, and bind up the wounds of a world that the great evangelical hymn writers almost always depicted in strikingly realistic terms.

The classic evangelical hymns, in other words, contain the clearest, the most memorable, the most cohesive, and the most widely repeated expressions of what it meant to be an evangelical. But why regard the religion of these hymns as evangelicalism at its best? The answer probably has as much to do with ancient understandings of Christianity as with contingencies of recent centuries. Conflicts with Roman officials, internal battles over the character of the faith, strenuous apologetics against Jews and pagans, and (in time) learned discourses exegeting and synthesizing Scripture all played their part in the emergence of Christianity during the first centuries after Christ. Wise commentators long since, however, have realized that the *lex credendi* was the *lex orandi*, that the way the church formally defined itself depended ultimately on what and how the church prayed.

Similarly, for the evangelical tradition, great diligence in preaching, an incredible organizational energy, and more learned theology than evangelicals and the critics of evangelicals have recognized went into the creation of modern evangelicalism. But nothing so profoundly defined the *lex credendi* of evangelicalism as the *lex cantandi*; what evangelicals have been is what we have sung.

Just as in the early church, the *lex orandi*, the law of prayer, did not guarantee that the early Christians would live up to the sublime faith expressed in their liturgies, so too with modern evangelicals the possession of a *lex cantandi*, a law of song, has not guaranteed that evangelical practice lives up to the Christ-centered, biblical piety about which evangelicals sing. In the early church, the liturgy, constructed primarily from the words and concepts of Scripture, defined a religion of beauty, charity, serenity, magnanimity, holiness, and realistic hope that far outshone the often tawdry realities of actual church practice. So too the hymnody of evangelicalism, perhaps because it so obviously is a creature of the Bible's salvific themes, defined a religion that was clearer, purer, better balanced, and more sharply focused than much evangelical practice. The religion of the classic evangelical hymns is evangelicalism at its best, we might say, because Christian movements in general are at their best in worship, prayer, and hymn.

In at least three specific ways the classic hymns display evangelicalism at its best. First, a Christ-centered picture of redemption is the scarlet thread running through these hymns. This picture of redemption insists upon the death of Christ on the cross as the only ultimate source of human salvation. The hymns display evangelicalism at its best because in them the boundary of offense is restricted narrowly to the scandal of the cross. Second, the classic evangelical hymns, as well as more general evangelical practice with respect to hymnody, define an unusually broad, unexpectedly gracious ecumenicity. Third, the social vision that constitutes a prominent subtheme in the classic evangelical hymns evokes a remarkably winsome vision of altruistic Christian charity.

The Scandal of the Cross

The history of modern evangelicalism could be written as a chronicle of calculated offense. Those who know even a little evangelical history know how prone evangelicals have been to violate decorum, compromise integrity, upset intellectual balance, and abuse artistic good taste. In specifically theological terms, the evangelical movement, including many of its subcanonical hymns, offers the spectacle of a luxurious expanse of weeds, with multiple varieties of gnosticism, docetism, manicheanism, modalism, and wild eschatological speculation, not to speak of confusion over doctrinal details and manifold outbreaks of unintended Unitarianism, springing up as a threat to the good seed of classic orthodoxy.

The great hymns are not like that. They do not meander theologically. Whatever else they may lack, they possess the virtue of clarity. In turn, by focusing on the great hymns of evangelicalism, proponents, opponents, and the merely curious can see clearly the essence of evangelicalism with a minimum of distraction. That essence is the central theme in a vast panoply of classic hymns.

Professor Stephen Marini of Wellesley College has twice in recent years tallied the most often reprinted hymns in American Protestant hymnbooks from the colonial era to the decades after the Second World War. Because of the different range of hymnals he sampled for the two surveys, he has identified two different hymns as the most often reprinted in American Protestant history.[10] Because the message of one of those two is so often repeated in so many of the other classic hymns of evangelicalism, its compact, forceful lines are an especially good record of the center of evangelical concern. That hymn appeared in 1776, and I say, with calculated awareness of what else was going on in that year in Philadelphia and in Scotland, where Adam Smith published his *Wealth of Nations,* that of all world-historical occurrences in that year the publication of August Montagu Toplady's hymn may have been the most consequential:

> Rock of Ages, cleft for me, Let me hide myself in Thee;
> Let the water and the blood, From Thy riven side which flowed,
> Be of sin the double cure, Cleanse me from its guilt and power.
> Not the labours of my hands, Can fulfill Thy law's demands;
> Could my zeal no respite know, Could my tears for ever flow,
> All for sin could not atone: Thou must save, and Thou alone.
> Nothing in my hand I bring, Simply to Thy Cross I cling;
> Naked, come to Thee for dress; Helpless, look to Thee for grace;
> Foul, I to the fountain fly; Wash me, Saviour, or I die.

Toplady's theme was never put more succinctly, with more theological acumen, and greater dramatic power than in a hymn Charles Wesley wrote at the very beginning of the evangelical movement:

> And can it be that I should gain An interest in the Savior's blood?
> Died he for me, who caused his pain? For me? Who him to death pursued?
> Amazing love! How can it be That thou, my God, shouldst die for me?
> 'Tis myst'ry all: th'Immortal dies! Who can explore his strange design?
> . . .
> Long my imprisoned spirit lay, Fast bound in sin and nature's night.
> Thine eye diffused a quck'ning ray; I woke; the dungeon flamed with
>   light.
> My chains fell off, my heart was free, I rose, went forth, and followed thee.
> No condemnation now I dread, Jesus, and all in him, is mine.
> Alive in him, my living head, And clothed in righteousness divine,
> Bold I approach th'eternal throne, And claim my crown, through
>   Christ my own.

It is impossible to illustrate quickly the fixation of evangelical hymnody on the saving death of Christ. The theme is prominent even in many songs written specifically for children:

> Jesus loves me, this I know, For the Bible tells me so. . . .
> Jesus loves me! He who died Heaven's gate to open wide;
> He will wash away my sin, Let his little child come in.

It remained a fixture in the memorable, though more sentimental, hymns of the Victorian era, as from Philip P. Bliss:

"Man of Sorrows," what a name for the Son of God, who came
Ruined sinners to reclaim! Hallelujah! what a Savior!
Bearing shame and scoffing rude, in my place condemned he stood;
Sealed my pardon with his blood: Hallelujah! what a Savior!

Or Horatio G. Spafford's "It Is Well with My Soul":

My sin – O, the bliss of this glorious thought, my sin – not in part but
    the whole,
Is nailed to the cross and I bear it no more:
Praise the Lord, praise the Lord, O my soul!

Even in the much more therapeutic concerns of the modern praise
chorus, emphasis upon the redemption won by Christ on the cross is by
no means absent.

The classic evangelical hymns do not offend on doctrines of the
church and the sacraments because they touch on these matters only
indirectly, if at all. Neither do they offend by promoting the particular
doctrines of a faction. The Arminian Charles Wesley and the Calvinist
A. M. Toplady both wrote hymns excoriating the theological positions
of the other – these hymns died long before their authors, while com-
positions like "Rock of Ages" and "And Can It Be" are found in the
hymnals of almost all Protestants and, since the 1970s, some Roman
Catholics as well. While the great hymns everywhere betray implicit
trust in the Scriptures, they do not offend by insisting on a particular
definition of biblical authority. Again, the classic evangelical hymns have
virtually no politics. Charles Wesley thought the American Revolution
was sinful through and through, but American patriots hardly noticed
as they went on reprinting his hymns in edition after edition. I could go
on – different evangelicals of different sorts and at different times have
tolerated or advocated racism, they have cheered attacks on the intellect,
they have indulged unimaginable vulgarity in the production of religious
kitsch, they have been callous to the dispossessed, they have confused
their political allegiances with divine mandates, they have equated
middle-class decorum with sanctification in the Holy Spirit, and they
have tried to pass off gratuitous nonsense as if it were gospel truth – as
Toplady, for example, did in the essay where he first published "Rock of
Ages" by claiming that the average number of sins committed by each
individual in his or her lifetime was 2,522,880,000.[11]

Such failings, as well as the particular dogmas and practices insisted
upon by different evangelical churches, have been the occasion for oceans

of offense. Whether all or some of these offences are justified is an open question deserving a degree of serious attention.

The classic evangelical hymns, by contrast, are virtually innocent of such offenses. Rather, their overriding message and the single offense upon which they insist is compacted into the four words that best summarize their message: *Jesus Christ Saves Sinners*. These hymns, in other words, proclaim a particular redemption of substitutionary atonement through a particular act of God accomplished in the particularities of the birth, life, death, resurrection, ascension, and kingly rule of Jesus Christ.

Evangelicalism at its best is an offensive religion. It claims that human beings cannot be reconciled to God, understand the ultimate purposes of the world, or live a truly virtuous life unless they confess their sin before the living God and receive new life in Christ through the power of the Holy Spirit. Such particularity has always been offensive, and in the multicultural, postmodern world in which we live it is more offensive than ever. But when evangelicalism is at its best, as it is in its greatest hymns, that declaration of a particular salvation is its one and only offense.

The Ecumenicity of the Gospel

Evangelicals, in point of historical fact, may never have been as factious, fissiparous, and sectarian as is commonly thought. To be sure, leaders of evangelical groups have indulged in their fair share of back-stabbing, power-mongering, petty minded polemicizing, gratuitous boundary-marking, and schismatical devilment. Although I am convinced that lay evangelicals have done better than their leaders in preserving the unity of the Body of Christ, there is enough fragmentation in the evangelical world to go around for all. I have often heard said in my circles what is no doubt said about different issues in other communions as well: the presence of three confessional Presbyterians guarantees at least four potentially schismatic opinions on the doctrine of predestination.

Evangelicalism at its best, however, embodies a kind of gospel ecumenicity which, while it does not overcome the fragmentation to which evangelicalism is prone, nonetheless speaks forcefully against it. In this case, evangelical hymnody has been more an eschatological sign of a unity to come than one of a unity realized. Specifically, it is not so much the message of the hymns as how they are used that displays most clearly their ecumenical potential.

John Wesley, for example, eventually broke with the Moravians: they were too passive, too mystical, perhaps too cheerful. But he did not hesitate to translate a few of their hymns. The result is that generations of evangelicals to this day have joined their voices in singing the cooperative efforts of Wesley the Methodist and Zinzendorf the Moravian long after the Moravians and Methodists went their separate ways. And what they have sung is, "Jesus, thy blood and righteousness / My beauty are, my glorious dress."

Some of the ecumenicity of the great evangelical hymns bridges even wider chasms. At the end of the nineteenth century, many evangelicals still regarded the pope as Antichrist and, if they thought of it at all, considered the Oxford Movement but a waystation toward Rome. Yet within the same generation that they were written, John Henry Newman's "Lead Kindly Light" and John Keble's "Sun of My Soul, Thou Savior Dear" were being sung by evangelicals. Moreover, a translation by the evangelical Presbyterian James Waddel Alexander of Paul Gerhardt's German translation of Bernard of Clairvaux's "O Sacred Head, Now Wounded" had become a fixture in evangelical hymnbooks. It is also ecumenically significant to ponder the translating history of Martin Luther's "Ein feste Burg," the very Marseilles Hymn of the Reformation that English-speaking evangelicals were also singing widely by the end of the nineteenth century. Two of the most popular translations of that great hymn were in fact made by individuals whose theological convictions would have excluded them from leadership in almost all evangelical churches – George McDonald, a renegade Scottish Congregationalist run off into Universalism, and Frederick Hedge, a graduate of the Harvard Divinity School and promoter of Unitarianism as a pastor and professor.

The ecumenicity of the classic evangelical hymns extends beyond ecclesiastical division to the polarities of gender and race as well. Although these hymns follow the conventions of their day in using masculine pronouns for all humans, they do not promote gender wars, and only a lunatic fringe of evangelicals has ever scrupled at not only singing, but singing with enthusiasm, the hymns of Fanny Crosby, Charlotte Elliott, Frances Ridley Havergal, Carolina Sandell, Cecil Frances Alexander, and Margaret Clarkson.

Race, the most intractable divider of Christians in the modern West, is not intractable enough to completely stifle the gospel ecumenicity of evangelical hymnody. Many of us whitebread evangelicals act uncomfortably in black churches, and I suspect that many African-Americans feel the same in white churches. Yet the white folk still try to sing "A Little Talk with Jesus Makes It Right" or Thomas A. Dorsey's "Precious Lord, take my hand, lead me on, let me stand, I am tired, I am weak, I am worn. Through the storm, through the night, lead me on, to the light, Take my hand Precious Lord, lead me home."[12]

Hymn-inspired racial inclusiveness goes way back in evangelical history. It was there in 1792, when eleven hundred African-Americans – some refugees from slavery in America, others escaping social harassment in a marginally freer Nova Scotia – waded ashore off the West African coast onto a strip of land purchased for their use by the British evangelicals of the Clapham Sect. As they came ashore, so it is said, the settlers joined their voices in Isaac Watts's "Awake, and Sing the Song of Moses and the Lamb," a hymn drawing on both Testaments and bearing great significance in that hour.[13]

On Whitsunday in 1862, when 5,000 South Sea Islanders from Tonga, Fiji, and Samoa gathered to inaugurate a new specifically Christian government with a professedly Christian king, they marked the occasion with a hymn that had become the missionary beacon of the evangelical movement. The consequences of Western imperialism have always been mixed, but it was the Islanders' own choice to appropriate an expressly evangelical gift to mark that day, as they sang Isaac Watts's christianized version of the Seventy-Second Psalm:[14]

> Jesus shall reign where'er the sun
> Doth his successive journeys run;
> His kingdom stretch from shore to shore
> Till moons shall wax and wane no more.

Although on ecumenical matters evangelicals have not always been at their best, in the spirit with which the classic evangelical hymns have been put to use, evangelicalism expresses an ecumenical vision shaped by the gospel itself. By so doing it illustrates in a specifically Christian way the truth of a German saying: "Wer spricht mit mir ist mein Mitmensch; wer singt mit mir ist mein Bruder"; that is, the folks I talk to are my fellow human beings, the ones I sing with are family.

A Social Vision

To return from hymnic practice to the substance of what is written, an important subtheme in the classic evangelical hymns is a persistent concern for the relief of suffering. Although this subtheme is almost never developed systematically or structurally, it is nonetheless there from the first, as in the hymn of Isaac Watts sung by the South Sea Islanders:

> Blessings abound where'er he reigns; The prisoner leaps to lose his chains,
> The weary find eternal rest, And all the sons of want are blest.

As J. R. Watson points out in his fine recent book *The English Hymn*, "Charles Wesley's hymns are forceful because they contain so many words which are physical: for him the life of a Christian was to be experienced in the body as well as in the soul."[15] Thus, the note struck in Wesley's "O for a thousand tongues to sing" is by no means untypical:

> Hear him, ye deaf, his praise, ye dumb, Your loosen'd tongues employ,
> Ye blind behold your Saviour come, And leap ye lame, for joy.

Nor is the challenge to this-worldly service found elsewhere in Wesley's hymns an oddity:

> A charge to keep I have, A God to glorify;
> A never-dying soul to save, And fit it for the sky:
> To serve the present age, My calling to fulfill;
> Oh, may it all my powers engage To do my Master's will.

In the Victorian era, Fanny Crosby expressed directly the care that at least some evangelicals showed to those for whom few others cared:

> Rescue the perishing, care for the dying,
> Snatch them in pity from sin and the grave;
> Weep o'er the erring one, lift up the fallen,
> Tell them of Jesus, the mighty to save.
> Rescue the perishing, care for the dying;
> Jesus is merciful, Jesus will save.

At its best, the evangelical desire to rescue the perishing has meant putting the perishing on their feet in the here and now as well as preparing them for eternity. Of course, we evangelicals are often not at our best, so the occasions are many of having been lured away from Christ-inspired social service by prejudice, class-consciousness, middle-class fastidiousness, blindness to the structural conditions of power that condition personal choices, and the many other forms of social sinfulness that beset the human race in general.

But at its best, evangelicalism is William Wilberforce, who for the sake of the kingdom of Christ devoted his life for the destruction of slavery. At its best, evangelicalism is the Grande-Ligne Mission of Madame Henriette Feller, who in Quebec patiently joined Protestant witness to educational exertion. At its best evangelicalism is the tireless, unpretentious, but absolutely stunning social achievements of the Salvation Army and the Mennonite Central Committee. And at its best evangelicalism is the motivation from the gospel of Matthew that has inspired many to establish shelters for pregnant women in distress and to march on pro-life picket lines: "Come to me, all who labor and are heavy laden, and I will give you rest. Take my yoke upon you, and learn from me; for I am gentle and lowly in heart, and you will find rest for your souls" (11:28–9); "Let the children come to me, and do not hinder them; for to such belongs the kingdom of heaven" (19:14, RSV).

Concern for the terrestial outworking of the Kingdom of God is not as fully developed in the classic evangelical hymns as it should be. But it is indubitably there, reflecting a vision of human need inspired by the love of Jesus and devoted not to extrinsic social or political causes, but to the good of the ones being served.

The researchable historical question as to when, how, in what proportion, and to what extent evangelicals have functioned at their best is too complex for easy adjudication. As an academic committed to the values of modern historical research when those values function at their best, I am reluctant to attempt a quick answer, since there is so much contradictory evidence.

In the history of evangelicalism, for every Jonathan Edwards dedicating the mind to discern the glories of God in the stuff of daily human existence, there are many James Davenports running amuck into mind-denying enthusiasm. For every William Jennings Bryan eager to judge the marketplace by the cross, there is a Russell Conwell eager to bury the cross in an acre of diamonds. For every Johann Albrecht Bengel or

Gordon Fee examining issues of biblical interpretation with painstaking care, there are many more evangelicals racing from slipshod plundering of the biblical text to bogus exegetical certainties. For every Wilberforce bringing the resources of evangelical faith to bear for spiritual and ter-restrial liberation there is a James Henley Thornwell bringing pretty much the same resources to bear for a now incomprehensible mixture of spiritual liberation and terrestrial enslavement. For every Billy Graham maintaining theological, financial, and sexual integrity as a traveling evangelist, there is a Marjo exploiting kerygmatic charisma for base ends. Or to take trenchant examples from Charles Marsh's captivating recent study of the dramatic civil rights confrontations of 1964 in the state of Mississippi, for every Fannie Lou Hamer who was sustained by thoughts of Jesus as she was being beaten in the Winona, Mississippi, city jail, there is a Sam Bowers, Imperial Wizard of the White Knights of the Ku Klux Klan, believing that he was defending the sovereignty of God and the resurrection of Jesus Christ by conspiring to murder three civil rights workers.[16]

From a historical perspective, therefore, I am reluctant to conclude too much about the question of whether evangelicals in practice have lived up to the vision of faith and life found in the great evangelical hymns. Yet as a historian who is also an evangelical, I must say more. Even if, historically considered, evangelicals have not always acted at our best, evangelical convictions are not compromised. In fact they may be strengthened.

It is evangelical to insist that humans are redeemed by God's grace rather than by the achievement of their own perfection; it is evangelical to claim that the righteousness on which we rely is a forensic gift rather than a personal possession; it is evangelical to claim that power resides in powerlessness and that the cross is a symbol both for human weakness as well as divine love. Holiness unto the Lord is a prominent evangelical theme, but it rests upon justification by faith alone.

Thus, even if evangelicals have acted at our best only inconsistently, there is nothing in that fact contradicting evangelical conviction. In fact, for evangelicals to confess how far short they have fallen of the divine beauty that they claim to honor is a very important first step toward real-izing evangelicalism at its best.

At the end of the twentieth century, all Christians, indeed all humans, have multiplied reasons to hope that evangelicalism will be at its best. As we have seen, sophisticated surveys suggest that about a fifth of all

American citizens are high participation adherents of evangelical churches (that is, about the same number as, or only slightly fewer than, active Roman Catholics and mainline Protestants combined). A recent survey by John N. Vaughan published in his newsletter, *Church Growth Today*, reported that nine out of the ten most rapidly growing non-Catholic churches in the United States, and 93 out of the top 100, are self-identified as evangelical, charismatic, pentecostal, Southern Baptist, fundamentalist, or by some other label usually considered as fitting under the broader evangelical umbrella. The situation for world Christianity reveals the same picture. Annual tabulations by the missiologist David Barrett suggest that of the world's nearly two billion people identified with Christian churches, something like 650 million are evangelical in a broad sense of the term (for Barrett, this category includes also some Roman Catholics).[17] His figures make clear that the only varieties of Protestantism growing with any concerted energy in the world are evangelical in general and most likely pentecostal in particular. Thus, it is important not just for the evangelical community, but for the world as a whole, that evangelicals live, think, and pray at their best.

That it might in fact be possible to hope for such a prospect is indicated by an account of two last hymns. Christian missions began among the Bor Dinka on the east side of the White Nile River in the southern Sudan in 1906.[18] But for the first seventy years and more of its activity the Anglican Church Missionary Society (CMS) experienced only scant results. From the 1970s, and with accelerating force in the 1980s and 1990s, however, Christianity under the guidance of the Episcopal Church of the Sudan has expanded with remarkable strength. The external circumstances of this expansion are tragic, for the Dinka have been caught in civil war with succeeding Muslim factions from the northern Sudan and have suffered great loss of life and property.

Precisely in those circumstances the Christian faith has taken root, but in a distinctively Bor Dinka manner. Everywhere in the new Dinka churches and among the burgeoning tide of converts is seen the cross. The display of the cross is particularly striking in massed processions on holy days when, as described by Marc Nikkel, "their crosses [create] a thick forest, surging with the crowds, thrusting heavenward with every beat of the songs they sing." The prominence of the cross in Bor Dinka life represents a Christianization of existing cultural forms, for the Dinka had historically put to use a wide variety of carved walking sticks, staffs, and clubs. Among Dinka converts, the Christian symbol has filled a form provided by traditional culture.

But the Dinka appropriation of the cross has also become a powerful expression of pastoral theology, expressed in a flourishing of fresh, indigenous hymnody. These hymns reprise historical evangelical emphases by pointing to the cross as a comprehensive reality of great power. The cross provides protection against hostile spirits, or the *jak*; the cross figures large in the baptisms that mark conversions; in hymns the cross becomes an ensign or banner raised high for praise and protection; the cross brings the great God, Nhialic, close to the Dinka in the person of Christ, whose suffering is appropriated with striking subjectivity; the cross is spoken of as the *mën*, or the solid central post that supports the Dinka's large, thatched cattle sheds; and the cross becomes a symbol of the potent Spirit who replaces the ancestral *jak* whose protective powers have so obviously failed in recent years. A song composed by Mary Nyanluaak Lem Bol is only one of many recent hymns illustrating the depth to which the cross has entered Dinka culture in desperate times:

> We will carry the cross. We will carry the cross.
> The cross is the gun for the evil *jok*.
> Let us chase the evil *jok* away with the cross.

This expression of Bor Dinka faith is in the great tradition of classical evangelical hymnody. It brings the saving work of Christ near; it is a sign of miraculous hope in a dark and threatening world. If such circumstances continue to lead to the writing of such hymns, it may be possible to think that evangelicalism can approximate its best.

In the second survey made by Professor Marini, "All Hail the Power of Jesus Name" emerges as the most-often reprinted hymn in American Protestant hymnbooks. This hymn's story reveals much that is typical of evangelicalism. As an indication of the kind of ecumenism that flourishes among evangelicals, the version of the hymn most often sung today actually represents an original composition of Edward Peronnet, who was a paedo-Baptist associated primarily with the Methodists, and John Rippon, a Baptist. In addition, the tune *Diadem*, the most lively of several tunes to which the hymn is sung, was composed by an 18-year-old Wesleyan hatmaker, James Ellor.[19]

Less auspiciously, Edward Perronet's career is also not untypical of
evangelicalism. Peronnet, it turns out, was not an easy chap to get along
with. As a young man he eagerly joined in the work of the Wesleys, but
his zeal for revival led him to bitter attacks on the Church of England
that soon alienated him from the Wesleys, who always saw their work as
a complement to official Anglicanism. Perronet next took one of the
chapels in the Countess of Huntingdon's Connection, but the violence
of his festering anti-Anglicanism remained so strong, he wore out the
Countess's patience and finally ended up pastoring a Congregational
church. Evangelicalism at its best is not the career of Edward Perronet.
Evangelicalism at its best, rather, is the hopes, dedication, aspirations,
and longing that have led tens, maybe hundreds, of millions of evangelicals to sing, decade after decade, and with all their hearts:

> All hail the power of Jesus' Name; Let Angels prostrate fall;
> Bring forth the royal diadem, To crown Him Lord of all. . . .
> Sinners, whose love can ne'er forget, The wormwood and the gall,
> Go spread your trophies at His feet, And crown Him Lord of all.
> O that, with yonder sacred throng, We at His feet may fall,
> Join in the everlasting song, And crown him Lord of all.

Notes

1 For an outstanding introduction to Charles Wesley's work as a hymnwriter,
see Frank Baker, ed., *Representative Verse of Charles Wesley* (Nashville, TN:
Abingdon, 1962), with the text and background for the hymn quoted in
the next paragraph from pp. 3–4. Full texts for the most important Charles
Wesley hymns may also be found in *A Collection of Hymns for the Use of
the People Called Methodists, volume 7* of *The Works of John Wesley*, eds
Franz Hilderbrandt and Oliver A. Beckerlegge (Nashville, TN: Abingdon,
1983).
2 See chapter 1 in this volume, p. 11.
3 Quotations from these and all other hymns in this chapter, unless noted
otherwise, are from Ian Bradley, ed., *The Penguin Books of Hymns* (London:
Penguin, 1989); or *Trinity Hymnal* (Philadelphia: Great Commissions
Publishing, 1961).
4 See Madeleine Forell Marshall and Janet Todd, *English Congregational
Hymns in the Eighteenth Century* (Lexington: University Press of
Kentucky, 1982); Donald Davie, *The Eighteenth-century Hymn in England*

(New York: Cambridge University Press, 1993); David Lyle Jeffrey, ed., *English Spirituality in the Age of Wesley* (Grand Rapids, MI: Eerdmans, 1987); and "The golden age of hymns," *Christian History*, 31, 1991. For general orientation to this subject, I am much indebted to Lionel Adey, *Hymns and the Christian Myth* (Vancouver: University of British Columbia Press, 1986); Adey, *Class and Idol in the English Hymn* (Vancouver: University of British Columbia Press, 1988); and J. R. Watson, *The English Hymn* (New York: Oxford University Press, 1997).

5   See especially Ian Bradley, *Abide with Me: the World of Victorian Hymns* (London: SCM, 1997).

6   See especially Dena Epstein, *Sinful Tunes and Spirituals: Black Folk Music to the Civil War* (Champaign: University of Illinois Press, 1977), from which the quotations below come, pp. 223–4, and 227; and James Weldon Johnson, *The Books of American Negro Spirituals* (New York: Viking, 1926).

7   See "A prayer for Joseph Scriven," *The Beaver*, August/September 1999, pp. 16–21.

8   See Bradley, *Abide with Me*, op. cit., n. 5, p. 91.

9   See especially Sandra Sizer, *Gospel Hymns and Social Religion: The Rhetoric of Nineteenth-century Revivalism* (Philadelphia: Temple University Press, 1978).

10   For his own use of such a list, see Stephen Marini, "Evangelical hymns and popular belief," in *Music and the Public Sphere, 1600–1900*, ed. Peter Benes (Boston: Boston University, 1998). Professor Marini's list are also being used for a multi-part project on Protestant hymnody in America directed by Edith Blumhofer at Wheaton College's Institute for the Study of American Evangelicals.

11   Bradley, *Penguin Book of Hymns*, op. cit., n. 3, p. 355.

12   See Michael W. Harris, *The Rise of Gospel Blues: the Music of Thomas Andrew Dorsey in the Urban Church* (New York: Oxford University Press, 1992).

13   Andrew Walls, "The evangelical revival, the missionary movement, and Africa," in *Evangelicalism*, eds Mark A. Noll, David W. Bebbington, and George A. Rawlyk (New York: Oxford University Press, 1994), p. 315.

14   Christopher Idle, *Stories of Our Favorite Hymns* (Grand Rapids, MI: Eerdmans, 1980), 315.

15   Watson, *English Hymn*, op. cit., n. 4, p. 261.

16   Charles Marsh, *God's Long Summer: Stories of Faith and Civil Rights* (Princeton, NJ: Princeton University Press, 1997).

17   David B. Barrett and Todd M. Johnson, "Annual statistical table on Global Mission: 2000," *International Bulletin of Missionary Research*, 24 (January), 2000, pp. 24–5.

18 The following account is from Marc R. Nikkel, "The cross of Bor Dinka Christians: a working Christology in the face of displacement and death," *Studies in World Christianity*, 1, 1995, pp. 160–85.
19 See Bradley, *Penguin Book of Hymns*, op. cit., n. 3, pp. 19–21.

Epilogue: The Future

And what of the future? Efforts at peering ahead are more difficult for a historian than looking backward. But with the trends of the recent past in mind, there are certain things we may expect from evangelicals in the future.

North American evangelicalism will almost certainly be characterized by more pluralism than unity. The passing of Billy Graham, who celebrated his eightieth birthday in November 1998, will mark the end of an important historical era. Unless unforeseen developments occur, the apparent unity that Graham's presence bequeathed to a diverse movement will be a thing of the past. In addition, evangelicalism will no doubt continue to fragment because of differences in response to the demise of "Christian America." Some may welcome America's more pluralistic society as a chance to shore up the inner life of the church, some may combat it as the loss of a treasured inheritance, and some may retreat back into inner realms of personal piety.

In theology evangelicalism will continue to witness a greater emphasis on practice than theory. In public life we are likely to see increasing cultural polarization. In intellectual life, evangelical populism will probably continue to prevail over intellectual breakthroughs. If these predictions are correct, it means that we should expect more of what has gone on throughout the past century. A few more words may be ventured on specific matters.

Demography and Cultural Influence

The size of evangelical constituencies might lead one to expect expanding evangelical influence in American society. But both the diversity and the demographics of the evangelical constituency make it unlikely that a united evangelicalism can translate large numbers of adherents into a cohesive national force. A general constituency that includes millions of Southern Baptists, as well as large numbers of conservative Reformed, Methodists, Lutherans, and adherents of many other denominations – all of whom may be more loyal to their particular churches than to a pan-evangelical ideal – will not be easy to mobilize for common goals.

The USA is a big country and its evangelical churches cover a wide spectrum. Christian Reformed parishioners in Grand Rapids, Michigan, Southern Baptists in Birmingham, Alabama, members of the Assemblies of God in Los Angeles, those committed to a Vineyard Fellowship in Tucson, Arizona, workers with the Salvation Army in New York, members of General Conference Baptists, the Evangelical Free Church, the Church of the Nazarene, and the Christian-Missionary Alliance throughout the American heartland – all are evangelicals, but they do not necessary act or think in concert.

The large numbers of African-Americans who share evangelical beliefs is a source of great potential for the movement as a whole. But as we saw in chapter 5, historic social separation has prevented black evangelicals from playing a major role in the national evangelical constituency. The growth of Hispanic evangelicalism, which is occurring mostly in pentecostal form, adds still more cultural diversity to the evangelical mosaic. In addition, as other details in chapter 5 suggested, evangelicals have been strongest precisely in those segments of the population that traditionally exert the least cultural influence in the United States – that is, among the young, the slightly less well educated, the less affluent, the Southern, and the non-white.

It is not clear if the demographic characteristics of American evangelicalism reflect a worldwide pattern. In at least some African and Latin American regions, evidence indicates that evangelicals may represent more cohesive elements in the rising middle class.[1] But whatever the case elsewhere, demographics of the evangelical situation in the United States suggest that evangelicals will have less cultural influence there than the size of the constituency might indicate.

Politicization

Given the political preoccupations of America's omnipresent media, there is considerable risk that in becoming politically active, evangelicals will corrupt their religion. At the end of the 1990s, it was relatively easy to stereotype white evangelicals as simply uncompromising pro-lifers and anti-gay zealots wholly locked up by the Republican Party. If evangelicals were ever as limited in their political concerns or as absolutely predictable in their political loyalties as this caricature suggests, it would not bode well for evangelical faith. The size of evangelical constituencies does mean that political parties and candidates cannot afford to overlook them. And as evangelicals continue to acquire greater wealth and more education, it is likely that their political participation will increase still more.

Yet barring unexpected events, it is unlikely that an evangelical political breakthrough will occur. Rather, as religious or quasi-religious values of the sort that once had greater force in North America decline, evangelicals must face the "end of Christian America." It is to be hoped that evangelicals will face this eventuality with firm theologies of society, politics, and economics, as also with strategies of integrity (perhaps a new Protestant monasticism; or a Lincoln-esque statesmanship transcending merely partisan rivalry?) rather than with a Lebanese or Northern Irish escalation toward cultural Civil War.

The Life of the Mind

An ambiguity has developed with respect to evangelical thinking about the world as a whole – that is, study from within a Christian framework devoted to nature, human institutions, and the products of human creativity. Currently, evangelical institutions, denominations, and publishers are relatively neutral concerning the prosecution of Christian learning. Most do not oppose it in the anti-intellectual fashion that prevailed for about a half-century after the mid-1920s, but most are not actively supporting it either. This relative inattention to higher learning may, in fact, be a strategic mistake, for, in an age characterized by deep structural change, guidance is needed from the best resources of Christian theology and other forms of learning. But evangelical institutions have responded only indifferently to that challenge.

On the other hand, a considerable amount of hard evangelical thinking is in fact going on, yet it is mostly sponsored by non-evangelical institutions: for example, the Lilly Endowment and the Pew Charitable Trusts (with many grants to evangelicals); the University of Notre Dame, Princeton University, Queen's University Ontario, and a few other research universities (whose faculties include first-rate scholars sympathetic to evangelicalism who are shaping at least some aspects of modern academic debate); many university presses and similar publishers that increasingly evaluate manuscripts involving Christianity on their merits and not by their ideological fit; religious thought journals like *First Things* and even the *Christian Century* (which frequently open their pages to learned expression of evangelical or classically Christian viewpoints). All these venues are, in their own ways, responding to the challenges of providing a distinctly Christian response to modern thought and culture. The end result is that in our day "evangelical scholarship" is actually advancing on many fronts, even if self-confessed evangelical institutions are not yet conspicuous by their leadership in this enterprise.

Black and White

The time is certainly far past for whites, African-Americans, and Hispanics who share evangelical convictions to pay more attention to each other. White evangelicals could bring their expertise in entrepreneurial mobilization, Hispanics an expertise in cross-cultural negotiation, and blacks their experiences at building up institutions in the face of opposition. As the larger culture slips further and further away from traditional Christian roots, it is the black evangelicals whose experience in slavery and oppression may well provide the most useful guide for evangelicals as a whole. At the same time, the rapid growth among Hispanic communities of evangelical convictions provides lessons for all believing Christians on issues of negotiation and selective adaptation between cultures. For their part, white evangelicals have money as well as experience in education, missionary sponsorship, and publishing that could aid all evangelical constituencies.

Secularization

Evangelicals, with other Americans, must come to terms with an increasingly secular culture marked by mindless or decadent popular media, a university world in which religious commitment is often ideologically suspect, and a political climate where religious values are regularly caricatured in debates over the public good. In this situation, sectarian religion of the sort once promoted by evangelicals may find it easier to withdraw into closed sanctuaries or to mount crude crusades rather than to engage the rest of society in persuasive public speech. Surveys, including some cited in chapter 2, suggest that between 20 and 30 percent of adults in the United States practice no religion (even though some in that number will tell pollsters they are Baptists, Catholics, or some other denomination, yet show no other signs of religious faith or practice). The proportion of such secularists in American society has been advancing fairly rapidly over the past quarter-century. Are evangelicals ready for a situation in which that proportion continues to rise? Are they ready to take responsible, constructive leadership of a "religious coalition" in a society increasingly characterized by religious/secular divisions? Time alone will tell.

In the end, it is difficult to characterize periods when cultures or movements experience escalating centrifugal force. North American evangelicals seem, at the start of the twenty-first century, to be living in such an era. Such times have often disoriented religious believers (as during the French Revolution, the Industrial Revolution, or the First World War). But such times have also, on occasion, witnessed evangelical renewal, as in the tenth- and thirteenth-century revivals of Roman Catholic monasticism, or among both evangelicals and Catholics in some parts of the Two-Thirds World today.

As the premier example of "culturally adaptive biblical experientialism" in the whole history of Christianity, American evangelicalism would seem well equipped to deal with the rapid changes that will doubtless characterize the twenty-first century. Almost certainly, however, the fate of evangelicalism will hinge on two circumstances. They can be phrased as questions. As a religion, can evangelicalism maintain the vitality of fresh religious experience in balance with the stability of traditional biblical authority? As a cultural force, can it preserve flexibility toward contemporary developments with integrity, and not careen off into a superficial Christianization of modernity or retreat into an isolated indulgence of merely sectarian faith? Historians of evangelicalism may be excused hope for the future, since to study evangelical history is to remember that great social, economic, political, and religious confusion characterized the era when, under the guidance of flexible traditionalists like John Wesley, Jonathan Edwards, and George Whitefield, modern evangelicalism first came into world.

Note

1   For a recent update, see David Martin, "The evangelical Protestant upsurge and its political implications," in *The Desecularization of the World: Resurgent Religion and World Politics* (Grand Rapids, MI: Eerdmans, 1999).

Guide to Further Reading

The following titles represent only samplings from a massive quantity of writing on the history and current manifestations of evangelical Christianity. The outline that follows provides some guidance through this material.

1 Reference and general treatments

1.1 Reference

Blumhofer, Edith L., and Joel A. Carpenter, eds, *Twentieth-Century Evangelicalism: a Guide to the Sources* (Garland, 1990).

Branson, Mark Lau, *The Reader's Guide to the Best Evangelical Books* (Harper & Row, 1982).

Burgess, Stanley M., and Gary M. McGee, eds, *Dictionary of Pentecostal and Charismatic Movements* (Zondervan, 1988).

Hart, D. G., ed., *Dictionary of the Presbyterian and Reformed Tradition in America* (InterVarsity, 1999).

Hill, Samuel S., ed., *Encyclopedia of Religion in the South* (Mercer, 1984).

Krapohl, Robert H., and Charles H. Lippy, *The Evangelicals: a Historical, Thematic, and Biographical Guide* (Greenwood, 1999).

Leonard, Bill, ed., *Dictionary of Baptists in America* (InterVarsity, 1994).

Lewis, Donald, ed., *The Blackwell Dictionary of Evangelical Biography, 1730–1860* (Blackwell, 1995).

Magnuson, Norris A., and William Travis, *American Evangelicalism: An Annotated Bibliography* (Locust Hill, 1990).

Reid, Daniel G., et al., eds, *Dictionary of Christianity in America* (InterVarsity Press, 1990).

Stout, Harry S., and D. G. Hart, eds, *New Directions in American Religious History* (Oxford University Press, 1997).

1.2 General treatments

Bloesch, Donald, *The Future of Evangelical Christianity: a Call for Unity Amid Diversity* (Doubleday, 1983).

Dayton, Donald W., and Robert K. Johnston, eds, *The Variety of American Evangelicalism* (Tennessee University Press/InterVarsity, 1991).

Hustad, Donald P., *Jubilate II: Church Music in Worship and Renewal* (Hope, 1989).

McGrath, Alister, *Evangelicalism and the Future of Christianity* (InterVarsity, 1995).

Schultze, Quentin J., *American Evangelicals and the Mass Media* (Zondervan, 1990).

Walls, Andrew F., *The Missionary Movement in Christian History: Studies in the Transmission of Faith* (Orbis, 1996).
Wells, Ronald A., ed., *History and the Christian Historian* (Eerdmans, 1998).

1.3 The special question of definition

Calver, Cline, Ian Coffey, and Peter Meadows, *Who Do Evangelicals Think They Are?* (Evangelical Alliance [of Great Britain], *c.*1995).
Chapman, Mark, "Identifying evangelical organizations: a new look at an old problem," *Studies in Religion/Sciences Religeuses*, 28, 1999, pp. 307–21.
Dayton, Donald W., "The search for historical evangelicalism: George Marsden's history of Fuller Seminary as a case study," *Christian Scholar's Review*, 23, 1993, pp. 12–33, 62–71; with commentary by George Marsden (pp. 34–40) and several others (pp. 41–61).
Dayton, Donald W., "Some doubts about the usefulness of the category 'evangelical,'" in *The Variety of American Evangelicalism* (see 1.2).
Johnston, Robert K., "American evangelicalism: an extended family," in *The Variety of American Evangelicalism* (see 1.2).
Marsden, George M., "Introduction," in *Evangelicalism and Modern America*, ed. Marsden (Eerdmans, 1984).
Sweeney, Douglas A., "The essential evangelicalism dialectic: the historiography of the early neo-evangelical movement and the observer–participant dilemma," *Church History*, 60 (March), 1991, pp. 70–84.
Tidball, Derek J., *Who Are the Evangelicals? Tracing the Roots of Today's Movements* (Marshall/Pickering, 1994).
Turnbull, Richard, "Evangelicalism: the state of scholarship and the question of identity," *Anvil*, 16, 1999, pp. 95–106 – focus on Britain.

2 History

2.1 General – international and transnational

Blumhofer, Edith L., and Randall Balmer, eds, *Modern Christian Revivals* (University of Illinois Press, 1993).
Carwardine, Richard, *Transatlantic Revivalism: Popular Evangelicalism in Britain and America, 1790–1865* (Greenwood, 1978).
Gäbler, Ulrich, *Auferstehungszeit: Erweckungsprediger des 19. Jahrhunderts* (C. H. Beck, 1991).
Geschichte des Pietismus, Vol. I: Das 17. und frühe 18. Jahrhundert, Vol. II: Der Pietismus im 18. Jahrhundert (Vandenhoeck & Ruprecht, 1993, 1995).

Gordon, Grant, *From Slavery to Freedom: the Life of David George, Pioneer Black Baptist Minister* (Baptist Heritage in Atlantic Canada, 1992).

Hollenweger, Walter J., *The Pentecostals* (Augsburg, 1972).

Noll, Mark A., David W. Bebbington, and George A. Rawlyk, eds, *Evangelicalism: Comparative Studies of Popular Protestantism in North America, the British Isles, and Beyond, 1700–1990* (Oxford University Press, 1994).

Rawlyk, George A., and Mark A. Noll, eds, *Amazing Grace: Evangelicalism in Australia, Britain, Canada, and the United States* (McGill-Queen's University/Baker, 1993).

Robbins, Keith, ed., *Protestant Evangelicalism: Britain, Ireland, Germany and America, c.1750–c.1950* (Blackwell, 1990).

Stoeffler, F. Ernst, *The Rise of Evangelical Pietism* (Brill, 1970).

Stoeffler, F. Ernst, *German Pietism during the Eighteenth Century* (Brill, 1973).

Ward, W. R., *The Protestant Evangelical Awakening* (Cambridge University Press, 1992).

2.2   General – American

Balmer, Randall, *Blessed Assurance: a History of Evangelicals in America* (Beacon, 1999).

Boyer, Paul, *When Time Shall Be No More: Prophecy Belief in Modern American Culture* (Harvard University Press, 1992).

Carpenter, Joel A., and Wilbert R. Shenk, eds, *Earthen Vessels: American Evangelicals and Foreign Missions, 1880–1980* (Eerdmans, 1990).

Dayton, Donald W., *Discovering an Evangelical Heritage* (Harper & Row, 1976).

Fulop, Timothy E., and Albert J. Raboteau, eds, *African-American Religion: Interpretive Essays* (Routledge, 1997).

Handy, Robert T., *A Christian America: Protestant Hopes and Historical Realities*, 2nd edn (Oxford University Press, 1984).

Harrell, David Edwin, Jr, ed., *Varieties of Southern Evangelicalism* (Mercer, 1981).

Hart, D. G., ed., *Reckoning with the Past: Historical Essays on American Evangelicalism from the Institute for the Study of American Evangelicals* (Baker, 1995).

Hatch, Nathan O., and Harry S. Stout, eds, *Jonathan Edwards and the American Experience* (Oxford University Press, 1988).

Keillor, Steven J., *This Rebellious House: American History and the Truth of Christianity* (InterVarsity Press, 1996).

Lincoln, C. Eric, and Lawrence H. Mamiya, *The Black Church in the African American Experience* (Duke University Press, 1990).

Marsden, George M., *Understanding Fundamentalism and Evangelicalism* (Eerdmans, 1991).

Ringenberg, William C., *The Christian College in America* (Eerdmans, 1984).

Robert, Dana Lee, *American Women in Mission: a Social History of Their Thought and Practice* (Mercer, 1996).

Shelley, Bruce, *Evangelicalism in America* (Eerdmans, 1967).

Sweet, Leonard I., ed., *The Evangelical Tradition in America* (Mercer, 1984).

2.3 American 1675–1758

Bushman, Richard L., ed., *The Great Awakening: Documents on the Revival of Religion, 1740–1745* (University Press of North Carolina, 1970).

Crawford, Michael J., *Seasons of Grace: Colonial New England's Revival Tradition in Its British Context* (Oxford University Press, 1991).

Guelzo, Allen C., "God's designs: the literature of the colonial revivals of religion, 1735–1760," in Stout and Hart, *New Directions* (see 1.1).

Hambrick-Stowe, Charles E., *The Practice of Piety: Puritan Devotional Discipline in Seventeenth-century New England* (University Press of North Carolina, 1982).

Lovelace, Richard F., *The American Pietism of Cotton Mather: Origins of American Evangelicalism* (Eerdmans, 1979).

Murray, Iain H., *Jonathan Edwards: a New Biography* (Banner of Truth, 1987).

O'Brien, Susan, "Eighteenth-century publishing networks in the first years of Transatlantic evangelicalism," in *Evangelicalism* (see 2.1).

Simonson, Harold, *Jonathan Edwards: Theologian of the Heart* (Eerdmans, 1974).

Stout, Harry S., *The Divine Dramatist: George Whitefield and the Rise of Modern Evangelicalism* (Eerdmans, 1991).

Stout, Harry S., *The New England Soul: Preaching and Religious Culture in Colonial New England* (Oxford University Press, 1986).

Westerkamp, Marilyn J., *Triumph of the Laity: Scots-Irish Piety and the Great Awakening, 1625–1760* (Oxford University Press, 1988).

2.4 American 1759–1815

Bilhartz, Terry D., *Urban Religion and the Second Great Awakening: Church and Society in Early National Baltimore* (Associated University Presses, 1986).

Calhoon, Robert M., *Evangelicals and Conservatives in the Early South, 1740–1861* (University Press of South Carolina, 1988).

Essig, James, *The Bonds of Wickedness: American Evangelicals Against Slavery, 1770–1808* (Temple, 1982).

Hatch, Nathan O., *The Democratization of American Christianity* (Yale University Press, 1989).

Heimert, Alan, *Religion and the American Mind from the Great Awakening to the Revolution* (Harvard University Press, 1966).

Heyrman, Christine Leigh, *Southern Cross: the Beginnings of the Bible Belt* (Knopf, 1997).

Isaac, Rhys, *The Transformation of Virginia* (University Press of North Carolina, 1982).

Juster, Susan, *Disorderly Women: Sexual Politics and Evangelicalism in Revolutionary New England* (Cornell University Press, 1994).

Kling, David W., *A Field of Divine Wonders: the New Divinity and Village Revivals in Northwestern Connecticut, 1792–1822* (Penn State University Press, 1993).

McLoughlin, William C., *New England Dissent, 1630–1833: the Baptists and the Separation of Church and State*, 2 volumes (Harvard University Press, 1971).

Marini, Stephen A., *Radical Sects of Revolutionary New England* (Harvard University Press, 1982).

Noll, Mark A., *Princeton and the Republic, 1768–1822* (Princeton University Press, 1989).

Noll, Mark A., "The American Revolution and Protestant evangelicalism," *Journal of Interdisciplinary History*, 23, 1993, pp. 615–38.

Richey, Russell E., *Early American Methodism* (Indiana University Press, 1991).

Sobel, Mechal, *The World They Made Together: Black and White Values in Eighteenth-century Virginia* (Princeton University Press, 1987).

West, John G., Jr, *The Politics of Revelation and Reason: Religion and Civic Life in the New Nation* (Kansas University Press, 1996).

Wigger, John, *Taking Heaven by Storm: Methodism and the Rise of Popular Christianity in America* (Oxford University Press, 1998).

2.5   American 1816–1870

Brekus, Catherine, *Strangers and Pilgrims: Female Preaching in America, 1740–1845* (University Press of North Carolina, 1998).

Brumberg, Joan Jacobs, *Mission for Life: the Judson Family and American Evangelical Culture* (New York University Press, 1980).

Butler, Diana Hochstedt, *Standing Against the Whirlwind: Evangelical Episcopalians in 19th-century America* (Oxford University Press, 1995).

Carwardine, Richard J., *Evangelicals and Politics in Antebellum America* (Yale University Press, 1993).

Caskey, Marie, *Chariot of Fire: Religion and the Beecher Family* (Yale University Press, 1978).

Conforti, Joseph A., *Jonathan Edwards, Religious Tradition, and American Culture* (University Press of North Carolina, 1995).

Dieter, Melvin Easterday, *The Holiness Revival of the 19th Century* (Scarecrow, 1980).

Foster, Charles I., *An Errand of Mercy: the Evangelical United Front, 1790–1837* (University Press of North Carolina, 1960).

Genovese, Eugene D., *A Consuming Fire: the Fall of the Confederacy in the Mind of the White Christian South* (Georgia University Press, 1999).

Genovese, Eugene D., *Roll, Jordan, Roll: the World the Slaves Made* (Random House, 1972).

Goen, C. C., *Broken Churches, Broken Nation: Denominational Schisms and the Coming of the American Civil War* (Mercer, 1985).

Gutjahr, Paul C., *An American Bible: a History of the Good Book in the United States, 1777–1880* (Stanford University Press, 1999).

Hambrick-Stowe, Charles E., *Charles G. Finney and the Spirit of American Evangelicalism* (Eerdmans, 1996).

Hanley, Mark Y., *Beyond a Christian Commonwealth: the Protestant Quarrel with the American Republic, 1830–1860* (University Press of North Carolina, 1994).

Hughes, Richard T., and C. Leonard Allen, *Illusions of Innocence: Protestant Primitivism in America, 1630–1875* (Chicago University Press, 1988).

Johnson, Curtis D., *Islands of Holiness: Rural Religion in Upstate New York, 1790–1860* (Cornell University Press, 1989).

Johnson, Curtis D., *Redeeming America: Evangelicals and the Road to Civil War* (I. R. Dee, 1993).

Lesick, Lawrence Thomas, *The Lane Rebels: Evangelicalism and Abolitionism in Antebellum America* (Scarecrow, 1980).

Loveland, Anne C., *Southern Evangelicals and the Social Order, 1800–1860* (Louisiana State University, 1980).

McLoughlin, William C., *Cherokees and Missionaries, 1789–1839* (Yale University Press, 1984).

Marsden, George M., *The Evangelical Mind and the New School Presbyterian Experience* (Yale University Press, 1970).

Mathews, Donald G., *Religion in the Old South* (Chicago University Press, 1977).

Miller, Randall, Harry S. Stout, and Charles Reagan Wilson, eds, *Religion and the American Civil War* (Oxford University Press, 1998).

Moorhead, James H., *American Apocalypse: Yankee Protestants and the Civil War, 1860–1869* (Yale University Press, 1978).

Murray, Iain H., *Revival and Revivals: the Making and Marring of American Evangelicalism, 1750–1858* (Banner of Truth, 1994).

Oden, Thomas C. ed., *Phoebe Palmer: Selected Writings* (Paulist, 1988).

Raboteau, Albert J., *Slave Religion: the "Invisible Institution" in the Antebellum South* (Oxford University Press, 1978).

Schneider, A. Gregory, *The Way of the Cross Leads Home: the Domestication of American Methodism* (Indiana University Press, 1993).

Smith, Timothy L., *Revivalism and Social Reform: American Protestantism on the Eve of the Civil War*, rev. edn (Johns Hopkins University Press, 1980).

Sutton, William R., *Journeymen for Jesus: Evangelical Artisans Confront Capitalism in Jacksonian Baltimore* (Penn State University Press, 1998).

Wyatt-Brown, Bertram, *Lewis Tappan and the Evangelical War Against Slavery* (Case Western Reserve, 1969).

Yee, Shirley J., *Black Women Abolitionists: a Study in Activism, 1828–1860* (Tennessee University Press, 1992).

2.6 American 1871–1949

Anderson, Robert M., *Vision of the Disinherited: the Making of American Pentecostalism* (Oxford University Press, 1979).

Beale, David O., *In Pursuit of Purity: American Fundamentalism since 1850* (Unusual, 1986).

Blumhofer, Edith L., *Aimee Semple McPherson: Everybody's Sister* (Eerdmans, 1993).

Blumhofer, Edith L., *Defending the Faith: the Assemblies of God, Pentecostalism, and American Culture* (Illinois University Press, 1993).

Bordin, Ruth, *Frances Willard* (University Press of North Carolina, 1986).

Brereton, Virginia Lieson, *Training God's Army: the American Bible School, 1880–1940* (Indiana University Press, 1940).

Campbell, James T., *Songs of Zion: the African Methodist Episcopal Church in the United States and South Africa* (University Press of North Carolina, 1998).

Carpenter, Joel A., *Revive Us Again: the Reawakening of American Fundamentalism* (Oxford University Press, 1997).

Carpenter, Joel A., ed., *Fundamentalism in American Religion, 1870–1950: a 45-Volume Facsimile Series* (Garland, 1988).

Dayton, Donald W., ed., *"The Higher Christian Life": Sources for the Study of Holiness, Pentecostal, and Keswick Movements*, 48 volumes (Garland, 1984).

Dorsett, Lyle W., *Billy Sunday and the Redemption of Urban America* (Eerdmans, 1991).

Dorsett, Lyle W., *A Passion for Souls: the Life of D. L. Moody* (Moody, 1997).

Findlay, James F., Jr, *Dwight L. Moody: American Evangelist, 1837–1899* (Chicago University Press, 1969).

Frank, Douglas W., *Less than Conquerors: How Evangelicals Entered the 20th Century* (Eerdmans, 1986).

Harris, Michael W., *The Rise of Gospel Blues: the Music of Thomas A. Dorsey in the Urban Church* (Oxford University Press, 1992).

Hart, D. G., *Defender of the Faith: J. Gresham Machen and the Crisis of Protestantism in Modern America* (Johns Hopkins University Press, 1994).

Longfield, Bradley J., *The Presbyterian Controversy: Fundamentalists, Modernists, and Moderates* (Oxford University Press, 1991).

Magnuson, Norris, *Salvation in the Slums: Evangelical Social Work, 1865–1920* (Scarecrow, 1977).

Marsden, George M., *Fundamentalism and American Culture, 1875–1925* (Oxford University Press, 1980).

Russell, C. Allyn, *Voices of American Fundamentalism: Seven Biographical Studies* (Westminster, 1976).

Sandeen, Ernest R., *The Roots of Fundamentalism: British and American Millenarianism, 1800–1930* (Chicago University Press, 1970).

Sizer, Sandra S., *Gospel Hymns and Social Religion: the Rhetoric of 19th-century Revivalism* (Temple, 1978).

Smith, Gary Scott, *The Seeds of Secularization: Calvinism, Culture, and Pluralism in America, 1870–1915* (Eerdmans, 1985).

Trollinger, William Vance, Jr, *God's Empire: William Bell Riley and Midwestern Fundamentalism* (Wisconsin University Press, 1990).

Wacker, Grant, "The Holy Spirit and the spirit of the age in American Protestantism, 1880–1910," *Journal of American History*, 72 (June), 1985, pp. 45–62.

2.7   American 1945–present

Ammerman, Nancy, *Bible Believers: Fundamentalists in the Modern World* (Rutgers University Press, 1987).

Balmer, Randall, *Mine Eyes Have Seen the Glory: a Journey into the Evangelical Subculture of America* (Oxford University Press, 1989).

Bergman, Susan, *Anonymity: the Secret Life of an American Family* (Warner, 1995) – memoir.

Berk, Stephen E., *A Time to Heal: John Perkins, Community Development, and Racial Reconciliation* (Baker, 1997).

Bush, Perry, *Two Kingdoms, Two Loyalties: Mennonite Pacifism in Modern America* (Johns Hopkins University Press, 1999).

Dobson, Edward (assoc. of Jerry Falwell), *In Search of Unity: an Appeal to Fundamentalists and Evangelicals* (Nelson, 1985).

Hadden, Jeffrey K., and Anson D. Shupe, *Televangelism, Power, and Politics on God's Frontiers* (Henry Holt, 1988).

Harrell, David Edwin, Jr, *All Things Are Possible: the Healing and Charismatic Revivals in Modern America* (Indiana University Press, 1975).

Harrell, David Edwin, Jr, *Oral Roberts: an American Life* (Indiana University Press, 1985).

Henry, Carl F. H., *Confessions of a Theologian: an Autobiography* (Word, 1986).

Howard, Thomas, *Christ the Tiger* (Lippincott, 1967) – memoir.

Marsden, George M., ed., *Evangelicalism and Modern America* (Eerdmans, 1984).

Marsden, George M., *Reforming Fundamentalism: Fuller Seminary and the New Evangelicalism* (Eerdmans, 1987).

Marsh, Charles, *God's Long Summer: Stories of Faith and Civil Rights* (Princeton University Press, 1997).

Martin, William, *A Prophet With Honor: the Billy Graham Story* (Morrow, 1991).

Nelson, Rudolph, *The Making and Unmaking of an Evangelical Mind: the Case of Edward Carnell* (Cambridge University Press, 1987).

Nelson, Shirley, *The Last Year of the War* (Harper & Row, 1978) – novel.

Poloma, Margaret, *The Assemblies of God at the Crossroads: Charisma and Institutionalization* (Tennessee University Press, 1989).

Quebedeaux, Richard, *The Worldly Evangelicals* (Harper & Row, 1973).

Quebedeaux, Richard, *The Young Evangelicals* (Harper & Row, 1974).

Robert, Dana, "From missions to mission to beyond missions: the historiography of American Protestant foreign missions since World War II," in Stout and Hart, *New Directions* (see 1.1).

Ruegsegger, Ronald W., ed., *Reflections on Francis Schaeffer* (Zondervan, 1986).

Shibley, Mark A., *Resurgent Evangelicalism in the United States: Mapping Cultural Change since 1970* (South Carolina University Press, 1996).

Stone, Jon R., *On the Boundaries of American Evangelicalism: the Postwar Evangelical Coalition* (St Martin's, 1997).

Warner, R. Stephen, *New Wine in Old Wineskins: Evangelicals and Liberals in a Small-town Church* (University of California Press, 1988).

Wells, David, "On being evangelical: some theological differences and similarities," in *Evangelicalism* (see 2.1).

Wells, David F., and John D. Woodbridge, eds, *The Evangelicals: What They Believe, Who They Are, Where They Are Changing* (Abingdon, 1975).

2.8   British (including Scottish and Irish)

Bebbington, D. W., *The Nonconformist Conscience: Chapel and Politics, 1870–1914* (George Allen & Unwin, 1982).

Bebbington, D. W., *Evangelicalism in Modern Britain: a History from the 1730s to the 1980s* (Unwin Hyman, 1989).

Bradley, Ian C., *The Call to Seriousness: the Evangelical Impact on the Victorians* (Macmillan, 1976).

Bradley, James E., *Religion, Revolution and English Radicalism: Non-conformity in Eighteenth-century Politics and Society* (Cambridge University Press, 1990).

Brady, Steve, and Harold Rowdon, eds, *For Such a Time as This: Perspectives on Evangelicalism, Past, Present and Future* (Scripture Union, 1996).

Brown, Stewart J., *Thomas Chalmers and the Godly Commonwealth in Scotland* (Oxford University Press, 1982).

Catherwood, Christopher, *Five Evangelical Leaders* (Hodder & Stoughton, 1985) – Stott, Lloyd-Jones, Schaeffer, Packer, Graham.

Garnett, Jane, and Colin Matthew, eds, *Revival and Religion since 1700: Essays for John Walsh* (Hambledon, 1993).

Heitzenrater, Richard P., *Wesley and the People Called Methodists* (Abingdon, 1995).

Hempton, David, *Methodism and Politics in British Society, 1750–1850* (Stanford University Press, 1987).

Hempton, David, *Religion and Political Culture in Britain and Ireland from the Glorious Revolution to the Decline of Empire* (Cambridge University Press, 1996).

Hempton, David, *The Religion of the People: Methodism and Popular Religion, ca. 1750–1900* (Routledge, 1996).

Hempton, David, and Myrtle Hill, *Evangelical Protestantism in Ulster Society, 1740–1890* (Routledge, 1992).

Hilton, Boyd, *The Age of Atonement: the Influence of Evangelicalism on Social and Economic Thought* (Oxford University Press, 1988).

Hindmarsh, Bruce, *John Newton and the English Evangelical Tradition between the Conversions of Wesley and Wilberforce* (Clarendon Press, 1996).

Hylson-Smith, Kenneth, *Evangelicals in the Church of England, 1734–1984* (T. & T. Clark, 1988).

Lewis, Donald M., *Lighten Their Darkness: the Evangelical Mission to Working-class London, 1828–1860* (Greenwood, 1986).

Murray, Iain H., *D. Martyn Lloyd-Jones*, 2 volumes (Banner of Truth, 1982, 1990).

Pollock, John, *Wilberforce* (Constable, 1977).

Rack, Henry D., *Reasonable Enthusiast: John Wesley and the Rise of Methodism* (Trinity, 1989).

Stanley, Brian, *The Bible and the Flag: Protestant Missions and British Imperialism in the 19th and 20th centuries* (Apollos, 1990).

Valenze, Deborah, *Prophetic Sons and Daughters: Female Preaching and Popular Religion in Industrial England* (Princeton University Press, 1985).

Walsh, John, "'Methodism' and the origins of English-speaking evangelicalism," in *Evangelicalism* (see 2.1).

Wolffe, John, *The Protestant Crusade in Great Britain, 1829–1860* (Oxford University Press, 1991).

Wolffe, John, *God and Greater Britain: Religion and National Life in Britain and Ireland, 1843–1945* (Routledge, 1994).

Wolffe, John, ed., *Evangelical Faith and Public Zeal: Evangelicals and Society, 1780–1980* (SPCK, 1995).

2.9   Canadian

Airhart, Phyllis D., *Serving the Present Age: Revivalism, Progressivism, and the Methodist Tradition in Canada* (McGill-Queen's University, 1992).

Burkinshaw, Robert K., *Pilgrims in Lotus Land: Conservative Protestants in British Columbia, 1917–1981* (McGill-Queen's University, 1995).

Christie, Nancy, and Michael Gauvreau, *A Full-orbed Christianity: the Protestant Churches and Social Welfare in Canada, 1900–1940* (McGill-Queen's University, 1997).

Elliott, David R., and Iris Miller, *Bible Bill: a Biography of William Aberhart* (Reidmore, 1987).

Gauvreau, Michael, *The Evangelical Century: College and Creed in English Canada from the Great Revival to the Great Depression* (McGill-Queen's University, 1991).

Marks, Lynne, *Revivals and Roller Rinks: Religion, Leisure, and Identity in Late-nineteenth-century Small-town Ontario* (Toronto University Press, 1996).

Noel, Jan, *Canada Dry: Temperance Crusades before Confederation* (Toronto University Press, 1995).

Rawlyk, George A., *The Canada Fire: Radical Evangelicalism in British North America, 1775–1812* (McGill-Queen's University, 1994).

Rawlyk, George A., *Is Jesus Your Personal Saviour? In Search of Canadian Evangelicalism in the 1990s* (McGill-Queen's University, 1996).

Rawlyk, George A., ed., *Aspects of the Canadian Evangelical Experience* (McGill-Queen's University, 1997).

Rawlyk, George A., ed., *The Canadian Protestant Experience, 1760–1990* (Welch, 1990).

Stackhouse, John G., *Canadian Evangelicalism in the Twentieth Century* (Toronto University Press, 1993).

Van Die, Marguerite, *An Evangelical Mind: Nathanael Burwash and the Methodist Tradition in Canada, 1839–1918* (McGill-Queen's University, 1989).

Westfall, William. *Two Worlds: the Protestant Culture of 19th-century Ontario* (McGill-Queen's University, 1989).

2.10   Australian

Dickey, Brian, ed., *The Australian Dictionary of Evangelical Biography* (Evangelical History Association, 1994).

Hutchinson, Mark, and Geoff Treloar, eds, *This Gospel Shall Be Preached: Essays on the Australian Contribution to World Mission* (Centre for the Study of Australian Christianity, 1998).

Hutchinson, Mark, E. Campion, and S. Piggin, eds, *Reviving Australia: Essays on the History and Experiences of Revival and Revivalism in Australian Christianity* (Centre for the Study of Australian Christianity, 1994).

Judd, Stephen, and Kenneth Cable, *Sydney Anglicans* (Sydney Anglican Information Office, 1987).

Piggin, Stuart, *Evangelical Christianity in Australia: Spirit, Word, and World* (Oxford University Press, 1996).

3 Evangelicals in relation to other forms of Christianity

Bellah, Robert N., and F. E. Greenspahn, eds, *Uncivil Religion: Interreligious Hostility in America* (Crossroad, 1987).

Blumhofer, Edith L., Russell P. Spittler, and Grant A. Wacker, eds, *Pentecostal Currents in American Protestantism* (Illinois University Press, 1999).

Bratt, James D., *Dutch Calvinism in Modern America* (Eerdmans, 1984).

Clendenin, Daniel B., *Eastern Orthodox Christianity: a Western Perspective* (Baker, 1994).

Colson, Charles, and Richard John Neuhaus, eds, *Evangelicals and Catholics Together: Toward a Common Mission* (Word, 1995).

Cox, Harvey, *Fire from Heaven: the Rise of Pentecostal Spirituality and the Reshaping of Religion in the 21st Century* (Addison-Wesley, 1995).

Dockery, David S., ed., *Southern Baptists and American Evangelicals* (Broadman & Holman, 1994).

Edwards, David L., and John Stott, *Essentials: a Liberal–Evangelical Dialogue* (Hodder & Stoughton, 1988).

Ellingsen, Mark, *The Evangelical Movement: Growth, Impact, Controversy, Dialog* (Augsburg, 1988).

Garrett, James Leo, Jr, and E. Glenn Hinson, eds, *Are Southern Baptists "Evangelicals"?* (Mercer, 1983).

Geisler, Norman, and R. A. MacKenzie, *Roman Catholics and Evangelicals: Agreements and Differences* (Baker, 1995).

Howard, Thomas, *Evangelical Is Not Enough* (Nelson, 1984) – from a convert to Roman Catholicism.

Kraus, C. Norman, ed., *Evangelicalism and Anabaptism* (Herald, 1979).

Martin, David, *Tongues of Fire: the Explosion of Protestantism in Latin America* (Blackwell, 1990).

Poewe, Karla, *Charismatic Christianity as a Global Culture* (South Carolina University Press, 1994).

Rudnick, Milton L., *Fundamentalism and the Missouri Synod* (Concordia, 1966).

4   The Bible

Abraham, William J., *Divine Revelation and the Limits of Historical Criticism* (Oxford University Press, 1982).

Barr, James, *Fundamentalism* (Westminster, 1978).

Cameron, Nigel M. de S., *Biblical Higher Critics and the Defense of Infallibilism in Nineteenth-century Britain* (Edwin Mellen, 1987).

Carson, D. A., *New Testament Commentary Survey*, 4th edn (Baker, 1993).

Carson, D. A., and J. D. Woodbridge, eds, *Scripture and Truth* (Zondervan, 1983).

Carson, D. A., and J. D. Woodbridge, eds, *Hermeneutics and Authority* (Zondervan, 1986).

Elwell, Walter A., ed., *Evangelical Commentary on the Bible* (Baker, 1989).

Elwell, Walter A., ed., *Bible Interpreters of the Twentieth Century: a Selection of Evangelical Voices* (Baker, 1999).

Green, Joel B., Scot McKnight, and I. Howard Marshall, eds, *Dictionary of Jesus and the Gospels* (InterVarsity Press, 1992).

Guthrie, Donald, *New Testament Introduction* (InterVarsity Press, 1970).

Hatch, Nathan O., and Mark A. Noll, eds, *The Bible in America* (Oxford University Press, 1982).

Hawthorne, Gerald F., R. P. Martin, and D. G. Reid, eds, *Dictionary of Paul and His Letters* (InterVarsity Press, 1993).

Johnston, Robert K., ed., *The Use of the Bible in Theology: Evangelical Options* (John Knox University Press, 1985).

La Sor, William Sanford, D. A. Hubbard, and F. W. Bush, *Old Testament Survey*, 2nd edn (Eerdmans, 1996).

Longman, Trumper, *Old Testament Commentary Survey*, 2nd edn (Baker, 1995).

Lundin, Roger, Anthony Thiselton, and Clarence Walhout, *The Promise of Hermeneutics*, 2nd edn (Eerdmans, 1999).

New Bible Dictionary, 3rd edn (InterVarsity Press, 1996).

Noll, Mark A., *Between Faith and Criticism: Evangelicals, Scholarship, and the Bible in America*, rev. edn (Baker, 1986).

Packer, J. I., *"Fundamentalism" and the Word of God* (Eerdmans, 1958).

Riesen, Richard Allan, *Criticism and Faith in Late-Victorian Scotland* (University Press of America, 1985).

Rogers, Jack, and Donald K. McKim, *The Authority and the Interpretation of the Bible* (Harper & Row, 1979).

Smith, Theophus, *Conjuring Culture: Biblical Formation of Black America* (Oxford University Press, 1994).

Thiselton, Anthony C., *The Two Horizons: New Testament Hermeneutics and Philosophical Description* (Eerdmans, 1980).

Warfield, Benjamin Breckinridge, *The Authority and Inspiration of the Bible* (Presbyterian and Reformed, 1948).

Woodbridge, John D., *Biblical Authority: a Critique of the Rogers/McKim Proposal* (Zondervan, 1982).

5 Evangelical religious experience

Bruce, Dickson D., Jr, *And They All Sang Hallelujah: Plain-folk Camp-meeting Religion, 1800–1845* (Tennessee University Press, 1974).

Bundy, David, "Keswick and the experience of evangelical piety," in Blumhofer and Balmer, *Revivalism* (see 2.1).

Campbell, Ted, *The Religion of the Heart: a Study of European Religious Life in the 17th and 18th Centuries* (South Carolina University Press, 1991).

Gordon, James, *Evangelical Spirituality from the Wesleys to John Stott* (Inter-Varsity Press, 1991).

Lovelace, Richard F., *Dynamics of Spiritual Life: an Evangelical Theology of Renewal* (InterVarsity Press, 1979).

McGrath, Alister, *Spirituality in an Age of Change: Rediscovering the Spirit of the Reformers* (Zondervan, 1994).

Sanders, Cheryl Jeanne, *Saints in Exile: the Holiness-Pentecostal Experience in African American Religion and Culture* (Oxford University Press, 1996).

Schmidt, Leigh Eric, *Holy Fairs: Scottish Communions and American Revivals in the Early Modern Period* (Princeton University Press, 1989).

Van Die, Marguerite, "The double vision: evangelical piety as derivative and indigenous in Victorian English Canada," in *Evangelicalism* (see 2.1).

6 Evangelical theologies and theologians

6.1 Reference

Carter, Charles W., ed., *A Contemporary Wesleyan Theology: Biblical, Systematic and Practical* (Zondervan, 1983).

Elwell, Walter A., ed., *Evangelical Dictionary of Theology* (Baker, 1984).

Elwell, Walter A., ed., *Handbook of Evangelical Theologians* (Baker, 1993).

Elwell, Walter A., ed., *Evangelical Dictionary of Biblical Theology* (Baker, 1996).

Ferguson, Sinclair B., D. F. Wright, and J. I. Packer, eds, *New Dictionary of Theology* (InterVarsity Press, 1988).

6.2 History

Bass, Clarence B., *Backgrounds to Dispensationalism* (Eerdmans, 1960).

Conser, Walter H., Jr, *Church and Confessions: Conservative Theologians in Germany, England, and America, 1815–1866* (Mercer, 1984).

Dayton, Donald W., *Theological Roots of Pentecostalism* (Hendrickson, 1987).

Guelzo, Allen C., *Edwards on the Will: a Century of American Theological Debate* (Wesleyan University Press, 1989).

Hart, D. G., and R. A. Mohler, Jr, eds, *Theological Education in the Evangelical Tradition* (Baker, 1996).

Holifield, E. Brooks, *The Gentlemen Theologians: American Theology in Southern Culture, 1795–1860* (Duke University Press, 1978).

Kuklick, Bruce, *Churchmen and Philosophers from Jonathan Edwards to John Dewey* (Yale University Press, 1985).

Madden, Edward H., and James E. Hamilton, *Freedom and Grace: the Life of Asa Mahan* (Scarecrow, 1982).

Noll, Mark A., ed., *The Princeton Theology, 1812–1921* (Baker, 1983).

Weber, Timothy P., *Living in the Shadow of the Second Coming: American Premillennialism, 1875–1982*, 3rd edn (Chicago University Press, 1987).

Wells, David F., ed., *Reformed Theology in America* (Eerdmans, 1985).

6.3 Landmarks, examples

Blaising, Craig A., and Darrell L. Bock, eds, *Dispensationalism, Israel and the Church* (Zondervan, 1992).

Cromartie, Michael, ed., *A Preserving Grace: Protestants, Catholics, and Natural Law* (Eerdmans, 1997).

Edwards, Jonathan, *Works*, eds, Perry Miller, John E. Smith, Harry S. Stout, et al. (Yale, 1957–). Connected with this edition are two anthologies: John E. Smith, Harry S. Stout, and Kenneth P. Minkema, eds, *A Jonathan Edwards Reader* (Yale University Press, 1995); and Wilson H. Kimnach, Kenneth P. Minkema, and Douglas A. Sweeney, eds, *The Sermons of Jonathan Edwards: a Reader* (Yale University Press, 1999).

Fackre, Gabriel, "The surge in systematics: a commentary on current works," *Journal of Religion*, 73 (April), 1993, pp. 213–37.

Henry, Carl F. H., ed., *Contemporary Evangelical Thought* (Channel, 1957).

Henry, Carl F. H., ed., *Revelation and the Bible* (Baker, 1958).

Henry, Carl F. H., ed., *Basic Christian Doctrines* (Holt, Rinehart, and Winston, 1962).

Henry, Carl F. H., ed., *Christian Faith and Modern Thought* (Channel, 1964).

Henry, Carl F. H., ed., *Jesus of Nazareth: Savior and Lord* (Eerdmans, 1966).

Henry, Carl F. H., ed., *Fundamentals of the Faith* (Zondervan, 1969).

Lewis, Donald, and Alister McGrath, eds, *Doing Theology for the People of God: Studies in Honor of J. I. Packer* (InterVarsity Press, 1996).

McGrath, Alister E., *The Genesis of Doctrine: a Study in the Foundations of Doctrinal Criticism* (Blackwell, 1990).

Noll, Mark A., and David F. Wells, eds, *Christian Faith and Practice in the Modern World: Theology from an Evangelical Point of View* (Eerdmans, 1988).

Phillips, Timothy R., and Dennis L. Okholm, eds, *The Nature of Confession: Evangelicals and Postliberals in Conversation* (InterVarsity Press, 1996).

Wells, David F., *No Place for Truth: Or, Whatever Happened to Evangelical Theology?* (Eerdmans, 1993).

Wesley, John, *Works*, eds Albert C. Outler, et al. (Oxford University Press/ Abingdon, 1984–).

7 Women (mostly recent)

Bendroth, Margaret Lamberts, *Fundamentalism and Gender, 1875 to the Present* (Yale University Press, 1993).

Brasher, Brenda E., *Godly Women: Fundamentalism and Female Power* (Rutgers University Press, 1998).

Brereton, Virginia Lieson, *From Sin to Salvation: Stories of Women's Conversions, 1800 to the Present* (Indiana University Press, 1991).

Deberg, Betty A., *Ungodly Women: Gender and the First Wave of American Fundamentalism* (Fortress, 1990).

Foh, Susan, *Women and the Word of God: a Response to Biblical Feminism* (Presbyterian and Reformed, 1979).

Griffith, R. Marie, *God's Daughters: Evangelical Women and the Power of Submission* (University of California Press, 1997).

Hardesty, Nancy A., *Women Called to Witness: Evangelical Feminism in the Nineteenth Century*, 2nd edn (Tennessee University Press, 1999).

Hardesty, Nancy A., and Leitha Scanzoni, *All We're Meant to Be: Biblical Feminism for Today*, 3rd edn (Eerdmans, 1992).

Juster, Susan, "The spirit and the flesh: gender, language, and sexuality in American Protestantism," in Stout and Hart, *New Directions* (see 1.1).

Malcolm, Kari Torjesen, *Women at the Crossroads: a Path beyond Feminism and Traditionalism* (InterVarsity Press, 1982).

Muir, Elizabeth Gillan, and M. F. Whitely, eds, *Changing Roles of Women within the Christian Churches of Canada* (Toronto University Press, 1995).

Piper, John, and Wayne Grudem, eds, *Recovering Biblical Manhood and Womanhood: a Response to Evangelical Feminism* (Crossway, 1991).

Van Leeuwen, Mary Stewart, *Gender and Grace: Love, Work, and Parenting in a Changing World* (InterVarsity Press, 1990).

Van Leeuwen, Mary Stewart, et al., *After Eden: Facing the Challenge of Gender Reconciliation* (Eerdmans, 1993).

8   Intellectual life

8.1   Historical and general

Bozeman, Theodore Dwight, *Protestants in an Age of Science: the Baconian Ideal and Antebellum American Religious Thought* (University Press of North Carolina, 1977).

Conser, Walter H., Jr, *God and the Natural World: Religion and Science in Antebellum America* (South Carolina University Press, 1993).

Marsden, George M., "The collapse of American evangelical academia," in *Faith and Rationality*, eds A. Plantinga and N. Wolterstorff (Notre Dame University Press, 1983).

May, Henry F., *The Enlightenment in America* (Oxford University Press, 1976).

Meyer, D. H., *The Instructed Conscience: the Shaping of the American National Ethic* (Pennsylvania University Press, 1972).

Noll, Mark A., "Common sense traditions and American evangelical thought," *American Quarterly*, 37, 1985, pp. 216–38.

Noll, Mark A., *The Scandal of the Evangelical Mind* (Eerdmans, 1994).

8.2   Science (including evolution and creationism)

Brooke, John Hedley, *Science and Religion: Some Historical Perspectives* (Cambridge University Press, 1991).

Dupree, A. Hunter, *Asa Gray* (Harvard University Press, 1959).

Gilkey, Langdon, *Creationism on Trail: Evolution and God at Little Rock* (Winston, 1985).

Hooykaas, Reijer, *Religion and the Rise of Modern Science* (Eerdmans, 1972).

Johnson, Phillip E., *Darwin on Trial* (InterVarsity Press, 1991).

Larson, Edward J., *Trial and Error: the American Legal Controversy over Creation and Evolution* (Oxford University Press, 1985).

Larson, Edward J., *Summer for the Gods: the Scopes Trial and America's Continuing Debate over Science and Religion* (Basic, 1997).

Livingstone, David N., *Darwin's Forgotten Defenders: the Encounter Between Evangelical Theology and Evolutionary Thought* (Eerdmans and Scottish Academic Press, 1987).

Livingstone, David, D. G. Hart, and Mark Noll, eds, *Evangelicals and Science in Historical Perspective* (Oxford University Press, 1999).

McGrath, Alister E., *The Foundations of Dialogue in Science and Religion* (Blackwell, 1998).

Moore, James R., *The Post-Darwinian Controversies: a Study of the Protestant Struggle to Come to Terms with Darwin in Great Britain and America, 1870–1900* (Cambridge University Press, 1979).

Moore, James R., "Interpreting the new creationism," *Michigan Quarterly Review*, 22, 1983, pp. 321–34.

Moore, James R., *The Darwin Legend* (Baker, 1994).

Morris, Henry M., *A History of Modern Creationism* (Master's, 1984).

Murphy, Nancy, *Theology in the Age of Scientific Reasoning* (Cornell University Press, 1990).

Noll, Mark A., and David N. Livingstone, eds, *Charles Hodge's What Is Darwinism and Other Writings on Science and Religion* (Baker, 1994).

Noll, Mark A., and David N. Livingstone, eds, *B. B. Warfield on Evolution, Scripture, and Science* (Baker, 2000).

Numbers, Ronald L., *The Creationists* (Knopf, 1992).

Numbers, Ronald L., ed., *Creationism in Twentieth-century America: a Ten-volume Anthology of Documents, 1903–1961* (Garland, 1995).

Numbers, Ronald L., *Darwin Comes to America* (Harvard University Press, 1998).

Ratzsch, Del, *The Battle of Beginnings: Why Neither Side Is Winning the Creation–Evolution Debate* (InterVarsity, 1996).

Van Till, Howard J., *The Fourth Day: What the Bible and the Heavens Are Telling Us about the Creation* (Eerdmans, 1986).

Young, Davis A., *The Biblical Flood: a Case Study in the Church's Response to Extrabiblical Evidence* (Eerdmans, 1995).

9 Contemporary politics and society

Bruce, Steve, *The Rise and Fall of the New Christian Right . . . 1978–1988* (Oxford University Press, 1988).

Cerillo, Augustus, Jr, and Murray W. Dempster, *Salt and Light: Evangelical Political Thought in Modern America* (Baker, 1989).

Cromartie, Michael, ed., *No Longer Exiles: the Religious New Right in American Politics* (Ethics and Public Policy, 1993).

Emerson, Michael, and Christian Smith, *Divided by Faith: Evangelical Religion and the Problem of Race in America* (Oxford, 2000).

Gay, Craig M., *With Liberty and Justice for Whom? The Recent Evangelical Debate over Capitalism* (Eerdmans, 1991).

Green, John C., James L. Guth, Corwin E. Smidt, and Lyman A. Kellstedt, *Religion and the Culture Wars: Dispatches from the Front* (Rowman & Littlefield, 1996).

Hunter, James Davison, *American Evangelicalism: Conservative Religion and the Quandary of Modernity* (Rutgers University Press, 1983).

Hunter, James Davison, *Evangelicalism: the Coming Generation* (Chicago University Press, 1987).

Lienesch, Michael, *Redeeming America: Piety and Politics in the New Christian Right* (University Press of North Carolina, 1993).

McCarthy, Rockne M., James W. Skillen, and William A. Harper, *Disestablishment a Second Time: Genuine Pluralism for American Schools* (Eerdmans, 1982).

Moberg, David O., *The Great Reversal: Evangelicals Versus Social Concern* (Lippincott, 1972).

Neuhaus, Richard John, and Michael Cromartie, eds, *Piety and Politics: Evangelicals and Fundamentalists Confront the World* (Ethics and Public Policy, 1987).

Noll, Mark A., *One Nation Under God? Christian Faith and Political Action in America* (Harper & Row, 1988).

Noll, Mark A., Nathan O. Hatch, and George M. Marsden, *The Search for Christian America*, rev. edn (Helmers & Howard, 1989).

Pierard, Richard V., *The Unequal Yoke: Evangelical Christianity and Political Conservatism* (Lippincott, 1970).

Skillen, James W., *The Scattered Voice: Christians at Odds in the Public Square* (Zondervan, 1990).

Smith, Christian, *American Evangelicalism: Embattled and Thriving* (Chicago University Press, 1998).

Smith, Christian, *Christian America? What Evangelicals Really Want* (University of California Press, 2000).

Wills, David W., "Beyond commonality and plurality: persistent racial polarity in American religion and politics," in M. A. Noll, ed., *Religion and American Politics* (Oxford University Press, 1989).

Wirt, Sherwood Eliot, *The Social Conscience of the Evangelical* (Harper & Row, 1968).

Index